The Literary Genres in the Flavian Age

Trends in Classics – Supplementary Volumes

Volume 51

The Literary Genres in the Flavian Age

Canons, Transformations, Reception

Edited by
Federica Bessone and Marco Fucecchi

DE GRUYTER

ISBN 978-3-11-065851-4
e-ISBN (PDF) 978-3-11-053443-6
e-ISBN (EPUB) 978-3-11-053330-9
ISSN 1868-4785

Library of Congress Cataloging-in-Publication Data
A CIP catalog record for this book has been applied for at the Library of Congress.

Bibliographic information published by the Deutsche Nationalbibliothek
The Deutsche Nationalbibliothek lists this publication in the Deutsche Nationalbibliografie;
detailed bibliographic data are available in the Internet at http://dnb.dnb.de.

This volume is text- and page-identical with the hardback published in 2017.
Logo: Christopher Schneider, Laufen
Printing: CPI books GmbH, Leck
♾ Printed on acid-free paper
Printed in Germany

www.degruyter.com

Table of Contents

VII   Epic and Other Genres

Introduction

A few decades after the construction of a new canon of classics, immediately accredited and acknowledged even today as one of the highest achievements of Roman culture, the Flavian age (69–96 CE) presents a highly dynamic scenery of the literary genres, traversed by productive tensions between tradition and innovation and stamped by strong self-consciousness.[1] The search for novelty by which the Augustan age itself, in its mature phase, had responded to the completion of a Latin library in the various genres, and the experimental spirit that had animated Neronian literature, do not fade in this cultural context, which a persistent critical prejudice, until the later twentieth century, labeled as Flavian 'classicism'.

This volume that collects papers presented at the conference *I generi letterari nell'età dei Flavi. Canoni, trasformazioni, ricezione*, held in Turin on September 18–19, 2013, intends to investigate the dynamics of genres in the literary production of the Flavian age as a whole: including prose and poetry, the main literary forms, all major authors. The explosion of Flavian studies in recent years,[2] promoted also by national and international research projects and teams well represented in this venue, has marked a substantial improvement in knowledge, while a more astute theoretical reflection has changed our way of considering an epoch that nobody today would any longer call 'Silver', which suggests a paradigm of decadence compared to the Augustan 'Golden Age'.

The time is ripe, we believe, to start considering how the literary system of this age is configured as a whole: the system of genres and their relations, in theory and practice. The theme is open to a plurality of methodological approaches and particular investigations concerning the way in which genres already canonized or with an ancient tradition evolve or see their status challenged, while new forms emerge, that are fit to answer the changing needs of imperial society, to interpret its expectations and direct its cultural orientations. Our aim has been to stimulate a complex reflection, carried out with a multiplicity of theoretical and critical instruments, that can help interpret a complex system of phenomena and changes. We have sought here a style of research which

---

1 The dynamic conception of literary genres presupposed by this volume has its points of reference above all in the reflection by Gian Biagio Conte (1984; 1985[2]; 1986; 1991, esp. 145–173; 1994) and Stephen Hinds (1998). On the notion of canon see Citroni 2003a; 2006a.

2 The most recent among the collective volumes dedicated to the Flavian age is Zissos 2016; imminent in the TCSV series are Coffee / Forstall / Galli / Nelis forthcoming and Ginsberg / Krasne forthcoming.

https://doi.org/10.1515/9783110534436-001

connects the evolution of literary forms to the transformations of society and culture. We intended to pay particular attention to a number of related issues: the genres' constant redefining themselves by reciprocal opposition, the instrumental reinterpretations of the literary past – from Virgil's poetic career to Callimachean aesthetics –, the relation between genres, power and audience, the link between forms of literature and ideas of empire, the role of literary communication in the construction of imperial ideology, the author's self-representation in different genres and the different proposals of his social function, and finally the reception of Flavian literature.

The contributions presented here do not offer a thorough and systematic treatment of the proposed theme (which is virtually inexhaustible), nor do they aim at theoretical redefinitions of the concept of 'genre', but represent, by the variety of analyses itself, a rich investigation of the dynamics in play, an exemplification of the critical issues emerging from them, and a stimulus for further thought in numerous directions.

The dialectic between reverence towards recognized models and innovative thrusts is an essential factor in the search for originality, and the confidence that this age expresses in the progress of literature provides the theoretical legitimation to its impulse of renewal: Quintilian's survey of Greek and Latin authors, ordered by genres, exemplifies the 'progressive' concept of literary evolution affirmed by one of the most authoritative personalities of Flavian culture.[3] There is now, in theory and practice, a capacity to look at the classics with respect, but without inferiority complexes; there appears a consciousness of one's own 'secondariness' that turns to a position of strength, whence an author can show his achieved autonomy and proudly claim the conquest of new spaces of artistic expression.[4] Also the immanent literary history, inscribed in the works of these authors, testifies to, and sometimes overtly declares, an attitude that is at the same time reverent and ambitious: the epilogue to the *Thebaid* is an emblem of this, a consecration of Virgil that is also a self-candidature to his succession in the role of national poet.[5]

The renewal of genres occurs, in short, in the full consciousness of the dynamic nature of the genres themselves. The keener the consciousness of the status as classics achieved by predecessors – particularly the Augustans –, the stronger the stimulus to do differently. The boldness and the thrust towards novelty are comparable to those by which, for instance, Ovid, and Lucan after him,

---

3 Citroni 2005a; 2006b.
4 On secondariness and self-consciousness see Hinds 1998, 91–98.
5 On Stat. *Theb.* 12.810–819 see Hardie 1993, 110f.; Rosati 2008.

had set the *Metamorphoses* or the *Pharsalia* against the *Aeneid*, revolutionizing the coordinates of epos. Statius will do the same in his turn, detaching himself from the *Aeneid* first with his – still most Virgilian – *Thebaid*, an epic of *nefas*, a negative poem imbued with the aesthetics of tragedy,[6] and then with the *Achilleid*, an epos ambiguous in genre and *gender*, light and ironical, even touching on effects of epic parody.[7]

As regards occasional poetry, the search for new paths continues that by which the late Ovid, at the height of his experiments in the elegiac genre, had converted happy elegy into sad elegy, and courtship poetry into court poetry.[8] That reconversion of minor poetry to a celebratory function (already elaborated in Calpurnius Siculus' bucolics)[9] is taken into account in different ways by both Martial and Statius, who moreover restate with different aims, in the *Epigrams* and the *Silvae* respectively, the refusal of the Callimachean principle of formal refinement displayed by the exile poet. The disavowal of the *labor limae* now occurs under the sign of the *festinatio* ('speed'), a creative adaptation to the conditions of imperial patronage, elaborating traditions of Greek epideictic poetry.[10]

In this new phase of Roman Callimacheanism,[11] in which the coordinates valid for the Augustan age are transformed and redefined, the epic poem – the most prestigious genre – is now watched at length and tortured by the file,[12] while minor poetry affects extraneity or declares contempt towards the hard work of elaboration. Statius' *libelli* present themselves as 'streamed from a sudden heat of inspiration and a sort of pleasure of hastening', while Martial's epigram proclaims impatience for stylistic refinements in the name of a ready and direct adhesion to the reality of occasions – the same adherence to reality that dictates the refusal of mythology.[13] Even the Augustan move of the *recusatio* ('refusal'), transplanted from minor genres into epic, changes its function: the Callimachean opposition between 'small' and 'large', already exploited by

---

6 Ganiban 2007; Bessone 2011.

7 On the Ovidianness of the *Achilleid* see Rosati 1992; 1994c; Barchiesi 1996; Heslin 2005; Bessone 2016; forthcoming a; b; c.

8 Labate 1987; Rosati 2003; 2005; 2014a.

9 Fucecchi 2009.

10 Merli 2013; Rosati 2015.

11 On the Callimacheanism of the archaic, the neoteric, and the Augustan poets see Labate 1990.

12 Stat. *Theb.* 12.811 f. ... *o mihi bissenos multum vigilata per annos / Thebai?*; *Silv.* 4.7.25 f. *nostra / Thebais multa cruciata lima*; Mart. *Ep.* 8.3.17 f. *scribant ista graves nimium nimiumque severi, / quos media miseros nocte lucerna videt.*

13 Stat. *Silv.* 1 *praef.* 2–4 *hos libellos, qui mihi subito calore et quadam festinandi voluptate fluxerunt*; Mart. *Ep.* 2.86.9 f. *turpe est difficiles habere nugas / et stultus labor est ineptiarum.*

Latin poets to set the minor genres against the grand ones, now becomes a contrast between 'less grand' and 'grander' internal to the epic genre, and serves to refuse before the emperor the historical-celebratory epos, perceived as more demanding (and risky) than the mythological one.[14]

The relation with epos is still at the centre of the programmatic statements of minor poetry. A humble genre, not officially 'recognized', aspires to enter the canon and, from the lowest level, challenges the literary forms that are on top of the system of genres.[15] By giving to the tradition of the Latin brief poem the definite form and stable name of *epigramma*, Martial claims the literary dignity, and success with the audience, of a poetic form devoid of prestige that is opposed to epos (as well as to tragedy).[16] On the contrary, the non-genre, hybrid and experimental, represented by the *Silvae*,[17] offers itself as a constant alternative to the epic production of the same author and, in fact, as a literary form complementing it, in a reciprocal implication and legitimation of the 'small' and the 'grand'. In the *praefationes* and the individual poems, Statius presents himself as the prestigious poet of the *Thebaid*, temporarily lent to a minor genre, but at the same time he sponsors an image of himself as a full-range professional poet, able to satisfy the cultural consumption of the élite; and, mixing the archaic with the contemporary, he portrays himself as an *aoidos* posing with lyre in hand, a performer ready for any occasion, a living myth invested with an outstanding social function in the Roman imperial world.[18]

The 'ascending' model of Virgil's poetic career, teleologically oriented toward the sublime,[19] is thus substituted by the parallel practice of 'grand' and 'small', high and humble poetry – where even the 'ephemeral' aspires to eternal glory, the 'occasional' hexameter can nourish ambitions of miniature epic, the Phalaecian hendecasyllable or the Sapphic and Alcaic strophe rise to the level of celebratory and Pindaric lyric. Thus, a polyvalent author awards in fact equal nobility to poetic forms of different rank, constantly alternating in his production: inside Statius' work, a new relativism of genres asserts itself, in response to the socio-cultural and economic conditions of the Flavian age. The

---

14 Stat. *Theb.* 1.15–40; *Ach.* 1.14–19; *Silv.* 4.4.93–100 (94–96 *Troia quidem magnusque mihi temp tatur Achilles, / sed vocat arcitenens alio pater armaque monstrat / Ausonii maiora ducis*). See Rosati 2002; Nauta 2006.
15 Mart. *Ep.* 12.94.9 *quid minus esse potest? epigrammata fingere coepi.*
16 Citroni 2003b; 2004. On Martial's polemics with contemporary epicists see most recently Henriksén 1998; Ripoll 2002; Camera 2007; Zissos 2003–2004.
17 Newlands 2002; 2008; 2012, 71–73 and *passim*.
18 Rosati 2013; 2014b; Bessone 2014.
19 See Hardie / Moore 2010.

proud Augustan vindication of the dignity of minor genres appears transformed: from opposite positions in the same socio-historical context, Martial and Statius, both of them in an instrumental and interested way, propose a new, idiosyncratic vision of the internal relationships within the system of poetic genres.

The reciprocal relations between epos and minor poetry are the object of a redefinition on the programmatic plane, and a field for experiments at the empirical level. Like Statius, Valerius and Silius also open the space of epos to different genres: while they go back from the Virgilian model to the Homeric archetype, or exploit the suggestions of Gigantomachy for a discourse on imperial power (nourished also with 'On kingship' literature),[20] on the other hand they let the antagonist urges of erotic elegy act in the narrative (as well as, in an opposite direction, those of tragedy). By putting into play a disturbing force like eros, already at work in the *Aeneid*, and unchained in the *Metamorphoses*,[21] the Flavian poets widen in turn the boundaries of the genre and make its arrangement more complex, enriching the narration with ideological implications and effects in character portrayal.[22]

The totalizing, all-inclusive vocation of epos has reached its apex with Ovid's work, which even proposes an 'encyclopedia of genres' and poses a true challenge to generic laws. There is no successive epic poet who does not reckon with the poem of the *mutatae formae* ('changed forms').[23] And the Flavian epicists react to Ovid's provocation with a range of attitudes that outlines their own personal reinterpretation of the genre of κλέα ἀνδρῶν ('the glorious deeds of the heroes').

Other post-Virgilian experiences interpose themselves decisively between the Flavian poets and the *Aeneid*. Lucan's poem, with its poetic exploration of civil war (a theme that is topical again, and dominant in the Flavian age), is for all the example of an *epos* that rethinks the Virgilian paradigm and plunges into crisis the providential vision of empire – a vision already exposed to problematic tensions, variously interpreted, in the *Aeneid*. The way in which we construct the relation of Valerius, Statius and Silius with Lucan's model can be decisive for our reading of their poems and of Flavian epic as a whole, mythological and histor-

---

20 Zissos 2002; 2014; Fucecchi 2013; 2014a.

21 Hinds 2000; Keith 2000.

22 Barchiesi 2001. Cf. e.g. Fucecchi 1996; 2014b. For the complex literary affiliations of the epos by Valerius, Silius and Statius see the rich documentation and the hints of general reflection in the essays collected in Augoustakis 2010b; Heerink / Manuwald 2014; Dominik / Newlands / Gervais 2015.

23 Keith 2014a; 2014b.

ical, in relation to Roman imperial discourse.[24] Thus the study of intertextuality, observing the tradition of a genre in its progressive making, can relate literary facts to the changing historical, social and cultural reality. Even the various engagements of the Flavian epicists with Seneca's tragedy renew the relation of epos with the tragic genre which, before Lucan, had been foundational for Virgil (with an impact on narrative structures and style even deeper than in Apollonius Rhodius).[25] The tragic reflection on absolute power, or the prefiguration of the tragic future of a heroine like Medea, confer to the Flavian *Thebaid* and *Argonautica* a new dimension, now also imprinted by the Senecan poetics of evil.

The relation between literature and society, and between literature and material culture, invests in a crucial way the evolution of literary forms. Since its beginnings the literature of the Flavian age confronts the issues of moral and cultural regeneration promoted by the new imperial dynasty and, in some fields, shows a marked consciousness of its social and pragmatic function: both as a channel of communication and exchange between author and patrons or addressees (the sovereign, the court, the officials and members of the leadership, or the patrons who made the choice of *otium*), and as an object of consumption by the anonymous audience of readers.

This consciousness of a literary piece's social utility is a key transformative factor of the literary system; within it, growing prestige is gained by those forms that identify 'usefulness' and adhesion to reality as their distinctive feature and programmatic goal. Thus, an encyclopedic intellectual like Pliny the Elder announces in the *praefatio* to the *Naturalis historia* – written under Vespasian and dedicated to his son, the future emperor Titus – his aim of 'being useful' (*prodesse*), and then in the second book, when talking about the *princeps*, he formulates the motto that is the guiding principle even of his own learned and monumental enterprise: *deus est mortali iuvare mortalem*.[26]

Again with a view to pursuing a socially useful goal, the remarkable flourishing of rhetorical precepts finds its maximum achievement in Quintilians' handbook, another successful literary product. The *Institutio oratoria* is not an instrument catering only to specialists and to the formation of 'technicians' attending the forum (i.e. lawyers). It addresses anyone who intends to refine his eloquence and attain the 'power of the word', something needed especially, but not exclusively, by those who occupy prominent positions in the administrative apparatus and the imperial bureaucracy. The work proves grandly 'useful' in a broader

---

24 Marks 2010; Bessone 2013; Fucecchi 2013; 2015 and forthcoming b.
25 Hardie 1997; Conte 2007b, 125–142; 2007a, 150–169.
26 Plin. *Nat.* 2.18.1. On Pliny's "inventory of the world" see Conte 1991, 95–144; 1994; Citroni Marchetti 1991, esp. ch. 1; Murphy 2004.

sense as well, as an instrument of cultural alphabetization, as it offers the reader an essential picture of the evolution of Greek and Latin literature and a critical survey of the main genres, trends and authors.

Poetic production more and more turns to celebrating the mature, wealthy imperial civilization and its most elegant expressions: encomiastic poetry configures Flavian society as "the best of all possible worlds".[27] Not only are events, deeds and characters celebrated, but also buildings, places and environments, public and private: imperial palaces and monuments, or villas and gardens of private patrons, reflecting the character, cultural tastes and ethical qualities of their owners. The ecphrastic poetry of the *Epigrams* and the *Silvae* is founded on a circle of reciprocal legitimation between poet and patron.[28] Responding to a growing demand for poetical celebration arising from concrete occasions is for the literary artist the best way to promote his social function before the imperial power and the élite, and to earn his living from the exercise of his profession; in turn, the eulogy of the addressees' lifestyle, and of their architectural and artistic achievements, provides moral legitimation to wealth and luxury, even of private patrons, and grants them, through poetry, the only possible form of immortality.[29]

1 Genres and literary history

The first section of this volume opens with a chapter by **M. Citroni**, who underlines the pragmatic character of Quintilian's handbook, as well as, in a diachronic perspective, its interest in the evolution and periodization of literary history, both Greek and Latin. Among the models of the past the *Institutio oratoria* highlights those which are still valid in the present as privileged – though not exclusive – objects of imitation: first of all Cicero and the Augustan writers. The more ancient authors who, despite their *ingenium*, appear lacking in *ars* and can no longer represent suitable paradigms of style and language, deserve the label 'archaic'. The classicist stance of the handbook insinuates no prejudice against novelties. Quintilian is very confident in the potential of oratory to make further steps and surpass its authoritative models (in this he differs from the more pessimistic view displayed in Tacitus' *Dialogus*). Such a notion of progress, involving every form of eloquence, is guaranteed by the specialists in this field, who are

---

27 Fabbrini 2007.
28 Nauta 2002; Zeiner 2005; Newlands 2008.
29 Newlands 2002; Rosati 2006; Bessone forthcoming d.

called upon to endorse the quality of technical innovations. Each 'conquest' entails the danger of relapsing – *utinam non peiora vincant!* Just for that reason, Quintilian intends to prevent the spread of aberrant tendencies resulting from excessive self-confidence (as was the case for Ovid and Seneca) and bordering on bad taste. Drawing upon tradition can be a deterrent from vice, and a constraint. The *vis* of the *veteres* should be added to the *cultus* of the moderns; the new must appropriate the best of the 'ancient' (sometimes even of the 'archaic'), recovering its vigour and energy. The goal to be attained is a style where modern qualities are enhanced by the strength of the ancients.

The following chapter, by **Baier**, also deals with Quintilian's attention to the *utilitas* of literature as a repository of examples for the training of the would-be orator. However, what is at stake here is rather how the Flavian rhetorician regards literary history from the viewpoint of reception. As a precursor of modern *Rezeptionstheorie*, Quintilian neither intends to assess the aesthetic value of Greek and Latin texts, nor to establish if and how they correspond to a schematic notion of genre. His aim is, rather, to judge their impact on the audience, with particular reference to their 'educational effect'. The would-be orator is invited to survey carefully previous literature in order to find useful examples of a persuasive, effective style: the construction of a canon of *auctores* is founded on just this pragmatic criterion. Selective imitation, however, is corroborated by individual contribution and original invention that must also meet the requirement of usefulness. Cicero drew abundantly on Demosthenes, Isocrates and Plato at the beginning; then, relying on his talent, he created something new and more suitable for his purposes (10.1.109). According to Baier, the first theorist of such a progressive, almost evolutionist, idea of literature may have been Epicurus, whose influence could reach Quintilian through Lucretius' mediation (in particular *De rerum natura* Book V).

2 Encyclopaedism and oratory

At the time of Pliny the Elder, the encyclopaedic scientific treatise was not properly a new genre. The author of the *Naturalis Historia* inserts himself in a *lignée* of antecedents (*prisci*, *veteres*), on whose work he intends to capitalize with particular care (*cura*). In so doing, as **S. Citroni Marchetti** argues, Pliny re-constructs the identity and self-awareness of a multidisciplinary literary creation, which he characterizes as a 'genre of peace', unlike (or even in opposition to) historiography, which privileges themes such as war and political struggle. After writing history (and military history), he devotes himself, as a humble, accurate compiler, to scientific divulgation: even before thinking of posterity, as some of his predecessors did, he wants to do something useful for the life of his contemporaries. He too privileges the criterion of usefulness and, by choosing the present as his goal, fully endorses the cultural propaganda of the new Emperors. Pliny's attitude displays a remarkable affinity to the so-called 'ethics of care', which acknowledges the vulnerability of the human race and argues for the necessity of benevolent relationships among men (e. g. *Nat.* 7.4). Emblematic of such a vision is Pliny's representation of Mother Earth (*Nat.* 2.154 ff.): she receives us at birth, she gives us nurture, she always supports us and even condescends to be ploughed by us when we become soldier-peasants. Earth can display a human sensibility even towards the nations defeated by Rome. Nonetheless Pliny – as a loyal, devoted officer – never really denies the paternalistic ethics of supremacy asserted by the Roman Empire through its armies.

Under Domitian the schools of rhetoric become the privileged seat of oratorical performances, their claustrophobic rooms replacing the forum and the senate as the arena of rhetorical exercise. Yet other factors combine to reduce the space of the oral word, like the diffusion of a new kind of trial, the *cognitio extra ordinem*. After surveying the (scarce) evidence of judicial oratory in the Flavian age, **Balbo**'s chapter deals with two letters of Pliny the Younger which both offer stimulating insights into this topic. As he recalls his defence of Iunius Pastor against the *potentissimi civitatis*, an episode of his youth (*Ep.* 1.18.3), Pliny implicitly compares himself to the young Cicero pleading the case of Roscius before Chrysogonus, Sulla's powerful freedman. The second example relates to a trial which took place a decade after the former (*Ep.* 1.5.5–7). In that instance Pliny had to deal with another influent member of the establishment: Aquilius Regulus, a notorious delator since the times of Nero. Once more Cicero's figure is evoked from the glorious past to provide a legitimizing term of reference. In both cases, Pliny aims to present himself as the author of a courageous effort to keep the hope for freedom alive. However, Pliny's self-congratulation seems to disguise his keen awareness that revitalizing such a dream is impossible, even after the death of the tyrant.

3 Tradition and poetics of the epigram

The tendency to simplify the literary canon through a polarization between the 'great' (*magnum*) and the 'small' (*parvum*) brings together various genres belonging to each of these categories. **Canobbio** analyses this phenomenon by considering the image of the literary system given in Martial's epigrams. As regards the *magnum*, epos exerts an attractive force over other great genres, like tragedy and lyric (at 5.5.8 *cothurnus* is associated with Virgil, while at 7.23.2 the lyre is connected with Lucan). In the area of the *parvum* the same polarizing role is played by the epigram, the smallest among the minor genres, but also the most capable of attracting and incorporating the others. For Martial, epigram even manages to prevail over epos, and this is a subversion of hierarchies in favour of the *parvum*. Following in the footsteps of Catullus, Martial specializes in the smallest form of the canon (12.94) and gains primacy in it (*Ep. 9. pr.* 5), thus matching the glory of Virgil, *maximus vatum*. More than Catullus, Martial broadens the scope, as well as the prestige, of lighter poetry, capitalizing on the Augustan experience in minor genres like satire, elegy and pastoral. The epigrammatic poet's success can have consequences for the canon of literary genres, according to the response of the anonymous affectionate reader and to his apparent socio-cultural profile. The individual dimension of literary consumption proves more important than the public, official one. In a different way, Statius offers with his *Silvae* a product characterized by *varietas* and generic interplay, involving minor forms as well as epic and lyric. Conversely, the *Thebaid* and the *Achilleid*, besides strong identity traits, show signs of infiltration by alternative forms, like elegy, satire and even comedy and bucolics.

Recurrent themes, such as ridiculous poverty or lack of virility, create allusive webs that provide an internal structure to a successful literary product like the book of epigrams. As a refounder of the genre in the Flavian age, Martial exploits this technique to organize the poetic collection and give unity to the whole. Sometimes he prefers to gather within a single epigram a series of allusions to a cluster of poems by Catullus, his undisputed 'genre-model'. This is the case of *Ep.* 1.92, where Mamurianus is the target of attacks which recall those launched against Mamurra, his almost homonymous Catullan *alter ego*, or other famous rivals like Furius and Aurelius (poem 23, but also 15, 21 and 26). The opposite can also occur, when a single poem by Catullus is dismembered by Martial into several epigrams that display, with only slight variations, the structuring theme and the most emblematic images of that poem. In his chapter, **Morelli** studies the case of Catullus 23, whose diffraction leaves traces in a number of Martial's epigrams, with particular frequency in Book XI, where the tradition of scoptic and erotic epigrams is recovered.

4 Occasional poetry and literary genres

Encomiastic poetry, responding rapidly and effectively to multiple occasions that involve the collective (like military triumphs) or a more limited audience (such as marriages and funerals), reaches a climax in the Flavian age. However, speedy composition (*carmina properata*) as an index of the use value of poetry had already been theorized in Ovid's exile elegy, which faced the physical limit of being far from Rome, the center of the world and the place where events and 'occasions' prompting literary responses emerge. **Merli**'s chapter analyses the notion of *festinatio* in Martial's epigrams and Statius' *Silvae*, defining the nature of this practice and distinguishing it from improvisation (which could also be the prerogative of an amateur) as well as from Catullus' *sprezzatura*. The *festinatio* specifically characterizes the professional poet and, at the same time, represents an added value, making minor genres more suitable than the great ones for the contemporary age. Useful poetry needs qualified professionals writers, who are called upon to combine celerity, quantity and even (relative) quality. The *lima*, on the contrary, belongs to higher level poetry, which is not bound to respect time limits, but is made to last and has to be appreciated by a restricted number of specialists.

A poet like Statius, who throughout his poetic career shifts with ease from the great genre *par excellence* (the epos) to a non-genre, resisting every attempt of classification (the *silvae*), offers a promising field for thinking about the relationship between two different forms: occasional poetry – *carmina properata*, motivated by specific occasions and primarily addressed to a definite addressee –, and poetry for a larger audience of readers, a product whose quality and duration depends mostly on *emendatio* (not *festinatio*). Claiming his achieved status as an epic poet, accredited by the anonymous public, is – according to **Bonadeo** – the core strategy of a preventive self-defence, by which the poet of the *Silvae* tries to legitimize his minor production and construct a new canon, complementary to the traditional one: a canon that has room for genres endowed with a relatively strong identity (such as the *epigramma*) as well as for others in search of a definition (like the *silvae*); a canon where the social function of poetry is an absolute, and fully recognized, value.

The chapter by **Newlands** deepens the reflection on the problematic status of the *Silvae*, highlighting the close connection and constant hosmosis that links epic to occasional poetry in Statius' literary production. The *Silvae* provide a kind of '*a posteriori* interpretive commentary' on the *Thebaid*; in turn, the great war epos anticipates the morphological fluidity of the *Silvae*. Such an anticipation is all the more meaningful as it occurs in a high genre, long codified. With his penchant for experimenting with new forms, a challenge to current conventions, Statius inverts the most consolidated type of poetic career: now the great enterprise of epos is no longer a final achievement. In a few centuries, Statius' *Silvae* will become a classic. The first author of late antiquity who explicitly mentions them as a genre model is Sidonius Apollinaris. In his poem 22, the Gallo-Roman poet exemplifies a new kind of celebratory poetry, which draws on the *Silvae* as regards the ecphrastic structure and transfiguration of reality into myth, while rejecting their improvisational quality, or rather their character of *carmen properatum*, to embrace the more comprehensive, wide-ranging scale of epic poetry.

5 Models and transformations of the epos

The critical debate of the last decades has definitively set aside the critical *vulgata* which regarded the epic revival of the first century CE as a mere classicist restoration. A label such as 'post-Virgilian' has acquired new meanings and increased in complexity, and, if we still feel comfortable in classifying Valerius' *Argonautica*, Silius' *Punica* and Statius' *Thebaid* (or even the *Achilleid*'s fragment) as epic poems, we can no longer ignore the transformations which affected their generic status.

The ambitious aim to revisit the archetypal myth of the Argonauts compels Valerius to confront a rather heavy legacy. This is true in the first place as regards the vast range of his *auctores*, where 'code models' like Homer and Virgil are no less important than 'exemplary models' like Apollonius of Rhodes, or the enigmatic Varro of Atax (not to mention Catullus). Even more problematic, however, is dealing with the ideological interpretation of this myth, which had undergone negative readings like that of Catullus 64, up to the more recent case of Seneca's *Medea*. Even Lucan's corrosive critique against the celebratory function of epos, as a *monumentum* of the national identity, made it difficult to take a definite position. Valerius Flaccus – as **Fabre** argues – seems to oscillate between two extremes. The emphasis on Jupiter's plan, in which *labor* is the privileged way to obtain glory and the Argo is destined to apotheosis, is indicative of a generally positive notion of fate. However, we may feel some discomfort as we find that the programmatic enthusiasm of the outset is not explicitly confirmed in the course of the poem (perhaps because of the sudden interruption of the text?).

Valerius' poem lends new epic dignity to certain characters. One of them is Hypsipyle, whose demonstration of *pietas* towards her father Thoas is extolled. As **Zissos** shows in his chapter, this episode is not only the most representative of Hypsypyle's mythical figure, but it also makes her the prototype of a genuinely Roman virtue: almost a 'female Aeneas', as well as the antithesis of Dido. Not by chance, Thoas' rescue is chosen by the queen of Lemnos as an iconographic subject of the cloak she offers to Jason, together with her father's sword: Hypsipyle's *pietas* must be celebrated and even repeated, while the sword represents the pledge of the future sharing of power over the island. Such a manifestation of heroic virility in a woman, a sign of Valerius' competitive attitude towards his Alexandrian model, is countered by Jason's apparent failure to understand the meaning of the gift. When, at Cyzicus' funeral, he throws this cloak into the pyre, the leader of the Argonauts is also symbolically cutting the link with *pietas* as exemplified by Hypsipyle. After causing (though indirectly and involuntarily) the death of his own parents, Aeson and Alcimede, once again Jason proves to be anything but a positive character.

6 War and generic tensions

Flavian epic poems, the *Thebaid* and *Punica* in particular, have often been negatively received because of their eagerness to represent bloody battle scenes, which display an almost morbid fascination with horrid details. **Lovatt** tries to dispel, or at least relativize, such a commonplace by focusing on the instants immediately preceding the beginning of hostilities; moments when armies are marching out to the battlefield which show the 'beautiful face' of war. This is not only a challenge to a consolidated opinion. Lovatt is mostly interested in underlining the visional quality of the war narratives that populate the new epic. For this purpose she selects passages where the Flavian poets draw directly upon Homer's *Iliad*. Sometimes, as is the case for the march-out in Statius, *Thebaid* 8 (the main focus of this chapter), several Homeric models are mobilized, from different books (*Il.* 2.445–487, the muster of the troops; 3.1–14, the two armies facing each other; 4.422–455, the clashing of the armies and the beginning of the battle). As regards Valerius, Lovatt concentrates on the great war parenthesis of Book VI, namely on Medea's *teichoskopia*. Such an effort to refresh epic by getting back to its origins – apparently bypassing Virgil's *Aeneid* – is another sign of the Flavian epicists' tendency to feature as 'models of their models'.

In Silius' *Punica* the remake of narrative situations and episodes which go back to Homer, and apparently lack Virgil's mediation, may be found even more off-putting. This happens, for example, when the battle of Trebia is transformed into an idiosyncratic recollection of the Iliadic *mache parapotamios* ('river battle', 4.638–703), with the consul Publius Cornelius Scipio, Africanus' father, as a protagonist. However, after the battle of Cannae – which represents the core of this hyper-heroic poem –, Hannibal dreams of fighting with Jupiter, when a voice is heard, intimating that he will never manage to conquer Rome (10.366–368). Hannibal's following hesitation in launching the decisive attack against the mortally wounded city risks endangering the coherence of the war epos and producing what **Littlewood** labels as an "illusion of generic instability". In fact, this is only a first warning: the Carthaginian leader will receive the second by Juno herself, under the walls of Rome (12.725). Yet – and this is even more interesting – such a forced slowdown in narrative rhythm proves to be another Homeric legacy, coming once more from the *Iliad*. In the Διὸς ἀπάτη of *Iliad* 14 Silius already found an example of intra-generic tension (this too having been discarded as a model by Virgil). When asking the god Sleep's intervention, Juno specifies that, this time, she does not aim to make Jupiter fall asleep (10.343–345); something easier and, at the same time, unprecedented is now at stake. Somehow like the elegiac-tragic nightmare announcing the death of Ceyx to his wife Alcyone in Ovid, *Metamorphoses* 11, Hannibal's *nova somnia* mark the beginning of his relentless decline.

Such a tension or, better, negotiation between epic tradition and other poetic forms runs throughout the *Punica* and concerns not only the core of the poem's architecture. In his chapter **Marks** offers the example of *Punica* 14, a 'peripheral' book, devoted to Marcellus' victorious military campaign in Sicily, and one which is granted relative autonomy, moreover, by its monographic character. After a geo-historical digression on Sicily, the book piles up a remarkable amount of antiquarian and literary references. Echoes from Greek poets (namely the Sicilian Stesichorus and Theocritus, but also Callimachus) and Latin ones (mostly the Augustan: Virgil, Horace, up to Ovid) join together so as to suggest the idea of a true anthology of texts and genres. It is an anthology, however, whose variety does not prevent a markedly indigenous colour from coming to the surface, as when we meet a descendant of the mythic bucolic hero Daphnis, or an ancestor with an Horatian air such as Pompeius Grosphus. This is perhaps the book of the *Punica* which best represents the author's taste for collecting memories from the past. Readers may feel almost like Marcellus himself before ancient Syracuse lying at his mercy, with all its treasures and works of art.

The section on generic tensions ends with a chapter that confronts the most intriguing of the Flavian epics, the great fragment of Statius' *Achilleid*. This is a text which can hardly be classified as war epic in a proper sense. The Apollinean portrait of the young Achilles as a lyre player, singing the deeds of heroes in Chiron's cave, and then teaching Deidamia as he courts her in Scyros, disguised as a girl, is almost an emblem of Statius' sustained engagement with the lyric genre in this poem. Throughout, as **Keith** argues, the narrator draws on Horace's *Carmina*, employs the technical diction of lyrics, and alludes to his own lyric poetry. Like the protagonist, with his Homeric and Pindaric image, in the proem the author of the *Achilleid* himself looks as if he had two faces: those of a lyric and epic poet at the same time, representing himself as a *vates* through the imagery of Augustan lyric (as well as elegy).

7 Epic and other genres

Epic and historiography are the genres that are most involved (though they are not the only ones) in Silius' recollection of the great national epos. At the end of the first century CE, the defeat of Carthage in the Second Punic War is still conceived of as the capital event of Roman history, which sanctions the *Urbs*' ability to rise from its own ashes and create the myth of an invincible power. A first victim of the making of this myth is apparently the worst enemy himself of the future World City. When paying tribute to the memory of the defeated Roman leaders, Hannibal already displays a sort of 'anxiety of influence'. By reflecting on these burial scenes and their ideological meaning, **Augoustakis** shows that the almost systematic recurrence of this trope throughout the *Punica* may also represent a way to stretch (or even manipulate) the historical tradition. A case in point is the *laudatio funebris* that Silius' 'Roman Hannibal' devotes to Marcellus (15.381–396), whose death was stigmatized by Livy and, particularly, Polybius as the consequence of a fatal lack of *prudentia*. The serial repetition of these 'Bestattungsszenen' plays an exemplary, as well as a consolatory, function: while glorifying the heroism of the Roman victims, historical epic, better than historiography, may also point to unsuspected traits of humanity – and Romanness – which progressively characterize the enemy.

Statius' *Thebaid* is built on a different kind of generic interplay: that between epos and tragedy. Here as in the *Punica*, however, there is room for a dialogue with further literary forms. A character *hors catégorie* like Capaneus, the cruel Argive hero, is charged with ideological implications, such as the relationships between nature and divinity, gods and humans. Statius' poem thus includes an internal discussion where epic interacts with philosophy and its Roman poetic (i.e. didactic epic) champion, Lucretius' *De rerum natura*. In her chapter **Reitz** reads through the exemplary history of this enemy of the gods, a subject which requires extraordinary poetic resources, as the narrator highlights from beginning (1.45 ... *alio Capaneus horrore canendus*) to end (10.829 *non mihi iam solito vatum de more canendum*). In Book X Capaneus' role reaches its climax with the great aristeia culminating in the death of the hero, struck by lightning. The cause of this phenomenon is expressed rather ambiguously by the puzzling phrase *toto Iove* (*Theb.* 10.927), on which Reitz concentrates. In fact, what is at stake in the ending of the *Thebaid* is the role of Jupiter and the Olympians themselves, whose apparent lack of authority and power is betrayed by the way they literally disappear from sight on the eve of the fraternal duel between Eteocles and Polynices.

I Genres and Literary History

Mario Citroni
Antiqui, *veteres*, *novi*: images of the literary past and the impulse to progress in the cultural program of Quintilian

1. The discourse structure of the *Institutio oratoria* is basically systematic, and not historical, as befits a treatise designed to provide practical guidance. References to writers, orators and authors of rhetorical treatises, and likewise to words, locutions and procedures, are generally synchronic in nature. What is important is not their chronology but the teaching they propose, the testimony they contribute, the model they provide for the current needs of orators. Very frequently, however, Quintilian introduces into this systematic, synchronic framework a brief historical digression, or a comparison between past and present, or a qualitative evaluation relating to the chronological position of the author, locution or procedure considered. The literary and cultural considerations associated with the situation in time we encounter in the *Institutio oratoria* can be tied in with different ambits, which may however intertwine and overlap to varying degrees: in particular, linguistic usages, the creative production that we describe as literary (and occasionally the figurative and musical kind as well), the expressive practices pertaining to oratory, rhetorical theory, and educational practices.

2. In the *Institutio* neither *vetus* nor *antiquus*, per se, indicate a definite age. *Antiquus*, *antiquitas* and *antiquitus* suggest a greater distance from the present with respect to *vetus* and *vetustas*.[1] *Vetustus* occurs just four times, three in the superlative (substituting *veterrimus* which, rare after Livy, is absent in Quintilian), and in each case emphasizes a remote antiquity (even if not so remote in 10.1.40). There are 41 instances of *antiquus* (and derivatives), referring in broad terms to cultural facts, compared to 102 of *vetus*, *vetustus*, *vetustas*.

All these terms can refer to situations located in a variously distant past,[2] and also to situations immediately prior to the current one, or to situations which began in the past and continue to apply into the present, concurrently with new situations. And so *vetera* in 1. *pr.* 2 indicates everything that has

---

1 Note that *vetustas* can indicate both the condition of what is *vetus* and 'the long passage of time'.
2 As already observed by Cova 1990, 44, in a rather imprecise note in a somewhat muddled essay.

https://doi.org/10.1515/9783110534436-002

been elaborated in rhetoric up to the present, in contrast to innovations that might be introduced from now on. *Antiquitus* in 12.2.29 and *antiquitas* in 12.11.22 refer to the repository of teachings, examples and models offered by the entire past up until today. In 12.1.25 *vetustas* is the entire course of history up to the present, a history which has not yet witnessed the figure of the ideal orator, in contrast to the future in which that figure might appear. In 1.5.26 and 29 *vetus* indicates a linguistic norm, established in the past and remaining in force, as opposed to a recent *consuetudo*, which may or may not gain such status. In 6.3.65 the witticisms of the *veteres* are those that have been uttered in the past until now (the example given immediately beforehand dates to the relatively recent time of Nero).

Sometimes, instead, these terms refer to ages whose remoteness they are meant to signal. Referring to mythical ages are *antiquus* (and derivatives) in 1.10.9; 1.10.30; 3.7.8; *vetustas* in 3.7.26. *Antiquitus* in 1.10.12 relates to traditions allegedly drawn on by Pythagoras, and, in 1.10.18, to forms of education discussed by Aristophanes. Obsolete uses of language are referred to by *vetustas* in 4.1.58 and 1.6.11, where the XII Tables are cited; by *vetus* in 1.7.12, with the citation of a (presumed) monument of 260 BCE; by *vetustus* in 1.4.16, with a generic allusion to inscriptions on ancient monuments. In 1.7.11 this distant age, which even used a different alphabet than the present one, is defined with the superlative: *vetustissima tempora*.[3] In 1.10.20 the making of music by the *veteres Romani* is situated in the age of Numa, of the *carmen Saliare* and of the *carmina convivalia*; in 1.11.18 the dancing of the *veteres Romani* is situated in the time of the establishment of the college of the Salii.[4]

On other occasions, *vetus*, or *antiquus*, refer to less remote ages, variously distant from the present: *vetus* in 2.4.41 relates to the methods of the orator's formation in Greece prior to Demetrius of Phalerum (who died around 280 BCE), and in Rome before the opening (circa 93 BCE) of the school of the *rhetores Latini*; in 1.4.18 to the age of Aristotle; in 1.4.3 to the Alexandrian grammarians of the III–II centuries BCE. In 3.4.1 *antiqui* is used to describe authors of rhetorical

---

3 In 8.2.12 *commentarios ... pontificum et vetustissima foedera* the reference is to the same remote phase of the production of the most ancient Latin texts, but the superlative almost certainly has a relative value ('the most ancient of the treatises'), like *antiquissimus* in 3.1.8 (the most ancient writers of rhetorical treatises); 8.5.3 (the most ancient type of *sententia*); 12.10.42 (according to some, the older a way of speaking, the more natural it is); 1.10.10 (music is the oldest of the *studia in litteris*). In this last example, reference is made to what is in any case a very ancient period, like *vetustissimus* in 8.2.12 cited at the beginning of this note.

4 Also in 3.7.24, with reference to moral practices, the use of *veteres* in relation to *Romani* who considered *luxuria* as the *summum crimen* is intended to stress great distance in time.

treatises subsequent to Aristotle (*Aristotelen secuti*), at least until Cicero. In 12.10.16, *antiqua* is used for the *divisio* between Attic and Asianic orators, which cannot have applied before the beginning of Hellenism. *Vetus* in 10.1.82 and 12.2.22, and *antiquus* in 10.1.65, refer to comedy in the age of Pericles: but in these cases the adjective is to be understood in contrast to the 'new' comedy of Menander.[5] *Priscus*, in its sole attestation (9.4.16), indicates the period of Greek prose before Plato and Demosthenes, when the technique of rhythmic prose had not yet been fully developed: in this context, Lysias, Herodotus and Thucydides are *prisci*.

In many passages, *vetus*, and, more rarely, *antiquus*, refer to that age of Latin literature – from Livius Andronicus to Accius – that we too are accustomed to defining as 'archaic', and which, as we shall see, was formalized in Quintilian himself as the 'archaic' age, in that its products reveal a not yet complete artistic development: 1.7.22 *veterum comicorum*; 6.1.52 *veteres tragoediae comoediaeque*; 9.3.14 *apud veteres tragicos comicosque*; 10.1.9 *scriptores ... veteris ... comoediae*; 10.1.97 *tragoediae scriptores veterum Accius atque Pacuvius clarissimi*; 1.5.21 *apud antiquos tragoediarum ... scriptores*. See also 10.1.88 *Ennium sicut sacros vetustate lucos adoremus, in quibus grandia et antiqua robora iam non tantam habent speciem quantam religionem* ('Ennius we should worship as we do groves whose age has made them sacred, and whose huge and ancient trees have come to have more sanctity about them than beauty' transl. by D.A. Russell[6]). In more general terms, *vetus* and *antiquus* refer to this same literary age in some passages to which we will return later: 1.8.8 (*veteres Latini*); 1.8.10 (*veterum poemata*); 2.5.21 (*antiquitas:* and, in it, Cato and the Gracchi) and 23 (*antiqui*); 10.1.43 *veteres*. In 1.6.31, *vetus* refers to annalistic works.[7] As in 2.5.21, so too in other passages, within the broad designation of *vetus* or *antiquus*, the examples come from this same age: 1.6.7–8 *antiqui* (among them: Lucilius); 8.5.33f. *veteres* (among them: Cato and the Gracchi).[8] In 9.4.38 the *antiqui* named by Cicero in the passage of the *Orator* referred to by Quintilian are Ennius and Lucilius. The *vetustissimi auctores, ingeniosi sed arte carentes*, whose usefulness, according to Quintilian in 10.1.40, had been asserted by Cicero, are Cato and other later orators valorized in *Brutus*. In 8.6.15 he cites a sentence of a *vetus orator:* for

---

5 Similarly, in 10.1.84, *Stoici veteres* is to be understood in contrast to more recent Stoics.

6 All translations of Quintilian's texts in this paper are by Donald A. Russell (Russell 2001).

7 In 1.7.23 and 9.4.39 the reference is not to the works of Cato, but to the books in which they are attested: it therefore indicates a distance from the present which is not as wide as the one from Cato, but is, if unspecified, at any rate considerable.

8 In 8.3.29 Cato is described as *antiquus* in an anonymous epigram cited by Quintilian. For the association of Cato with the Gracchi, see note 38.

readers able to recognize the author, *vetus* entailed a precise chronological reference which, as can be understood from the context, was in any case situated in
the pre-Ciceronian period. To it there belonged the *antiqui* that certain orators of
today believe they can emulate by speaking *horride atque incomposite* (10.2.17),
and the *antiqui* followed by Caesar in adopting now obsolete morphologies for
Greek names (1.5.63). The *veteres* in 10.7.14, 12.9.5, 12.10.48 (and see 4.1.9) are
the pre-Ciceronian orators.

Throughout the *Institutio* the examples of expressive choices proposed as
points of reference are drawn very prevalently from Cicero, who for Quintilian
therefore has current value as a model for would-be orators. And Caesar is contrasted with the *antiqui* and the *veteres* respectively in 1.5.63 and 1.7.21. Yet in
9.3.1, compared to certain uses of recent linguistic *consuetudo*, Cicero is also
placed among the *veteres* (... *ut omnes veteres et Cicero praecipue*); in 10.5.2 *veteres* includes the orators of the generation prior to Cicero, Cicero himself and
the orators of the Augustan age; in 11.3.143, with regard to the way of wearing
the toga, *veteres* refers to the time of Plotius Gallus, active around 100 BCE,
and of Nigidius Figulus, a contemporary of Cicero, but also to orators *qui post
Ciceronem fuerunt*. In 3.4.1–4, a position sustained by Aristotle and Cicero is associated with the *antiqui* (1), and described as *vetus* (4); in 9.3.74, Gorgias and
Isocrates in the Greek tradition, and Cicero in the Latin one, are placed
among the *veteres*. In 10.5.20, Cicero is already considered among the *veteres*
from the point of view of Cestius Pius, an Augustan rhetorician who composed
fictitious orations in response to, and confuting, those of Cicero. In 9.3.16, we
find Terence and Catullus associated together in the category of *antiqui*.[9] In
10.1.126, the *antiqui* from which Seneca was anxious to distance himself, evidently included, first of all, Cicero. In 10.1.118, the *veteres* to whom Quintilian likens
his admired master Domitius Afer, and, in 10.1.122, the *veteres* he is pleased to
see emulated by contemporary orators, are undoubtedly Cicero and the orators
of his generation, not the pre-Ciceronians, whom he does not regard as models.
In these two cases, we can chronologically circumscribe the reference only on the
basis of its coherence with other passages in the *Institutio*, in which the fully positive model of the past is always the oratory of Cicero and of the early Augustan
age: these are effectively the only two passages in the *Institutio* where *veteres*,
without further specification, conveys the idea of a superior quality.[10]

---

9 Also in 6.3.57 the *veteres* include a figure from the II century BCE and one from the age of Cicero.
10 See Cova 1990, 44, n. 69.

Thus far we have considered cases in which these terms indicate a somehow identifiable distance from the present. With similar frequency, however, they signal (as *prior* sometimes does as well) a distance that remains entirely undefined.[11] This can be said for at least 38 of the 83 pertinent occurrences of *vetus/vetustus*, for almost all the 19 pertinent occurrences of *vetustas*, for at least 15 of the 41 pertinent occurrences of *antiquus* (and derivatives).

A periodization of cultural ages is not therefore attainable from the terminology in itself but, from time to time, is discernable from context. However, in many of the cases in which *vetus* or *antiquus* indicate in a general way an outdated linguistic or stylistic usage in Latin, it is reasonable to assume that the reference should be understood as relating to the pre-Ciceronian period, to which, as we have seen, these terms often refer in an explicit way. I therefore believe it is mistaken to affirm that in Quintilian *antiquus* and *vetus* always – or with rare exceptions – refer to the whole past up to and including the Augustan age, as opposed to the post-Augustan age through to the Flavian present, deemed the age of the *novi*.[12] This is the meaning such terms usually have in the *Dialogus de oratoribus*, where the discourse is polarized into a clear-cut opposition between *antiqui* (or *veteres*) and *novi*, with the late Augustan orator Cassius Severus (c. 40 BCE – c. CE 35) called upon to represent the transition to the new age. In Quintilian's work the discourse develops, as we shall see, along more complex and therefore less clear-cut lines.[13]

Novus and *recens* (or *nos, nostri, nunc* etc.) also often have an indeterminate meaning in Quintilian, and may refer to phenomena whose beginning it would be difficult to establish. It is true, however, that very often they quite clearly

---

11 In some cases the opposite pair *vetus-novus* expresses entirety: 5.4.1 *orationes veterum ac novorum*; 12.4.1 *exemplorum copia cum veterum tum … novorum*; 12.11.29 *veteribus vel novis exemplis*. **12** As maintained by Peterson 1891, 42 and 43, who, as it seems, admits no exceptions, Colson 1924, 109, who admits as exceptions only 1.8.9, 2.5.23 and 10.1.43 (see below, note 39), and Calcante 2007, 121. **13** It is understood that also in the *Dialogus* the age of the *antiqui*, though regarded overall as being in opposition to that of the *novi*, is however conceived as evolving. Aper's speech (16–23) delineates a constant growth of oratory from the remote age of Maenenius Agrippa to the present and towards the future: in this *continuum*, the Ciceronian-Augustan period in any case takes on its own distinct form, if nothing else as a polemic target, in that it is isolated and celebrated by admirers of the *antiqui*, and by Messala's speech. Also emerging from the speeches of Aper and Messala is a clear awareness of the distance, in terms of artistic maturity, between the Ciceronian-Augustan age and previous ages in other genres: theatrical texts, poetry, historiography. Furthermore, the *Dialogus* interestingly calls into question the literary concept of 'antiquity' (and 'modernity'), linked to the time involved in the evolution of styles, which is different from the 'objective' time of history: see Citroni 2005b.

identify the post-Augustan phase of eloquence, literature and custom, through to the present, and the tendencies conditioned by the practice of declamation already present in the Augustan age: see, for example, *novus* in 2.5.23; 2.5.26; 8.5.15 (in this case Cicero is also included); 8.5.34; 9.2.42; 10.1.41 and the expression *recens haec lascivia* in 2.5.22 and 10.1.43.

3. A definition of the periodization of the literature of the past adopted by Quintilian has been attempted by Steinmetz in two useful discussions, one serious limitation of which, however, is that only the review of the writers in book X is taken into consideration.

As regards Greek literature, Steinmetz argues that it is considered all together in Quintilian, with no reference to a periodization, or rather, that the rare mentions of the different phases in Greek literature are not aimed at evaluating the cited authors' capacity to offer useful models of expression.[14] One can agree with this latter consideration, but only in relation to poetry. For the other genres of cultural production, things are rather different. Heldmann, in his important volume on the ancient concept of oratory's decadence, in the correct attempt to demonstrate an optimistic and progressive attitude in Quintilian, adopts, with different arguments, a similar position: he argues that Quintilian tones down the temporal breaks, does not emphasize the excellence of certain phases of oratory and of other genres of the past, and represents the Greek tradition as a basically uninterrupted flow through to the present.[15] I do not believe that is how things are at all.

In the review in book X the authors are ordered according to genre, and then, within each genre, possibly after an indication of the most representative one, they are generally presented in chronological order. In the course of the first proposed series, that of the epic poets, Quintilian signals at a certain point that the authors he is about to name (evidently unlike those mentioned previously) were not included in the lists drawn up by the Alexandrian grammarians, not because their value was less but because the grammarians had adopted the criterion of not including living authors (10.1.54 *Apollonius in ordinem a grammaticis datum non venit, quia Aristarchus atque Aristophanes, poetarum iudices, neminem sui temporis in numerum redegerunt*, 'Apollonius does not appear in the grammarians' list, because Aristarchus and Aristophanes, who evaluated the poets, included none of their contemporaries'). This annotation reminds the reader, albeit only indirectly, of the threshold represented by the Alexandrian period in

---

14 Steinmetz 1964, 463–466; Steinmetz 1982, 12.
15 Heldmann 1982, 137–141. See also below, end of note 18.

the history of Greek literature. Nonetheless, it is true that the evaluations concerning the Hellenistic poets do not allude to any diversity, or inferiority, connected with their relative lateness. If the appraisal expressed here about Apollonius of Rhodes, and in the following section on Aratus, appear somewhat reductive, it must be said that Quintilian, a few lines above, points out even more serious shortcomings in Hesiod and in Antimachus.

Instead, in the whole review of the Greek poets, the only evaluation of artistic inferiority explicitly associated with the temporal dimension concerns a condition of antiquity: I am referring to the serious reservations expressed about Aeschylus, whose *sublimitas* and *gravitas*, in Quintilian's appraisal, often go *usque ad vitium*, and who is mostly *rudis* and *incompositus* (10.1.66). These presumed defects are attributed to his antiquity: Quintilian, with cursory simplification, identifies him as the *primus inventor* of tragedy (*tragoedias primus in lucem ... protulit*), and *rudis* regularly refers to the immature phases of an art. Clear confirmation comes from the subsequent assertion that those defects were subsequently corrected by other poets, who were authorized to re-perform his dramas in an updated form, thus obtaining success and agonal victories.[16]

The situation is different for historiography and oratory. Greek historiography after Clitarchus, one of Alexander's historians, is judged to be simply nonexistent (10.1.74 f.): output is deemed to have been interrupted (*intermissa*), only to make a comeback in the age of Augustus, with Timagenes, who restarted historiography, earning for himself fresh glory (*intermissam historias scribendi industriam nova laude reparavit*). Here Quintilian adopts the pattern of total condemnation of Hellenistic production that had also been applied to other spheres: as various sources attest, the figurative arts and oratory had been declared 'dead' after Alexander by Greek intellectual and artistic movements which, at least from the middle of the second century BCE onwards, had begun to advocate their 'rebirth' through a return to pre-Hellenistic forms.[17]

---

16 An extensive discussion of this problematic piece of information can be found in Biles 2006–2007, esp. 218 and 240, with bibliography.

17 See D.H. *Orat.Vett.* 1.1ff. (high-quality oratory, which declined after Alexander almost to the point of disappearing, is now, under Augustus, experiencing new development); Petr. 2.7 (oratory, with the advent of new corrupting trends from Asia, *stetit et obmutuit*); Philostr. *VS.* 1.19 (oratory, exhausted after Aeschines, was reborn in the second half of the first century CE with Nicetas, considered to be the founder of what we call New Sophistic). For sculpture: Plin. *Nat.* 34.52 *cessavit deinde ars, ac rursus ... revixit* (the revival was due to artists active in the middle of the second century BCE). See Preisshofen 1979, 269–277; Heldmann 1982, 126–131; Coarelli 1996, 521–526, with further bibliography.

Quintilian is only a little less drastic regarding oratory: he declares (10.1.80) that Demetrius of Phalerum (who concluded his political activity in 307 BCE), a highly talented orator (*multum ingenii habuisse et facundiae fateor*) with whom, however, the beginning of the decline of eloquence is made to coincide (*quamquam is primus inclinasse eloquentiam dicitur*), was the last of the Attic orators (*ultimus est fere ex Atticis qui dici possit orator*). After him, therefore, a genuine Attic oratory no longer existed.[18] And in fact, in all of his work, Quintilian does not cite any Greek orators or historians later than the first decades after the death of Alexander.[19] By contrast, he frequently cites, and in very positive terms, recent and very recent Greek authors of treatises on oratory, almost right up to the very years in which the *Institutio oratoria* was written.[20]

In short, it would not be right to say that Greek literature is seen by Quintilian as a monolith, with an absence of chronological depth. He shows his awareness that before Lysias there had been less elaborate forms of oratory (12.10.21)

---

18 From various passages in Cicero (*De orat.* 2.95; *Brut.* 36–38; 285; *Orat.* 92; 94; *Off.* 1.3) and Quintilian (10.1.33) we know that Demetrius was considered to have initiated a new form of eloquence – calm and gentle, sophisticated and flowery – which placed him in an ambiguous position on the boundary between the Attic tradition and the innovations of Asianism. He might have been considered the initiator of Asianism, and therefore, from the Atticistic point of view, the initiator of the corruption of eloquence (a responsibility attributed on other occasions to Hegesias), or as the last exponent of the great Attic oratory, as affirmed by Cicero (*Brut.* 285) and Quintilian (10.1.80), reacting to the opposing viewpoint, which, however, they themselves markedly attest (Quintil. *ibid.*; Cic. *Brut.* 37). For an in-depth discussion of the ancient judgements on Demetrius, see Heldmann 1982, 98–122; 134–139: I am unconvinced, however, by his thesis that Quintilian's inclusion of Demetrius among the Attics expresses a conception of Attic oratory as being open to future evolutions and in continuity with them; in Quintilian's language as well, the word 'Attic' expresses a qualitative idea, and so the end of Attic oratory means the end of high-quality oratory.
19 Empylos of Rhodes, a contemporary of Cicero, is recalled in 10.6.4 only for his exceptional memory; Glycon Spyridion, a declaimer of the Augustan age often cited by Seneca the Elder, is mentioned in 6.1.41 only as the protagonist of an episode in which he made himself look ridiculous. Posidonius is cited in 3.6.37 as a philosopher, not as a historian. Eratosthenes (III BCE), Apollodorus of Athens (II BCE) and Apelles (or Apollas) of Pontus (III BCE?) are referred to in 11.2.14 as authorities only with regard to some specific information about the poet Simonides.
20 Often mentioned are Hermagoras of Temnos (II BCE) and various authors of the Augustan age, including Dionysius of Halicarnassus and, above all, Caecilius of Caleacte, Apollodorus of Pergamum and Theodorus of Gadara. There are also occasional references to other Greek rhetoricians from the second century BCE to the first century CE. The most recent are Theon and Hermagoras, a pupil of Theodorus, who some contemporaries of Quintilian had known personally (3.1.18). In the history of Greek rhetorical theory outlined in 3.1.8–18 the contribution made by authors of the Ciceronian and Augustan age, through to this more recent Hermagoras, receives great prominence.

and that the advent of Asianism marked a turning point in Greek oratory.[21] If, in rhetorical treatise writing, the elaborations ranging from the origins of the science through to the contemporary period are considered useful for the present, oratory appears instead to be an appropriate point of reference only in the production preceding the flourishing of Asianism. This delimitation certainly reflects his opting for a composed and disciplined oratorial model. But I do not believe one can draw from this any significant support for the idea of a presumed fundamental 'classicism' in Quintilian. In the Roman schools and in the culture of the time there was probably never a significant presence of Greek oratorical texts other than those – at any rate, very large in number – representing the Attic oratory of the fifth and fourth centuries, which the Greek tradition had already somehow judged to be canonical, and had passed down. Also Cicero, in his polemics against Roman Atticism, certainly does not refer to exemplary representatives of Hellenistic oratory, but rather to what, for him, was the loftier Atticism of Demosthenes. It is very surprising, on the other hand, that authors like Polybius and Timaeus, repeatedly praised by Cicero, seem here to have sunk into the sea of the Hellenistic death of history.

As far as poetry is concerned, the review is dominated by the pre-Hellenistic poets already rendered canonical by Greek tradition and who had been great models for the Roman poets from the start. Only for poetry in hexameters does the review consider the Hellenistic age: basically in continuity and in the same line with the more ancient poets (10.1.55 f.), there come three of the main exponents of the first Alexandrian generation: Apollonius of Rhodes, Theocritus and Aratus, then followed by Euphorion and the more recent Nicander (II BCE). These two latter poets are explicitly cited, together with Tyrtaeus, as figures of reference for the great Augustan poets, who, having imitated (*Nicandrum ... secuti Macer atque Vergilius*) or cited them (Virgil, in citing Euphorion, showed his approval, while Horace placed Tyrtaeus beside Homer), now functioned, in the Flavian present, as guarantors of their value and testified to their status as mod-

---

21 It must be acknowledged, however, that in 9.4.16 f. (see above, p. 21) Quintilian, departing from Cicero, interprets the different rhythmic modalities of Lysias, Herodotus and Thucydides with respect to Plato and Demosthenes as being due not to chronological distance, and thus to a different degree of maturity of the art, but as the result of the different artistic criteria adopted. His treatment of Asianism and Atticism in 12.10.16–26 also stresses the diversity of styles, not their evolution over time, which in any case is also suggested within Attic oratory itself: ranging from the maximum of simplicity in Andocides, to Lysias, to the greater richness of Isocrates and on to the fullness and perfection of Aeschines and, above all, Demosthenes.

els.[22] For the three Hellenistic poets cited previously, there had been no need to render explicit this guarantee, but in fact they too had been well-known models of Virgil. If the Greek poets, from Homer to Nicander, seem here to be a unitary and chronologically-indistinct whole, it is exactly because they are seen through the filter put in place by Latin literature of the past: they represent the treasure trove, preselected by the Greek tradition, in which the whole of Latin literature had found its own points of reference, and in which they still had to be sought in the present and future. But it cannot be said, as Steinmetz does, that the Latin poets, insofar as they simultaneously took, within a single work, archaic, 'classical' and Hellenistic Greek authors as their models, demonstrated that they had a vision of Greek literature which was not correlated with its historic development, and that Quintilian reflected this vision in his review. The Latin poets knew how to distinguish the difference between the epic of Homer and that of Apollonius, between the iambics of Archilochus and those of Callimachus, whom they took at the same time as models: the Hellenistic poets themselves, and above all Callimachus, had taught how to recognize the differences in their programmatic and polemic passages, frequently echoed and re-elaborated by the Latin poets. Signs of this awareness of the diversity of historical phases in Greek literature can be discerned, as I believe I have demonstrated, also in Quintilian, and in his review of poets as well.

The lively influence that recent and contemporary Greek epigrammatists, especially Lucillius (active in the age of Nero), were having in those same years on the poetry of Martial was not regarded by Quintilian as worthy of consideration.

4. The picture presented of the Latin literary past is much more complex.

Let's begin with the language. Quintilian sees it as being in continual transformation, and makes no reference to general periodizations or chronological thresholds: every single phenomenon has its own history, sometimes with alternating phases of eclipse and recovery. The instability and constant mutation of usages appears particularly evident in orthography (1.7.11). *Vetustas* may be a guarantee of the validity and correctness of linguistic choices in current use (1.5.72; 1.6.32), or may refer to what we call archaisms – outdated forms whose

---

22 10.1.56 *Euphorionem transibimus? Quem nisi probasset Vergilius … numquam certe conditorum Chalcidico versu carminum fecisset in Bucolicis mentionem. Quid? Horatius frustra Tyrtaeum Homero subiungit?* ('Shall we leave out Euphorion? If Virgil had not approved of him, he would never have mentioned those 'songs wrought in Chalcidic verse' in his *Eclogues*. And has Horace no reason for putting Tyrtaeus next to Homer?'). With an allusion to Verg. *Ecl.* 10.50 and Hor. *Ars*. 402.

recovery may be justified for particular ends.[23] For Quintilian, current *consuetu-do*, provided it is understood as *consensus eruditorum* (1.6.45), must outweigh, in general, every other criterion of legitimacy in the choice of language (1.6.3): both criteria relating to the coherence (*ratio*) of the language system (*analogia* and *etymologia*) and those regarding usages attested in the past: *auctoritas* (uses of the *summi in eloquentia viri*, normally taken as points of reference and as models: 1.6.2) and *vetustas* (outdated 'archaisms'), to the point of judging as erroneous usages present also in illustrious *auctores* like Lucilius (1.6.7–9), Asinius Pollio, Messala, Cato (1.6.42).[24] It would be ridiculous to prefer the *consuetudo* of the past to current *consuetudo* (1.6.43), at the expense of clarity (*perspicuitas*), which is the chief virtue of discourse (1.6.41). Yet Quintilian shows he has a good understanding of the subtle reasons of expressive efficacy that may in some cases suggest the adoption of archaizing forms. *Vetustas*, understood as archaism, confers *maiestas* (1.6.1; 1.6.39), *religio* (1.6.1), *dignitas* and *sanctitas* (8.3.24), *auctoritas* (8.3.25). And there is also a further reason, acutely noted in

---

23 The first of these two meanings of *vetustas* in Quintilian is not considered by von Fritz 1949, nor, it seems to me, in later studies on the matter. Von Fritz does however deserve credit for having precisely identified the second meaning, that of the studied archaism, and for having perceptively analysed its relationship with the other criteria of legitimation of language choices. We are also indebted to him for sustaining that Quintilian is completely coherent and autonomous in the grammatical chapters, a position that ran contrary to other scholars, who, though authoritative, entertained some misunderstandings in this respect.

24 On *vetustas*, *auctoritas* and *consuetudo* as criteria of legitimacy in linguistic choices alongside and, potentially, in conflict with, *ratio*, see 1.5.5; 1.6.1; 9.3.3. In turn, *consuetudo* may come into conflict with *vetustas* and *auctoritas*. Grebe 2000, 207 does not seem to grasp that in Quintilian *consuetudo* is current usage, in constant evolution, and considers it to be a conservative principle similar to *vetustas*. *Auctoritas* and *vetustas*, though clearly distinct, as shown by von Fritz 1949, 345–352, arguing against those who did not see, or misunderstood, the difference, are however closely connected: the writers who, with their prestige, act as authorities, generally belong to the past (see 1.6.39 *verba a vetustate repetita ... magnos adsertores habent:* however, in Ax 2011, 296 and 298, *magnos adsertores* is understood as referring not to the great ancient authors, but to the great archaizers, such as Virgil), and *vetustas* itself may constitute *auctoritas:* see 3.7.26 *multum auctoritatis adfert vetustas*; 4.2.118 *auctoritate veterum*; 8.3.25 *vetustatis inimitabilem ... auctoritatem*; 1.6.39 *auctoritatem antiquitatis*. The frequently affirmed idea that *auctoritas* in Quintilian denotes the attestations of the Ciceronian and Augustan ages, regarded as normative, as opposed to *vetustas*, which refers to pre-Ciceronian attestations, was confuted by Siebenborn 1976, 95, on the basis of the observation that, in 1.6.42, *auctoritas* is represented by Cato (further bibliography in Grebe 2000, 204). The idea also conflicts with the fact, ascertained above (§ 2), that *vetustas* in Quintilian does not refer to a definite age as such. A useful discussion of *vetustas* and *auctoritas* in Quintilian can be found in Lomanto 1994, 240 and 247–249, who, however, does not make a really clear distinction between the two concepts. The treatment of the topic in Ax 2011 is too cursory.

1.6.39: archaisms (*verba a vetustate repetita*) also create, together with a sense of *maiestas*, a special *delectatio* (*adferunt orationi maiestatem aliquam non sine delectatione*) in that, no longer being in use (*quia intermissa sunt*), they paradoxically combine the authoritativeness of antiquity with the allure of novelty (*et auctoritatem antiquitatis habent et ... gratiam novitati similem parant*). Aside from the subtlety of the observation, which anticipates Fronto's notion of archaism as a generator of surprise and which would be echoed in Gellius,[25] it is worth noting that Quintilian is affirming here – and he confirms it in other contexts, as we shall see – that there is a specific pleasure, worthy of being pursued, inherent to *novitas*.

Searching for this pleasure by reproposing what is old and no longer used must not, however, become a norm of discourse. On the contrary, it should be the exception (1.6.40): moderation is required (*opus est modo*), and archaisms must neither be frequent nor too showy (*neque crebra sint haec nec manifesta*), because nothing is more displeasing than ostentation (*nihil est odiosius adfectatione*). And at any rate, they must not be drawn from too remote an antiquity (*nec utique ab ultimis et iam oblitteratis repetita temporibus*), the risk being that of incomprehensibility (*qualia sunt ... Saliorum carmina vix sacerdotibus suis satis intellecta ...*).

A similar appreciation of archaism recurs in book VIII: *antiquitas* confers dignity and sacredness, and stirs wonder in that it employs terms extraneous to *consuetudo*: 8.3.24 ... *dignitatem dat antiquitas. Namque et sanctiorem et magis admirabilem faciunt orationem, quibus non quilibet fuerit usurus.*[26] And here too there is immediately an invitation to exercise moderation in resorting to this expedient, and to avoid using terms from remote antiquity: 8.3.25 *Sed utendum modo nec ex ultimis tenebris repetenda.*

Note that the *ultima et iam oblitterata tempora* in 1.6.40, that age whose language, as attested by the *Carmen Saliare*, is incomprehensible today and which Quintilian therefore believes is inadmissible to draw upon, the *ultimae tenebrae* in 8.3.25, and the *vetustissima tempora* in 1.7.11 (when even the alphabet was not the same), represent the only chronological period identified as such in the treat-

---

25 Calcante 2007, 112 rightly refers to the well-known passages of Fro. p. 57.18 f. v.d.H.[2] *insperatum ... atque inopinatum verbum appello quod praeter spem atque opinionem audientium aut legentium promitur* and Gell. 11.7.2 *Nova autem videri dico etiam ea quae sunt inusitata et desita, tametsi sunt vetusta* (see Lomanto 1994, 247 and n. 47).

26 *Sanctus* and *admirabilis* are tied in by Calcante 2007, 113 f. to the Aristotelian concepts of σεμνόν and θαυμαστόν, pertaining to the ξενικόν, that is, the 'unusual', in language. In this way, then, according to Calcante, we again encounter the same paradox of an effect of novelty induced by an archaic element.

ment of the language: but it is done so 'negatively', in that it is a phase without any contact with or relevance for the present.

All this constant changing of spoken and written forms over time (see also 8.3.26, 34; 10.2.13) is considered from the point of view of a powerful idea of the present. It is clear to Quintilian that in the present, as in any given moment, there coexist usages corresponding to different periods in the evolution of the language: innovative uses that are becoming established, and the survival, spontaneous or intentionally sought, of usages that are fading away.[27] Looking to the past, the evolution appears to him as a whole to be a path that now makes it possible, choosing in a reasoned and measured way on the basis of a sensible weighing of the options offered by tradition and usage, to employ a more coherent, effective and clear language.[28] But in the case of language, as in those of literary trends, style and oratorial practices, which we shall come to presently, the author also knows that the tendencies which have led to this progress are also accompanied by contrary and aberrant ones. In 9.3.1, observing the constant transformation imposed upon language by *consuetudo*, he exclaims: *Utinam ... non peiora vincant.* In language, as in oratorial and literary style, he feels it is his task and responsibility to guide contemporaries and posterity towards the choice of the best possibilities that have matured over the course of tradition, and to thwart opposing impulses, confident that he knows how to interpret what is most authentic in the requirements of the present.[29]

5. In relation to Latin literature, Steinmetz,[30] on the basis of the review in book X alone, thought he could discern a five-phase periodization in Quintilian: 1) from the beginnings to Terence; 2) from the second half of the II century BCE until Accius; 3) the age of Cicero and Virgil; 4) from the end of the Augustan age to Quintilian's older contemporaries; 5) the living authors (never named, with the exception of Domitian in his capacity as epic poet). However, the distinction between phases 1) and 2) is not recognizable in book X. We find it, but only in relation to

---

27 See 1.5.21, 27–29; 8.3.27.

28 This is not an explicitly formulated principle, but an overall attitude in his treatment of the language. At any rate, see 1.7.6, 27.

29 *Peiora* is also read as 'worse than the examples cited'. The generic *et mille alia* with which the series of examples ends rules out this interpretation, as Shackleton Bailey 1983, 226, notes; he proposes the expunction of *vincant* (*et mille alia utinam non peiora*): but the cited examples are not presented as degenerations compared to which other cases must be considered 'worse'. Russell 2001 interprets in the sense I have accepted above: 'Let us hope the worse usages do not prevail!' 2.12.12 expresses the old master's sense of dejection regarding the eventuality that an uncultured oratory will totally prevail in the future.

30 Steinmetz 1982, 21–25.

the development of oratory, in two passages from book XII that are not considered by Steinmetz: in 12.10.11, Quintilian, in relating the development of Greek sculpture to that of Roman oratory, distinguishes between a primitive phase, from Cato to the Gracchi, and an intermediate phase represented by Crassus and Hortensius (who, however, was a contemporary of, and not much older than, Cicero);[31] in 12.11.27 as well, Crassus and Hortensius represent the phase preceding the full Ciceronian maturity (surprisingly, no mention is made of Antonius, whom Cicero, in *De oratore*, placed alongside Crassus as the leading figure of that generation). Then, in 12.10.11, comes the Ciceronian-Augustan phase (Steinmetz's phase three) and, in close continuity with it, the period of the authors personally known to Quintilian (from Seneca to no longer living contemporaries), corresponding approximately to the fourth phase of Steinmetz. Actually, in 10.1, on which Steinmetz relies, this phase is divided into two: 10.1.118 mentions authors of the previous generation that Quintilian had known personally, and 10.1.119–121 some slightly older contemporaries who were no longer living.[32] In 8.5.33 and 12.10.45 Quintilian identifies a period of oratory predating Cato, not considered by Steinmetz, who also does not consider the whole phase that produced the most ancient documents in other genres (XII Tables, *Carmen Saliare*, etc.) which, in Quintilian, as we have seen, is often identified as a separate phase, unsuited to providing models for the present.[33]

In truth, in the review of book X, although the names of the authors in each genre are for the most part listed in chronological order, the explicit references situating them in time are few in number, and by no means do they enable us to affirm that Quintilian regarded the same chronological framework as pertinent for all genres. Among the epic poets, Ennius is described as ancient compared to Lucretius, Varro of Atax, Macer and Virgil; then comes a single phase of *propiores* running from Ovid to contemporaries. For satire, Lucilius is a more ancient author than Horace; next comes Persius and then the contemporaries,

---

31 Irrespective of the objective chronology, Heldmann 1982, 153 rightly observes that in *Brutus* Cicero too presents Hortensius as a transitional figure.

32 This distinction is recorded by Heldmann 1982, 155. In his analysis of Quintilian's view of the development of Roman oratory, Heldmann (151–156, 160 f.) correctly identifies 5 phases, of which only the last 3 are considered in the review of book X (the Ciceronian-Augustan phase and the following two we have just mentioned); in 12.10, the first two – the period from Cato to the Gracchi, and the one from Crassus to Hortensius – are considered as well, while the final two are run together. Heldmann, like Steinmetz, says nothing about the pre-Catonian phase (see following note).

33 1.6.11; 1.6.40; 1.7.11; 8.2.12, 8.3.25, cited above on pp. 20 and 30 f. Pre-Catonian oratory appears, together with the XII Tables, as a paradoxical model of contemporary hyper-archaists in Sen. *Ep.* 114.13.

who are not named. For lyric verse, Quintilian names Horace, then Caesius Bassus (specifying that he is an older contemporary of himself: 10.1.96 *quem nuper vidimus*), after which he says there are other living poets, much better than Bassus, though without mentioning their names. As regards tragedy, he distinguishes the ancient phase, represented here by Pacuvius and Accius (the only mention of earlier periods in Latin tragedy is in 5.10.84, a citation from the beginning of Ennius' *Medea*, often used in rhetorical treatises; of the 9 quotations of tragic verse for which the author is not indicated, some could be traced back to Ennius), and then recalls the Augustans Varius and Ovid, and finally his own older contemporaries, among whom he names Pomponius Secundus. Of the historians, he refers to Sallust and Livy, and then some older contemporaries; finally, he mentions a great living author, but does not give his name. After the review of the orators from the age of Cicero and Augustus, mention is made of the older contemporaries, then, as we have said, other, more recent but already dead ones, and finally some who are still living, who remain unnamed. No reference is made to a chronology or to temporal phases for writers of elegiacs, iambics and comedies, or for philosophers. In any case, in his review in book X, Quintilian does not set out to delineate historic phases of literary production, but only, in the cases we have mentioned, to position the authors he speaks about in a chronological timeframe. A reference to developmental phases can only be glimpsed for the archaic nature of Ennius' epic verse and the tragedies of Pacuvius and Accius, and for the modernity of Seneca.

It is important to underline that in Quintilian, for the first time, we find an explicit formalization of the category of 'archaic Latin literature' for pre-Ciceronian production. This comes partly in the review of book X, but above all in other passages of the *Institutio:* the passage in book XII mentioned at the beginning of this section, to which we will return, the passages already cited on p. 21 f. regarding the use of *vetus* or *antiquus* with reference to this age of Latin literature, and others which we will now examine.

Naturally, in his Epistle to Augustus, Horace had already judged, without the possibility of appeal, all output prior to neoterism to be archaic, understood negatively as artistically inadequate: all that literature which, in the final years of Horace's own life, was still considered in traditionalist cultured circles to be fully up-to-date and the only valid kind, just as it undoubtedly had been, only a few years earlier, by Cicero and Varro.[34] After Horace we occasionally encounter, from Ovid to the Flavian age, more or less severe observations on the shortcomings in *ars* of the poets before Catullus, and on their unsuitability for modern

---

34 On the Ciceronian and Varronian canon, see Citroni 2006a, 216–220.

taste.[35] But only in Quintilian is there a clearly defined concept of archaic Latin literature. We must, however, also acknowledge that he seems to be referring to a notion already known and familiar to his public.

In the review in book X, the category of archaic literature is presupposed, and not rendered truly explicit. Only a few 'archaic' authors are cited, indubitably because they are, generally speaking, not suited to acting as expressive models for the present. Of the epic poets, only Ennius is mentioned, with a very reductive judgment entirely conditioned by where he fits chronologically: antiquity makes him venerable rather than fine, just as oak trees in woods are considered sacred because of their antiquity (10.1.88, cited above, on p. 21). It is therefore more useful to look at poets more recent than Virgil rather than his predecessors: *propiores ... magis utiles ...* The tragedians Pacuvius and Accius receive glowing appreciation: 10.1.97 *clarissimi gravitate sententiarum, verborum pondere, auctoritate personarum* ('the most distinguished of the ancients for seriousness of thought,weightiness of expression, and the dignity of their characters'), while their lack of polish is justified by their antiquity; it was not a personal shortcoming, but one of their time, a time which was still ignorant of these values: *nitor et summa in excolendis operibus manus magis videri potest temporibus quam ipsis defuisse...* ('Their lack of polish and of those finishing touches which perfect a work may well be the fault of the times they lived in rather than of themselves'). In the appraisal of Lucilius (10.1.93), the chronological position enters into play in a more veiled way. Quintilian attests that in the Flavian age he has *adhuc* admirers who consider him not only to be the best satirist, but even the greatest of all the poets. Only *adhuc* suggests that one would expect a less positive judgement by virtue of his antiquity. Quintilian considers Horace's criticism of Lucilius to be unjustly severe, and highly praises the qualities of the latter's content (94 *et eruditio in eo mira et libertas atque inde acerbitas et abunde salis* 'Lucilius has both remarkable learning and remarkable freedom, and hence a sharp edge and an abundance of wit'). The reasons why he nonetheless regards Horace as superior are based on qualities regularly associated with the modernity opened up by neoterism: *multum est tersior et purus magis.* His severe appraisal of the comic playwrights (1.10.99–100; Plautus, Caecilius, Terence and Afranius are named) is not related to when they were active, but to the presumed inability of the Latin language to replicate the charm of Attic comedy. It is at any rate noteworthy that the best of them is considered to be Terence, on the basis,

---

35 The passages from Ovid are cited in note 37. See also Val. Max. 8.14.2; Pers. 1.76–78; Sen. *Ep. fr. ap.* Gell. 12.2.2–12; Stat. *Silv.* 2.7.75; Mart. 11.90 and also the *Dialogus* of Tacitus, written at a later date but set in the same Flavian age: 20.5; 21.7; 23.2.

once again, of a quality associable with greater modernity: *elegantia* (*Terenti scripta ... sunt in hoc genere elegantissima*). In the sections on prose writers (historiography, oratory, philosophy), no pre-Ciceronian author is mentioned at all. His judgement of Asinius Pollio, whose lack of *nitor* and *iucunditas* makes him seem a century older than his contemporary Cicero (10.1.113), presupposes as a given in Quintilian and his readers the idea that the oratory of the II century is artistically immature.[36]

A full-blown general category of 'archaic literature' is identified in the review of the poets that the *grammaticus* will get his young pupils to read (1.8.5–12). The review initially considers Greek and Latin authors together, and lists which genres are recommended and which are not, rather than discussing individual poets. Only a few very prestigious names are mentioned: Homer, Virgil, Horace, Menander. As far as the Greeks are concerned, there is a complete absence of chronological references, and the genres listed, which besides epic, tragedy, lyrical verse and comedy, also include erotic elegy, hendecasyllabic and sotadic verse, suggest that here too in general Hellenistic poetry is considered together with what came before (even if, given the youthful age of the pupils, for moral reasons sotadic verse is prohibited and hendecasyllabic verse and erotic elegy heavily discouraged). The comments on comedy and on Menander prompt a specific mention of Latin comedy, judged to be not without utility (1.8.8 *Latini quoque auctores adferent utilitatis aliquid*). From here, almost as an appendix to the discourse, Quintilian begins to reflect on how the *veteres Latini* can be useful in general. The passage opens with a broad acknowledgement, which reiterates and extends the one just granted to comedy: 1.8.8 *Multum autem veteres etiam Latini conferunt...* An apologetic note can be detected in the words of Quintilian, as if he knew he had to address readers' distrust of these texts. In fact, he immediately concedes that in general they are worth more for *ingenium* than for *ars* (*quamquam plerique plus ingenio quam arte valuerunt*), with an allusion to Ovid's well-known judgement of Ennius,[37] but declares that they can make a big contribution to the *copia verborum* (the specific aim also of the proposed readings in the review of book X). The tragedies offer models of *gravitas*, the comedies of *elegantia* and *attikismòs* (here they are rated much more positively than in book X). The *veteres* are even exemplary in terms of care of composition (*oeconomia*), in which they are superior to the majority of the *novi*, as well as in terms of *sanctitas* and *virilitas*: 1.8.9 *Oeconomia quoque in iis diligentior*

---

36 A similar judgement of the anachronistic stylistic archaism of Asinius Pollio can be found in Tac. *Dial.* 21.7.

37 Ov. *Tr.* 2.424 *Ennius ingenio maximus, arte rudis*, and cf. *Am.* 1.15.19 *Ennius arte carens*. See also Quint. *Inst.* 10.1.40 *ingeniosis quidem sed arte carentibus* (p. 21 above).

*quam in plerisque novorum erit, qui omnium operum solam virtutem sententias pu-
taverunt. Sanctitas certe et, ut sic dicam, virilitas ab iis petenda est...* ('They are
also more careful about organization than most of the moderns, who have
come to think that clever phrases are the only virtue in any work. Certainly a
high moral tone, and, if I may say so, manliness, has to be sought from
them'). The qualities which Quintilian claims for the *veteres* are contrasted
with the deplorable characteristics of the majority of contemporary authors (*plerique novi, nos*) who, instead of attending to composition, aim only to achieve
the virtuosity of striking sentences, and who yield to every vice stemming
from pleasure in style, as is now common practice in personal behaviour: *quando nos in omnia deliciarum vitia dicendi quoque ratione defluximus.* So, from an
initially defensive position inviting the refined people of today to acknowledge a
series of significant qualities in the *veteres*, Quintilian moves on to denounce the
decadence of current literature, with regard to which the *veteres* represent positive models. And the *veteres* can be identified with certainty. In fact, Quintilian
cites (1.8.11) the most significant names, which are the customary ones of the Ciceronian and Varronian canon contested by Horace: Ennius, Accius, Pacuvius,
Lucilius, Caecilius, Terence. Indeed, he lists them precisely insofar as they are
often cited for their quality of *veteres* by Cicero himself, by Asinius Pollio and
by other orators of that time (1.8.10–12) – not just to display erudition, but to
add credibility and embellishment to their speeches, and also to bring the relief
of aesthetic pleasure to audiences tired of the harshness of the court.

The chronological position of the *novi* is less clear-cut. The craze for impressive *sententiae* and voluptuousness of style point towards the methods employed
above all by declaimers from the Augustan age onwards, and then by Neronian
literature, frequently criticized by contemporaries themselves. Between the decadent *novi* and the *veteres* who, for their lack of *ars*, can only be praised with
reserve, there stretches the span of the great literature from the Ciceronian
and Augustan age (the latter inasmuch as it has not already been tainted by
the 'decadent' features displayed by Ovid and the declaimers), in the ambit of
which there are effectively the only authors that Quintilian, in all of his work,
praises and recommends unconditionally.

Analogously, with regard to the prose texts that the master of rhetoric will get
his pupils to read, Quintilian in book II warns his readers to avoid two opposing
risks (2.5.21 *Duo autem genera maxime cavenda pueris puto*). If entrusted to a
master with an excessive admiration for antiquity (*antiquitatis nimius admirator*),

the young, by imitating Cato and the Gracchi,[38] would become *duri, horridi* and *ieiuni,* and even before being able to understand the *vis* that is the merit of those authors, would acquire a style that was excellent for those times but entirely extraneous to the present age (*elocutione, quae tum sine dubio erat optima, sed nostris temporibus aliena est*). Moreover – and this is the worst thing (*quod est pessimum*) – they would feel that they were on a par with those great authors. On the other hand, it will also be important to avoid being seduced by the depravity of the flowery flourishes indulged in by recent usage: 2.5.22 *Alterum, quod huic diversum est ... ne recentis huius lasciviae flosculis capti voluptate prava deleniantur.*

Only after the pupil has acquired a sure taste, evidently on the basis of the models from the intermediate phase represented by the prose of the Ciceronian age, and has therefore eluded these risks (2.5.23 *Firmis autem iudiciis iamque extra periculum positis*), will it be possible to advise him to read the *antiqui* and the *novi* (*suaserim et antiquos legere ... et novos*). Even the latter do, in fact, have great value (*quibus et ipsis multa virtus adest*). As for the *antiqui,* the student must avoid the carelessness belonging to an age that had not yet reached artistic maturity (*deterso rudis saeculi squalore*) and must draw on their force of inspiration instead (*si adsumatur solida ac virilis ingenii vis ...*). If we are able to do so, Quintilian suggests, our modern excellence itself will gain further lustre: *tum noster hic cultus clarius enitescet.*

And once again in book X, before proceeding with the review of authors, Quintilian proposes the same outline of literary ages, and the same evaluation of qualities. There are those who believe only the *veteres* should be read, the sole models of natural and virile energy: 10.1.43 *quidam solos veteres legendos putant, neque in ullis aliis esse naturalem eloquentiam et robur viris dignum arbitrantur.* Others just love the self-satisfied affectedness of recent eloquence, designed to seduce the inexpert majority: *alios recens haec lascivia deliciaeque et omnia ad voluptatem multitudinis imperitae composita delectant.* Between the two extremes lies the *rectum dicendi genus;* those who follow it (10.1.44 *qui rectum dicendi genus sequi volunt*) can evidently find models, which will vary according to the different stylistic trends adopted, in the intermediate period between the *veteres* and the *recens lascivia.*

This repeated presentation of an intermediate segment in time – between an inadequate ancient phase and a recent one marked by decay in taste – as the locus for the most certain models of style, seems to justify, or indeed to demand,

---

38 Cato and the Gracchi are also put together as canonical figures of the archaic phase of Latin prose in 8.5.33; 12.10.45; Plin. *Ep.* 1.20.4; and then on various occasions in Fronto and Gellius.

the customary labelling of Quintilian as a 'classicist',[39] both in that he is the advocate of a formal model pertaining to the past, and insofar as he upholds a formal ideal of measured balance between opposites. The two temporal extremes of ancient and modern also represent, in fact, two extremes on the plane of formal typology (virility-voluptuousness, roughness-affectedness, etc.).

The reality is more complex. Not only are the *veteres* acknowledged each time as having significant qualities, as we have seen. Many merits are attributed to the moderns as well. In the review in book X, Quintilian is generous in his praise of recent authors, and confident in the abilities of his contemporaries.[40] Throughout the *Institutio* the recurrent condemnation of the degradation and corruption of educational practices, of oratorial praxis, and of stylistic and formal choices, are interwoven with references to improvement upon the past and faith in the future.[41] In the passage from book II considered above, Quintilian goes so far as to sustain, with emphasis, that even in the most recent past (*nuper*), and among the living as well, there are figures worth pointing to as models without any reservations at all: 2.5.25 *Quosdam vero etiam quos totos imitari oporteat et fuisse nuper et nunc esse quidni libenter non concesserim modo verum etiam contenderim?* ('I am of course happy to admit – indeed, I should positively contend – that there have been in recent times, and still are, orators who ought to be imitated in all their features'). Great appreciation for recent and very recent authors (for example, his master and model Domitius Afer, or his friend and peer Iulius Secundus), and some unconditional acclaim for living writers,[42] also recur for rhetorical treatise writing.

In effect, Quintilian too, like Cicero and Horace, adopts a model of artistic evolution towards an enrichment and maturing of expressive means and taste. And Quintilian too, like Cicero (*Brutus* 70 f., 75 f.), relates technical progress in the figurative arts to that of literary style and oratory (12.10.1–12). The many differences between individual works, figurative and oratorial (in 12.10.11 he lists 15 Latin orators of great quality, from the time of Cicero to the present, Cicero him-

---

39 Already Colson 1924, 109, in a note on 1.8.9, refers to 2.5.23 and 10.1.43, and writes that in these passages "the 'veteres' and the 'novi' stand at the two ends, with the true classics in between" (the "true classics", for Colson, are the authors of the Ciceronian and Augustan age). A different view is taken by Peterson 1891, 42 and 43, who wrongly retains that Quintilian always posits a clear-cut opposition between *veteres* (through to and including the Augustans) and *novi* (see above, note 12).

40 See 10.1.41, 89–90, 102–104, 118–122.

41 For example, in 5.12 a gloomy picture of decadence (17–18) is followed by perspectives marked by greater faith (19– 22), which it is the responsibility of masters to sustain by preventing the young from being guided *ad peiora*.

42 See 3.1.21; 9.3.89.

self not included, identifying each one with a specific characteristic of style), are due both to differences between the personalities of the artists and the local traditions in which they are situated, and between the different techniques employed, which also vary in relation to the different phases of development of *ars*. Thus the *genera dicendi* of the period from Cato to the Gracchi are *horridiora* for the *condicio temporum*, even though they already show *magna ingenii vis* (12.10.10). The oratory of Cato and the Gracchi had in turn been preceded by an even less elaborate (*simplicior*) *ratio loquendi* (8.5.33). Quintilian, like Cicero (*De orat.* 3.98), knows that there are those, in the figurative arts as in oratorial style, who favour the more ancient works, executed with more primitive techniques (12.10.3). However, he believes that it is just a snobbish affectation, and, like Cicero (*Orat.* 169), does not accept the production of works today that are not suited to the modern development of *ars*.

As can be seen in the passages illustrated above, the inadequacy for current needs of prose from Cato to the Gracchi, and likewise of the tragedies of Accius and Pacuvius, is due to the fact that less sophisticated formal models were employed in their age: in the time of Accius and Pacuvius, *nitor* and *summa in excolendis operibus manus* (1.10.97) were still unknown; the *elocutio* of Cato and the Gracchi was *sine dubio optima* for their time, *sed nostris temporibus aliena* (2.5.21). For Quintilian's time they may become a positive example of *solida ac virilis ingeni vis* only by removing the *squalor* connected with their age, which was still initial and immature (*rudis*: 2.5.23). Just as the linguistic *consuetudo* of the past is now out of date (above, p. 29), so too the criteria of literary and oratorial expression evolve, are perfected and become increasingly refined. In fact, those with a fondness for archaism in Quintilian's day not only recover obsolete locutions, but also reject any artistic elaboration in the name of a rough naturalism presumed to belong to the ancients, but which is now unacceptable (11.3.10). In the generation prior to Cicero, oratorial technique was still so little developed that it could be dissimulated in order not to make the judges suspicious, as Antonius recommends in *De oratore*, but its current power is such that it would be impossible to conceal it (12.9.5). The precept not to display *ars* retains its value (and is referred to on various occasions: see, for example, 4.2.127), but must be adapted to the new times (4.1.57 *aliquatenus temporum condicione mutatur*) because a judge today (*iam*) could take offense if he thought the orator had not devoted all the resources of his *ars* to his task.

Quintilian, as we have just seen (2.5.23), recommends combining the *vis* of the *veteres* with the *cultus* of the present times. This, enriched by that ancient *vis*, will shine even brighter. His ideal is not, therefore, a 'classicistic' return to a specific past – the chronologically intermediate one between antiquity and modernity, and the typologically intermediate one between rigidity and self-satisfied affectation. The ideal is to construct methods and styles suited to the times, which use in the best possible way what is offered by the whole tradition. The ideal, in short, is a modern style, whose modern qualities are valorized (valorized, not toned down: 2.5.23 *noster hic cultus clarius enitescet*) by an ancient robustness. Our intellectual capacities are not inferior to those of our predecessors;[43] if anything, Quintilian suggests, what are inferior are the goals, the ideals of style (*dicendi genus*) we set ourselves: 24 *neque enim nos tarditatis natura damnavit, sed dicendi mutavimus genus et ultra nobis quam oportebat indulsimus: ita non tam ingenio illi nos superarunt quam proposito*. And this has come about exactly because the search for new expressive modes (in itself, necessary and praiseworthy, as we shall see) has resulted in excesses of intemperance: *ultra nobis quam oportebat indulsimus*.

6. The phenomenon of the distortions resulting from an excess of self-indulgence in the admittedly necessary and productive search for *novitas* is often deplored by Quintilian in relation to literary and oratorial expression, formative practices and rhetorical theory. In 2.10, for instance, declamation, though judged to be the most recent innovation in the field of rhetoric and by far the most useful (1), has become the primary cause of the corruption of eloquence (3), due to the exhibitionism of the masters (7 f.). The preponderance of *adfectus* and the privileging of the *voluptas* of the public are aspects of the recent corruption induced by declamation (5.12.17–23), but eloquence could not do without *adfectus* and *voluptas* (or *delectatio*), also for the purpose of convincing the judges, and therefore for the purpose of *utilitas*. It had therefore been right and necessary to value these elements, presumed to be absent in an *antiquus* and obsolete model of oratory, for which Attic oratory is considered to be the paradigm (5.14.29–35; 6.1.7 and 9–50 *passim*, 52; 6.2.1–7, 26–36). Quintilian himself is proud of having made a contribution in this direction with his teaching (6.2.25) and oratory (6.2.36). In the course of book VIII he emphasizes the idea (esp. 8.*pr.*; 8.2.12–24) that eloquence is corrupted by an excessive use of *ornatus* and tropes, often for their own sake, which leads to a loss of contact with its content, diminishes the credibility of the speech and thus becomes counterproductive for trial purposes. *Cacozelon*, or *mala adfectatio*, is a *vitium* that lies *ultra virtutem*, in other words a form of *corrupta oratio* (see also 2.3.9) stemming from an immoderate quest for *virtus* and

---

43 *Illi* is translated as 'the ancients' by Russell 2001, and similarly, for example, by Cousin 1976 ('les anciens'), Corsi 1997 ('gli antichi'), Reinhardt / Winterbottom 2006, 140 ('early writers'). The translation is acceptable, provided it is borne in mind that *illi* does not refer to the authors described as *antiqui* a few lines earlier, namely the pre-Ciceronians, but to the predecessors superior to us, among whom Cicero was certainly prominent.

bonum in *ornatus* (8.3.56–58). But *ornatus* in itself, which in any case involves going beyond common usage (8.3.61), is an essential requirement of eloquence, and is developed through the search for new effects (8.*pr.*24). Similar considerations crop up in book IX with regard to the use of *figurae*, which is necessary, but if excessive becomes inopportune and counterproductive; and similar considerations again lie at the heart of the judgements on the excess of self-indulgence in one's *ingenium*, not adequately curbed, in Ovid and Seneca (10.1.88, 98 and 130).[44] The virtuosic ambition of orators, writers and masters of rhetoric leads to the excogitation of spectacular but overly extravagant solutions lacking in communicative efficacy: indeed, for the most part they are hard to understand, and therefore counterproductive for the purposes of persuasion,[45] even though capable of attracting great praise. *Ars* must not pursue spectacular effects; on the contrary, it should be suited to the *utilitas* of trial, an idea referred to constantly, in contrast to the craze for the *ostentatio* and *iactatio* of oratorial prowess.[46]

It is precisely in the incapacity of setting a limit for this inherently positive impulse to innovation that Quintilian sees the fundamental reason why oratory faces the risk of decadence (admittedly, alongside other reasons, due to a lack rather than an excess of expressive research, such as disinterest in or contempt for the rules of the art and the hard study and elaboration they entail; see 2.11 and 12). It does not seem to me that due importance has been given to the fact that in two of the rare cases in which he refers to his *De causis corruptae eloquentiae* (8.3.58 and 8.6.76), it is to remind us that in the treatise he had iden-

---

44 See also 11.3.57–60, on the excesses in artistic modulation of the voice, designed to seduce listeners: however, referring each time to Cicero, Quintilian in 12.10.45–46 affirms the licit nature of the quest for *voluptas*; in 12.5.5–6 he extols an oratorial theatricality superior even to that of the tragic actors; in 8.3.3–14 he also accepts as a virtue the search for success, applause and the *voluptas*, or *delectatio*, of listeners (see also 8.5.32; 9.2.4; 9.4.116 and 129), provided they are subordinate to, or in keeping with, the efficacy of persuasion. Otherwise, as is often repeated, it is one of the chief causes of the decay of eloquence. Heldmann 1980 grasps very well the disproportion between the power of *ingenium* and the lack of *iudicium* in Seneca (and Ovid), a representative element, according to Quintilian, of the constant danger of corruption to which eloquence is exposed, but he does not identify the positive nature of the impulse towards innovation that lies at the origin of the risks of aberration.

45 See 4.2.39; 4.2.127; 8. *pr.* 23. Excesses of indulgence in the search for novelties by theorists of rhetoric are signalled in 3.1.7; 3.3.8; cf. also 3.11.21 f.

46 In 2.13.6 Quintilian goes so far as to affirm that the whole teaching of rhetoric has been dictated by *utilitas*, and that this, in turn, in individual trial situations, must prevail over the general principles taught by rhetorical doctrine even though these are founded upon it. See also 12.9.1 (and 5–6): the *utilitas causae praesentis* must come before the *cupido laudis* of the orator.

tified as one cause of the decay in eloquence the absence of temperance in the search for artistic effects (in themselves positive).

Not to innovate, would, on the other hand, be a sign of laziness, of a lack of a sense of responsibility. Without *novitas*, in fact, neither literature nor civilization would have developed. And it cannot be accepted that the present age is the only one not to contribute to human progress:

> 10.2.4 ... pigri est ingenii contentum esse iis quae sint ab aliis inventa. Quid enim futurum erat temporibus illis quae sine exemplo fuerunt si homines nihil nisi quod iam cognovissent faciendum sibi aut cogitandum putassent? Nempe nihil fuisset inventum... 7 ... Nihil in poetis supra Livium Andronicum, nihil in historiis supra pontificum annales haberemus; ratibus adhuc navigaremus, non esset pictura nisi quae lineas modo extremas umbrae quam corpora in sole fecissent circumscriberet. 8 Ac si omnia percenseas, nulla mansit (mansit *Meister*, sit *codd.*) ars qualis inventa est, nec intra initium stetit: nisi forte nostra potissimum tempora damnamus huius infelicitatis, ut nunc demum nihil crescat...

> only a lazy mind is content with what others have discovered. What would have happened in the days when there were no models, if men had decided to do and think of nothing that they did not know already? Nothing of course would have been discovered ... We should have nothing in poetry better than Livius Andronicus, nothing in history better than the Annals of the *pontifices*; we should still be going to sea on rafts, and the only painting would consist in drawing outlines round the shadows cast by objects in the sun. Take a comprehensive view: no art has remained as it was when it was discovered, or come to a stop in its early stages. Or are we to condemn our own age to the unique misery of being the first period in which nothing grows?

Being capable of departing from common and current expressive usage – *recedere a consuetudine vulgari* – is a *virtus*, and *novitas* may be especially *laudabilis:*

> 2.13.10 Quid tam distortum et elaboratum quam est ille discobolos Myronis? Si quis tamen ut parum rectum improbet opus, nonne ab intellectu artis afuerit, in qua vel praecipue laudabilis est ipsa illa novitas ac difficultas? 11 Quam quidem gratiam et delectationem adferunt figurae, quaeque in sensibus quaeque in verbis sunt. Mutant enim aliquid a recto, atque hanc prae se virtutem ferunt, quod a consuetudine vulgari recesserunt.

> What is so contorted and elaborately wrought as Myron's famous Discobolus? But would not any critic who disapproved of it because it was not upright show how far he was from understanding its art, in which the very novelty and difficulty of the pose are what most deserve praise? The same grace and charm are produced by Figures, whether of Thought or of Speech. They represent a deviation from the norm, and make a virtue of their distance from common or vulgar usage.

Only the objective of improving on the past justifies study (3.6.65) – a highly significant affirmation for a man who dedicated his life, and this great work of his, to teaching. Lexical innovation also finds in him a spirited supporter (8.3.31–36;

8.6.31 f.; in 1.5.72 he is instead very cautious).[47] It is the thrust of innovation that has created the extraordinary progress of all human arts, including literature, eloquence and its theory, leading them to attain great achievements in a long and glorious process that he proudly extols on various occasions.[48] This process, which continues still (2.16.18 ... *et adhuc augeri potest*), and to which he regards himself as contributing (see especially 6.2.25), in reality makes all past models relative, and means that the present always exceeds the past – provided, that is, that one is capable of repelling the corrupting elements that have undermined much of recent oratory and which represent a constant threat, all the more so in that they are largely due to an excess in the just search for more effective expressive means.

I do not therefore share the position, still prevalent today, that Quintilian regards Cicero as a model of perfection which has been succeeded, thus far, only by decadence, or as an ideal point of equilibrium between *veteres* and *novi*.[49] In the Flavian present, as seen by Quintilian, there coexist, in every aspect of language and culture, different and contrasting inclinations: forced effects of archaism or of modernism, tendencies correctly relating to the real needs of the present and aberrant ones. In 10.2.17, without claiming to be exhaustive, he lists five

---

47 For *novitas* as a value in language and style, see also 8.3.74; 8.6.51; 9.2.66; 9.3.5, 12, 58.
48 See 2.16.18; 2.17.3; 3.1.7–21; 5.12.1; 10.3.4; 9.4.3–5.
49 This latter view is, for example, the position of Calcante 2007, 121. Cicero's oratory is continually held up as exemplary by Quintilian, and on one occasion even as inimitable (11.1.93), yet he declares a number of times that the ultimate goal of his work is the creation of a perfect orator, which not even Cicero had managed to be. Quintilian knows that Cicero was the target of criticism by contemporaries and successors (12.1.14–22 and 12.10.12 f.), and points out that, over time, the nature of the criticisms has changed: if he had previously seemed superabundant, now, in the changed taste of the new generations, he seems too arid and spare (but Aper's speech in Tac. *Dialogus* shows that, even among the 'moderns', Cicero might seem too verbose; a mention also in Quint. 10.2.17). In Quintilian's view, these criticisms are unjust, founded on unhealthy criteria. It is clear that for him the perfect orator is to be shaped by innovating on the basis of the Ciceronian model. The optimistic nature of his vision of oratory, in contrast to that of the Tacitian figure of Messala, is forcefully affirmed in Heldmann 1980 and 1982 (pp. 138 f.; 143; 155–157), and is in due evidence in Raina 2008, 1397 f., 1408, but in the long run it found (and continues to do so) only occasional and timid acknowledgement in readings dominated by the idea of his more or less delayed classicism and neo-Ciceronianism: see, for example, Kennedy 1969, 23 f., 34, 111–12, 114 f., 130; Kennedy 1972, 495, 509; Winterbottom 1975, 90, 92; Adamietz 1986, 2234 f. Heldmann 1980 very rightly denies the 'classicism' of Quintilian, but he ends up reverting to this idea when he affirms that Quintilian's vision of post-Ciceronian oratory is not one of a progressive development (as in the Aper of the *Dialogus*), but rather that of a series of repeated attempts to achieve perfection by moving beyond the Ciceronian model, which is situated in a dimension of a non-temporal exemplarity.

different models of oratory inspired by different figures and phases of the Greek and Roman past that compete in the panorama of the eloquence of his age, each bringing varying degrees of value and risk of corruption.[50] And in the case of Seneca, he evidences, in the same person, the coexistence of a positive and a decadent modernity (10.1.131). But the overall picture is one of progress, a progress which ensures that the current age stands at the culmination of a path and possesses, taking into account the different models proposed by tradition, the greatest number of possible options, and therefore the greatest possibility of creating glorious things (10.2.28; 12.11.22). In at least one instance (12.10.46) Quintilian identifies a specific feature in which contemporary oratory represents progress upon Cicero: the use of *sententiae* (though this too, naturally, runs the risk of corrupting excess). And if part of contemporary oratory seems to him to be *corrupta*, positive trends are still well represented by the best contemporary orators, who are by no means part of a picture of decline.

The work ends with an impassioned reference to the fact that after what appears to us to be perfect not only must we not fear a necessary decline, but we must instead always believe in the possibility of further improvement, because no art has ever stopped once a goal has been reached, even though each time it seemed *optimum* (12.11.25–28): Virgil and Cicero represented a step forward with respect to authors who might already have seemed great, such as, respectively, Lucretius and Macer, Crassus and Hortensius. Likewise, the greatness already attributed to Cicero did not stop Pollio and Messala from earning their own glory in the history of eloquence. And as is known, Quintilian believed that the near future held the possibility of creating the perfect orator.[51] For Quintilian, it is the responsibility of cultural players – a responsibility he himself felt to a very great degree – to contribute to this progress. This means combatting aberrant tendencies: *utinam non peiora vincant*, he affirms in 9.3.1 (already discussed

---

50 The deliberate roughness inspired by the *antiqui*, the sobriety of the 'Attics', the obscure concision of Sallust and Thucydides, the dry harshness of Pollio, the expansive breadth of Cicero. See also 12.10.40–48, against an intransigent, still-surviving Atticism totally lacking in *ars*. Austin 1965, 185, on the basis of a comparison with 10.1.44, considers this hyper-archaism as a form of Atticism (also adding: "the point of view is clearly Stoic"); similarly, though with greater caution, Kennedy 1969, 120; however, I doubt that the lack of art can be related to Atticism: better Austin himself, ibid., p. xxi: "critics with Stoic leanings". The solution is to adopt a plurality of models to create an appropriate style each time: 10.2.23–26; in truth, the Latin models recommended here are all from the Ciceronian and Augustan age, and in 12.10.11–12, after the list of 15 orators that have each distinguished themselves for their own specific quality of style, Quintilian affirms that Cicero encapsulated the ability to excel in all these qualities: *in omnibus quae in quoque laudantur eminentissimus*.
51 1.*pr*.9, 18–20; 1.10.4–8; 2.15.33, 38; 10.2.9, 28; 12.1.9,19,24–25,31; 12.2,9,27,31; 12.9.8.

above);[52] and in 10.1.125, with regard to the polemic practiced at the time against Senecan style, Quintilian presents himself as striving to curb what he felt to be a dangerous drift: ... *dum corruptum et omnibus vitiis fractum dicendi genus ad severiora iudicia contendo.* And this also means promoting, with the great Ciceronian model being taken as a reference, those choices that prove actually to correspond each time to *utilitas.* After all, the orator's criterion for making the best expressive choice does not correspond to a model classically assumed to be ideal, but must pursue the efficacy of persuasion in the concrete present context, and the capacity to engage the whole complex of the logical-rational, emotive and aesthetic dimensions of the listeners whom it is the orator's task to convince.

---

52 See p. 31 and note 29, and see 10.2.15 *utinam tam bona imitantes dicerent melius quam mala peius dicunt.*

Thomas Baier
Quintilian's approach to literary history via *imitatio* and *utilitas*

1 What is literary history good for?

Since the late sixties of the last century literary history has been considered a "provocation in literary criticism", as Hans Robert Jauß put it.[1] The usual classification of literature according to literary genres or literary ages has since been replaced by problem-oriented or systematic approaches.[2] This 'structural turn' in literary criticism is due to a more 'scientific' view of literary history which aims to avoid the historical perspective and applies general categories which transcend literary epochs. Classical literary history is usually confronted with the dilemma of either delivering just an annalistic summary or writing about the important authors and adding the minor ones as an appendix. The last method is often a consequence of the fragmentary transmission of texts. However, a classification according to historical epochs is not a history of literature, but tends to subdue literature to politics; a concentration on the 'big' authors tends to neglect historical aspects.

What is the purpose of writing on literary history? A first answer may be found in Wilhelm von Humboldts "Über die Aufgabe des Geschichtsschreibers" (1821), which focusses on national particularity as being the basis of any kind of culture, such as the 'Englishness' of English literature, and on the uniqueness of the historical moment. The 20th century, after the Great War, adopted a more sober point of view and restrained itself to 'Quellenforschung'. This kind of positivism viewed literature as a conglomeration of innumerable influences ("Bündel beliebig vermehrbarer 'Einflüsse'").[3] Continuity became more important than the singular historical moment. Literary works were no longer seen as the product of an ingenious individual author, but rather the focus lay on the tradition from whence he sprang.

---

1 Jauß 1974.
2 Jauß 1974, 145.
3 Jauß 1974, 153.

https://doi.org/10.1515/9783110534436-003

2 What are categories good for?

Categorization is a precondition for any general statement. The pivotal question is: "are these categories real or are they only a means of understanding? Do they exist in the tangible world or only within our minds?"[4] The answer depends on the perspective. At first sight it seems to be easy to define literary genres. But on the other hand, one never finds these genres in a pure and unpolluted state. Most literary works comprise elements of different genres, and in an author like Ovid one wonders whether a clear attribution to literary genres is possible. Things are even more complicated when one adds to the discussion questions of meaning: since Hans Robert Jauß' theory of reception (*Rezeptionstheorie*) we know that not only the author but also the reader is responsible for the meaning of a literary text. This argument, however, is not as new as it seems. Already Terentianus Maurus' winged word, *pro captu lectoris habent sua fata libelli*,[5] states the fact that books depend on the knowledge and horizons of their readers.

All this conveys the notion of contingency. If the impact of a literary work is dependent on its reception and reverberates beyond the author's lifetime, the process of original production becomes less interesting, bordering on meaninglessness. The author effectively loses any control over his work. The famously fraught question of authorial intention becomes an all but moot point. Some have even claimed, with Roland Barthes, the "death of the author".

But again, these ideas are not new: the provocative idea of an all-embracing contingency is for the first time insinuated by Ovid. In *Metamorphoses* XI, at the transition from historical to mythical times, he narrates the story of Aesacus, but he does so in a very significant way: he puts it into the mouth of two old anonymous men. One of them – Ovid does not specify which – tells that Aesacus had originally been a son of Priam, before he was turned into a kingfisher (*mergus*). Ovid parodies and, in a way, outdoes the so-called '*tis*-speech', i.e. the speech of a nameless person, by introducing two *anonymi* (11.758–760):

> frater fuit Hectoris iste:
> qui nisi sensisset prima nova fata iuventa,
> forsitan inferius non Hectore nomen haberet.

---

4 These questions have already been raised in Porphyry's introduction to Aristotle's *Categories*, without having been answered exhaustively (Porph. *Intr.* p. 1 B.): αὐτίκα περὶ τῶν γενῶν τε καὶ εἰδῶν τὸ μὲν εἴτε ὑφέστηκεν εἴτε καὶ ἐν μόναις ψιλαῖς ἐπινοίαις κεῖται εἴτε καὶ ὑφεστηκότα σώματά ἐστιν ἢ ἀσώματα καὶ πότερον χωριστὰ ἢ ἐν τοῖς αἰσθητοῖς καὶ περὶ ταῦτα ὑφεστῶτα [...].
5 Ter. Maur. 1286.

he (*scil.* Aesacus) was the brother of the great illustrious Hector; and, if he had not been victimized by a strange fate in youth, he would have equalled Hector's glorious fame.

From these words we understand that even the struggle between Hector and Achilles, the actual core of the *Iliad* and the very beginning of European literature, was purely accidental. It is even fortuitous that we hear about Aesacus, as Ovid gives the impression that someone – we do not know who – overheard the chatter of the two old boys by chance, which enabled him to write it down. Not only does Ovid shatter the foundation-stone of ancient epic, but he also deconstructs literary genres. As a consequence, we cannot subsume the *Metamorphoses* either under didactic or under heroic epic. They belong to both. Other works, especially the *Heroides*, do not fit into any traditional stereotype. The anarchic creativity and subversive playfulness of the *tenerorum lusor amorum* makes any sort of categorization a failure.

If we follow Ovid's implicit theses, that everything is fortuitous, why then do works of art outlive the circumstances of their genesis? A possible answer to this originally Marxist question has been attempted by Karel Kosík: "a work of art lives as long as it has an effect on the recipients or consumers, i. e. as long as it is being interpreted".[6]

3 Quintilian on literary history

The 20th century has seen a shift from the perspective of production to the perspective of reception. Literary genres are no longer "given by nature", but are determined by their function and effect. Yet, one might see already in Quintilian's *Institutio oratoria* Book X a classification of literature according to its effect – in this case, its educational effect. It is not astonishing that Quintilian would classify authors according to their usefulness for the orator. He is not interested in literature for its own sake, but categorizes it under the topic '*De copia verborum*' (10.1.46–131). Quintilian provides the reader with a catalogue of Greek and Roman writers, whom he characterizes in brief. His judgement of poetry does not aim at being 'objective' in a wider sense; rather, he tries to expose what the future *orator* can learn from each author, as he puts it in his own words (10.1.37):

Credo exacturos plerosque, cum tantum esse utilitatis in legendo iudicemus, ut id quoque adiungamus operi, qui sint ⟨legendi⟩, quae in auctore quoque praecipua virtus.

---

6 Quoted in Jauß 1974, 163.

> Most of my readers will, I think, demand that, since I attach so much importance to reading, I should include in this work some instructions as to what authors should be read and what their special excellences may be.[7]

The central criterion is *utilitas*, the purpose of reading an author is to profit from his *praecipua virtus*, i. e. his main quality. In his judgement, Quintilian is utterly pragmatic. He does not ask whether an author is 'good' or 'bad', but whether he is useful for the rhetorician to be or whether he is not. A good example is his treatment of Greek tragedy. In the light of the ancient discussion on the subject, Quintilian's dispatch is short and apodictic (10.1.67):

> sed longe clarius inlustraverunt hoc opus [*scil.* tragoediam] Sophocles atque Euripides, quorum in dispari dicendi via uter sit poeta melior, inter plurimos quaeritur. idque ego sane, quoniam ad praesentem materiam nihil pertinet, iniudicatum relinquo. illud quidem nemo non fateatur necesse est, iis, qui se ad agendum comparant, utiliorem longe fore Euripiden.

> Sophocles and Euripides, however, brought tragedy to far greater perfection: they differ in style, but it is much disputed as to which should be awarded the supremacy, a question which, as it has no bearing on my present theme, I shall make no attempt to decide. But this much is certain and inconvertible, that Euripides will be found of far greater service to those who are training themselves for pleading in court.

Quintilian neither contributes to this particular literary discussion nor does he give any specifically literary reasons for his preference for Euripides. His predilection for the latter is adumbrated in very broad terms, first when he claims that 'for defence and attack [he] may be compared with any orator that has won renown in the courts' (*in dicendo ac respondendo cuilibet eorum qui fuerunt in foro diserti comparandus*), and then when he praises his emotional appeal (*in adfectibus* [...] *mirus*) and his power to excite pity (*in iis qui miseratione constant* [...] *praecipuus*, 10.1.68). Sophocles and Euripides used different *viae dicendi*, but only one is worthy of imitation. Quintilian gives the impression that the Greek authors had tested various forms of communication, whence it becomes his task to choose the best. He does not appreciate the quality of drama, but considers what use can be made of its language for the sake of improving one's rhetorical abilities.

Quintilian establishes a very simple, but probably rather realistic pattern for the emergence of cultural achievements. The first step is one of trial and error, the second consists in selective imitation. In 5.12.21 Quintilian attributes this scheme not only to literature, but also to the most celebrated sculptors and

---

7 This and the following translations of Quintilian are taken from Butler 1922.

painters of antiquity: *ut pictura poesis*, what is true for art is also true for literature. In paralleling visual arts and literature he inserts himself into a long tradition. In treatises on rhetoric, the metaphors from sculptural modelling are very frequent. Cicero himself applies them when he compares the teacher to an artist and the pupil to his medium.[8] A good teacher works with the medium "in choosing the form (*genus dicendi*) to be aimed at, and *against* it, in the sense that he eliminates the excesses that disfigure it, modifying it toward the best version of the form".[9] Cicero realizes an organic development from rude beginnings to the height of the art which is due to imitation and selection: *et nescio an reliquis in rebus omnibus idem eveniat: nihil est enim simul et inventum et perfectum* (*Brut.* 71).[10] Quintilian shares Cicero's view and has adopted it. For Quintilian, literature becomes a playground – or perhaps a junkyard – where the orator can find his material. The selection of the best examples leads to the establishment of a canonized standard. For the rhetorician, this standard is, of course, represented by Demosthenes and Cicero (10.1.105 f.). The canonization of certain authors and the *praeteritio* of others has first of all pragmatic justification.[11] But probably Quintilian does not feel as uneasy about it as some scholars thought.[12] Imitation and selection is rather to be seen as something natural. This becomes clear from Quintilian's next chapter (10.2), where he deals with the problem of *imitatio*.

---

8 For instance Cic. *Brut.* 70; *De orat.* 3.36.

9 Fantham 2011a, 248.

10 Cicero seems to like the parallels with visual arts. In *Off.* 3.10 he quotes Rutilius Rufus comparing Panaetius to Apelles and his philosophical treatise to an unfinished statue of Venus. One might also compare Cic. *Inv.* 2.1 where he refers to the anecdote of Zeuxis who is reported to have 'combined' the picture of Helen from several models, because he couldn't find all the ideal parts *uno in corpore.*

11 See 10.1.44 f. *interim summatim quid et a qua lectione petere possint qui confirmare facultatem dicendi volent attingam. paucos (sunt enim eminentissimi) excerpere in animo est: facile est autem studiosis qui sint his simillimi iudicare, ne quisquam queratur omissos forte aliquos (quos) ipse valde probet; fateor enim pluris legendos esse quam qui a me nominabuntur,* 'For the moment I shall restrict myself to touching briefly on what the student who desires to consolidate his powers of speaking should seek in his reading and to what kind of reading he should devote his attention. My design is merely to select a few of the most eminent authors for consideration. It will be easy for the student to decide for himself what authors most nearly resemble these: consequently, no one will have any right to complain if I pass over some of his favourites. For I will readily admit that there are more authors worth reading than those whom I propose to mention'.

12 Schwindt 2000, 157: "Die lange Vorrede zeugt lebhaft vom Unbehagen des Kanonikers am Kanon: als Redelehrer und Erzieher muß er pragmatisch verfahren".

4 The philosophical background of Quintilian's concept of *imitatio*

The chapter on *imitatio* follows directly Quintilian's 'literary history'. Obviously, he sees imitation as a vital concept in the development of literature. He therefore embeds his treatise on imitation within a broader context. *Invenire* and *imitari* are seen at the very heart of all sorts of cultural development. According to Peterson, Quintilian is dependent on "Aristotle's general theory of art" in order "to introduce the subject of imitation (μίμησις, ζῆλος) in the sphere of oratory".[13] But Quintilian does not seem to refer to *mimesis* as a part of human nature, as does Aristotle. He rather wants to focus on invention and imitation as necessary and complementary steps which are thrust upon mankind; there is a notion of constraint, which is absent from Aristotle's account. Art consists mostly in imitation, as Quintilian points out, because most things have been done already and need not be invented again (10.2.1):

> neque enim dubitari potest quin artis pars magna contineatur imitatione. nam ut invenire primum fuit estque praecipuum, sic ea quae bene inventa sunt utile sequi.

> For there can be no doubt that in art no small portion of our task lies in imitation, since, although invention came first and is all-important, it is expedient to imitate whatever has been invented with success.

In the following Quintilian refers explicitly to the men of old, whose privilege it was to invent everything, to act as πρῶτοι εὑρεταί. He takes this as an argument for his generation to combine new inventions with the imitation of the approved and time-tested. He even claims the right for his contemporaries to be innovative (10.2.4 f.):[14]

> quid enim futurum erat temporibus illis quae sine exemplo fuerunt si homines nihil nisi quod iam cognovissent faciendum sibi aut cogitandum putassent? nempe nihil fuisset inventum. cur igitur nefas est reperiri aliquid a nobis quod ante non fuerit? an illi rudes sola mentis natura ducti sunt in hoc, ut tam multa generarent: nos ad quaerendum non eo ipso concitemur, quod certe scimus invenisse eos, qui quaesierunt?

---

13 Peterson 1903, 82 *ad* Quint. 10.2.1.
14 See Kennedy 1969, 114, who argues against Quintilian's alleged classicism: Quintilian "is thus led to write a very significant passage cautioning against the dangers and limitations of imitation (10.2.4–13). Imitation of literary classics is not enough; literature would never have arisen in the first place if there had been nothing but imitation, and why should we not be as inventive and original as primitive man?"

For what would have happened in the days when models were not, if men had decided to do and think of nothing that they did not know already? The answer is obvious: nothing would ever have been discovered. Why, then, is it a crime for us to discover something new? Were primitive men led to make so many discoveries simply by the natural force of their imagination, and shall we not then be spurred on to search for novelty by the very knowledge that those who sought of old were rewarded by success?

The theory of the emergence of culture developed in this chapter appears to have an Epicurean background. The passage in question is Epicurus, *Epistula ad Herodotum* 75. Epicurus begins with general observations on the beginning of culture, and he proceeds to the problem of how language came into existence. The section runs (*Ep. Hdt.* 75 f.):[15]

Ἀλλὰ μὴν ὑποληπτέον καὶ τὴν φύσιν πολλὰ καὶ παντοῖα ὑπὸ αὐτῶν τῶν πραγμάτων διδαχθῆναί τε καὶ ἀναγκασθῆναι, τὸν δὲ λογισμὸν τὰ ὑπὸ ταύτης παρεγγυηθέντα ὕστερον ἐπακριβοῦν καὶ προσεξευρίσκειν [...]. Ὅθεν καὶ τὰ ὀνόματα ἐξ ἀρχῆς μὴ θέσει γενέσθαι, ἀλλ' αὐτὰς τὰς φύσεις τῶν ἀνθρώπων καθ' ἕκαστα ἔθνη ἴδια πασχούσας πάθη καὶ ἴδια λαμβανούσας φαντάσματα ἰδίως τὸν ἀέρα ἐκπέμπειν στελλόμενον ὑφ' ἑκάστων τῶν παθῶν καὶ τῶν φαντασμάτων, ὡς ἄν ποτε καὶ ἡ παρὰ τοὺς τόπους τῶν ἐθνῶν διαφορὰ εἴη. ὕστερον δὲ κοινῶς καθ' ἕκαστα ἔθνη τὰ ἴδια τεθῆναι πρὸς τὸ τὰς δηλώσεις ἧττον ἀμφιβόλους γενέσθαι ἀλλήλοις καὶ συντομωτέρως δηλουμένας.

Moreover, we must suppose that human nature too was taught and constrained to do many things of every kind merely by circumstances; and that later on reasoning elaborated what had been suggested by nature and made further inventions [...]. And so names too were not at first deliberately given to things, but men's natures according to their different nations had their own peculiar feelings and received their peculiar impressions, and so each in their own way emitted air formed into shape by each of these feelings and impressions, according to the differences made in their different nations by the places of their abode as well. And then later on by common consent in each nation special names were deliberately given in order to make their meanings less ambiguous to one another and more briefly demonstrated.[16]

Epicurus had distinguished two steps: in the first, learning is a necessity of survival. Human nature (φύσις) has to adapt itself to life's circumstances (πράγματα). In a second step, the λογισμός refines the newly acquired knowledge and makes "more accurate what has been provided by nature, adding new discoveries".[17]

---

15 The famous passage in the *Letter to Herodotus* 75 f. represents an abridged version of the relevant section in Epicurus' *On nature*; for the table of contents of this treatise see Erler 1994, 96–98.
16 Translation by Bailey 1975, 47–49.
17 Reinhardt 2008, 127.

Quintilian's model is very similar. In his account, Roman writers were taught by Greek models, but then they improved what they had learned according to their talent. While in Epicurus human nature is being taught and, in a way, 'constrained' by πράγματα, Roman writers are being 'forced' to comply with Greek literary genres. For Quintilian *Athenae doctrices* have substituted the Epicurean way of ὑπὸ αὐτῶν τῶν πραγμάτων διδαχθῆναί τε καὶ ἀναγκασθῆναι. The principal idea is the same in both cases: earlier, 'natural' conceptions determine further development. Obviously, Quintilian sees the Greek literary genres as 'natural'.[18] He thus embeds the Roman development of literary genres within the broader context of the development of culture; he uses the same method in approaching literature as in approaching the field of "Kulturentstehungslehre".

One prominent example illustrates the above point well. In 10.1.107 Quintilian compares Cicero to Demosthenes and comes to the conclusion (10.1.108):

> cedendum vero in hoc, quod [*scil.* Demosthenes] et prior fuit et ex magna parte Ciceronem quantus est fecit. nam mihi videtur M. Tullius, cum se totum ad imitationem Graecorum contulisset, effinxisse vim Demosthenis, copiam Platonis, iucunditatem Isocratis.

> But, on the other hand, there is one point in which the Greek [Demosthenes] has the undoubted superiority: he comes first in point of time, and it was largely due to him that Cicero was able to attain greatness. For it seems to me that Cicero, who devoted himself heart and soul to the imitation of the Greeks, succeeded in reproducing the force of Demosthenes, the copious flow of Plato, and the charm of Isocrates.

It is commonly accepted that Demosthenes and Isocrates, and in a certain respect even Plato, are predecessors of Cicero. But Quintilian portrays this as an organic development, with Cicero adopting from each of these authors their respective prevailing virtues. The imitation of these distinctive qualities marks only the first step. In the second step he will have added the mellifluous gifts of his own immortal talent (10.1.109):

> nec vero quod in quoque optimum fuit studio consecutus est tantum, sed plurimas vel potius omnis ex se ipsa virtutes extulit immortalis ingenii beatissima ubertas. non enim 'pluvias', ut ait Pindarus, 'aquas colligit, sed vivo gurgite exundat', dono quodam providentiae genitus, in quo totas vires suas eloquentia experiretur.

> But he did something more than reproduce the best elements in each of these authors by dint of careful study; it was to himself that he owed most of, or rather all his excellences, which spring from the extraordinary fertility of his immortal genius. For he does not, as Pindar says, "collect the rain from heaven, but wells forth with living water," since Provi-

---

18 So did Winckelmann and the protagonists of 'classicism'.

dence at his birth conferred this special privilege upon him, that eloquence should make trial of all her powers in him.

This second step, as it were, is not a refinement of what the Greeks had already invented, but consists in new inventions, and is meant as a corroboration of Quintilian's claim that new inventions are still possible and still allowed. Quintilian, who is often denounced as an 'archaist' and conservative, reveals himself to be an advocate of permanent innovation.[19]

This attitude is distinctly different from Cicero's high-handed claim in the *Tusculanae disputationes* 1.1, where – with respect to philosophy – invention is attributed to the Greeks and the Romans alike, refinement only to the Romans.[20] Cicero implies that the era of invention has passed, because everything has already been created. And with the Romans having improved (*fecisse meliora*) and led to perfection (*elaborare*) their Greek models the evolution of culture has come to its acme and, therefore, to an end. Cicero sees himself at the heyday of philosophy – and, of course, even more of rhetoric. His task is to preserve what has been inherited from the Greeks, and to adopt it for and adapt it to the Romans. He does not, though, open up new fields. Cicero is driven by the idea that rhetoric and philosophy have gotten as good as they could, and thus seeks merely to maintain the ideal *status quo*.[21]

This static interpretation of cultural maturity can also be seen in Cicero's theory on the relation between literature and rhetoric.[22] In *De orat.* 2.87–90 Cic-

---

19 This innovative approach may be due to the fact that Quintilian sees the main purpose of literature in education. Citroni 2006a, 214 sees an "essential part" of Roman literature in "the foundation of an educational system". But he maintains: "The affirmation that these texts were written with a view to their use in education does not undermine their cultural and artistic awareness".

20 *Sed meum semper iudicium fuit omnia nostros aut invenisse per se sapientius quam Graecos aut accepta ab illis fecisse meliora, quae quidem digna statuissent, in quibus elaborarent*, 'it has always been my opinion that our countrymen have, in some instances, made wiser discoveries than the Greeks, with reference to those subjects which they have considered worthy of devoting their attention to'.

21 The generation of Cicero's teachers was probably mainly influenced by Greek models, but grew up to be themselves teachers for the younger generation. For Cicero "there were now two competing forms of imitation": the Roman orators on the one hand, and the classical representatives of the *Atticum genus* separated from them by some three centuries (Fantham 2011a, 244 f.).

22 Gombrich 1966, 30 rightly points out that Cicero carefully distinguishes his own art of persuasion from poetry where very different standards apply. In his view, the poet writes to the few and elect. Quintilian, however, seems rather insensitive to this aspect of poetry; he sees poetry as a field of learning for the many.

ero talks about *imitatio* in its practical and pedagogical aspects. In 2.91, he moves on to literary subjects without providing any formal transition. The underlying idea is that in each generation "a common style, a nucleus of characteristics shared by all the orators of that day" was prevalent.[23] Cicero's imitation resembles Aristotelian μίμησις, although his context is quite different from Aristotle's.

In Quintilian's account, however, invention is an everlasting process. Imitation is not, like Aristotelian μίμησις, a natural human desire, but is forced upon mankind by necessity. But μίμησις /*imitatio* alone is not enough. Imitators strive to go beyond their models. The development of culture never comes to an end. According to Quintilian, every generation is entitled to fresh ideas. He thus sees the development of literature as a continuous improvement. An 'archaist' though he may be, Quintilian is not the typical *laudator temporis acti*. He sees very clearly that a revival of the old models would not fit his time. Not only is departure from the canon allowed, it is even highly desirable.[24]

5 The problem of *imitatio*, *inventio* and *natura*

In his theory of instruction, Quintilian puts an emphatic accent upon human nature, *natura humani ingenii* (1.12.2). This is, of course, a very common topic in classical rhetoric and philosophy. In ancient thought, the authority of nature is beyond any question; the requirements of nature can easily stand as a moral imperative.[25] At first sight, however, there appears to be a contradiction between the primacy of nature and the necessity of imitating others and even inventing new things.[26] If nature is perfect and has the right to claim the highest authority, its followers have to raise the banner of purity and to condemn all innovation and progress as symbols of corruption and decay.[27] Elaine Fantham has dealt in an article with this "apparent opposition between nature and imitation".[28] In her eyes, Quintilian has built "his own doctrine of the complementar-

---

23 Fantham 2011a, 249.

24 The innovative character of Quintilian's model becomes clear in a comparison with the more traditional "concept of the classical" and conventional ideas of "Latin literary canons", see Citroni 2006a, 211–227.

25 E. g. Cic. *Part.* 111, *Top.* 73; see Fantham 2011b, 333.

26 On the relationship between *natura* and *inventio* see Varwig 1976, 62–65.

27 Gombrich 1966, 26.

28 Fantham 2011b, 333.

ity of nature and care",[29] understanding by care (*cura*) something like craftsmanship and training.[30] We have to understand that the most ingenuous artists, be they painters, sculptors or poets, find or develop their nature by training. But still, this harmonization of *natura* on the one hand, and *diligentia* and *imitatio* on the other, is probably not what Quintilian intended. It would fit very well into the Socratic or Platonic concept of divine ideas which are being hidden and which have to be unveiled and 'remembered' by the practice of *anamnesis*. In Platonic philosophy, instruction is the development – or rather the unveiling or 'unwrapping' – of one's own nature, a return to hidden origins. In this line of thought there exists no possibility of real progress, since any refinement is under the suspicion of corruption, of hiding the truth rather than uncovering it. Or, in other words, the only acceptable progress in the Platonic universe is re-form, the return to an assumed original state, *ad instar primitivae aetatis*. Nature is supposed to provide the perfect pattern, and it is man's duty to preserve it by imitating the 'natural'. Under such conditions the innovator has to take the disguise of a reformer.

Also, Quintilian, like his predecessors, attributes the very origin of culture to what he calls *natura*. Moreover, he makes it clear that the art of rhetoric sprang from nature itself. But at this point, parallels with the Platonic concept of φύσις end. Instead, his distinctly Epicurean interpretation of the *rerum natura* becomes evident (3.2.1):

> Nec diu nos moretur quaestio quae rhetorices origo sit. nam cui dubium est quin sermonem ab ipsa rerum natura geniti protinus homines acceperint (quod certe principium est eius rei), huic studium et incrementum dederit utilitas, summam ratio et exercitatio?

> The question as to the origin of rhetoric need not keep us long. For who can doubt that mankind received the gift of speech from nature at his birth (for we can hardly go further back than that), while the usefulness of speech brought improvement and study, and finally method and exercise gave perfection?

Quintilian pretends to deal with the *rhetorices origo*, but then he starts with the *sermo* which is in this context 'language', i.e. the ability to talk as an innate potentiality. This means that every man is capable of uttering sounds with his mouth and tongue. These sounds may have correlated with feelings humans undergo and they may have served for signifying things. They were, however, ambiguous in terms of meaning, and totally ungrammatical. So they could not yet

---

29 Fantham 2011b, 338.
30 Quintilian (10.1.86) praises e.g. Virgil for his *natura caelestis atque immortalis* and his even greater *cura et diligentia*: see Fantham 2011b, 336.

be used as a basis for interaction. It was only *utilitas*, the need and at the same time the convenience to interact with others, that made man invent language as a means of communication.[31] Indistinct utterances turned into a grammatical system of meaningful sentences.[32] Human beings understood that it was practical to be able to communicate with their fellow men.[33] Their *ratio*, which is in this case 'common sense', told them what was beneficial and what was not (3.2.3):

> Initium ergo dicendi dedit natura, initium artis observatio. Homines enim sicut in medicina, cum viderent alia salubria, alia insalubria, ex observatione eorum effecerunt artem, ita cum in dicendo alia utilia, alia inutilia deprenderent, notarunt ea ad imitandum vitandumque, et quaedam secundum rationem eorum adiecerunt ipsi quoque: haec confirmata sunt usu.

> It was, then, nature that created speech, and observation that originated the art of speaking. Just as man discovered the art of medicine by observing that some things were healthy and some the reverse, so they observed that some things were useful and some useless in speaking, and noted them for imitation or avoidance, while they added certain other precepts according as their nature suggested. These observations were confirmed by experience.

We can infer that the development of language – and, on a higher level, the development of rhetoric – is based on trial and error. The same is true for the primitive beginnings of medicine. With this theory Quintilian puts himself into open contradiction with Cicero. Cicero had, as Quintilian himself points out, attributed the beginnings of rhetoric to the founders of cities and the first legislators (3.2.4):[34]

> Cicero quidem initium orandi conditoribus urbium ac legum latoribus dedit, in quibus fuisse vim dicendi necesse est: cur tamen hanc primam originem putet non video […].

---

31 It is rather difficult to understand the exact meaning of these verses and to sever the two stages in the development of language. This ambiguity is exacerbated if one takes into consideration the comparison with human gestures which follows in Lucretius' account: *non alia longe ratione atque ipsa videtur / protrahere ad gestum pueros infantia linguae* (5.1030 f., see below at n. 36). Dahlmann 1928, 16 f. made clear that there is no evident analogy between the sounds uttered by the first humans on the one hand and children's gestures on the other. He was followed by Spoerri 1959, 153 f. For the latest discussion see Verlinsky 2005, 83–85.
32 Reinhardt 2008, 132, following Ax 1986, 253–257, observes that Lucretius in his account seems to be using the terminology of grammatical handbooks.
33 Sedley 1973, 18: "Men utter sounds instinctively in reaction to objects and feelings, and, noticing that they have one sound to correspond with each object or feeling, they find it useful to employ the sounds as labels."
34 Quintilian refers to Cic. *Inv.* 1.2 and *De orat.* 1.8.33.

Cicero, it is true, attributes the origin of oratory to the founders of cities and the makers of laws, who must [...] have possessed the gift of eloquence. But why he thinks this the actual origin, I cannot understand [...].

There is a controversy between two theories on the development of rhetoric, the one tracing it back to *natura* and *utilitas*, the other claiming a πρῶτος εὑρετής. The debate between the two viewpoints calls to mind the discussion about the origin of language in Lucretius: in 5.1028 f. the Epicurean poet maintains: *at varios linguae sonitus natura subegit / mittere et utilitas expressit nomina rerum*, 'but nature 'twas urged men to utter various sounds of tongue and need and use did mould the names of things'. Sounds were given by nature, necessity formed the language.[35] *Infantia linguae ipsa*, the 'childhood' of language, pushes mankind to the invention of language.[36] We may interpret the 'infancy' of language to be a longing for communication which does not yet own the necessary instruments and which is, in the strict sense of the word, still *infans*. In a second step the mere sounds became *nomina rerum*, i.e. sounds which are associated with a particular referent.[37] Lucretius goes on: *proinde putare aliquem tum nomina distribuisse / rebus et inde homines didicisse vocabula prima, / desiperest* 'that in those days some man apportioned round to things their names, and that from him men learned their first nomenclature, is foolery' (1041–1043). He calls the idea preposterous that one single man could have invented all languages. The scepticism towards wise legislators, ingenious inventors and innovative creators of language is shared by Quintilian. Both adopt a very down-to-earth view on the development of culture. Both believe in *utilitas* as the basis of all progress. It is highly probable that Quintilian took the model for his Epicurean concept from Lucretius himself. He may have transferred the account on the emergence of language in *De rerum natura* Book V into his own treatise on the beginnings of literature.

The method of transferring a theory from one area into another by analogy is very well attested in Epicurus and his followers.[38] It is, so to speak, the hallmark

---

35 Plat. *Prot.* 322 a 3–6; see Dahlmann 1964, 96.

36 1030–1033: *non alia longe ratione atque ipsa videtur / protrahere ad gestum pueros infantia linguae, / cum facit ut digito quae sint praesentia monstrent. / sentit enim vis quisque suas quoad possit abuti*, 'about in same wise as the lack-speech years compel young children unto gesturings, making them point with finger here and there at what's before them. For each creature feels by instinct to what use to put his powers'. See Verlinsky 2005, 85: "Lucretius may imply a semantic and/or articulary difference between *sonitus linguae* and *nomina rerum*, but what concerns him, is the change from gesture to sound as means of signifying".

37 This corresponds to the emergence of ὀνόματα in Epicur. *Ep. Hdt.* 75.

38 For the understanding of analogy in Epicurean philosophy see De Lacy 1941, 129.

of an Epicurean background.[39] Here, it is the case of cognition διὰ λόγου θεωρητικῶς.[40] This conclusion by analogy was originally designed in order to investigate those domains which are ἄδηλα, i.e. imperceptible or intangible, as for example celestial phenomena.[41] But it also serves for any kind of theoretical research, ἐάν τις καλῶς τοῖς φαινομένοις ἀκολουθῶν περὶ τῶν ἀφανῶν σημειῶται, 'if one successfully follows the lead of seen phenomena to gain indications about the invisible' (Epicur. *Ep. Pyth.* 104).[42]

Quintilian, of course, is not the first to construct a model of how Roman literature came into existence. His Epicurean approach has a parallel in Horace. Quintilian's history of literature recalls the Augustan poet's account of how Greek literature and art came into existence and how the Romans dealt with it: after the Persian wars the Greeks began to experience all genres in a playful way (*nugari*, Hor. *Ep.* 2.1.93) and behaved like children: *sub nutrice puella velut si luderet infans, Ep.* 2.1.99). The Romans instead saw it as their duty to find out *quid Sophocles et Thespis et Aeschylus utile ferrent* (*Ep.* 2.1.163). Their main interest was the *utile*. Horace, of course, gave a mocking version of Roman literary history with a clear satirical point. But satire only works if the concept under attack is widely accepted. Quintilian closely follows the path where Horace had shed his irony. He takes seriously what the poet was mocking, and inserts his theories into the context of Epicurean epistemology.

6 Conclusion

We could see that Quintilian does not discuss literature according to traditional categories or literary genres. He rather advocates the idea of contingency and denies the natural authority of Greek genres. He is not so much interested in the origins of Roman literature (as many writers of the Augustan age were), but in the function of poetry and its usefulness for the education of future orators. The key concept in his account of the development of literature and culture as a whole is *imitatio*. His concept of *imitatio* is not derived from Aristotelian μίμησις. Quintilian may well have taken the inspiration for his model from Lucretius and other Epicurean sources. The stimulus for imitation is given by *utilitas*. All cultural achievements came into being because they were seen as useful. Imitation goes hand in hand with innovation. In dealing with tradition Quintilian

---

39 Kullmann 1980, 98–100.
40 Epicur. *Nat.* 29.14.25 f. and 29.15.1–9 Arr.; see Arrighetti 1965, 565.
41 Epicur. *Ep.Pyth.* 87.
42 Translation by Bailey 1926, 71.

never stares with awe at the great men of old, but he calculates very soberly what is useful (*utile*) and what is not. In judging literature, his yardstick is comprised of the needs of his own time. He measures literature from the point of view of reception. And it has to be emphasized that his assessment is never authoritarian nor even harsh, but always appreciative and sympathetic.[43] His literary judgement is more innovative and his attitude towards the Roman past less sentimental than it appears to be at first sight. We may enrol him among the modernizers in the Flavian age.

---

43 No one has recognized this better than Seel 1977, 66: "ich meine die völlige Freiheit Quintilians von jedem starren Doktrinarismus, von aller Rechthaberei, Verhärtung, Übellaunigkeit und Herbheit! Eine Aura von Gutartigkeit liegt über dem gesamten Werk, von Verstehensbereitschaft, Nachgiebigkeit, Einsicht in die Mehrdeutigkeit der meisten Probleme."

II Encyclopaedism and Oratory

Sandra Citroni Marchetti

Contingat aliqua gratia operae curaeque nostrae: an ethic of care in the *Naturalis historia*

According to the prefatory letter, after reading two thousand volumes, Pliny chose twenty-thousand topics to include in his thirty-six book work. The *Naturalis historia* is presented, then, as a highly selective reduction of book material, to which the author added further information absent from those books due to their authors' lack of knowledge or because it was the result of later discoveries. The selection made by Pliny within the mass of book material was, in a certain sense, imposed upon him. In fact, he re-presented the information and facts that had presented themselves to him when he read them in his sources as deserving attention, as 'worthy of care' (Plin. *Nat.pr.* 17 f.):

> XXM rerum dignarum cura … lectione voluminum circiter IIM, quorum pauca admodum studiosi attingunt propter secretum materiae, ex exquisitis auctoribus centum inclusimus XXXVI voluminibus, adiectis rebus plurimis, quas aut ignoraverant priores aut postea invenerat vita … subsicivisque temporibus ista curamus, id est nocturnis.

> by perusing about 2000 volumes, very few of which, owing to the abstruseness of their contents, are ever handled by students, we have collected in 36 volumes 20000 noteworthy facts obtained from one hundred authors that we have explored, with a great number of other facts in addition that were either ignored by our predecessors or have been discovered by subsequent experience … and we pursue this sort of interest in our spare moments, that is at night. (transl. by H. Rackham)

And to the invitation of the books that present things 'worthy of care', the author in turn responds with his own *cura*, which he depicts himself as being engaged in during the night-time hours (*pr.* 18 *subsicivis … temporibus ista curamus, id est nocturnis*).

The expression *dignus cura* is not a common one. There is some likeness here to a passage in Quintilian recommending that chosen passages be learnt by heart in *volumina ea cura digna*. In the *Naturalis historia*, therefore, the first reference to *cura* is in a sentence that presents the author in direct relationship with books, and contains an expression which, in the same age and in the field of rhetorical instruction, denoted a criterion of selection regarding books themselves.[1]

---

1 Quint. *Inst.* 2.7.2 *Nam ut scribere pueros plurimumque esse in hoc opere plane velim, sic ediscere*

https://doi.org/10.1515/9783110534436-004

Pliny's declaration contains a reference to later discoveries that he attributes directly to the ongoing course of life (*postea invenerat vita*). Among the cases of information available personally to Pliny with respect to the 'discoveries of life', the most evident one concerns the new geographic information acquired following the eastern expeditions of Domitius Corbulo (*Nat.* 6.23):

> in quo multa aliter ac veteres proditurum me non eo infitias, anxia perquisita cura rebus nuper in eo situ gestis a Domitio Corbulone regibusque inde missis supplicibus au⟨t⟩ re⟨g⟩um liberis obsidibus.

> I do not deny that my description of it will differ in many points from that of the old writers, as I have devoted much care and attention to ascertaining them thoroughly in consequence of the recent events in that region from Domitius Corbulo and the kings sent from there as suppliants or king's children sent as hostages. (transl. by H. Rackham, modified)

Suppliants and hostages, then, arrived in Rome from Pontus. Announcing that what he had to say about these territories would differ from the ancient authors, Pliny describes his own information from such figures as being sought after with an anxious *cura* (*anxia ... cura*). If in the case of the book information the author's *cura* was a response, as it were, to what the books contained (it was the books that offered topics 'worthy of care'), here the term *cura* refers to a personal, emotively connoted condition of the author: 'anxious care' is a trait of the author in the way he relates to others in the difficult task of obtaining information that might be considered reliable even if in contrast to received wisdom. To the

---

electos ex orationibus vel historiis aliove quo genere dignorum ea cura voluminum locos multo magis suadeam ('For while I certainly believe in boys writing and being mainly occupied with this, I should much prefer them to learn by heart selected passages of speeches or histories or some other type of book that is worth treating in this way'; transl. by D.A. Russell). Of the five examples we have of this expression, four, including Pliny's, are clustered in the period between Seneca and Quintilian, and relate to culture: the other three pertain more specifically to the field of teaching. In two cases (respectively in Seneca and Quintilian) the issue is the relationship between tutor and pupil, where the pupil is described as *dignus cura*: Sen. *Ben.* 6.16.3 *Ne praeceptorem quidem habeo cur venerer, si me in grege discipulorum habuit, si non putavit dignum propria et peculiari cura, si numquam in me derexit animum* ('Nor is there any reason why I should venerate a teacher if he has considered me merely one of his many pupils, and has not deemed me worthy of any particular and special consideration, if he has not directed his attention to me'; transl. by J.W. Basore); Quint. *Inst.* 1.1.24 *Fingamus igitur Alexandrum dari nobis, impositum gremio dignum tanta cura infantem (quamquam suus cuique dignus est)*, 'So let us imagine that Alexander is entrusted to our care, that the child placed in our lap deserves as much attention (though of course every father thinks this of his son)'. Transl. by D.A. Russell). The remaining example, which is separate, is from Frontinus (*Aq.* 119.1 *rem enixiore cura dignam*).

degree to which the fear of falling into error emotively colours the scholar's quest for accuracy, the term *cura* (with the adjective *anxia*) moves away from the sphere of positive 'caring', that is attention for and labours in relation to things, towards the ambit of anxieties and cares, which the same term was equally capable of conveying.[2] As we shall see, *cura* as anxiety is significantly present in Pliny. But let's look now at the 'caring' dimension, especially insofar as it distinguishes the scholar. Pliny ascribes this dimension to himself, without, however, considering himself in isolation but as part of a tradition instead.

According to Pliny, the ancient scholars (*prisci*, *veteres*, whose extensive number he stresses) deserve admiration for the *cura* which, combined with *diligentia* and *labor*, they devoted to their researches: 23.112 *Non est satis mirari curam diligentiamque priscorum*; 25.1 *in admirationem curae priscorum diligentiaeque*; 3 *cura eorum mira*; 27.1 *adorare priscorum in inveniendo curam*; 29.140 *admirationem ... priscorum ... curae*. But the *cura* of the ancients was met with ingratitude by later authors, who neglected science in favour of less useful studies (*Nat.* 2.43):

> non sumus profecto grati erga eos qui labore curaque lucem nobis aperuere in hac luce, miraque humani ingeni peste sanguinem et caedes condere annalibus iuvat, ut scelera hominum noscantur mundi ipsius ignaris.

> We forsooth feel no gratitude towards those whose assiduous toil has given us illumination on the subject of this luminary, while owing to a curious disease of the human mind we are

---

2 The dimension of anxiety may be considered intrinsic to the concept of *cura*: cf. *De differentiis, Gramm. Lat.* VII p. 528 K. *Diligentiam et curam. Diligentia a diligendo singula, huic neglegentia opponitur, nec recipit errorem: cura animi est, quae anxium facit hominem et tam honestae quam inhonestae rei est*. In the course of the *Naturalis historia*, it is in the field of art that care, devoted to the execution of a work, appears to be exercised in an overly anxious manner: 34.92 *Callimachus, semper calumniator sui nec finem habentis diligentiae ... memorabili exemplo adhibendi et curae modum* ('Callimachus, he was unfairly critical of his own work, and was an artist of never-ending adsiduity ... a notable warning of the duty of observing moderation even in taking pains'); 35.80 *Protogenis opus inmensi laboris ac curae supra modum anxiae* ('the immensely laborious and infinitely meticulous work of Protogenes'); cf. 35.103 (by throwing a sponge the painter obtains by chance what he had not managed to produce with care) *spongeam inpegit ... et illa reposuit ablatos colores qualiter cura optaverat*. The connection between anxiety and care can in fact be seen as indissoluble: see Non. 72 M. *Ubi cura est, ibi anxitudo acerba*. Only rarely does the adjective *anxius* appear directly combined with *cura* (e. g., Liv. 1.56.4 *anxiis curis*). More commonly, *anxius* defines the spirit of the person dominated by care. The more strictly positive aspect of care is effectively expressed by Cicero, when he identifies it with the active part (that which 'looks outwards') of moral life: Cic. *Fin.* 5.67 *inest in omni virtute cura quaedam quasi foras spectans* (for Cicero, avoiding *cura* because of the anxiety it might cause is even equivalent to fleeing from virtue: *Amic.* 47 *Quodsi curam fugimus, virtus fugienda est*).

pleased to enshrine in history records of bloodshed and slaughter, so that persons ignorant
of the facts of the world may be acquainted with the crimes of mankind. (transl. by H. Rackham)[3]

and above all assumed an attitude of erudite narrow-mindedness (*Nat.* 25.1 f.):

Ipsa quae nunc dicetur herbarum claritas ... in admirationem curae priscorum diligentiaeque animum agit. Nihil ergo intemptatum inexpertumque illis fuit, nihil deinde occultatum
quodque non prodesse posteris vellent. At nos elaborata (i)is abscondere ac supprimere cu-
pimus et fraudare vitam etiam alienis bonis. Ita certe recondunt qui pauca aliqua novere,
invidentes aliis, et neminem docere in auctoritatem scientiae est. Tantum ab excogitandis
novis ac iuvanda vita mores absunt, summumque opus ingeniorum diu iam hoc fuit, ut
intra unumquemque recte facta veterum perirent.

This peculiar glory of plants which I am now going to speak of ... rouses in one's mind admiration for the care and industry of the men of old; there was nothing left untried or un-
attempted by them, and furthermore nothing kept secret, nothing which they wished to be
of no benefit to posterity. But we moderns desire to hide and suppress the discoveries
worked out by these investigators, and to cheat human life even of the good things that
have been won by others. Yes indeed, those who have gained a little knowledge keep it
in a grudging spirit secret to themselves, and to teach nobody else increases the prestige
of their learning. So far has custom departed from fresh research and assistance to life;
the supreme task of our great minds has long been to keep within individual memory
the successes of the ancients, so allowing them to be forgotten. (transl. by W. H. S. Jones)

Pliny believes he is exercising the same *cura* as the ancients, but in an intellectual setting inclined to denigrate him. The care he takes in his researches may
appear to some to be *frivola*, in that it is applied to humble and generally neglected aspects of nature (*Nat.* 25.22):

Tanta res videbatur herbam invenire, vitam iuvare, nunc fortassis aliquis curam hanc nos-
tram frivolam quoque existimaturis.

It was thought a great honour to discover a plant and be of assistance to human life, although now perhaps some will think that these researches of mine are just idle trifling.
(transl. by W. H. S. Jones)

The fundamental link Pliny establishes between himself and the ancient scholars, and on the basis of which he rejects the charge that his care is *frivola*, con-

---

3 Pliny describes the genre of historiography negatively, in that it contains accounts of wars. It
is remarkable that in a scientific work this condemnation should come precisely from an author
of historical works, also specifically devoted to narrating wars.

sists of the desire to 'benefit life': 25.22 *Tanta res videbatur ... vitam iuvare.*[4] In other words, Pliny attributes to the ancients (to some extent projecting onto them) the same philanthropic ideal, expressed by the terms *iuvare, prodesse,*

---

[4] The *cura* of the new author ties in with that of the ancients by going back over and beyond the time that saw the blameworthy neglect of studies: 14.3 *non reperiuntur qui norint multa ab antiquis prodita. Tanto priscorum cura fertilior aut industria felicior fuit, ante milia annorum inter principia litterarum Hesiodo praecepta agricolis pandere orso subsecutisque non paucis hanc curam eius, unde nobis crevit labor, quippe cum requirenda sint non solum postea inventa, verum etiam ea quae invenerant prisci, desidia rerum internecione memoriae indicta ...; 7 Sed nos oblitterata quoque scrutabimur, nec deterrebit quarundam rerum humilitas* ('we do not find people acquainted with much that has been handed down by the writers of former days: so much more productive was the research of the men of old, or else so much more successful was their industry, when a thousand years ago at the dawn of literature Hesiod began putting forth rules for agriculture, and not a few writers followed him in these researches – which has been a source of more toil to us, inasmuch as nowadays it is necessary to investigate not only subsequent discoveries but also those that had already been made by the men of old, because general slackness has decreed an utter destruction of records ... We, however, will carry our researches even into matters that have passed out of notice, and will not be daunted by the lowliness of certain objects'; transl. by H. Rackham). Cf. 18.24, where Pliny contrasts his own careful working method, which (as he also says elsewhere) takes account both of the ancient authors and of more recent discoveries, with the one commonly in use: *Apud Romanos multo serior vitium cultura esse coepit, primoque, ut necesse erat, arva tantum coluere, quorum a nobis nunc ratio tractabitur, non volgari modo, verum, ut adhuc fecimus, et vetustis et postea inventis omni cura perquisitis* ('Vine-growing began among the Romans much later, and at the beginning, as of necessity, they only practised agriculture, the theory of which we will now deal with, not in the common method but, as we have done hitherto, by making an exhaustive research into both ancient practices and subsequent discoveries ...'; transl. by H. Rackham). Virgil serves as a reference in two ways, both as an author who dealt only with 'the flower of things' (14.7 *videmus Vergilium ... flores modo rerum decerpsisse, beatum felicemque gratiae quindecim omnino generibus uvarum nominatis*) and as an author familiar with the difficulty of treating humble topics with literary dignity: 19.59 *contingat aliqua gratia operae curaeque nostrae Vergilio quoque confesso, quam sit difficile verborum honorem tam parvis perhibere*, 'some gratitude may attach to our labour and research on the ground that Virgil also confessed how difficult it is to provide such small matters with dignified appellations'; transl. by H. Rackham). Nonetheless, the position expressed on various occasions by Pliny concentrated more on utility than on *gratia* (*pr.* 16 *Equidem ita sentio, peculiarem in studiis causam eorum esse, qui difficultatibus victis utilitatem iuvandi praetulerint gratiae placendi*, 'For my own part I am of opinion, that a special pace in learning belongs to those who have preferred the useful service of overcoming difficulties to the popularity of giving pleasure'; transl. by H. Rackham; 28.2 *omnemque insumemus operam, licet fastidii periculum urgeat, quando ita decretum est, minorem gratiae quam utilitatium vitae respectum habere* 'Surely I must, and I shall devote all my care to the task, although I realize the risk of causing disgust, since it is my fixed determination to have less regard for popularity than for benefiting human life'; transl. by W.H.S. Jones).

with which he programmatically motivated the *Naturalis historia*, and which was also in line with the political programme of the Flavian family.[5]

There are, however, differences between the ways in which Pliny pictures the ancient scientists and those he employs in identifying himself as an author. Adopting the viewpoint of those who came later, Pliny attributes to the ancient scientists a precise intention to benefit 'posterity' (2.118 *posteros iuvandi*; 25.1 *prodesse posteris*): an attitude he never assumes for himself. It is by looking around him in the current age that he decides on the treatment of individual topics: 2.118 *scrupulosius ... tractabo ventos, tot milia navigantium cernens*. The knowledge he spreads also seems in general to be oriented to the present, and it is reasonable to think that his attention to the contemporary age ties in closely with the policy of the Flavians. On the other hand, the fact that he makes the relationship with posterity the privileged ideal of the ancient discoverers is indicative of how keenly aware Pliny was of the idea of duration in time; and if, in relation to himself, he does not speak of activities beneficial for the future, he perhaps chooses not to do so out of modesty, avoiding an explicit declaration of faith in the survival of his work. There is another difference as well, a more important and programmatic one, which Pliny establishes between himself and the ancient authors. The activities of the latter are related by Pliny to the sphere of original discovery (*invenire, excogitare nova, eruere*). He pictures them at work outdoors, in sometimes dangerous and fraught environments, engaged in that *cura* from which the discovery will arise: 2.117 *miror ... tot viris curae fuisse tam ardua inventu, inter bella praesertim et infida hospitia, piratis etiam ... terrentibus*, 'this makes me all the more surprised that so many people devoted themselves to these abstruse researches, especially when wars surroundend them and hosts were untrustworthy, and also when rumours of pirates ... terrified intending travellers'; transl. by H. Rackham); 25.3 *cura ... mira ... culmina quoque montium invia et solitudines abditas fibrasque omnis terrae scrutati*. Pliny continues the 'caring' of the ancients: but the vast majority of his own subject matter, as announced in the prefatory epistle, is drawn from previous authors and not, as with the ancients, from the direct study of nature.

---

5 I am referring here to the well-known passage in book 2 (2.18 *Deus est mortali iuvare mortalem, et haec ad aeternam gloriam via. Hac proceres iere Romani, hac nunc caelesti passu cum liberis suis vadit maximus omnis aevi rector Vespasianus Augustus fessis rebus subveniens*, 'For mortal to aid mortal – this is god; and this is the road to eternal glory: by this road went our Roman chieftains, by this road now proceeds with heavenward step, escorted by his children, the greatest ruler of all time, His Majesty Vespasian, coming to the succour of an exhausted world'; transl. by H. Rackham), and to other passages in Pliny, regarding which see Citroni Marchetti 1982 and 1991, passim.

Pliny's depiction of earlier authors sometimes involves another figure: a *princeps* who looks favourably upon their labours.[6] Of particular significance in this mode of representation is the picture Pliny paints of Aristotle as a zoologist (*Nat.* 8.44):

> Alexandro Magno rege inflammato cupidine animalium naturas noscendi delegataque hac commentatione Aristoteli, summo in omni doctrina viro, aliquot milia hominum in totius Asiae Graeciaeque tractu parere iussa, omnium quos venatus, aucupia piscatusque alebant quibusque vivaria, armenta, alvaria, piscinae, aviaria in cura erant, ne quid usquam genitum ignoraretur ab eo. Quos percunctando quinquaginta ferme volumina illa praeclara de animalibus condidit. Quae a me collecta in artum cum ⟨i⟩is, quae ignoraverat, quaeso ut legentes boni consulant, in universis rerum naturae operibus medioque clarissimi regum omnium desiderio cura nostra breviter peregrinantes.

> King Alexander the Great being fired with a desire to know the natures of animals and having delegated the pursuit of this study to Aristotle as a man of supreme eminence in every branch of science, orders were given to some thousands of persons throughout the whole of Asia and Greece, all those who made their living by hunting, fowling, and fishing and those who were in charge of warrens, herds, apiaries, fishponds and aviaries, to obey his instructions, so that he might not fail to be informed about any creature born anywhere. His enquiries addressed to those persons resulted in the composition of his famous works on zoology, in nearly 50 volumes. To my compendium of these, with the addition of facts unknown to him, I request my readers to give a favourable reception, while making a brief excursion under our direction among the whole of the works of Nature, the central interest of the most glorious of all sovereigns. (transl. by H. Rackham)

Pliny abbreviated Aristotle's books, adding what the latter did not know – this is the procedure announced in the letter to Titus. But in this case, the author's *cura* is designed to inform readers not only about the works of nature but also about the role of Alexander as the promoter of those studies. Introducing the regal figure into a passage in which Pliny reiterates the programme of the preface renders explicit what, in the latter, had been entrusted to the very act of the dedication: that is, the ideal of collaboration between *princeps* and scholar to promote scientific knowledge. It should be stressed that both in this passage and in the preface Pliny sees himself as an epitomist, capable of adding some information of

---

6 In such cases, the care of authors and the care of the *princeps* corresponded: the measuring of mountains by Dicaearchus was requested by the *cura regum* (2.162 *Dicaearchus, vir in primis eruditus, regum cura permensus montes*); the *cura* of Agrippa in surveying lands was shared by Augustus himself (3.17 *Agrippam quidem in tanta viri diligentia praeterque in hoc opere cura, cum orbem terrarum orbi spectandum propositur(u)s esset, errasse quis credat et cum eo Divum Augustum?*, 'Agrippa was a very painstaking man, and also a very careful geographer; who therefore could believe that when intending to set before the eyes of the world a survey of the world he made a mistake, and with him the late lamented Augustus?' Transl. by H. Rackham, modified).

his own to what is available in books. But one should also note the modesty of Pliny, who, just as he does not arrogate any role as a benefactor of posterity, does not even claim to have the ability – which he does actually possess – of the 'writer', capable of representing in a personal fashion the material gathered from books. There is another respect in which the passage on Aristotle ties in with the programme outlined in the preface: the reference to human activities. Many men who deal with animals (who make them the object of their *cura: quibus ... in cura erant*) relate their experiences to Aristotle. In the preface Pliny speaks of nature as 'life', peopled by human beings and sustained by the basic activities of *agricolae* and *opifices* (*pr.* 13; cf. 6). The active presence of men is essential to the *rerum natura* as conceived by Pliny: nature not as a separate entity but as part of an interaction. And I do not believe one can say (as is often said) that of this *vita* Pliny saw only the reflection of it found in books.[7]

In the *Naturalis historia*, the area of activity in which the word *cura* is used most frequently is agriculture,[8] and obviously the term *curare* is very much present in discussions of medical matters. I refer to medicine simply to highlight one feature of Pliny's ideology. He does not present himself as a physician, but as an intermediary between man and nature: his goal is to promote knowledge of the medicinal potential of nature's products, rather than leading readers to the practical application of the product.[9] The goal of knowledge is, however, underpinned by a philanthropic stance, which stems in turn not from a generic benevolence but from a vision of man as an exposed and vulnerable creature. At the beginning of book VII, devoted to man, Pliny, in an emotionally engaged tone, makes the observation that although new medicines are constantly being

---

7 It is noteworthy, for example, that Pliny attributes the attention towards celestial phenomena not only to scientists and traditional groups such as farmers and navigators, but also to merchants motivated by the desire for profit: 18.225 *servantque id sidus etiam vestis institores, et est in caelo notatu facillimum: ergo ex occasu eius de hieme augurantur quibus est cura insidiandi, negotiator(e)s avari*, 'and even clothes-dealers go by that constellation, and it is very easy to identify in the sky; consequently dealers out to make money, who are careful to watch for chances, make forecasts as to the winter from its setting' (transl. by H. Rackham), and see 18.273, where those contemptuous of this *cura* prove to be financially penalized. In turn, an individual product of nature may need to be dealt with by the author with particular care due to its capacity to enrich the nations that produce it: 17.42 *candidam argillam ... Gallias Britanniasque locupletantem cum cura dici convenit*. It seems characteristic that Pliny, in speaking of cockerels, attributes to them the task of calling men 'to care and toil': 10.46 *ad curas laboremque revocant*.
8 For some useful remarks on the use of *cura* in the domain of agriculture in Latin authors see Hauser 1954, 2ff.
9 A comprehensive overview of the link between the medical matters dealt with in the *Naturalis historia* and Pliny's overall vision of nature can be found in Doody 2009.

found, they are defeated by ever newer illnesses: 7.4 *iam morbi totque medicinae contra mala excogitatae, et hae quoque subinde novitatibus victae!* This passage, besides expressing a piteous vision of man as a vulnerable being, seems to be at odds with a precise position of medical professionals. According to Celsus, the representatives of empirical medicine maintained that sufficient medicines had already been found, and that no need was felt to discover others, because there were no new illnesses to warrant them: Cels. 1 *pr.* 36 *Primo tamen remedia exploranda summa cura fuisse; nunc uero iam explorata esse; neque aut nova genera morborum reperiri, aut novam desiderari medicinam* ('Nevertheless, at first remedies had to be explored with the greatest care; now, however, they have been explored already; there were neither new sorts of diseases to be found out, nor was a novel remedy wanted'; transl. by W. G. Spencer). In all likelihood Pliny was familiar with this debate within medicine.[10] He is not taking sides in a debate between physicians, but, as a competent and informed author, refers to it in expressing his own existential vision.

Pliny's compassion towards man as an exposed and vulnerable being finds direct expression in the comparison with animals. Animals only care about procuring food, without concerning themselves either with abstract or material goods or with death: 2.25 ... *nec quicquam miserius homine aut superbius. Ceteris quippe animantium sola victus cura est ... de gloria, de pecunia, ambitione superque de morte non cogitant.* On the other hand, man is so assailed by illnesses and distressing cares that he ends up 'invoking' death: 7.167 *tot periculorum genera, tot morbi, tot metus, tot curae, totiens invocata morte, ut nullum frequentius sit votum.* And yet he extends his cares into a future that will no longer concern him (see 7.5 *uni animantium luctus est datus ... uni inmensa vivendi cupido, uni superstitio, uni sepulturae cura atque etiam post se de futuro,* 'On man alone of living creature is bestowed grief ... he alone has ... immeasurable appetite for life, superstition, anxiety about burial and even about what will happen after he is no more'; transl. by H. Rackham). In the descriptions of animals given by Pliny at various points, the difference between them and man becomes less marked: not only do they display multiple forms of humanization in their behaviour, but a certain capacity for care is also explicitly attributed to them. Insects even devote care to the future: 11.7 *habere sensum victus, generationis, operis atque etiam de futuro curam ... quis facile crediderit?* And some talking birds love words, and devote *cura* and *cogitatio* to them: 10.118 *adamant verba quae*

---

[10] The idea that medicine was already complete was in reality shared by dogmatists and empirics, while there was disagreement regarding the appearance of new illnesses: see Cels. *praef.* 17, and see also Mudry 1982.

loquantur nec discunt sed diligunt meditantesque intra semet cura atque cogita-
tione, intentionem non occultant ('these birds get fond of uttering particular
words, and not only learn them but love them, and secretly ponder them with
careful reflexion, not concealing their engrossment' ; transl. by H. Rackham).[11]

The presence of *cura* in the *Naturalis historia* relates to a way of positioning
oneself in the world that is inspired by concerned sharing. It will perhaps not be
arbitrary here to refer to the line of moral philosophy developed in the 1980s,
known as the 'ethics of care'; providing, of course, one is careful not to force
the ancient text into patterns and schemes extraneous to it, using instead this
cultural experience to heighten our sensitivity to the text.[12] What above all
else enables us to compare Pliny with the ethics of care is his choice to engage
with others in a benevolent relationship based on acknowledgement of the weakness and vulnerability of the other, and also the scope of emotion that defines
that relationship in terms of compassion and identification. It is precisely this
emotional engagement that seems to differentiate Pliny's position from the patriarchal 'care' (both in specific sectors of human activity and in social relations,
with the exchange of favours attested most fully by the letters of Cicero) dominant in Roman society, which arose from a general sense of responsibility and
a respect for roles.[13] It would be wise, however, to regard this capacity for differ-

---

11 For the *cura* of which animals were capable, see also 8.8 (on elephants taking care of their
teeth) *circa hos beluis summa cura*; 10.103 (the partridge) *libera ac materna vacan(s) cura*; 11.109
(on the habits and organization of bees) *et his rei p(ublicae) ratio, memoria, cura*; 8.86 (on the
conjugal sentiment of the asp, which takes revenge for the death of its mate) *unus huic tam pes-*
tifero animali sensus vel potius affectus est ... alterutra interempta incredibilis ultionis alteri cura.
It is interesting to note that the connection between *cura* and *cogitatio* is characteristic of Cicero,
who mainly employs it in significant contexts, in relation to oratory, politics, social relations and
moral life. For the importance of this connection in Cicero's thought, one needs only cite *Off.* 1.79
Honestum ... totum est positum in animi cura et cogitatione. The relation between *cogitatio* and
cura is explained in Vitr. 1.2.2 *cogitatio est cura studii plena*; for their shared derivation from *di-*
ligentia, see Cic. *de Orat.* 2.149 *ut sit cura et cogitatione intentus (animus) diligentia est.*
12 Reference can be made here to the now classic works of Gilligan 1982; Noddings 1984; Held
2005.
13 The degree to which Pliny himself was aware of the necessary presence of *cura* in social relations is attested by the prefatory letter. The decision to give the *Naturalis historia* a table of contents (a choice which was of great programmatic significance) stemmed from Pliny's regard for
the *princeps*, whom he takes pains not to distract from his affairs: *pr.* 33 *Quia occupationibus tuis*
publico bono parcendum erat, quid singulis contineretur libris, huic epistulae subiunxi summaque
cura, ne legendos eos haberes, operam dedi. Tu per hoc et aliis praestabis ne perlegant ('As it was
my duty in the public interest to have consideration for the claims upon your time, I have ap-
pended to this letter a table of contents of the several books, and have taken very careful precautions to prevent your having to read them. You by these means will secure for others that they

entiation as having serious limits. To try to gauge how close Pliny came to an effective 'ethic of care', we can turn to an important point of comparison. The modern ethic of care values the female universe, and regards the mother-child relationship as a model for 'caring'.[14]

Pliny speaks explicitly of female care (*cura feminae*) on just one occasion, in relation to the tending of a vegetable patch: we are at any rate in a highly valued context, that of the ancient family-run farm (*Nat.* 19.57):

> Hortorum Cato praedicat caules. Hinc primum agricolae aestimabant prisci et sic statim faciebant iudicium, nequam esse in domo matrem familias – etenim haec cura feminae dicebatur –, ubi indiligens esset hortus, quippe e carnario aut macello vivendum e(sse).

> Cato sings the praises of garden cabbages. People in old days used to estimate farmers by their garden-produce and thus at once to give a verdict that there was a bad mistress in the house where the garden, which used to be called the woman's responsibility, was neglected, as it meant having to depend on the butcher or the market for victuals. (transl. by H. Rackham, modified)

As for the mother-child relationship, it is present in Pliny by way of the Mother Earth myth.

That the connection between care and the Earth, the entity from which human materiality depends, was present in the culture of the age is attested to by one of Hyginus' fables, sometimes cited in relation to the ethics of care and used by Heidegger as well, who considered care to be a primary ontological phenomenon. *Cura* fashions an image of man from mud, then asks Jove to give it life; in the ensuing dispute over the name, they are joined by Earth, who claims

---

will not need to read right through them either'; transl. by H. Rackham). As the dominant point of reference in the preface is the *princeps*, the *cura* takes the form of a meticulous concern to give the *princeps* what is due to him: therefore, just as the author shows great respect for his affairs, so those approaching the *princeps* must take great care in behaving appropriately, in a way befitting the great distance separating them: *pr.*11 *Te quidem in excelsissimo generis humani fastigio positum ... religiose adiri etiam a salutantibus scio, et ideo curari, quae tibi dicantur ut digna sint*, 'You yourself indeed, I know, being placed on the loftiest pinnacle of all mankind ... are approached with reverential awe even by persons paying a visit of ceremony, and consequently care is taken that what is dedicated to you may be worthy of you' (transl. by H. Rackham). **14** The connection between women and the ethic of care, propounded by Gilligan, Noddings and Held, has been widely disputed. For a firm and highly authoritative critique, see Tronto 1993, 81ff. A position that recognizes as necessary the link between women and the ethic of care both at a concrete level and at a cultural and symbolic one, can be found in Clement 1996 (see especially 2: "We need not make any false generalization about women to recognize that women's traditional activities and experiences are especially relevant to a study of the ethic of care"; 51 "there is a strong symbolic connection between femininity and the ethic of care").

to have provided the material for man's body. Ruling on the matter, Saturn gives *Cura* possession of man during life, but ascribes a name to the new creature on the basis of his origin: *homo vocetur quoniam ex humo videtur esse factus* (Hyg. *Fab.* 220):

> Cura cum quendam fluvium transiret, vidit cretosum lutum, sustulit cogitabunda et coepit fingere hominem. Dum deliberat secum quidnam fecisset, intervenit Iovis; rogat eum Cura ut ei daret spiritum, quod facile ab Iove impetravit. Cui cum vellet Cura nomen suum imponere, Iouis prohibuit suumque nomen ei dandum esse dixit. Dum de nomine Cura et Iovis disceptarent, surrexit et Tellus suumque nomen ei imponi debere dicebat, quandoquidem corpus suum praebuisset. Sumpserunt Saturnum iudicem; quibus Saturnus †secus† videtur iudicasse: Tu Iovis quoniam spiritum dedisti *** corpus recipito. Cura quoniam prima eum finxit, quamdiu vixerit Cura eum possideat; sed quoniam de nomine eius controversia est, homo vocetur quoniam ex humo videtur esse factus.

> When Cura was crossing a certain river, she saw some clayey mud. She took it up thoughtfully and began to fashion a man. While she was pondering on what she had done, Jove came up; Cura asked him to give the image life, and Jove readily grant this. When Cura wanted to give it her name, Jove forbade, and said that his name should be given it. But while they were disputing about the name, Tellus arose and said that it should have her name, since she had given her own body. They took Saturn for judge; he seems to have decided for them: Jove, since you gave him life [take his soul after death; since Tellus offered her body] let her receive his body; since Cura first fashioned him, let her posses him as long as he lives, but since there is controversy about his name, let him be called homo, since he seems to be made from humus. (transl. by M. Grant)

In Pliny's depiction, Earth is a mother who sustains the whole life of man (*Nat.* 2.154–159):[15]

> 154. Sequitur terra, cui uni rerum naturae partium eximia propter merita cognomen indidimus maternae venerationis. Sic hominum illa, ut caelum dei, quae nos nascentes excipit, natos alit semelque editos sustinet semper, novissime conplexa gremio iam a reliqua natura abdicatos, tum maxime ut mater operiens, nullo magis sacra merito quam quo nos quoque sacros facit, etiam monimenta ac titulos gerens nomenque prorogans nostrum et memoriam extendens contra brevitatem aevi, cuius numen ultimum iam nullis precamur irati grave, tamquam nesciamus hanc esse solam quae numquam irascatur homini ... 155. ... At haec benigna, mitis, indulgens ususque mortalium semper ancilla ... 156. Quin et venena nostri miseritam instituisse credi potest, ne in taedio vitae fames, mors terrae meritis alienissima, lenta nos consumeret tabe ... Ita est, miserita genuit id, cuius facillimo haustu inlibato corpore et cum toto sanguine exstingueremur nullo labore, sitientibus simi-

---

15 Pliny appears particularly close to Lucretius in the way both resort to the term *meritum* to explain in a rationalistic way the attribution of the name Mother Earth to the Earth: see Lucr. 5.795 f. *Linquitur ut merito maternum nomen adepta / terra sit*; 821 f. *Quare etiam atque etiam maternum nomen adepta / terra tenet merito*. On the passage in Lucretius, see Campbell 2003.

les ... 157. Verum fateamur: terra nobis malorum remedium genuit, nos illud vitae facimus venenum. Non enim et ferro, quo carere non possumus, simili modo utimur? nec tamen quereremur merito, etiamsi maleficii causa tulisset. Adversus unam quippe naturae partem ingrati sumus. Quas non ad delicias quasque non ad contumelias servit homini? in maria iacitur aut, ut freta admittamus, eroditur. Aquis, ferro, igni, ligno, lapide, fruge omnibus cruciatur horis multoque plus, ut deliciis quam ut alimentis famuletur nostris ... 159. ... Placatiore tamen dea ob haec, quod omnes hi opulentiae exitus ad scelera caedesque et bella tendunt, quodque sanguine nostro rigamus insepultisque ossibus tegimus, quibus tamen velut exprobrato furore tandem ipsa se obducit et scelera quoque mortalium occultat.

154. Next comes the earth, the one division of the natural world on which for its merits we have bestowed the venerable title of mother. She belongs to men as the sky belongs to God: she receives us at birth, and gives us nurture after birth, and once brought forth she upholds us always, and at the last when we have now been disinherited by the rest of nature she embraces us in her bosom and at that very time gives us her maternal shelter; sanctified by no service more than that whereby she makes us also sacred, even bearing our monuments and epitaphs and prolonging our name and extending our memory against the shortness of time; whose divinity is the last which in anger we invoke to lie heavy on those who are no more, as though we did not know that she is the only element that is never wroth with man ... 155. But earth is kind and gentle and indulgent, ever a handmaid in the service of mortals ... 156 Nay, even poisons she may be thought to have invented out of compassion for us, lest, when we were weary of life, hunger, the death most alien to earth's beneficence, should consume us with slow decay ... So is it! In mercy did she generate the potion whereof the easiest draught – as men drink when thirsty – might painlessly just blot us out, without injury to the body or loss of blood ... 157. Let us own the truth: what earth has produced as a cure for our ills, we have made into a deadly poison; why, do we not also put her indispensable gift of iron to a similar use? Nor yet should we have any right to complain even if she had engendered poison to serve the purpose of crime. In fact in regard to one of nature's elements we have no gratitude ... For what luxuries and for what outrageous uses does she not subserve mankind? She is flung into the sea, or dug away to allow us to let in the channels. Water, iron, wood, fire, stone, growing crops, are employed to torture her at all hours, and much more to make her minister to our luxuries than our sustenance ... 159. Yet that shows the goddess all the kinder towards us, because all these avenues from which wealth issues lead but to crime and slaughter and warfare, and because we besprinkle with our blood and we cover her with unburied bones, over which nevertheless, when at length our madness has been finally reproached, she draws herself as a veil, and hides even the crimes of mortals. (transl. by H. Rackham, modified)

What characterizes Earth is the generosity of her gifts, but also indulgence and compassion: she is *benigna, mitis, indulgens*, and on occasion *miserita*.[16] Earth

---

16 Among the mythicized forms of the female figure found in Pliny, Earth has a more reassuring maternal status than Nature, which sometimes appears a cruel stepmother (7.2 *non ut sit satis aestimare, parens melior homini an tristior noverca fuerit*); but it is Pomona who takes on the role of spoiling man, not only with the delightfulness of her fruits but also by encouraging laziness, in that she does not demand the care and toil required by Earth: 23.2 *Plurimum, inquit,*

represents a maternal universe in which the paternal code of responsibility and justice is not applied. This picture may seem very close to the current ethic of care, which affirms its diversity with respect to the ethic of justice. But some elements in the picture limit its comprehensiveness. Through its own suffering as well, Earth aids and supports activities, goals, and ways of life and death that are fundamentally male (i.e. plowing, mining, digging, warring, etc). And where, at the beginning of the passage, the merit of Earth with respect to man seems to exceed the materiality typical of their relation, the transcendence conferred by Earth is that which is obtained with the *monimenta* and *tituli* that she supports on her body: symbols of a male universe, and of great importance in the universe of the Roman man.

In the *Naturalis historia* the personified depiction of Earth brings to light an important problematic issue. Following the presence of the word *cura*, let's try to make a brief foray into agriculture, as we already have with medicine. Reflecting on the limited fertility of the Italic lands, Pliny focuses on the figures (identified as *imperatores*) who once practiced agriculture: their success depended on their condition as warriors capable of applying the same care to cultivation as they did to war. Pliny also suggests (but there is no real difference) that everything done by honourable hands (*honestae*) yields happier results because it is carried out with more care (*curiosius*) (*Nat.* 18.19):

> quaenam ergo tantae ubertatis causa erat? ipsorum tunc manibus imperatorum colebantur agri, ut fas est credere, gaudente terra vomere laureato et triumphali aratore, sive illi eadem cura semina tractabant, qua bella, eademque diligentia arva disponebant, qua castra, sive honestis manibus omnia laetius proveniunt, quoniam et curiosius fiunt.

> What therefore was the cause of such great fertility? The fields were tilled in those days by the hands of generals themselves, and we may well believe that the earth rejoiced in a laurel-decked ploughshare and a ploughman who had celebrated a triumph, whether it was that those farmers treated the seed with the same care as they managed their wars and marked out their fields with the same diligence as they arranged a camp, or whether everything prospers better under honourable hands because the work is done with greater attention. (transl. by H. Rackham)

---

homini voluptatis ex me est ... neque, ut Tellus, omnia per labores ... ex me parata omnia nec cura laboranda, sed sese porrigentia ultro et, si pigeat attingere, etiam cadentia, 'Man, she says, enjoys through me a very great amount of pleasure ... I am unlike Mother Earth, all of whose gifts must be earned by toil ... But my gifts are perfect before they leave me, and need no laborious preparation. They proffer themselves unasked, and if it be too much trouble to reach them, they actually fall of themselves' (transl. by W. H. S. Jones).

The earth enjoyed being ploughed by the farmer warrior. The relation here is not between mother and child, but is a conjugal relationship that the earth accepts because in the man who possesses her she recognizes the triumphant warrior (*gaudente terra vomere laureato*).[17] Pliny's depiction of the current situation is radically different: the earth is no longer the benevolent mother nor the consensual bride, but a woman attempting to repel the violence inflicted on her by men (*invita ea et indignante*). What image of man is given to us here? The cultivators of the age are depicted as the basest of slaves: neuter *ergastula*, the opposite of *imperatores*. Their physical figure as men is broken up, with the single parts carrying derogatory overtones (*Nat.* 18.21):

> At nunc eadem illa vincti pedes, damnatae manus inscriptique vultus exercent, non tam surda tellure, quae parens appellatur colique dicitur ips⟨o⟩ honore his absumpto, ut non invita ea et indignante credatur id fieri. E⟨t⟩ nos miramur ergastulorum non eadem emolumenta esse, quae fuerint imperatorum!

> But nowadays those agricultural operations are performed by slaves with fettered ankles and by the hands of malefactors with branded faces! Although the Earth who is addressed as our mother and whose cultivation is spoken of as worship is not so dull that when this honour has been bestowed to them one can believe that this is not done against her will and to her indignation. And we forsooth are surprised that we do not get the same profits from the labour of slave-gangs as used to be obtained from that of generals! (transl. by H. Rackham, modified)

We are a long way here from an ethic of care that moves towards acknowledgement of the other and the possibility of relating to him. The other is no longer even recognized as man. Examining the *Naturalis historia* for the possible presence of a female model, we found instead a discriminatory warrior male principle. We might say that it is a protective male principle, in that it is in the moment in which there is a perceived danger or damage (invasion from abroad, crumbling of ancient customs, etc.) that a depersonalizing hostility towards the other is triggered in Pliny. And yet the emotiveness that the representation of the Earth as suffering woman brings into play is precisely what obscures and thwarts a possible reflection about the causes of suffering and the historic responsibilities of warrior paternalism: that is, about the fact that those who are abhorred as aggressors gained access to Italic lands through wars promoted by those same *imperatores* invoked as the Earth's fitting grooms.[18]

---

17 On the application of the term *arare* to the sexual sphere on the part of Latin authors, see Dieterich 1905. The term *vomer* is used with such a meaning in Lucretius 4.1272f.

18 A warning about the danger that commiseration for people seen as victims may reinforce positions of paternalistic domination comes from Robinson 2011 (see especially p. 165: "When care

Pliny's concrete experience of war, as reflected in the *Naturalis historia*, adds something useful for the understanding of his position. Pliny is willing to acknowledge the fragility and unhappiness of the other, even an enemy in arms: '*Misera gens*' is his comment about a German people he sees exposed to the inclemency of the natural environment (*Nat.* 16.2–4):[19]

> sunt vero et in septentrione visae nobis C(h)aucorum (gentes) qui maiores minoresque appellantur ... Illic, misera gens, tumulos optinent altos aut tribunalia exstructa manibus ad experimenta altissimi aestus ... Et hae gentes, si vincantur hodie a populo Romano, servire se dicunt! ita est profecto: multis fortuna parcit in poenam.

> but so also are the races of people called the Greater and the Lesser Chauci, whom we have seen in the north ... There this miserable race occupy elevated patches of ground or platforms built up by hand above the level of the highest tide experienced ... And these are the races that if they are nowadays vanquished by the Roman nation say that they are reduced to slavery! That is indeed the case: Fortune oft spares men as a punishment. (transl. by H. Rackham)

Pliny believed that these populations could not but benefit from being conquered by the Romans. That Roman arms brought civilization and wellbeing is one paternalistic view that Pliny certainly accepted in good faith.

At a conceptual level, Pliny did not choose, and could never have chosen, to uphold a relational ethic based on benevolence at the expense of a paternalistic ethic of dominion. But the personality of Pliny (especially his 'writer's' persona) and also the peculiar character of the work nonetheless favour the embracing of an ethic open to recognizing vulnerability, however it might present itself. It can undoubtedly be said that Pliny displays a sense of involvement in the world (the human world, but also that of animals, and the natural environment) that is hard to find in ancient authors.[20]

---

is understood as benevolence, charity, or attention to the 'victims' or the 'vulnerable' in societies, an ethics of care could serve to reinforce existing patterns of domination and dependency"). Along the same lines as Tronto 1993 and Sevehuijsen 1998, Robinson regards care as a 'social practice' of political value, through which to overcome traditional binary opposites (like that of gender). Sevehuijsen and Robinson offer a valid recognition of the debate stirred by the works of Gilligan, Noddings and Held.

19 For an examination of the passage, see Citroni Marchetti 1982.

20 Pliny's conception of the natural environment, which I cannot look into now, can, I believe, be readily associated with what is postulated on a general level by Robinson 2011, 144: "seen through the lens of care ethics, the health and flourishing of the natural environment must be understood as inextricably connected with the health and flourishing of persons ... we can make moral sense of the environment only in the context of our association with it".

By way of conclusion I would like to refer to one of Pliny's descriptions. Among the depictions of animals in the *Naturalis historia* one of the most striking is that of a tiger, who, having pursued the men who had stolen her cubs, vents her rage in vain on the shore (*Nat.* 8.66):

> At ubi vacuum cubile reperit feta – maribus enim subolis cura non est – fertur praeceps odore vestigans. Raptor adpropinquante fremitu abicit unum ex catulis; tollit illa morsu et pondere etiam ocior acta remeat iterumque consequitur ac subinde, donec in navem regresso inrita feritas saevit in litore.

> But when the mother tiger finds the lair empty (for the males do not look after the young) she rushes off at headlong speed, tracking them by scent. The captor when her roar approaches throws away one of the cubs. She snatches it up in her mouth, and returns and resumes the pursuit at even a faster pace owing to her burden, and so on in succession until the hunter has regained the ship and her ferocity rages vainly on the shore. (transl. by H. Rackham)

This story crops up in other authors as well, but I would say that in none of them is there such an effective representation of frustrated motherhood.[21] Pliny's account explains why the mother is alone in protecting her young: among tigers 'males do not care for the offspring'. In Roman life it was customary for men (the fathers) to devote such care. The care exercised by the Roman male took many forms, and impinged strongly on the world. The tiger on an African shore evokes other contexts. Someone carries off her cubs. They are men, and they take the tigers to exhibit them in spectacles. Tigers, like other animals. When Marcus Caelius Rufus wrote to Cicero in Cilicia, he continually asked to be sent panthers: he asked that Cicero 'should devote care' to sending him panthers (Cic. *fam.* 8.2.2):

> ut tibi curae sit quod ⟨ad⟩ pantheras attinet rogo; 8.4.5 de pantheris ... cures ... ut mi vehantur; 8. 6.5 Turpe tibi erit pantheras Graecas me non habere; 8.9.3 Fere litteris omnibus tibi de pantheris scripsi.

> I beg you to be taking measures as to the panthers; 8.4.5 so also about the panthers ... see ... that they are shipped to me; 8.6.5 it will be a disgrace to you if I have no Greek panthers; 8.9.3 In nearly every letter I have mentioned the subject of the panthers to you. (transl. by W. W. Glynn)

---

21 See above all Mela 3.43 (note that in Mela the story is told from the point of view of the hunter, building up a picture of his intentions and the ways in which he frustrates the animal). An elaborate dramatization can also be found in the poets: see Stat. *Theb.* 10.820 ff., who describes not the anger but the grief of the tiger (and likewise, briefly, V. Fl. 6.149), and V. Fl. 1.489 ff., who instead describes the fear of the pursued abductor.

Pliny's work, by virtue of its subject matter, occupies a central position with respect to Roman civilization. It represents it as a whole, in that each individual topic refers to other forms and features of the Roman world. At the centre of the work ('at the heart' of the work) is a sense of care which, though relating to specific (and for us also alien) aspects of the patriarchal society to which the author belonged, has an affinity with our own notion of a care ethic. It is towards this ethic of care that Pliny, with his sensitivity for the vulnerability, weakness and frustration of the other, moves, even simply through the effectiveness of his writing.

Andrea Balbo
Roman oratory and power under the Flavians: some case studies from Pliny the Younger

1 In the crossfire

The history of oratory in the first century CE is not easy to write. From a structural point of view, eloquence seems to maintain in this century its important
role in Roman society.[1] Indeed, in the domain of education, rhetoric plays a fundamental role in the school system: the schools of declamation are flourishing[2]
and, by the end of the century, prominent teachers receive a public salary from
the Emperor, as the well-known case of Quintilian shows. Throughout the Roman
Empire, rhetorical education was considered the best way to train young elites.
But what about oratory? Our sources tend to divide into two main positions on
this issue. One side gives the impression that oratory is in a terrible state of crisis, in which it is possible to observe clearly the gulf between theory and practice, between scholastic training on one side, and court and Senate debates on
the other.[3] To the contrary, other sources show great confidence in the high quality of contemporary oratory. We may compare two examples of these opposing
views:

Quint. *Inst.* 10.1.122:
Habebunt qui post nos de oratoribus scribent magnam eos qui nunc
vigent materiam vere laudandi: sunt enim summa hodie quibus inlus-
tratur forum ingenia. Namque et consummati iam patroni veteribus aemulantur et
eos iuvenum ad optima tendentium imitatur ac sequitur industria.

I wish to thank Thomas Frazel for his help in the revision of the English form of this paper.

1 See Cavarzere 2008[2], 225.
2 "Declamation is the first major literary movement of the Roman empire" (Bloomer 2010, 297).
See also Orentzel 1978a.
3 The distance between school and real life is effectively described in the dialogue between Encolpius and Agamemnon in the first preserved fragment of Petronius, *Sat.* 1–5. The bibliography
on this section of Petronius' work is huge, due to its connection with the problem *de causis corruptae eloquentiae* (cf. below, n. 4). See, for instance, Cizek 1975 and Kennedy 1978; a reappraisal
in Courtney 2001, 54–61; recently on chapter 5 see Vannini 2009.

https://doi.org/10.1515/9783110534436-005

Subsequent writers on the history of oratory will find abundant material for praise among the orators who flourish to-day: for the law courts can boast a glorious wealth of talent. Indeed, the consummate advocates of the present day are serious rivals of the ancients, while enthusiastic effort and lofty ideals lead many a young student to tread in their footsteps and imitate their excellence. (transl. by H. E. Butler)

Tac. *Dial.* 1.1
Saepe ex me requiris, Iuste Fabi, cur, cum priora saecula tot eminentium oratorum ingeniis gloriaque floruerint, n o s t r a   p o t i s s i m u m   a e t a s   d e s e r t a   e t   l a u d e   e l o q u e n t i a e   o r b a t a   v i x   n o m e n   i p s u m   o r a t o r i s   r e t i n e a t ; neque enim ita appellamus nisi antiquos, horum autem temporum diserti causidici et advocati et patroni et quidvis potius quam oratores vocantur.

You often ask me, Justus Fabius, how it is that while the genius and the fame of so many distinguished orators have shed a lustre on the past, our age is so forlorn and so destitute of the glory of eloquence that it scarce retains the very name of orator. That title indeed we apply only to the ancients, and the clever speakers of this day we call pleaders, advocates, counsellors, anything rather than orators. (transl. by W. Peterson)

According to Quintilian, contemporary Rome can rely on many orators of the highest quality (*summa ingenia*),[4] while Tacitus, in the context of the debate *de causis corruptae eloquentiae*,[5] posits a break in continuity between the oratory of ancient times and that of his own day; he even goes so far as to declare that the very name of oratory is in crisis. A two-part caveat is necessary: Quintilian is strictly connected to the Flavian emperors in a patronage context, which positively colours his judgments of the Flavian present, while Tacitus evinces hostility towards the dictatorial hand of Domitian and the idea of autocratic degeneration implied in the development of empire. Wherein lies the truth? Kennedy explains that "in the upshot the truth was somewhere between Tacitus' and Quintilian's position. Oratory and traditional rhetoric were not quite so dead as Tacitus thought, nor did any orator as great as Cicero come again as Quintilian hoped".[6] But what is the real situation of Flavian oratory and what exactly do we know about it? How did oratory relate to Flavian imperium, and how did it affect power dynamics in Flavian Rome? In this paper, I would like to give an initial answer to these questions by dealing with two points: (1) first, by briefly

---

4 An expression of evident rhetorical origin: with the exceptions of Pl. *Capt.* 165 and Acc. *Trag.* 362, *summum ingenium* is used above all by Cicero and Seneca the Elder.
5 The problem has been deeply studied: I refer only to Kennedy 1972, 446–465; 1994, 186–192; and Cavarzere 2008[2], 215–238.
6 Kennedy 1972, 523. For Pliny's statements about his contemporary oratory see Gamberini 1983, 49–52.

examining the landscape of Flavian oratory; (2) second, by analysing two cases that provide information about both oratory and rhetoric in the Flavian age and about the connection between power and oratory.

2 Oratory in Flavian times: a short critical survey

Research on Flavian oratory is still an open field. If we look at the scholarship from the second part of the twentieth century until today, Kennedy 1972, Leeman 1974 and Orentzel 1974 have offered important studies that have improved our knowledge of the cultural system and of the oratorical world in the years 69–96 CE, while Gamberini 1983 has described Pliny's view on contemporary oratory. More recently, Rivière 2002, Cavarzere 2008[2], Bäblitz 2009, Dominik 2010, Mastrorosa 2010a and 2010b, and Procchi 2012 have pursued three main objectives: (1) to reassess the role of Flavian oratory in the history of Roman eloquence; (2) to pay attention to the juridical context of orations and, consequently, to trials; (3) to highlight the presence of real oratory outside the rhetoric schools. Despite these efforts, we do not have at our disposal a definitive work on the art of public speaking in this period.

First of all, as is well known, we cannot read any complete speech from this era,[7] but we can find traces of judicial oratory, especially pertaining to the centumviral court, as well as evidence of *contiones militares*.[8] In the domain of strict deliberative oratory, there exists less evidence of senate debates, while epideictic speeches largely survive only after Domitian's death, as is shown for example by the burial speech for Verginius Rufus[9] and Pliny's panegyric.

What could be the reasons for such a situation? The first problem is a lack of documents. We have to deal with a dearth of consistent sources, above all among the Latin historiographers. Moreover, in accordance with the tradition derived from the Alexandrian grammarians, Quintilian does not quote any living orator.[10] Finally, we see a deliberate reticence in dealing with the period between 81 and

---

7 Pliny's panegyric to Trajan dates back to 100 CE; Ps. Quintilian's *Declamationes maiores* are later, perhaps of II–III century CE: see for instance Stramaglia 2013, 34–37.

8 About the *contiones militares* see Abbamonte 2009.

9 See Trisoglio 1973, 256 n. 3 with bibliography and Levick 1985, Gibson / Morello 2012, 104–108 and 126–135.

10 See Orentzel 1978b, Citroni 2005a and Rutledge 2010, 109 f.

92 by some sources, such as Pliny the Younger, who is eager to distance himself from the *pessimus princeps*, Domitian.[11]

If we move away from information concerning the activity of the orators and turn our attention to juridical contexts, i.e. the trials, the situation does not change. Bleicken 1962, for instance, records only three trials *de repetundis* in the Flavian age; in fact, apart from the numerous *maiestas* cases,[12] trials based on other charges seem to be rarer in the years between 70–97/98 CE, and this could explain the rarity of orations in that period. But the unfortunate political context of the late first century and the subsequent loss of literary texts from the period may perhaps not entirely explain this lack of data; other long-term phenomena, in my opinion, should be considered.

The first of these is the gradual transition from the system of *quaestiones* to the *cognitio extra ordinem:* a phenomenon, already underlined by Cavarzere 2008[2], which had a particular impact on the first and second century CE, because it reduced the space for the conduct of the trial, consequently causing a decrease in the space available for judicial oratory. The second is partially a consequence of the first: in the *cognitio extra ordinem* and in civil trials the time reserved for the orators' speeches was cut. For example, Pliny the Younger observes (*Ep.* 6.2.4 f.):

> Sed utcumque se habent ista, bene fecit Regulus quod est mortuus: melius, si ante. Nunc enim sane poterat sine malo publico vivere, sub eo principe sub quo nocere non poterat. Ideo fas est non numquam eum quaerere. Nam, postquam obiit ille, increbruit passim et invaluit consuetudo binas uel singulas clepsydras, interdum etiam dimidias et dandi et petendi. Nam et qui dicunt, egisse malunt quam agere, et qui audiunt, finire quam iudicare. Tanta neglegentia tanta desidia, tanta denique inreverentia studiorum periculorumque est.

> But for all that, Regulus did well to die though he would have done still better had he died sooner; since he might now be alive without any danger to the public in the reign of princeps under whom he could do no mischief. I need no scruple therefore to say I sometimes miss him: for since his death, the custom has grown widely prevalent of not allowing, nor indeed asking, more than an hour or two to plead in, and sometimes not half that time. The truth is, our advocates are better pleased to have got through a cause, than to be engaged in it; and our judges are more bent on concluding, than on deciding it. Such is their negligence, their sloth, nay, disrespect for both the profession and the grave issues fo the Law. (transl by W. Melmoth)

---

11 Orentzel 1980, 49.
12 Rogers 1960 and Bauman 1974 list a consistent number of these trials mainly under Domitian. Sometimes it is not easy to understand if some characters were involved into one trial or many, as in the case of the persecution of philosophers in 93: see Rogers 1960.

Tacitus also confirms that the duration of speeches was shortened (*Dial.* 38):

> Transeo ad formam et consuetudinem veterum iudiciorum. quae etsi nunc aptior est [ita erit], eloquentiam tamen illud forum magis exercebat, in quo nemo intra paucissimas horas perorare cogebatur et liberae comperendinationes erant et modum in dicendo sibi quisque sumebat et numerus neque dierum neque patronorum finiebatur.

> I pass on to the organization and procedure of the old law courts. It may nowadays have become more practical, but all the same the forum as it then was provided a better training-ground for eloquence. There was no obligation on any speaker to complete his pleading within a very few hours; adjournments were always in order; as regards a time-limit, every man was a law to himself and there was no prescribed number of days or of counsel. (transl. W. Peterson, with some changes)

Quite clearly, the *paucissimae horae* of Tacitus reveal that lawyers of his day had to prepare their performances relying on the use of much less time than Cicero had enjoyed.

The second phenomenon is the restriction on freedom of speech: the problem arose in Augustus' time, got worse during the government of Tiberius and the other Julio-Claudian emperors, and reached a high under Domitian, who persecuted Stoics and Cynics, exhibited cruelty on a variety of occasions, and expelled the philosophers from Rome.[13] Closely connected to this is the rise of the *delatores*,[14] who became a real threat for anyone who could be suspected to be an enemy of the Roman order (to use the phrase of R. Mac Mullen) or who was simply rich enough to attract the interest of false witnesses.

If we use a pictorial metaphor, we now have at our disposal enough information to draw preparatory outlines for a fresco representing the art of eloquence in this period that would allow us to understand the general meaning of the scene, but we still cannot paint the details of the characters with sufficient precision. Metaphors aside, we do not even have a detailed list of the orators who were active in this period. Heinrich Meyer, in his *ORF²*, records the following speakers working at this time: Quintilian, Pliny the Younger, Tacitus, Vibius Crispus, Galerius Trachalus, Sextus Iulius Gabinianus, Pompeius Saturninus, Domitian

---

13 See Plin. *Ep.* 4.11; about the problem of Domitian's cruelty see Bauman 1996, 92–99, who argues that he used such a terrifying way to punish the Vestals who broke their chastity vote "as a means of propagating *correctio morum*, his policy of moral reform. It was an extreme use of the *poenae metus*" (99).

14 See Rivière 2002, *passim.*

and a mysterious Donatianus.[15] To these we should probably add the followers of the schools of declamation; among them, Meyer places Calpurnius Flaccus who, however, lived later, according to the most recent studies.[16] A few other characters are attested, in the face of a much larger number of speakers active in the Julio-Claudian era (more than 50 during Tiberius' reign alone). Nevertheless, Meyer's list is far from exhaustive and already Syme had suggested that it be supplemented at the very least with Aquilius Regulus, Eprius Marcellus, Salvius Liberalis, Silius Italicus, Paccius Africanus, Didius Gallus Fabricius Veiento, Valerius Catullus Messallinus, and a vague Pompeius *delator*, perhaps Cn. Pompeius Catullinus consul in 90.[17] Moreover, I would add Curiatius Maternus, Marcus Aper, Vipstanus Messalla, Marcus Antonius Primus and the emperors Vespasianus and Titus;[18] about their oratorical activity, there is still much work to do.[19] If the situation is uncertain concerning the orators, the case of the speeches is similar, as we can see from the following scheme (Table 1):[20]

Table 1: Orators and cases attested in the Flavian era

Orator	Hypothetical topic	Date	Source
Salvius Liberalis	*Pro reo divite*	70–79 CE	Suet. *Vesp.* 13
Quintilian	*Pro regina Berenice*	75 CE	Quint. *Inst.* 4.1.1
Quintilian	*Pro rea de falso testamento*	Flavian age	Quint. *Inst.* 9.2.73
Pliny the Younger	*Pro Iunio Pastore*	Under Titus or Domitian	Plin. *Ep.* 1.18
Pliny the Younger	*Pro Arrionilla*	Before 93 CE	Plin. *Ep.* 1.5

15 *ORF²*, nn. 135–143, 591–607. *Donatianus* was the original reading of the manuscripts of Priscian's *De nomine* (*GL* 2, 225, 10). Putschius proposed to read *Domitianus*, a correction which however is far from convincing. Finally Heinrich Keil restored *Donatianus* and so we should take this name into account.
16 See Håkanson 2013, 47–130.
17 Syme 1958, 2, 667 f.
18 I hope to implement the list further during the inquiries I am making for the edition of *Oratorum Romanorum Fragmenta* from Augustus to Symmachus that I am preparing for Teubner/De Gruyter. At the moment, I have to thank very much the works of Münkel 1959 and Orentzel 1974, who provided me with important materials. We have no information after 70 about many of the orators registered by Münkel. I do not discuss here the problem of the nature of the fragments, whether they were published or not, but I deal with them only as witnesses of oratorical activity.
19 About them, the reference work for the fragments is still *ORF²*.
20 See *ORF²*, Orentzel 1974, Procchi 2012. According to Dominik 2010, 335, Pliny "in his *Epistles* refers specifically to twenty-seven speeches that he had given between 79/80 and 108", but most of them date after Domitian's death.

Table 1: Orators and cases attested in the Flavian era *(Continued)*

Orator	Hypothetical topic	Date	Source
Pliny the Younger	*Contra Baebium Massam*	93 CE	Plin. *Ep.* 6.29; 7.33
Pliny the Younger	*De bibliothecae dedicatione*[21]	Perhaps 96 CE	Plin. *Ep.* 1.8

The landscape appears very barren and needs reappraisal. This paper aims to make a first step towards the reconsideration of Roman imperial oratory.

3 Two case studies from Pliny the Younger

Despite such a difficult backdrop, the relationship between the orators and Flavian power is certainly an interesting topic, and suggests several stimulating hints. Let us examine two Plinian cases from which, perhaps, we may discern some indication of larger trends.

3.1 Pliny the Younger[22] stands up for Iunius Pastor (*Ep.* 1.18.3)

> Susceperam causam Iuni Pastoris, cum mihi quiescenti visa est socrus mea advoluta genibus ne agerem obsecrare; et eram acturus a d u l e s c e n t u l u s adhuc, eram in quadruplici iudicio, eram contra p o t e n t i s s i m o s c i v i t a t i s atque etiam Caesaris amicos, quae singula excutere mentem mihi post tam triste somnium poterant. Egi tamen λογισάμενος illud
> εἷς οἰωνὸς ἄριστος ἀμύνεσθαι περὶ πάτρης.
> Nam mihi patria, et s i q u i d c a r i u s p a t r i a, fides videbatur. Prospere cessit, atque adeo illa actio[23] mihi aures hominum, illa ianuam famae patefecit.

> I had undertaken a brief for Julius Pastor, when there appeared to me in my sleep a vision of my mother-in-law, who threw herself on her knees before me and begged that I would not plead. I was quite a young man at the time of the action, which was to be heard in the Fourfold Court, and I was appearing against the most powerful men of the State, including some of the Friends of Caesar. All these things or any one of them might well have shattered my resolution after such an ominous dream. Nevertheless, I went on with the case, remembering the well-known line of Homer: 'But one omen is best, to fight on behalf of one's country.' For in my case the keeping of my word seemed to me as important as fighting on behalf

---

21 On the date see Dix 1996.

22 As regards Pliny's oratory and eloquence see the still fundamental study of Picone 1977 and, more recently, Mayer 2003.

23 Here *actio* is used in the sense of speech in front of the judges: see Trisoglio 1973, 1390.

of my country or as any other still more pressing consideration – if any consideration more pressing can be imagined. Well, the action went off successfully, and it was the way that I conducted that case which got me a hearing with men and opened the door to fame. (transl. by W. Melmoth)

Pliny writes to Suetonius to reassure him that a nightmare cannot influence the results of a trial in which he is involved. He relates an episode from his youth: after accepting to undertake the defence of a certain Iunius Pastor,[24] he dreamt that his mother-in-law[25] begged him not to plead the case. Pliny did not pay any attention to the portent and won the trial.

Pliny is the only source for this case and his testimony leaves several areas uncertain. First of all, the date of the trial itself is a matter of discussion. Stein[26] situates it simply "under Domitian", but Sherwin-White 1966, 128 posits a date between 79 and 81, a very early date for Pliny, possibly identifying it with his *exordium* into forensic activity, which Pliny himself places in *undevicesimo aetatis anno* (i.e. 80 CE).[27] But there is no certainty here. Surely Pliny was very young: though the term *adulescentulus* does not mark a precise age, Pliny apparently uses it to describe people younger than twenty.[28] The presence of *adhuc* also seems to suggest a slightly older age, but I will return to this point later.

The trial took place in the centumviral court and was held in multiple sections (*quadruplex iudicium*), which would have made Pliny's defense particularly difficult.[29] The *centumviri* had jurisdiction in matters of both inheritance and property,[30] so the specific nature of the charge against Pastor is uncertain. However, we do know the result: Pastor was acquitted.

---

24 This character could be identified with the *Pastor* portrayed by his friend Martial in 9.22: see Procchi 2012, 33 n. 58.

25 The identity is uncertain, because Pliny had three wives. Perhaps she was the mother of his first wife, whom he married very early and about whom we know nothing: see Sherwin-White 1966, 128. For Shelton 2013, 260 and 293, this woman could be Pompeia Celerina.

26 A. Stein, *RE* XIX 1918, *Iunius Pastor* n. 117, col. 1073.

27 *Ep.* 5.8.8. Perhaps he came from *Transpadana* (*Patavium?*): see Mratschek 2003, 237.

28 Pliny employs *adulescentulus* 9 times with a denotative meaning and in the Imperial age he is the author who uses the word most frequently (Slusanschi 1974, 284 and 367). Also the late-antique data from digilibLT (www.digiliblt.uniupo.it) – not taken into consideration by Slusanschi – confirm both the rarity of the word (30 occurrences, 4 in Iulius Valerius and 3 in Iulius Paris) and Pliny's predilection for it.

29 "I casi trattati 'a sezioni riunite' dovevano essere abbastanza rari, visto che l'autore li cita soltanto sporadicamente" (Procchi 2012, 33 n. 60).

30 See in general David 1983 and Gagliardi 2002; further bibliography in Procchi 2012. I do not concentrate on the problem whether the trial could be postponed, as Pliny seems to suggest

In this speech Pliny stresses the fact that his adversaries are the most powerful and influential men of Rome: the *amici Caesaris*. This definition refers to
some friends of the emperor who, as part of the *consilium principis*, played a significant role in administration and politics.[31] Pliny's statement and the reaction
of his mother-in-law highlight the perception of the high risk the young orator
had taken by agreeing to oppose such men.

But the situation and the expression used by the author both reveal, in my
opinion, an intertextual relationship that has not yet been fully explored. Pliny
refers to these Emperor's friends as *potentissimi civitatis:* a very rare phrase in
Latin as the following survey will show:

a. Cic. *Pro Sexto Roscio Amerino* 6:
Bona patris huiusce Sex. Rosci quae sunt sexagiens, quae de viro fortissimo et clarissimo L.
Sulla, quem honoris causa nomino, duobus milibus nummum sese dicit emisse adulescens
vel p o t e n t i s s i m u s h o c t e m p o r e n o s t r a e c i v i t a t i s , L. Cornelius Chrysogonus.

The property of the father of this Sextus Roscius, which is six millions of sesterces, which
one of the most powerful young men of our city at this present time, Lucius Cornelius
Chrysogonus, says he bought of that most gallant and most illustrious man Lucius Sulla,
whom I only name to do him honour, for two thousand sesterces. (transl. by C. D. Yonge)

b. Val. Max. 9.4.1:
Cum admodum locupleti L. Minucio Basilo falsum testamentum quidam in Graecia subie-
cisset eiusdemque confirmandi gratia p o t e n t i s s i m o s c i v i t a t i s n o s t r a e v i r o s , M.
C r a s s u m e t Q . H o r t e n s i u m , quibus Minucius ignotus fuerat, tabulis heredes inse-
ruisset, quamquam evidens fraus erat, tamen uterque pecuniae cupidus facinoris alieni
munus non repudiavit. quantam culpam quam leniter retuli! l u m i n a c u r i a e , o r n a -
m e n t a f o r i , q u o d s c e l u s v i n d i c a r e d e b e b a n t , i n h o n e s t i l u c r i c a p t u r a
i n v i t a t i a u c t o r i t a t i b u s s u i s t e x e r u n t .[32]

(1.18.6): *nam iudicium centumvirale differri nullo modo, istuc aegre quidem sed tamen potest*; see
Sherwin-White 1966, 129 and Méthy 2007, 305 n. 136.

31 For their role and functions see Crook 1955; for a list of known members of the consilium see
ibidem, 149–190.

32 Valerius Maximus is retelling a story already narrated by Cic. *Off.* 3.73 *sed haec consideremus,
quae faciunt ii, qui habentur boni. L. Minuci Basili locupletis hominis falsum testamentum quidam
e Graecia Romam attulerunt. Quod quo facilius obtinerent, scripserunt heredes secum M. Crassum
et Q. Hortensium, homines eiusdem aetatis potentissimos. Qui cum illud falsum esse suspicarentur,
sibi autem nullius essent conscii culpae, alieni facinoris munusculum non repudiaverunt. Quid
ergo? Satin est hoc, ut non deliquisse videantur? Mihi quidem non videtur, quamquam alterum
vivum amavi, alterum non odi mortuum.* ('But let us study here the conduct of those who have
the reputation of being honest men. Certain individuals brought from Greece to Rome a forged
will, purporting to be that of the wealthy Lucius Minucius Basilus. The more easily to procure
validity for it, they made joint-heirs with themselves two of the most influential men of the

L. Minucius Basilus was a very rich man. A certain person in Greece produced a forged will and for confirmation of the same put in as heirs two very powerful persons in our community, M. Crassus and Q. Hortensius, who did not know Minucius. The fraud was apparent, but in their greed for money neither of the two repudiated the gift of another's misdeed. What guilt, how lightly here reported! Luminaries of the Senate house, ornaments of the Forum, lured by getting of disgraceful gain they covered with their authority a crime that they ought to have punished. (transl. by D. R. Shackleton Bailey)

c. Tac. *Dial.* 8.3:
Nam quo sordidius et abiectius nati sunt quoque notabilior paupertas et angustiae rerum nascentis eos circumsteterunt, eo clariora et ad demonstrandam oratoriae eloquentiae utilitatem inlustriora exempla sunt, quod sine commendatione natalium, sine substantia facultatum, neuter moribus egregius, alter habitu quoque corporis contemptus, per multos iam annos potentissimi sunt civitatis ac, donec libuit, principes fori, nunc principes in Caesaris amicitia agunt feruntque cuncta atque ab ipso principe cum quadam reverentia diliguntur, quia Vespasianus, venerabilis senex et patientissimus veri, bene intellegit [et] ceteros quidem amicos suos iis niti, quae ab ipso acceperint quaeque ipsis accumulare et in alios congerere promptum sit, Marcellum autem et Crispum attulisse ad amicitiam suam quod non a principe acceperint nec accipi possit.

The meaner and the more humble was the origin of those two men, and the more notorious the poverty and want that hemmed in their young lives, so the more brightly do they shine as conspicuous examples of the practical advantage of oratorical power. Though they had none of the recommendations of birth, or the resources of wealth, though neither of the two was of preeminent high moral character, while one of them had an exterior that made him even an object of derision, yet after being now for many years the most powerful men in Rome and – so long as they cared for such success – leaders of the bar, they take today the leading place in the emperor's circle of friends and get their own way on everything, and even the leading man himself of the State esteems and almost reverences them. Vespasian indeed, our aged and venerable emperor, who never shuts his eyes to facts, is well aware that while all the rest of his favourites owe their position to the advantages they have received from him – advantages that he finds quite easy to amass on himself and to lavish on others – Marcellus and Crispus, on the other hand, have brought to the friendship that unites them to him an element which they never got from an Emperor and which could not be received from a prince. (transl. by W. Peterson, with some changes)

---

day, Marcus Crassus and Quintus Hortensius. Although these men suspected that the will was a forgery, still, as they were conscious of no personal guilt in the matter, they did not spurn the miserable boon procured through the crime of others. What shall we say, then? Is this excuse competent to acquit them of guilt? I cannot think so, although I loved the one while he lived, and do not hate the other now that he is dead', transl. by W. Miller). Cicero's phrase (*homines eiusdem aetatis potentissimos*) highlights the worldwide fame of Crassus and Hortensius, while Valerius Maximus' slight variation (*potentissimos civitatis nostrae viros*) rather hints at their authoritative influence in Rome, where the validity of the (false) will had to be confirmed.

Pliny's letter is rich in quotations[33] as well as further, more or less explicit, references;[34] so an allusion to Cicero could hardly be surprising. Cicero, in fact, is very relevant here.[35] He characterizes the powerful freedman of Sulla, Chrysogonus, as *potentissimus civitatis* and presents him as his real opponent in the case of Sextus Roscius Amerinus;[36] thus he often attacks Chrysogonus.[37] Some decades later, Valerius Maximus uses the phrase for M. Crassus and Q. Hortensius Hortalus,[38] who, in the situation described, behave in a cowardly and criminal way, again in a case of a forged will, a context not very different from Pliny's trial. Moreover, Eprius Marcellus and Vibius Crispus, *delatores* and close collaborators of the imperial power, are called *potentissimi* by Tacitus. He describes them as *neuter moribus egregius*; for the historian, they were *principes fori, nunc principes in Caesaris amicitia*.[39] Therefore, Pliny too labels as *potentissimi civitatis* some characters who are closely related to political power and notable for their dishonest or deceitful conduct.

However, what is even more important, Pliny's possible reference to Cicero's *Pro Roscio Amerino* is also corroborated by many 'parallelisms of context':

---

33 See his quote of Hom. *Il.* 12.243, a passage whose celebrity is stressed by the intensive *illud*.
34 E. g. *quid carius patria*, perhaps a memory of Catul. 82 (*Quinti, si tibi vis oculos debere Catullum / aut aliud si quid carius est oculis, / eripere ei noli, multo quod carius illi / est oculis seu quid carius est oculis*) which, for the concept, rather recalls Cic. *Catil.* 1.27 *etenim si mecum patria, quae mihi vita mea multo est carior, si cuncta Italia, si omnis res publica loquatur*, quoted also by Quint. *Inst.* 9.2.32. To the dossier offered by Sherwin-White and Trisoglio, I would add Cic. *Fin.* 3.64 *ex quo fit, ut laudandus is sit, qui mortem oppetat pro re publica, quod deceat* cariorem nobis esse patriam *quam nosmet ipsos*; Ov. *Ep.* 4.108 *iam nunc est* patria carior illa mea; *Pont.* 2.8.27 *per patriae numen, quae te tibi carior ipso est*.
35 As Marchesi 2008, 220 f. observed, the Homeric quotation strictly connects Pliny with Cicero: the verse appears in *Att.* 2.3.4.60, a letter in which Cicero declares his will to work for the restoration of good relationships with Caesar and Pompey and reconcile himself with his enemies. In the same letter Cicero quotes three verses of his *De consulatu suo: haec mihi cum in eo libro in quo multa sunt scripta* ἀριστοκρατικῶς *Calliope ipsa praescripserit, non opinor esse dubitandum quin semper nobis videatur* "εἷς οἰωνὸς ἄριστος ἀμύνεσθαι περὶ πάτρης" ('these verses Calliope herself dictated to me in that book, which contains much written in an aristocratic spirit, and I cannot, therefore, doubt that I shall always hold that "The best of omens is our country's cause"', transl. by E. O. Winstedt). Marchesi 2008 finds that Pliny "can be shown to conform to an intertextual rhetoric of understatement".
36 von der Mühll 1914, 1117; see also Shackleton Bailey 1992², 83.
37 See e. g. *Sex. Rosc.* 146; 150. About Chrysogonus in Cicero see Buchheit 1975a, who explains that, for Cicero, Chrysogonus' *dominatio* should be interpreted as a tyranny. Updated information on Sulla and Chrysogonus are also in Eckert 2016, but without references to Pliny's passage.
38 On Hortenius Hortalus and his relationship with Cicero see Dyck 2008.
39 About them, see Cavarzere 2008², 221–225.

a. Pliny is very young, even younger than Cicero, who was 26–27 years old at the time of Sextus Roscius' trial;[40] the orators were both at the beginning of their careers;
b. Pliny is as conscious of the risks of the trial as Cicero was, and he shows his anxiety by using the metaphorical verb *excutere*;[41]
c. Pliny's opponents were as close to the emperor as Chrysogonus was to Sulla;
d. the role of Caesar was very similar to Sulla's: both were considered to be very near to tyrants.

So, if Pliny's *potentissimi* have these features, it seems possible to compare them with Chrysogonus and, perhaps, the emperor with Sulla.[42] The name Caesar here probably identifies Domitian and not Titus: consequently, the date of the trial should be placed after 81, as Sherwin-White himself inclines to admit.[43]

The allusion may seem to be quite hidden in the text, but it is strengthened by the repeated insistence on the national import of the case: Pastor's defense against the *potentissimi* becomes a real patriotic action to protect Rome against her real enemies. If this scenario is reasonable and Pliny wanted to develop a comparison between himself and the young Cicero, then it seems probable that Pliny too wanted to highlight the political meaning of the trial: in other words, even in centumviral trials it was possible to find a space for politics. So civil cases may have been more dangerous than we would normally think. Pliny reads his past activity in light of the present day and describes his behavior towards Domitian from the Trajanic perspective. We actually cannot know if he deliberately acted as the young Cicero: however, the example of the greatest Republican orator was a useful and viable one for him in shaping his own relationships to imperial power.

3.2 Pliny stands up for Arrionilla

Plin. *Ep.* 1.5.5–7:
Aderam Arrionillae Timonis uxori, rogatu Aruleni Rustici; Regulus contra. Nitebamur nos in parte causae sententia Metti Modesti optimi viri: is tunc in exsilio

---

40 The exact date of the trial is discussed: Alexander 1990, n° 128 thinks it may have been at the end of 81 and the beginning of 80 BC; the majority of the scholars place it in 80 (see *Ephemerides Tullianae* s.v. [www.tulliana.eu]); less probably Carcopino 1931, 156 n. 4 dates it to 79.
41 See Trisoglio 1973, 232 n. 332 and Méthy 2007, 305 n.134.
42 Buchheit 1975b highlights the critical judgment of Cicero against Sulla. See also Fuhrmann 1997.
43 Sherwin-White 1966, 128: "a date in the early years of Domitian is possible".

e r a t, a D o m i t i a n o r e l e g a t u s. Ecce tibi Regulus 'Quaero', inquit, 'Secunde, quid de Modesto sentias.' Vides quod periculum, si respondissem 'bene'; quod flagitium si 'male'. Non possum dicere aliud tunc mihi quam deos adfuisse. 'Respondebo' inquam 'si de hoc centumviri iudicaturi sunt.' Rursus ille: 'Quaero, quid de Modesto sentias.' Iterum ego: 'Solebant testes in reos, non in damnatos interrogari.' Tertio ille: 'Non iam quid de Modesto, sed quid de pietate Modesti sentias quaero.' 'Quaeris' inquam 'quid sentiam; at ego ne interrogare quidem fas puto, de quo pronuntiatum est.' Conticuit; me laus et gratulatio secuta est, quod nec famam meam aliquo responso utili fortasse, inhonesto tamen laeseram, nec me laqueis tam insidiosae interrogationis involveram.

I defended Arrionilla, the wife of Timon, at the request of Rusticus Arulenus, and Regulus was conducting the prosecution. We on our side were relying for part of the defence on a decision of Metius Modestus, an excellent man who had been banished by Domitian and was at that moment in exile. This was Regulus's opportunity. "Tell me, Secundus," said he, "what you think of Modestus." You see in what peril I should have placed myself if I had answered that I thought highly of him, and how disgraceful it would have been if I had said that I thought ill of him. I fancy it must have been the gods who came to my rescue. "I will tell you what I think of him," I said, "when the Court has to give a decision on the point." He returned to the charge: "My question is, what do you think of Modestus?" Again I replied: "Witnesses used to be interrogated about persons in the dock, not about those who are already convicted." A third time he asked: "Well, I won't ask you now what you think of Modestus, but what you think of his loyalty." "You ask me," said I, "for my opinion. But I do not think it is in order for you to ask an opinion on what the Court has already passed judgment." He was silenced, while I was congratulated and praised for not having smirched my reputation by giving an answer that might have been discreet but would certainly have been dishonest, and for not having entangled myself in the meshes of such a crafty question. (transl. by W. Melmoth, with some changes)

Pliny writes this letter to Voconius Romanus, an equestrian writer from Saguntum in Spain and one of his best friends and addressee of many Plinian epistles.[44] Here he harshly attacks M. Aquilius Regulus, one of the most notorious *delatores* of the Flavian age. Regulus[45] was very active in the trials both under Nero and the Flavian emperors and accused many prominent members of Roman society, such as Sulpicius Camerinus[46] and Cornelius Orfitus.[47] Regulus receives very negative judgment by Pliny, who says of him that, under Domitian, *non minora flagitia commiserat quam sub Nerone, sed tectiora.*[48] In the letter –

---

44 About him see Schuster 1961, Sherwin-White 1966, 93, Trisoglio 1973, *passim* and, recently, Frass 2009.
45 See von Rohden 1895, 331 f., Sherwin-White 1966, 93 f., Heurgon 1969; Scarcia 1984; Gibson / Morello 2012, 68– 73.
46 Miltner 1931, 745 f. He was *consul suffectus* in 46 CE and a member of the *collegium* of *Arvales*.
47 Groag 1931, 1506 f. He was consul in 51 CE and an important senator.
48 *Ep.* 1.5.1.

the "account of his long-standing hostile relationships with Regulus"[49] – Pliny describes the case of Arrionilla,[50] the wife of Timon, perhaps one of the philosophers who gathered around Arulenus Rusticus.[51] Rusticus[52] was a close friend of Pliny, as were Herennius Senecio and Helvidius Priscus. All these men shared an attitude of opposition towards the imperial system[53] and were considered as models of behaviour by Pliny: for him, Arulenus was a *summus vir* (Ep. 1.14.1). It was plain that he could not refuse the request of his old friend, and so defended the woman against Regulus. The date of the civil trial cannot be later than 93, because Rusticus was still alive.[54] This trial is therefore almost ten years later than Iunius Pastor's and, as we see, Pliny shows perfect control of the scene because of his greater experience. The trial took place in the centumviral court, and though we do not know the precise charge, it was surely a question of estate and properties, perhaps complicated by the presence of a will.[55] The outcome is not clear, but in light of Pliny's claims about his cleverness, it was probably favourable for Arrionilla.

Pliny recalls that during the trial there was a harsh exchange of words with Aquilius in the form of an *altercatio:* Regulus wanted to catch Pliny in the trap[56] of declaring his hostility to the emperor. To do so, he kept posing questions[57] about Pliny's thoughts on Mettius Modestus,[58] a former governor of Lycia

---

49 Shelton 2013, 157.

50 We do not know anything about this woman. From her name, Sherwin-White 1966 supposed that she was connected with the family of Arria, but we have no evidence about this. Shelton 2013, 157 rightly argues that, in this case, her name should have been Arrianilla, but this argument is not decisive, because there is an inscription about Arria Arrianilla (CIL 6 12404), already indicated by Syme 1968 a, 146. On the contrary, Shelton 2013 is right in underlining that Arrionilla was married to a man with a foreign name, a condition that was very dangerous in Domitian's times. The old suggestion to emend Arrianilla to Aristylla from the letters of Timoxenus and Aristylla in Plut. *praecept. conviv.* 46 (already considered unnecessary by Sherwin-White 1966) has not found any support. About the case, see Mastrorosa 2010b, 127–136, who concentrates mainly on the juridical problems posed by the trial.

51 Sherwin-White 1966, 97. We do not have any further information about him.

52 Rogers 1960.

53 See Wistrand 1979.

54 His death dates exactly to 93: see Tac. *Agr.* 45 and Shelton 2013, 157.

55 According to Sherwin-White 1966, 97: "the case concerned a provincial property which had come under the jurisdiction of Modestus as legate in Lycia".

56 About Regulus' project see Picone 1977, 154.

57 Using the technique of *repetita percontatio* described by Quint. *Inst.* 5.7.27 (Mastrorosa 2010a).

58 Stein 1950, 1499–1502.

whose career is not well known. At the time of the trial Mettius was in exile,[59] but we do not know why. Nevertheless, Aquilius' insistence makes it possible to argue that he was sent away from Rome for charges related to *maiestas*.[60] Basically, the charge of this case was a pretext and became an opportunity for Aquilius Regulus to embarrass Pliny by calling into question his attitude towards Domitian.

Pliny has to fight against the attempt of Aquilius to transform a civil case into a political one. For this reason, he deliberately aims to discuss the case strictly within the boundaries of the civil law. He demonstrates considerable expertise both in centumviral questions[61] and in general trial problems, as shown when he refers to the rule that prohibits re-trying an issue already judged.[62] Pliny underlines the importance of preserving two limits in his discussion of the case: he does not exceed the legal boundaries of the trial and he emphasizes the idea of an ethically correct attitude. Aquilius Regulus, however, does just the opposite: he is eager to exceed the limits of the trial and is not interested in preserving correct behaviour. Indeed, his flattering attitude compels him to accept an unsat-

---

59 According to Sherwin-White 1966, 97, here and in other passages of his letters Pliny does not distinguish between *exilium* and *relegatio*, a "less severe penalty". Nonetheless, the problem is a little bit different: as a matter of fact, the juridical meaning of *exilium* changed between Republic and Empire: in Republican times it connoted a practice that allowed the guilty to leave Rome's territory before the final sentence was pronounced and was followed by the formal *interdictio aqua et igni*: see, for instance, Santalucia 1998, 88 and 252 with bibliography; Kelly 2006, *passim*; and, for the limits of this practice, Jonca 2009. Later, with the *cognitio extra ordinem* – which is the case in Pliny's times – it became a real penalty; nevertheless, the word *exilium* seems to be more generic and sometimes inclusive of penalties such as *relegatio*, sometimes not. Washburn 2013, 6, quoting Grasmück 1978, highlights that in the early Empire "*deportatio* and *relegatio* became new coercion techniques, signaling a contrast to the traditional role of exile as a volitional option. Thus it became a punishment rather than a perk". Pliny, nonetheless, does not use the word *deportatio*. Mastrorosa 2010b, 128 investigates *relegatio*.

60 Two clues seem to strengthen the hypothesis. First, the accuser explicitly admitted to Pliny that he wanted to attack Modestus because he had written in a letter read in front of Domitian: *Regulus, omnium bipedum nequissimus*, perhaps alluding to the wren (*regulus*), a bird of little value. Domitian could have seen the attack to Aquilius as an attack against himself. Secondly, Aquilius asks Pliny what he thinks about the *pietas* of Modestus: as Bauman 1974 observes, *impietas* was the precise word used to accuse someone for *maiestas*. See also Mastrorosa 2010b, 128 n. 12 and Rivière 2002, 85.

61 See *Ep.* 6.12.2 *Itaque Bittio Prisco quantum plurimum potuero praestabo, praesertim in harena mea, hoc est apud centumviros.*

62 Commonly known as *bis de eadem re ne sit actio* (e.g. Quint. *Inst.* 7.6.3). Pliny refers to it with the words *ego ne interrogare quidem fas puto de quo pronuntiatum est* (7). It is interesting that this rule does not properly exist in the Roman jurists: according to Liebs 1967, it took its origin in Attic law and passed into the praxis of Roman orators. See also Mastrorosa 2010b, 132, n. 25.

isfactory line of argument that will be condemned by the applause and outcry of the public. While this debate surely owes much to fictional scholastic debates about tyranny,[63] when Pliny highlights the antithesis between the *utile* and the *honestum*, he also vividly engages with Cicero's *De officiis:*[64] *quod nec famam meam aliquo responso utili fortasse, inhonesto tamen laeseram.*[65] In this *altercatio* Pliny avoids taking an explicit position contra Domitian – it would have been unwise and imprudent, especially in 93, the very year of the prosecutions against philosophers – but, with his insistence on the right limits of the law, he takes a clear political position on behalf of the *honestum*, implicitly criticizing the prevalence of utility (and flattery) betrayed by Regulus. At the same time, Pliny does not miss an opportunity for self-praise in exercising his ability to force Regulus into silence;[66] but even this tribute to personal vanity can be seen as an example of political cleverness.

Arrionilla's trial is a valuable document that confirms how politics could also influence the centumviral courts and how it required orators to pay careful attention to imperial power. Yet Pliny also wants to show that the power of *delatores*, although significant, was not absolute and that the force of right could prove greater than tyrannical actions. He made it through this difficult situation by preferring to make use of a "regola giuridica, quale quella contraria alla ripetizione di un processo già chiuso con sentenza definitiva, piuttosto che di un linguaggio ambiguo, per fronteggiare le insidie di Regolo".[67]

4 Some conclusions

It is almost impossible to draw definitive conclusions from this short inquiry of a few case studies. So, I only aim to propose some reflections derived from my analysis. Even from our exiguous traces of orations – significant and worthy

---

63 Mastrorosa 2010b, 133.

64 Trisoglio 1973, 184 n.76 refers to Sen. *Nat.* 4a *praef.* 15, where the philosopher is praising himself for having fought against the pressures of the emperor Gaius, Narcissus and Messalina, who however did not change their *propositum.*

65 Already Korfmacher 1946 had shown the presence of views common to Pliny and Cicero's *De officiis.* In this letter there is also the famous statement by Pliny, *mihi est cum Cicerone aemulatio nec sum contentus eloquentia saeculi nostri* (*ep.* 1, 5, 12). On Pliny and Cicero see Kennedy 1972, 530, Pflips 1973, Trisoglio 1973, 186 n. 84 with bibliography, Leeman 1974, Winniczuk 1982, Weische 1989, Riggsby 1995 and, now, Gibson / Morello 2012, 86 f.

66 About Pliny's art of self-praising see Gibson 2003.

67 Mastrorosa 2010b, 135.

of further research in themselves – we can see that the relationship between power and oratory is still a very lively one in the Flavian age.

The great difficulty of saying something about Vespasian's and Titus' influence on the courts – at least at the present state of research – inevitably leads us to concentrate on Domitian. Civil courts, too, are interested in this relationship and orators cannot avoid confronting the *imperium*, whether explicitly or implicitly present. As a matter of fact, the presence of Domitian lingers in the persons of the *delatores* and compels orators to assume an attitude of strategic distance: Pliny does not explicitly refer to imperial power, but, via the kinds of allusions and references that we have tried to detect, he assumes an antityrannical position by underlining the importance of the *honestum* and the law against the claims of his opponents, as in the cases of Iunius Pastor and Arrionilla. This relationship with power is difficult and requires not only balance, but also prudence and a keen diplomacy to avoid irritating the Emperor. Pliny seems to emphasize as often as possible the antithesis between the orator, who, while practicing the 'savoir vivre', seeks to preserve the *honestas* (thus restating the importance of his ethical function as pointed out by Quintilian, *Inst.* 12), and the *delatores*, who, as Mastrorosa 2010b recalls, "a vario titolo ricorsero alla retorica per intessere con spregiudicato pragmatismo relazioni organiche con il potere imperiale". Key political topics of the century – *libertas*, attitudes towards the emperor, opposition, relationship between ethics and politics – are clearly present also in the fragmentary oratory, offering a strong but silent contrast to dictatorial attitudes toward power.

In this context, Cicero plays a central role. The allusions to the Arpinate are quite clear both in the cases of Iunius Pastor and Arrionilla. In these Plinian texts, I think, Cicero features as a defender of freedom and the Republican constitution, and suggests an implicit but pointed comparison between Republic and Empire, obviously favourable to the former. In other words, through Cicero's image, Pliny cautiously manifests his preference for a former political era, that of the Roman Republic.

III Tradition and Poetics of the Epigram

Alberto Canobbio

Bipartition and non-distinction of poetical genres in Martial: *magnum* vs *parvum*

Among the various Saturnalician gifts listed in Martial's *Apophoreta*, there are also the books (183–196).[1] This section begins with Homer and Virgil and ends with a work of Calvus, most likely Licinius Calvus, about the use of cold water (14.196).[2] This wittily malicious evaluation is an *unicum* within the book section, otherwise eulogistic; given its final position, it is also a kind of final surprise that creates an antithesis with the greatest poets of Greek and Latin literature named at the beginning. Moreover, it is an ironical comment about the gift of bad books such as the *horribilem et sacrum libellum* ('horrible and cursed little book') passed off by Calvus to Catullus during the Saturnalia (cf. Catul. 14.12–15).

According to the typical alternation of the *Apophoreta* between gifts for the rich and gifts for the poor (14.1.5 f.), Calvus' work represents a cheap gift, which forms a pair with Catullus' *liber*, celebrated in the previous epigram as a source of glory for the native town of the poet (14.195): CATULLUS. *Tantum magna suo debet Verona Catullo, | quantum parva suo Mantua Vergilio* ('Great Verona owes as much to her Catullus as does little Mantua to her Virgil'). By an evident parallelism, Martial underlines a paradox: Catullus, who devoted himself to the minor genres, was born in a big town like Verona; the author of the *Aeneid*, a poem belonging to the *genus grande* and hailed by Propertius as *maius Iliade* (2.34.66), came to light near the small Mantua. This is the only epigram in the book section which makes a comparison between two authors; it is clear that Martial wanted to put Catullus, his *auctor*,[3] and Virgil, the poet whom he defines

---

Martial is quoted and translated according to Shackleton Bailey 1993. I thank the editors and Dr. Elena Tosi for their help with the English translation of my text. A more extended version of this paper is Canobbio 2014.

1 About these epigrams cf. Pini 2006; Prioux 2008, 311–328; Neger 2012, 30–48; Mindt 2013, 25–29.

2 Cf. Mart. 14.196 CALVI DE AQUAE FRIGIDAE USU. *Haec tibi quae fontes et aquarum nomina dicit, | ipsa suas melius charta natabat aquas* ('CALVUS ON THE USE OF COLD WATER. These pages that tell you of fountains and the names of rivers were better swimming in their own waters'). According to Shackleton Bailey 1993, III, 303 *suas aquas* alludes instead to the water "from which the papyrus came".

3 On Catullus and Martial see Fedeli 2004; Lorenz 2007; Mattiacci 2007a, 162–177; Mattiacci 2007b, 177–183; Neger 2012, 54–73; Mindt 2013, 131–161.

https://doi.org/10.1515/9783110534436-006

as *vatum maximus* (8.55[56].11), on the same level. Above all – and this is the main point – the absolute character of this comparison between the two poets, as well as the presence of two antonyms (*magna*; *parva*) probably endowed with eidetic sense, suggest a simplified and bipartite view of the whole literary system. According to such a view, the 'grand' poetry (in terms of size, style, and purpose) stands in contrast to the area of the *parvum*, whose absolute champion is Catullus.

This bipartite view is already discernible when considering Homer's and Virgil's works, i. e. the subjects of the first two epigrams in this section: the *Iliad* and *Odyssey* are combined with the *Batrachomachia*[4] (14.183 and 184); a *Vergilius in membranis* is paired with the far less serious *Culex* (14.185 and 186). In both cases the epic poems are intended for the *pauperes*; instead, the gifts for the *divites* are two shorter, funny texts which represent a parody and miniaturization of epic: the war between frogs and mice gets the unexpected honor of the first place in the book section, whereas the pseudovirgilian epyllion is presented as preferable to the *Aeneid* during the Saturnalia.[5]

The bipartition *magnum / parvum* has its roots in Callimachean aesthetics, endorsed by Catullus and the *neoteroi* and then received by the Augustan poets. This approach implies an evaluation which subverts the 'natural' order of things (the big should prevail over the small) and challenges the older literary hierarchy. Apollo, god of poetry, spoke *apertis verbis* in favour of the *parvum* in replying to Envy at the end of the hymn dedicated to him, and in admonishing both Callimachus in the *Aitia* prologue and Tityrus-Virgil in the proem to the sixth *Bucolic*, where the two poets recall their artistic beginnings.[6]

Now, if we read 14.195 from a Callimachean viewpoint, we see that it unbalances the outwardly balanced presentation of Catullus and Virgil, thus acting in synergy with the *titulus* (the epigram entitled *Catullus* aims at celebrating the poet from Verona, not the Mantuan). Indeed, Catullus was a more faithful interpreter of Apollo's will than Virgil: the latter does not hesitate to shift from the *Culex* to the *Aeneid* (i. e. from the *parvum* to the *magnum*) when Maecenas offers

---

4 Shackleton Bailey 1993, III, 298 reads *Batrachomyomachia* (Calderini).

5 Cf. Mart. 14.185 VERGILI CULEX. *Accipe facundi Culicem, studiose, Maronis, / ne nucibus positis 'Arma virumque' legas* ('Virgil's "Gnat". Accept, studious reader, the "Gnat" of eloquent Maro; no need to read "Arms and the Man," when you put away your nuts').

6 Cf. Call. *hymn.* 2.108–112; *aet.* fr. 1.22–24 Pf.; Verg. *Ecl.* 6.3–5; Nauta 2006, 24 observes that the prologue to the *Aitia* "alludes to a number of different genres and poetological discussions, thus establishing a frame of reference in which the opposition between the 'small' and the 'grand' is not limited to a single genre", as against Virgil, who shifts onto the eidetic level (*epos* vs bucolic) an opposition which in Callimachus was mainly stylistic.

him *divitias* and a beautiful boy like Alexis, according to the humorous recon-struction Martial makes of the first encounter between the poet and the *Tuscus eques*.[7]

Virgil and Catullus are depicted as the champions of two opposite regions of the literary space in 4.14 too: Martial sends his poems to Silius Italicus, inviting him to lay his *Punica* aside during the Saturnalia and devote himself to the re-laxing texts that he got as a gift (13 f.): *sic forsan tener ausus est Catullus / magno mittere Passerem Maroni* ('thus, it may be, did tender Catullus venture to send his Sparrow to great Maro').

The high poetry is evoked in a very generic way at 1.107, where a friend ad-dresses to Martial this reproach (2): *scribe aliquid magnum: desidiosus homo es* ('write something big. You are a lazybones'). Martial replies that he would write 'grand' poetry if he had the same economic security that Maecenas guar-anteed to Virgil and Horace, who both represent the *magnum* here within Mar-tial's opportunistic straining of the literary history. Virgil actually passed from the *parvum* to the *magnum*; Horace's 'grand' poetry (i. e. lyric) represents instead a well circumscribed moment in a poetical career otherwise devoted to minor genres.[8] The Callimachean pattern that Martial wittily recalls at the end of book one, where he applies the *mega biblion mega kakon* concept to the epigram-matic genre,[9] undoubtedly simplifies the literary system. This view polarizes lit-erary space and promotes a unilateral placement of authors like Virgil and Hor-ace, who could stay with full rights in both categories (the *magnum* and the *parvum*), as well as a trend of non-distinction among the genres belonging to the same area.

In this regard it is important to consider Martial's self-presentation at the end of the epigram which we find in the *praefatio* to book nine (5–8):

---

7 Cf. Mart. 8.55(56).7–12 and 19 f. *protinus Italiam concepit et 'Arma virumque', / qui modo vix Culicem fleverat ore rudi* ('Forthwith he conceived Italy and "Arms and the man," though his prentice lips had but lately with difficulty mourned the Gnat').

8 Horace himself, however, places his lyric on the side of *parvum* in *Carm.* 3.3.70–72 *quo, Musa, tendis? Desine pervicax / referre sermones deorum et / magna modis tenuare parvis* ('What are you saying, Muse? This theme doesn't suit the happy lyre. Stop wilfully repeating divine conver-sations, and weakening great matters with these trivial metres'); 4.2.31–34 *operosa parvus / car-mina fingo. / Concines maiore poeta plectro / Caesarem* ('I, a diminutive creature, compose elab-orate verses ... You, a poet of sublimer style, shall sing of Caesar'); 4.15.1–4; likewise in *Carm.* 1.6.1–12 (esp. 9) he 'refuses' the high poetry saying that his *tenuis* inspiration does not allow him to write *grandia*.

9 Cf. Mart. 1.118 *Cui legisse satis non est epigrammata centum, / nil illi satis est, Caediciane, mali* ('He for whom reading a hundred epigrams is not enough, will never have enough of a bad thing, Caedicianus').

Ille ego sum nulli nugarum laude secundus,
    quem non miraris sed, puto, lector, amas.
Maiores maiora sonent: mihi parva locuto
    sufficit in vestras saepe redire manus.

I am he whose trifles are praised second to none, who, reader, you do not wonder at, but whom, methinks, you love. Let greater men sing greater themes: I speak of little things, and am content to come back often to your hands.

In 1.1 Martial claims to have achieved a worldwide fame thanks to his *epigrammaton libelli*;[10] in this important text, he uses the technical term he himself promotes to identify his work,[11] thus defining – as shown by Citroni[12] – its specific genre identity in the context of Latin literary tradition. On the contrary, at the beginning of Book IX Martial presents himself as the author of much more indefinite 'little things' (*parva*), alternative to 'grand' and bombastic poetry, towards which he shows complete disregard. The emphasis on the concept of *magnum* at line 7 (*maiores maiora sonent*) suggests, first of all, an allusion to Flavian epic, which – according to Barchiesi –[13] may be considered as a sort of hyper-epic for its tendency to accentuate the identity of the *genus grande*. As regards the area of the *parvum*, the reference point continues to be Catullus: *nugarum*, put in evidence in the middle of line 5, leaves no doubt. However, Martial, who in 7.99.7 already proclaimed himself not much inferior to Catullus, here proudly claims to be actually the first in the composition of *nugae*. This is a very suggestive word, but with much less defining force (from an eidetic viewpoint) than a more expected 'technical' reference to the epigrammatic genre. Such a boast, unattested elsewhere,[14] may cause surprise; however, it is a well-founded one, if we think that Martial actually developed the various expressive options of the *parvum* even more than Catullus. Indeed, the epigrammatist had the chance to con-

---

10 Cf. Mart. 1.1.1–3 *Hic est quem legis ille, quem requiris, / toto notus in orbe Martialis / argutis epigrammaton libellis* ('You read him, you ask for him, and here he is: Martial, known the world over for his witty little books of epigrams'); this text together with the *praefatio* and epigram 1.2 most likely belonged to a second edition of book one, published when Martial had become a successful poet; it is indeed very difficult that the epigrammatist's fame was already widespread *toto orbe* at the time of the first edition of book one (see Citroni 1975, 4 f.; 7; 12–14; 17 f.).
11 About the innovative use made by Martial of the term *epigramma* see Puelma 1997, 207 f.
12 Citroni 2003b; Citroni 2009.
13 Barchiesi 2001, 351.
14 In Book X Martial will return to recognize himself inferior to Catullus (10.78.14–16); at the most he will suggest his own ability to equal the poet from Verona in the glory which his native town got thanks to him, cf. 10.103.4–6.

front his poetic task also with the poetical genres which came to full maturity in Rome only in the Augustan age: satire, elegy, bucolic.

The literary categories of 'grand' and 'small' become anthropological data in another epigram of book nine (9.50):[15] a certain Gaurus[16] insults Martial, claiming that he must have a 'tiny mind' (1 *ingenium ... pusillum*), as he writes texts marked by *brevitas*; but then, conversely, Gaurus himself should be a great man only because he sings *grandia Priami proelia* in twelve books – and this is obviously not true! In the last couplet, Gaurus' epic poem is compared to a muddy giant (6 *tu magnus luteum, Gaure, Giganta facis* 'you, Gaurus, great man that you are, make a giant of clay'); instead, Martial's epigram is compared to two little statuettes characterized by smallness, fame, and intrinsic vitality: the so-called *Bruti puer* type, famous despite its small size as it was loved by Caesar's murderer,[17] and the unidentified *Langon vivus*, perhaps another *puer*.[18] The translation of a literary controversy into effective images is a typically Callimachean act: the mention of the mud, in particular, recalls Horace's criticism of Lucilius (*lutulentus, S.* 1.4.11), whereas the opposition between short poetry and the epic *mega biblion* creates an evident continuity with the huge quantity of mud dragged along by the great Assyrian river at the end of the *Hymn to Apollo*.

Also the brothers Memor, a glory of the Roman tragedy (11.9 *Romani fama cothurni*, 'fame of the Roman buskin'), and Turnus, who despite his epic name and *ingentia pectora* prefers to write satires in order to avoid a contest with his brother (11.10), operate in opposite areas of the literary system. The diptych that Martial dedicated to the two brother-poets corresponds once again to the Callimachean bipartition *magnum / parvum*, as well as what we read in 12.44: Unicus, a relative of Martial who continues the Catullan and Ovidian erotic tradition, is told to display *pietas* towards his brother, because he does not venture into the *mare magnum* of a more prestigious genre (most likely the epic). Indeed, Unicus applies himself to minor poetry, which is the *amor* of both brothers and is alluded to in this epigram through the metaphor of inshore navigation.[19] Accord-

---

15 See Canobbio 2008, 187–189.

16 A nickname for 'Statius' according to Friedländer, but more likely the embodiment of the type of the ordinary epic poet; on Gaurus see Canobbio 2008, 187 n. 46; Canobbio 2011a, 585.

17 See Canobbio 2008, 178 n. 25.

18 See Canobbio 2008, 188 n. 48.

19 Cf. Mart. 12.44.7 f. *nec deerant Zephyri, si te dare vela iuvaret; / sed tu litus amas. Hoc quoque fratris habes* ('And if you had wished to spread your sails, Zephyrs were not wanting; but you love the shore. This too you owe your brother').

ing to Shackleton Bailey,[20] the epigram makes sense only if Unicus' brother is not an elegiac poet but cultivates a different literary genre, unidentified but certainly *parvum*; however that may be, Martial seems to feel a kinship, even on a literary level, with Unicus, to whom he attributes at line 2 *corda propinqua meis.*

The recognized proximity among different genres belonging to the same area promotes a habit of non-distinction. Martial provides a very interesting evidence of this trend when he associates both the tragic buskin to Virgil (first inside a comparison between the *Aeneid* and Domitian's *Bellum Capitolinum*, then speaking about Silius' *Punica*)[21] and the lyre to Lucan (7.23.1 f.): *Phoebe, veni, sed quantus eras cum bella tonanti / ipse dares Latiae plectra secunda lyrae* ('Come, Phoebus, but come in might, as when in person you gave the second quill of the Latin lyre to him who thunders wars'). Martial obviously did not see a lyric feature in Lucan's poem (defined by the Callimachean expression *bella tonare*); rather, we should think that either Lucan is considered as the second Latin poet (with *lyra* = poetry; the first is Virgil), or that – within the epic genre – his *Pharsalia* is second only to the *Aeneid.* Anyway, what really matters is Martial's use of '*lyra*' as a technical term when expressing an evaluation about a text (the *Pharsalia*) which belongs to a 'grand genre', though different from lyric. Epic, tragedy and lyric tend to become blurred in Martial's work. This is confirmed by 8.18, where it is said that Virgil would have been able to surpass Horace in Pyndaric lyric as well as Varius Rufus in tragedy, but that he did not practise these genres out of regard for his two friends. Both tragedy and lyric, two genres recently brought nearer to one another by Seneca's *cothurnatae*, are cultivated by an otherwise unknown Varro whom Martial in 5.30 invites to suspend his usual poetical activity during the Saturnalia and relax himself with lighter texts: in particular, Martial recommends Varro not to read mimes or elegies, but the epigrams sent to him as a gift.

Martial relates his epigram to other minor genres in 8.3. In this important and much studied text,[22] starting from line 11, the Muse – cast in the role of an elegiac *relicta* – attacks Martial: she fears that the poet may betray her by

---

20 Shackleton Bailey 1993, III, 126 f.

21 Cf. Mart. 5.5.7 f. *ad Capitolini caelestia carmina belli / grande cothurnati pone Maronis opus* 'Beside the celestial lay of the Capitoline ware place the great work of buskined Maro' (about Domitian's lost *epos*, focused on the Capitol's siege by Vitellius' troops, see Canobbio 2011a, 114 f.); 7.63.5 f. *sacra cothurnati non attigit ante Maronis / implevit magni quam Ciceronis opus* 'He did not put his hand to buskined Maro's mysteries before he filled the measure of great Cicero's work' (Silius dedicated himself to the *Punica* after retiring from public life and oratory activity).

22 See Canobbio 2005, 137–145; Nauta 2006, 38–40; Mattiacci 2007a, 186–191; Mattiacci 2007b, 192–195; Canobbio 2011b, 445–450; Neger 2012, 150–156.

shifting from the *dulces nugae* to tragic and epic poetry, once more indicated respectively through the metaphor of the buskin and the Callimachean expression *bella tonare* (11–14):

> Tune potes dulcis, ingrate, relinquere nugas?
> > Dic mihi, quid melius desidiosus ages?
> An iuvat ad tragicos soccum transferre cothurnos
> > aspera vel paribus bella tonare modis [...]?

> Ingrate, can you abandon your sweet trifles? Tell me, what better will you find to do in your idleness? Or do you wish to exchange your slipper for tragic buskins or thunder hard-fought wars in equal measures [...]?

At the end of the poem – when defining how Martial's poetry should be – the Muse does not label it simply and univocally as *epigrammata*. Remarkably, taking into account eidetic affinity with other minor genres, she instead talks about symbolic objects and strong marks of identity which evoke texts and poetical genres belonging to the area of the *parvum* (19–22):

> At tu Romano lepidos sale tinge libellos:
> > agnoscat mores vita legatque suos.
> Angusta cantare licet videaris avena,
> > dum tua multorum vincat avena tubas.

> But do you dip your witty little books in Roman salt; let life recognize and read of her ways. Never mind if you seem to sing a narrow pipe, so long as your pipe outmatches many people's trumpets.

At line 19 the Catullan *lepidus libellus* is to be flavoured with the salt used by Lucilius in order to rub Rome (cf. Hor. *S.* 1.10.3 f. *sale multo / urbem defricuit* 'he lashed the town with great humor'). The following verse too (20 *agnoscat mores vita legatque suos*) is suitable to satire, or perhaps even more to comedy, the traditional *speculum vitae*[23] which the *soccum* mentioned at 13 can also be referred to. In the final couplet Martial marks the *avena*, the pipe of Virgil's shepherds,[24] with the same adjective, *angustus*, used by Propertius to characterize

---

23 Remember the famous judgement of Aristophanes of Byzantium about Menander (quoted in Nauta 2006, 39 n. 51, with further references), who – according to Quintilian (10.1.69) – *omnem vitae imaginem expressit* ('so perfect is his representation of actual life').

24 Cf. Verg. *Ecl.* 1.2 *silvestrem tenui Musam meditaris avena* ('wooing the woodland Muse on slender reed') and 10.51 *pastoris Siculi modulabor avena* ('I will play on a Sicilian shepherd's pipe'), but also 6.8 *agrestem tenui meditabor harundine Musam* ('now will I woo the rustic Muse on slender reed').

Callimachus' *pectus* in a famous *recusatio* of 'thundering epic poetry'.[25] This is symbolized at line 22 by the war trumpets, which will be defeated by Martial – so the Muse predicts – provided that he continues to be faithful to her.

This text presents Martial's epigram as a poetic form which is enabled by its Muse to move within the whole area of the *parvum*; thus Martial controls a wide literary space, encompassing the legacy of poetical traditions very far from one other: the Callimachean-neoteric *lignée* represented in epigram 8.3 by Catullus and Propertius is characterized by formal and sentimental refinements which have little to do with the notorious aggressiveness of the *lutulentus* founder of the Roman satire; the distance between elegy and bucolic was measured by Verg. *Ecl.* 10, and the world of the pastoral song is very different also from the *tranches de vie* staged by comedy, a typical urban genre. The key to hold all this together consists in applying to epigram the Callimachean *poikilia:* a book of Martial is a multiform and changing literary object, a sort of Proteus which, depending on circumstances, may incorporate elements from many poetical genres (satire, comedy, elegy, bucolic),[26] yet always keeping and preserving the epigrammatic identity of its individual poems. Epigram 8.3 makes us understand that the idea of multiplicity which characterizes Martial's work (starting from its title, twice plural, *Epigrammaton libri*) not only fosters a more complete representation of contemporary society, but, from a purely literary viewpoint, is also the *passepartout* which allows the poet to access the themes and expressive resources of the other genres belonging to the area of the *parvum*; in this way his poetry displays a much higher *varietas* than the epigrammatic genre considered *stricto sensu.*

---

25 Cf. Prop. 2.1.39–42 *sed neque Phlegraeos Iovis Enceladique tumultus / intonet angusto pectore Callimachus, / nec mea conveniunt duro praecordia versu / Caesaris in Phrygios condere nomen avos* and 45 *nos contra angusto versamus proelia lecto* ('But Callimachus's frail chest could not thunder out Jupiter's struggle with the giant Enceladus, over the Phlegrean Plain, nor have I the strength of mind to carve Caesar's line, back to Phrygian forebears, in hard enough verse').

26 In Martial's work satire and comedy are the most natural reference points for the description of Roman everyday life and its human types; from Augustan elegy the epigrammatist takes not the sentimental side (Martial's approach to *eros* has rather an iambic character), but the attitude to self-representation, self-consciousness and literary polemic, as well as the exploration of the relationships between books and readers; finally, the bucolic, which is read also in an erotic key, attracts Martial mainly as a celebration of Virgil's patrons: from this viewpoint, this genre represents an authoritative precedent in the area of the *parvum* for epigrams celebrating imperial power. On the relationships between Martial's epigram and other minor genres see Canobbio 2005, esp. 137 ff. (elegy and bucolic); Merli 2006a (satire; see also Merli 2008, 309–313); Canobbio 2011b (elegy).

Martial profits from such a bipartite and, so to speak, fluid view of the literary system in integrating his epigram with the other genres. This is also shown indirectly by an epigram like 12.94, which, on the contrary, offers a rigorous classification of poetical forms: in order to avoid the competition with Tucca, a poet who persistently imitates him, Martial continues to change genre, shifting each time towards a less prestigious literary form; after leaving behind epic, he passes from tragedy to Horatian lyric and then, entering the area of the *parvum*, from satire to elegy. The last genre so entered is the epigram (9 *quid minus esse potest?* 'What can be humbler?'), the smallest poetical form not only from a dimensional viewpoint but also from an axiological one. Towards this kind of classification, which dooms the epigram to remain absolutely marginal (also in the area of the *parvum*), Martial evokes irony rather than approval; indeed, according to this text, both he and Tucca would gain success in any kind of poetical genre: too good to be true! Intertextuality confirms that this is nothing but an ironical joke: at line 1 (*Scribebamus epos; coepisti scribere: cessi* 'I was writing an epic; you started to write one. I gave up') Martial represents himself as an epic poet forced to abandon the genre which otherwise he would have practised; this picture suggests an analogy with Verg. *Ecl.* 6.3–5, where Tityrus, who was already singing *reges et proelia*, is pushed by Apollo towards a *deductum carmen*. The god of poetry, as everybody knows, will also stop Propertius' epic ambitions, by moving him away from the source whence *pater Ennius* drank (3.3.5f. and 13–18), as well as the ambitions of Horace, who must set aside the project of singing *proelia* and *victas urbes* (*Carm.* 4.15.1–4). On the contrary, it is Cupid who thwarts Ovid's ambitions by crippling his hexameters, ready to run the road of *epos* in the first elegy of the *Amores* (1.1.1–4).

These famous scenes, where the greatest Augustan poets dramatize their (provisional or definitive) refusal of the high genres, implicitly legitimize Martial's own self-presentation as an epic poet (or better, as a 'handyman poet'); at the same time, the remake of the Augustan *recusatio* in playful terms[27] offers the reader a further key to understanding that Martial is looking ironically at a hierarchy of poetical genres with which he does not agree.

In the Flavian age, therefore, there are different views of literary topography. On one hand, we have the bipartite, 'Callimachean' view picked up by Martial, following in the footsteps of Augustan minor poetry: Martial consolidates the eidetic identity of his own poetry by stressing its differences from the *magnum*[28],

---

27 On the *recusatio* in Flavian poetry see Nauta 2006, esp. 37–40 as regards Martial.
28 But with a polemical attitude towards epic and tragedy not present in the Augustan poets, who are not polemically situated against the 'refused' genres. Tityrus-Virgil has no objection to

but he also suggests an affinity between the new Latin epigram, still 'under construction', and the other more 'established' genres belonging to the area of the *parvum*. Thus, Martial helps his poetry to be fully legitimized as literature. On the other hand, we find a more articulated classification (which someway recalls Quintilian's work), like that displayed by Mart. 12.94 and later attested elsewhere, with a few changes (e. g. Tac. *Dial.* 10.4).[29] But there is also a third and, so to speak, more modern way of thinking about the relationships among literary genres. That way is embodied by Statius.

In the preface to *Silvae* Book I (1 *praef.* 5–9), Statius seems perfectly aware that his new work cannot match the *Thebaid*'s grandeur; but, at the same time, he defends this 'lighter' side of his production by assimilating the *Silvae* to the *Batrachomachia* and the *Culex*, which stand in stark contrast to epic poetry also in Martial's *Apophoreta*. As is noticed by Aricò,[30] Statius relies on the authoritative examples of Homer and Virgil in order to leave behind the drastic, Callimachean opposition between epic and non-epic poetry. At the same time, he recognizes legitimacy and importance to the latter, though not challenging, as Martial does, the 'first place' of the oldest literary genre. The opening lines of the ode to Vibius Maximus (*Silv.* 4.7) account for the superiority of epic and confirm the existence of a hierarchy of poetic genres (as well as of different interpretations of the same genre). At first, Statius asks Erato, the Muse *iam diu lato sociata campo* ('who long have wandered the widening plain', 1), to reduce the *ingens opus* of epic in *minores gyros* (3–4). Then, he apologizes with Pindar, the 'leader of the lyric host' (5), for making his own poetry more 'thin' (9 *tenuare*) after singing the great Thebes: indeed, the present poem is a Sapphic ode, not a Pindaric one. On the contrary, in *Silv.* 1.3, among the various poetical options available to the *chelys* of Manilius Vopiscus, there is also the option of raising the Pindaric lyric to heroic *epos* (101 f.), whereas afterwards, i. e. in subordinate position, two 'minor' genres such as satire and verse epistle are mentioned (103 f.). Finally, a hierarchy within the epic genre itself is detected by Aricò[31]

---

other poets singing the *laudes* of Varus and *tristia bella* (*Ecl.* 6.6 f.). Horace in *Carm.* 1.6 shirks the celebration epic practised by his friend Varius by speaking of *pudor* and *culpa ingeni* (9–12), whereas in *Carm.* 2.12 he invites Maecenas to give a literary form to the *proelia Caesaris* (9–11). Propertius, who celebrates Virgil as an epic poet (2.34.65 f.), acknowledges himself to be unsuitable for war epic, which he regrets not being able to cultivate (2.1.17 f. and 25 f.). Finally, in Ovid's case, tragedy, delayed until the elegiac inspiration goes on (*Am.* 3.1.69 f. *teneri properentur Amores,* / *dum vacat; a tergo grandius urguet opus* 'quick, tender Amores: a greater work is pushing on behind!'), will be realized with the *Medea*.

29 About the similarity between these two passages see Citroni 1968, 263.

30 Aricò 1972, 46 and 50 f.; Aricò 2008, 2.

31 Aricò 1996, 187.

in the phrase *magnusque tibi praeludit Achilles* ('great Achilles plays the prelude unto thee'), which Statius addresses to Domitian in the proem to the *Achilleid* (19), after 'refusing' the task of celebrating the emperor in the *Thebaid*'s proem (16–22 and 32–34): "su un piano più alto sta il poema storico-panegiristi-co, la celebrazione del principe, supremo obiettivo ancora una volta rinviato, più in basso il poema mitologico imperniato su Achille, che di quello costituisce il 'preludio'".

Statius has a hierarchical, but neither 'isolationist' nor polemical view of the various literary genres, a view that can be considered authentically Flavian. On the other hand, Martial seems to make a revival of Augustan ideas. According to his more modern views, Statius moves freely throughout literary space, so that his own production is characterized by the contamination of poetical forms, both *magna* and *parva*. The *Thebaid* is an epic *mega biblion* on a tragic subject,[32] but it also leaves room for an elegiac voice like that of Argia.[33] The story of the couple formed by Deidamia, seduced and abandoned, and Achilles, deceitfully introduced into Lycomedes' court in female dress, brings not only elegy but also comedy into the second Statian *epos*.[34] The *Silvae*, whose 'occasional' character fits in with lyric despite the majority of hexameter poems,[35] are read by Newlands as a renewed form of bucolic, more open to panegyric.[36] Nevertheless, this peculiar work also renders features which recall two other hexametrical genres: epic[37] and, to a limited degree, satire.[38] The *Silvae* contain texts belonging to very different kinds of occasional poetry, together with *leves libellos quasi epigrammatis loco scriptos*, 'trifling pieces dashed off like epigrams', as is the case of *Silv.* 2.2 and 2.3 (about the tree and the *psittacus* of Atedius Melior respectively), and even other examples of *stili facilitas* (e.g. *Silv. 2.5 leo mansuetus*).[39]

---

32 On epic and tragedy in the *Thebaid* see Bessone 2011, 11 f.; 19–22; 75–101.

33 See Bessone 2002; Bessone 2011, 200–223.

34 See Rosati 1994c, esp. 16 f., 25 and 42 ff.

35 The exceptions are four poems in Phalecean, the Catullan metre (*Silv.* 1.6; 2.7; 4.3; 4.9), and two odes in the Horatian mode: *Silv.* 4.5 (Alcaic strophe) e 4.7 (Sapphic strophe).

36 See Newlands 2002, 36–38 esp. 37 "the title *Silvae*, far from indicating trivial, light verse, offers a new version of pastoral for the Flavian age in its recurring dialectic within the collection between city and country, court and villa, withdrawal and engagement" and 197 f. "indeed, the *Silvae* are a new kind of pastoral poetry if we accept that pastoral poetry is a dialectic mode that constructs and contests different views of society and history". As a starting point of this assimilation we can take the famous *si canimus silvas, silvae sint consule dignae* ('if your song is of the woodland, let the woods be worthy of a consul', Verg. *Ecl.* 4.3),

37 See Gibson 2006a; van Dam 2006.

38 See Laguna Mariscal 2006.

39 Cf. Stat. *Silv.* 2 *praef.* 14–16.

The *Silvae* of Statius, a renowned exponent of a tendency to *polyeideia*[40] that seems rather common in his times,[41] as well as the epigrams of Martial, who returns *pro domo sua* to the Callimachean bipartite view, have connections with many literary genres and display particular inclination for *varietas:* their success shows that they are both fully in line with the culture and expectations of their contemporaries.[42] At the end of the first century, after two very rich seasons such as the Augustan and Neronian ages, the literary public has at its disposal a large and varied *corpus* of Latin works which are awarded a status of excellence; this public enjoys finding in the same work elements that recall different texts stored in its memory. On the other hand, the author seems more interested in stimulating the literary competence of the reader than in keeping absolute faith to eidetic orthodoxy: this is a factor of order and legitimation within the literary system, which can also become, however, a dangerous selector as regards the tastes of the readers.

Statius' epic poetry is a case in point: on one hand, it strengthens its identity as a product of the *genus grande* by establishing connections with tragedy; at the same time, it takes in (like so many antibodies) both elegiac *eros*, which the Augustan *recusationes* marked as 'non epic', and comedy, that is the other face, the smiling one, of scenic poetry. A similar crossing between traditionally antagonistic genres such as war epic and erotic elegy has been noted also in Valerius Flaccus and Silius Italicus.[43]

---

40 Statius wrote also a third epic poem (*De bello Germanico*) to celebrate the war deeds of Domitian, and a *fabula saltica* (*Agave*), cf. Iuv. 7.82–87.

41 The practice of various poetical genres, both *magna* and *parva*, is attested for Canius Rufus, about whom Mart. 3.20.1–7 mentions (besides historiography) fable and elegy as well as epic and tragedy, and Manilius Vopiscus, whose name is connected by Statius on one hand to lyric and epic and on the other to satire and verse epistle (*Silv.* 1.3.99–104). Pliny the Younger tells us that he tried various genres before devoting himself to light poetry in Phalaceans, which was preceded by a juvenile tragedy and poems in hexameters, *elegos* and *plura metra* (*epist.* 7.4.2f. and 6–8). Such an eclecticism was probably not uncommon in Flavian amateur poetry (on which see Mattiacci 2007a, 195–218); Merli 2009, 53f. (esp. 54) rightly speaks of a loss of drama about the choice of genre, a choice "non necessariamente esclusiva né frutto di opposizione polemica".

42 The variety, but not of metres, characterized also the Pliny's *hendecasyllabi*, cf. *Ep.* 4.14.3 *ipsa varietate temptamus efficere, ut alia aliis, quaedam fortasse omnibus placeant* ('my object has been to please different tastes by this variety of treatment, and I hope that certain pieces will be liked by everyone').

43 The mix of serious and facetious, *epos* and *eros*, *magnum* and *parvum*, is present throughout Flavian epic, as shown by Barchiesi 2001; on the elegiac component in post-Virgilian epic see Bessone 2002, 189 n. 18; 192 n. 28; 198 n. 48; 206 nn. 62 and 64, with several textual references and further bibliography.

As for 'minor' poetry, the concept of literary genre does not represent a problem when dealing with products like Statius' *Silvae:* their shifting character (*varietas*) is already highlighted in the prefaces which give unity to each book and provide them with an index of contents.[44] In Martial's *Epigrammaton libri* the opposition to 'grand' poetry still remains a notable feature. More important, however, is that the definition of the epigram's eidetic identity – already well focused by Citroni[45] – develops into a less marked distinction from the other minor genres. In this regard, two important programmatic texts are placed at the beginning of the last two Domitianic books: epigram 8.3 and the epigram included in the *praefatio* to book nine. In these texts, instead of showing the eidetic identity of his *libelli*, which, however, is reasserted in other passages of these same books,[46] Martial openly alludes to the Catullan roots of his own poetry (8.3.11 *dulcis … nugas* and 19 *lepidos … libellos*; 9 *praef.* 5 *nugarum*). And he does so while declaring that his epigram belongs to the wider and less defined area of the *parvum.* Similarly, Martial presents himself as a 'small' (not explicitly epigrammatic) poet in another, already mentioned, text of book nine where he mocks the *magnus* Gaurus and his colossal epic (9.50). Martial appears more interested in suggesting literary contiguities than in confirming the epigrammatic identity of his poetry also in another contemporary poem (8.73), where the humorous request to a patron to have a *puella* or a *puer delicatus* as a gift goes along with a catalogue of love poets where Catullus and the Augustan elegists are linked to Virgil's bucolics and Martial himself (5–10):

> Cynthia te vatem fecit, lascive Properti;
>   ingenium Galli pulchra Lycoris erat;
> fama est arguti Nemesis formosa Tibulli;

---

44 Newlands 2008, 231: "each collection of poems is presented not as a random miscellany but as a poetry book, carefully ordered and packaged for publication and posterity" and 232 "by giving a brief summary of each poem, the preface takes into account an audience unfamiliar with the original occasion; the preface opens the door to Statius' social world". The summary is not present only in the fifth (and last) book, probably posthumous.

45 Cf. note 12.

46 Cf. Mart. 8 *praef.* 10 *epigrammata* and 19 f. *brevissimo … epigrammate*; 9 *praef.* 1 *epigramma … extra ordinem paginarum.* The eidetic identity of Martial's work is indirectly inferred also from 8.18.1 f., where the poet claims that the *epigrammata* of his friend Cerrinius have a value equal, if not superior, to his own texts, as well as from 8.55(56).23 f. *ergo ero Vergilius, si munera Maecenatis / des mihi? Vergilius non ero, Marsus ero* ('Well then, shall I be a Virgil if you were to give me the gifts of a Maecenas? I shall not be a Virgil, I shall be a Marsus'), where Domitius Marsus, a poet belonging to the Maecenatian circle, acts as "*exemplum* di un possibile e proficuo rapporto di patronato tra un epigrammista e la corte che si avviava a diventare imperiale" (Canobbio 2005, 151).

> Lesbia dictavit, docte Catulle, tibi:
> non me Paeligni nec spernet Mantua vatem,
> si qua Corinna mihi, si quis Alexis erit.

Cynthia made you a poet, sprightly Propertius; fair Lycoris was Gallus' genius; beauteous Nemesis is the fame of clear-voiced Tibullus; Lesbia, elegant Catullus, dictated your verse. My poetry neither the Paelignians nor Mantua will spurn, if I find a Corinna or an Alexis.[47]

The Flavian poets – be they engaged in a literary genre whose identity is strong and well recognizable (epic), or in course of construction and legitimization (epigram), or even hard to classify (*Silvae*) – tend to blur the boundaries among the various genres in different ways and measures: these boundaries are perceived not as absolute limits, but rather as an opportunity for a productive and enriching comparison among different poetic forms.

---

47 This text shows well Martial's intention to put his epigram in a line of continuity not only with Catullus, but also with Augustan poetry (Canobbio 2005, 145f.; 2011b, 440–445; see also Neger 2012, 156–161; Mindt 2013, 120–124 esp. 123, where she speaks of an "indirekten Selbstkanonisierung Martials" inside a "Klassikerliste").

Alfredo Mario Morelli

Catullus 23 and Martial. An epigrammatic model and its 'refraction' throughout Martial's *libri*

This paper focuses on connections between thematic networks in the books of Martial and allusions (especially the 'continuous' ones) to a single poetic model. In recent years, much attention has been devoted to the arrangement of Martial's books, resulting from the identification of thematic and verbal connections;[1] it is in this context also that intertextuality has to be envisaged, especially when it involves the *aemulatio* of a single author, if not of a single text. By activating the reader's memory at more than one point of a *liber*, allusions to a literary model bolster the artistic self-presentation of the book.

Catullus 23 marks a special case within the complex relationship between Martial and his favourite epigrammatic *auctor*.[2] The poem is a well-appreciated one by Martial, who often alludes to it by reproducing single features or poetic *iuncturae*, if not its overall framework.[3] I believe that there is more than one reason for this predilection. Thematic aspects are crucial here, because Catullus 23 is perhaps the most important poem of the *Liber* concerning a topic on which Martial often draws: ridiculous poverty.[4] But features in style and arrangement of the poem also have their importance. Catullus 23 puts at Martial's disposal not only an extraordinary collection of resources in speech and expression, but also, on the whole, a paradigm of *epigramma longum* skillfully and thoughtfully constructed:[5]

---

1 After Barwick 1932 and esp. 1958, which opened the path to further investigation, see at least Merli 1993 and 1998; Scherf 1998 and 2001; Lorenz 2004; Moreno Soldevila 2004; Scherf 2008; Sapsford 2009; Morelli 2009.
2 On the relationships between Martial and Catullus, see Paukstadt 1876; as regards recent discussion, see Ferguson 1963; Offerman 1980; Newman 1990, 75–103; Sullivan 1991, 95–97; Swann 1994 and 1998; Watson 2003; Fedeli 2004; Gavi 2007, and above all Mattiacci 2007a, esp. 162–195.
3 The noteworthy *Nachleben* of Catullus' poem did not reach modern times: apart from commentaries and large-scale essays on Catullus, almost only Németh 1971 and O' Bryhim 2007 focus on Catul. 23.
4 See, on this, Watson 2004, 315 f., who remarks that – as regards Martial's background – we should consider the influence of Catul. 23 as well as that of Catul. 21 (see below), 26 (on Furius' *villula:* about this topic, see Morelli 2003) and Fur. Bib. 1 f. Mor. (= Blans.; = Courtn.).
5 I adopt the text of Thomson 1997, 114: I only have doubts at l. 21, where Thomson prints *lupillis* (conjectured by Ianus Gulielmius in *Lampas*, ed. J. Gruter, III, Frankfurt 1604, pars II, 446) in-

https://doi.org/10.1515/9783110534436-007

Furi, cui neque servus est neque arca
nec cimex neque araneus neque ignis,
verum est et pater et noverca, quorum
dentes vel silicem comesse possunt,
est pulchre tibi cum tuo parente   5
et cum coniuge lignea parentis.
Nec mirum: bene nam valetis omnes,
pulchre concoquitis, nihil timetis,
non incendia, non graves ruinas,
non facta impia, non dolos veneni,   10
non casus alios periculorum.
Atqui corpora sicciora cornu
aut siquid magis aridum est habetis
sole et frigore et esuritione.
Quare non tibi sit bene ac beate?   15
A te sudor abest, abest saliva,
mucusque et mala pituita nasi.
Hanc ad munditiem adde mundiorem,
quod culus tibi purior salillo est,
nec toto decies cacas in anno;   20
atque id durius est faba et lupillis,
quod tu si manibus teras fricesque,
non umquam digitum inquinare possis.
Haec tu commoda tam beata, Furi,
noli spernere nec putare parvi,   25
et sestertia quae soles precari
centum desine, nam sat es beatus.

Furius, you who have neither a servant nor a moneybox, neither a bedbug nor a spider-web nor a fire, but have a father and step-mother, whose teeth even are able to eat hard rock: things are sweet to you, with your father, and with the tough wife of your father. Do not be amazed: for you are all well, you digest well, you fear nothing – not fires, not severe ruin, not wicked deeds, not plots of poison, nor other dangerous accidents. And you have bodies drier than horn, or whatever is drier than horn; and they are accustomed to both cold and hunger. Why then is everything not well and blessed for you? Sweat also is absent from you, and saliva, and mucus and other bad nasal emissions. To this cleanliness add more cleanliness, because you have an anus more pure than a saltcellar, nor in the entire year do you defecate ten times, and even then it is more solid than a bean or pebble – if you rubbed it with your hands, you wouldn't even be able to make your hands dirty. These advantages are so beautiful, Furius, don't spurn them or think them worthless, and stop begging the hundred thousand sesterces as you are accustomed to: for you are blessed enough.
(transl. by C. Bradley)

---

stead of *lapillis* (**V**), which can perhaps be defended; and also at l. 27, where *satis beatus* (**V**, defended by Fraenkel 1966) has been corrected (already by Calpurnius and by most modern editors) in *sat es beatus*.

The ring-composition is based on the repetition of the addressee's name in the vocative case (*Furi*, 1 and 24), a very common feature also in Martial's poetry. Bipartition of the central, scoptic segment (5–23, with the central 'navel' of 12–14 + 15) is also frequently found in Martial's *epigrammata longa* (see below the example of Mart. 11.56). Final *aprosdoketon* is not a necessary feature, but is nevertheless a very common one even in the 'long' poems of Martial.[6]

As concerns Catul. 23, readers may be surprised by the sudden final pun on the 'denied loan' (a very favorite theme also in Martial): in Catul. 24 Furius is the lover of Iuventius; his fellow Aurelius (see Catul. 11 and 16) is also a rival of Catullus, an *amator* of the same boy (cc. 15 and 21).[7] In the present arrangement of the *Liber Catulli*, the poem 24 immediately follows 23, and Furius is once again mocked as an indigent (the same happens to Aurelius in the poem 21, and therefore both Aurelius in 21 and Furius in 24 are depicted as unsuitable lovers for Iuventius): 24.4–6 *mallem divitias Midae dedisses / isti, cui neque servus est neque arca, / quam sic te sineres ab illo amari* ('I had rather you had given the riches of Midas to that fellow who has neither servant nor money-box, than so allow you to be courted by him'). This echoes the opening jingle of Catul. 23.

Therefore, erotic rivalry could have been also expected in Catul. 23 as the most probable starting point for a convenient final pun against Furius (something like: 'hey, Furius, you are happy and poor, over a barrel: please, leave in peace my Iuventius'), but the topic is absent. Nevertheless, it is reasonable to think that such details, as that concerning the *culus ... purior salillo* (18–23, esp. 19), are not completely innocent: 'impurity' of oral and anal orifices is a widespread topic in Catullus' scoptic *nugae* and epigrams against rivals (23.19 can be compared with 97.4 *verum etiam culus mundior et melior*). Therefore, there is probably an irony implied regarding the 'cleanness' of Furius' buttocks, as well as on the 'hardness' and 'dryness' of Furius' body:[8] in Catul. 16, Furius

---

6 See Morelli 2008a, esp. 32–38 (on the structure of Martial's *epigrammata longa*).

7 Beck 1996 assumes that there was a *libellus Iuventi*, which contained a "cycle of rivals" (viz., "of Furius and Aurelius"). About this theory, see Bellandi 2007, 72–74 (with further bibliography).

8 O' Bryhim 2007 cleverly interpreted Furius' 'lack of fluids' as related to the condition of financial distress, in short, to the absence of 'liquid' money (not so different is the interpretation already proposed by Wray 2001, 74, who also insists on the similarities between the pair formed by Catul. 23–24 and the other one dedicated to Ameana, Catul. 41 and 43). Catullus grotesquely uses ancient medical theories about hassles that the excess of body fluids can cause, leading the argument to paradox: privations Furius and family are subjected to lead to a total loss of humors, and this extreme dryness is taken as a symbol of health (see also Syndikus 2017[4] *ad loc.*). It must be said that the notion that a very 'dry' temperament is the most healthy is not the dominant one in ancient medical doctrine: fluid balance and consequent diet are more often recommended,

and Aurelius mocked Catullus' 'mild' verses (*molles ... versiculos*) and so generated the harsh reaction of the *ego*, who reverses the charge and argues that his rivals are in fact the 'soft' ones (viz., they are a *pathicus* and a *cinaedus*).[9] If we also consider Catul. 15 and 21 (Aurelius tries to seduce Iuventius and is threatened by the *ego* with *raphanidosis* and *irrumatio*), we may conclude that there is a cluster of topics (which implies erotic and literary rivalry between *Catullus* and his fellows Furius and Aurelius, poverty and lack of masculinity of both rivals) which are consistently elaborated within a small group of poems (15, 16, 21, 23, 24, perhaps 26).[10] Burlesque 'didactic' cares of the Catullan *ego* are also part and parcel of this thematic cluster: in Catul. 21.9–11 there is a comic 'concern' for Iuventius' educational corruption: *atque id si faceres satur, tacerem: | nunc ipsum id doleo, quod esurire | a temet puer et sitire discet* ('If you had your belly full I should say nothing; as it is, what annoys me is that my lad will learn from you how to be hungry and thirsty');[11] the same 'anxiety' appears in Catul. 24.4–6 and 9 f.

It is an open question whether Martial and his contemporaries could appreciate Furius' and Aurelius' poems in the same arrangement in which we read them today (or in a similar one). However, we know for sure that Martial read Catul. 23 in association with the other poems of this group:[12] this is demonstrated by Mart. 1.92:[13]

> Saepe mihi queritur non siccis Cestos ocellis,
>   tangi se digito, Mamuriane, tuo.
> Non opus est digito: totum tibi Ceston habeto,

---

see e.g. Cels. *med.* 1.3.14. Nevertheless, a widespread prejudice against humors in excess (considered an emblem of poor control and self-care, a result of excessive intake of food and drink) is evidenced for instance by Cic. *Tusc.* 5.99 f. or by *Sen.* 34 and already by Pl. *As.* 857.
9 On Catul. 16 and, more generally, on the opposition *mollis / durus* in Catullus, there are recent, excellent remarks in Bellandi 2007, 51–61; see also Agnesini 2012, 191–193, Morelli 2012, 476 f., and Morelli forthcoming a.
10 In Roman culture, the *esuritio* is connected to the lack of manhood (particularly strong is the connection between hunger and *irrumatio*), but some remarks are necessary. Peek 2002 argues that in Catul. 21 Aurelius is attacked as a 'passive' homosexual, subjected to (oral) penetration: he wants to 'dominate' Iuventius (and indirectly even Catullus), but his hunger reveals that he is actually a *pathicus*, who will be conveniently penetrated by the *ego* (however, it should be noted that Peek's interpretation of *CIL* XI 6721,34 a,b,c is wrong; see App. *BC* 5.35 and Osgood 2006, 166 f. and related plate).
11 I accept Froehlich's emendation *a temet*; **V** has *me me*; Thomson 1997, 112, prints *a te mi.*
12 See already Paukstadt 1876, 14–16.
13 I adopt the text of Lindsay 1929[2]. I always take into consideration also Heraeus 1976[2] and Shackleton Bailey 1990.

si dest nil aliud, Mamuriane, tibi.
Sed si nec focus est nudi nec sponda grabati   5
    nec curtus Chiones Antiopesve calix,
cerea si pendet lumbis et scripta lacerna
    dimidiasque nates Gallica paeda tegit,
pasceris et nigrae solo nidore culinae
    et bibis inmundam cum cane pronus aquam: 10
non culum – neque enim est culus, qui non cacat olim –
    sed fodiam digito qui superest oculum:
nec me zelotypum nec dixeris esse malignum.
    Denique pedica, Mamuriane, satur.

Often Cestos complains to me with overflowing eyes that he is pawed by your finger, Mamurianus. No need of a finger: take Cestos altogether to yourself if he, Mamurianus, is all that you lack. But if you possess no fire, nor frame of a bare truckle-bed, nor a broken cup like Chione's and Antiope's; if a cloak, white with age and threadbare, hangs over your loins, and a Gaulish cape covers but half your buttocks; and if you batten on the steam only of a sooty kitchen, and on all fours like a dog drink from dirty puddles, I will not prod that latter-end of yours – it isn't a latter-end, being unused – but I will gouge out your remaining eye. And don't say I am jealous or malicious. In a word, follow your bent, Mamurianus, – on a full stomach!
(transl. by Ker 1919–1920)

Verbal and thematic hints at Catul. 23 and other poems related to Furius and Aurelius have been already detected in the past.[14] Mamurianus enacts his attempt at seduction exactly as Aurelius did in Catul. 21, and he is starving like him; as it happens in Catul. 21, the ego would not blame his rival if he had made his *avances* as 'sated' (the last word of the poem, *satur*, is an obvious allusion to Catul. 21.9 *atque id is faceres satur tacerem:* see already above, Mart. 1.92.3 f. *totum tibi Ceston habeto, | si dest nil aliud, Mamuriane, tibi*). The characterization of Mamurianus' poverty (exactly in the center of the poem, ll. 5–10) recollects features of both Catul. 21 and 23. If there is emphasis on the *esuritio* suffered by the tattered lover (see especially ll. 9 f., nearly a reworking of the Catullan theme of Aurelius' hyperbolic hunger), the initial catalogue, with its insistent anaphora (*nec focus est nudi nec sponda grabati | nec curtus* eqs.), certainly recalls the opening sequence of Catul. 23 *neque servus est neque arca | nec cimex neque araneus neque ignis:* it is noteworthy that the first element of Martial's series is the last one in the Catullan chain (*nec focus ~ neque ignis*).

Hints at Catul. 23 become even clearer at Martial's l. 11: *non culum – neque enim est culus, qui non cacat olim* exaggerates the hyperbolic sentence of the model (Catul. 23.19 f. *culus tibi purior salillo est, | nec toto decies cacas in*

---

14 See Friedländer 1886, 220; Citroni 1975 *ad loc.*; Howell 1980 *ad loc.*

anno). Martial is treating a set of Catullan poems (those concerning Furius and Aurelius) as a coherent whole; in particular, he provides the reader with a 'reinterpretation' of the theme of Furius' poverty in Catul. 23, because it clearly interacts with the erotic motif, viz. 'the courtship of the *puer*'. In this sense, Martial exploits the contiguity among Catul. 15, 21, 23, and 24 (we do not know in which arrangement Martial read those poems, but they were definitely for him thematically and stylistically interconnected).

We should not miss another important element. As has been brilliantly noted in a recent paper,[15] the name of the main character is not elsewhere present in Martial, and this cannot be an accident: it refers to another character found in Catullus' *Liber*, Mamurra. In Mart. 1.92.11f. the threat of sexual punishment mostly alludes to the famous ending of Catul. 15 (the threat of *raphanidosis* addressed to Aurelius). However, that model is comically transformed: Martial's *ego* does not hit (with a finger; it is a perfect retaliation, if we consider l. 2 *tangi se digito*) the *culus* of the victim, but rather the only eye he has. This detail is given almost in passing (Mamurianus is *luscus*) and it seems completely incongruous (in the long poem there are no other references to the physical features of Mamurianus). In fact, it is extremely significant: Mamurianus is graphically depicted as a great *Mentula* (the penis is often the 'one-eyed' in the poetry of Martial: think of 2.33; 3.8 and 11; 9.37.10; 12.22),[16] just like Catullus' Mamurra, who in a cluster of poems has precisely the nickname *Mentula* (see 94, 105, 114, 115: see already 29.13). Mamurra is also described as a third-rate gallant in Catul. 29.6–8, and is mocked as *cinaedus* in Catul. 57 (in this poem, the pair of pretentious *erudituli*, Caesar/Mamurra, matches the couple of *pathici* in Catul. 16, Furius/Aurelius, who also have literary ambitions). Mamurra himself, while not being poor as a church mouse, is anyway the *decoctor Formianus* in Catul. 41.4 and 43.5, and is teased for his estate, which ruins him in poems 114–115.[17] Finally, Mamurra is also threatened with *raphanidosis* (this is the most probable meaning of *ipsa*

---

15 Sparagna 2010; see already O' Connor 1990; Vallat 2008, 355 f. (he correctly remarks that in other poems of Martial the name *Mamurra* is clearly connected with the Catullan character, see Mart. 9.59; 10.4; Newman 1990, 95 f., and below, n. 17) and 615; see now Fusi 2013, 102. On the comical 'law of retaliation' that characterizes the poem (*digito*, ll. 2.3, and 12) see the remarks in Obermayer 1998, 87 f.

16 On the *lusci* in Martial see Watson 1982 (though she actually neglects the point we are interested in) and Sparagna 2010.

17 Vallat 2008, 329 f., argues that the indigent *Mamurra* in Mart. 9.59 imitates *in opponendo* the Catullan *Mamurra* (a very rich person), but in Catul. 41, and 114–115 (and already in Catul. 29), this character is a prodigal and bankrupt one, and this may already contain the seeds of interesting ideas for Martial's characterization of *Mamurra* and *Mamurianus*: see the excellent considerations of Watson 2006, 276 and n. 26 (on Mart. 9.59).

olera olla legit at Catul. 94.2).[18] We may conclude that Martial, by depicting Mamurianus, definitely combines a sophisticated 'horizontal' reading of Furius' and Aurelius' 'cycle' and malicious hints at the 'cycle' of Mamurra. Martial achieves an effect of hyperbole, drawing a character who is affected by the most remarkable features of Catullan seducers: poverty, *invenustas* (or only apparent *venustas*), exhibited, but also equivocal and humiliated manhood (the final 'blinding' at ll. 11 f. is a symbol not only of violation, but even of castration, because it reduces to impotence Mamurianus/*Mentula*'s eye ...).

Hyper-characterization and imitation of more than one Catullan 'cycle' are also found in Mart. 1.77:

> Pulchre valet Charinus, et tamen pallet.
> Parce bibit Charinus, et tamen pallet.
> Bene concoquit Charinus, et tamen pallet.
> Sole utitur Charinus, et tamen pallet.
> Tingit cutem Charinus, et tamen pallet.   5
> Cunnum Charinus lingit, et tamen pallet.

Charinus has good health, and yet he is pale. Charinus drinks moderately, and yet he is pale. Charinus has good digestion, and yet he is pale. Charinus enjoys the sunshine, and yet he is pale. Charinus rouges his skin, and yet he is pale. Charinus indulges in every debauchery, and yet he is pale.

Allusions to Catul. 23 are well known and registered in current commentaries. The description of Charinus' paradoxical 'good health' (1 and 3 *pulchre valet ... bene concoquit*) clearly hints at Catul. 23.7 f. *bene nam valetis omnes / pulchre concoquitis* ('you all enjoy the best health, your digestions are excellent'); the character's name itself, Charinus, also seems allusive to relevant lexemes in Catul. 23 such as *bene, pulchre, mundus* etc.[19] However, the interpretation of Catullus' poem is once again mischievous, because repulsive sexuality and disgusting vices are involved.[20] This also causes a paradoxical reversal of the Catullan

---

18 See Hartz 2007, 79–82.

19 See also Vallat 2008, 557 f. (the name *Charinus* is often connected with repulsive vices, see Mart. 4.39; 6.37 and 7.34, and Friedländer 1886, 214). The adverb *pulchre* is rarely used in the poetry of Flavian age (see also below, on 11.31 and the term *venustus*), with the exception of Martial, who is certainly influenced by Catullus and neoteric poetry: see also 2.58.1; 3.95.13; 12.17.9 and Citroni 1975, 248 (*ad* 1.77.1); Williams 2004, 197 (*ad* 2.58.1). The *incipit* of 1.77 (*pulchre valet*) is perhaps influenced by Catul.57.1 *pulchre convenit improbis cinaedis* (repeated at the end, l. 10, with ring-composition).

20 Lorenz 2002, 138–140 deals with the arrangement of 1.77: the poem is set just at the end of a scoptic sequence (71–77), interrupted by 1.78 (which concerns the *exitus* of an *illustris vir*, seriously ill in his face: there is a clear contrast with 1.77). The scoptic series goes on with 1.79–81.

motif: notwithstanding his good health, Charinus is sickly pale because of his sexual practice (he is a *cunnilictor*). Together with Furius, other Catullan features and characters are recalled: the singsong structure with final scomma reproduces (and exaggerates) the framing of Catul. 78, centered on the figure of Gallus (*Gallus habet fratres ... Gallus homo est bellus ... Gallus homo est stultus*);[21] other thematic aspects remind us of Catul. 80 (at the end of which the 'pale' Gellius turns out to be a *fellator*) and 89 (in which Gellius' 'thinness' is the result of his nocturnal revelry with the whole family).

Through a 'horizontal' reading of more than one Catullan 'cycle', the characterization of Martial's Charinus reaches paradoxical and hyperbolic effects. He is as healthy as Furius is (he does not show, apart from his inexplicable 'whiteness', any of the typical symptoms of lover's melancholy: thinness, emaciation, sadness, and suffering), but his perversion goes even beyond that of Gellius, the Catullan champion of sexual vice. Moreover, Charinus' practices are by far more disgusting than the effeminacy of the *pathicus* Furius or even more nauseating than Gellius' *fellatio*. Martial's readers perceive this dense and articulated background, which is passed into new dynamics of rhetorical construction and thematic organization: a consistent, new paradigm of vice is proposed, based on a plurality of Catullan suggestions. It is also remarkable that, in order to describe Mamurianus and Charinus, Martial has extrapolated two distinct sets of features, which coexist in Catul. 23: extreme poverty is thematized in 1.92, paradoxical good/bad health is the topic of 1.77. This is what I call the 'diffraction' of the Catullan model: Martial alludes to Catul. 23 at two different times and in two completely different ways within his Book I. There is a consistent strategy of allusiveness and a keen sense of variation in alluding to the same model, in order to draw a variegated tableau of the human failings in the course of the book. In both cases themes taken from Catul.23 are intertwined with other Catullan motifs and serve to characterize sexual vices (a component which is absent in Catullus' poem).

Catullus 23 then remains a constant point of reference: just consider Mart. 2.51,[22] and 3.89.[23] However, it is in Book XI that the most impressive effects of 'dif-

---

21 See Fedeli 2004, 165. On Martial's use of repetition as a structural device, see Laurens 2012[2], 273–281, and Watson 2006, 273 f.

22 See Paukstadt 1876, 15; Williams 2004, 178–181, both for comparison with Catul.23 and 33 and for the 'internal' allusion to Mart. 2.44.9 *et quadrans mihi nullus est in arca* ('I don't have a farthing in the money box'). On the massive presence in Book II of epigrams that treat the same erotic and 'financial' motifs, see Lorenz 2002, 120, with bibliography.

23 See Fusi 2006, 512.

fraction' of the Catullan model are recorded. I will focus on the aspects related to the 'construction' of a coherent and well-articulated poetic discourse through verbal and thematic connections throughout the book.

First, it should be considered that the book is characterized (already in the long initial sequence of poems) by a return of Saturnalian topics. There are 'apologetic' reasons for this: Martial seems to go back to the profound and original issues of his epigrammatic art, now that the long 'courtesan' relationship with Domitian is over. Nerva is the ideal patron for an ideological change,[24] which consists in re-evaluating the 'Roman' roots of the genre. Thanks to the renewed atmosphere of the Saturnalia, the epigram goes back to Italic simplicity, wisdom, spiciness, and 'sincerity', mobilizing a set of (mainly, but not exclusively) erotic and scoptic themes belonging to the Latin tradition. Models are to be found mostly in Catullus, but also in other authors and genres, from Horace's satire to elegy.[25] I previously wrote a paper on the allusive strategies by which Martial sketches a malicious, parodic reinterpretation of Ovid's didactic elegy,[26] but references to Catullus and other Latin epigrammatists are likewise continuous. Yet nowhere else, as in this case, do intertextual strategies blend in with those related to the artistic arrangement of the book. It is in this context that allusions to Catul. 23 should be considered.

I begin with Mart. 11.32:

> Nec toga nec focus est nec tritus cimice lectus
>   nec tibi de bibula sarta palude teges,
> nec puer aut senior, nulla est ancilla nec infans,
>   nec sera nec clavis nec canis atque calix.
> Tu tamen adfectas, Nestor, dici atque videri   5
>   pauper, et in populo quaeris habere locum.
> Mentiris vanoque tibi blandiris honore.
>   Non est paupertas, Nestor, habere nihil.

You have neither toga, nor fire, nor bug-haunted bed, nor have you a mat stitched of thirsty rushes, nor boy, nor older slave; you have no maid, nor infant, nor door-bolt, nor key, nor

---

24 There are obviously some ambiguities in drawing the image of the elderly emperor, who comes close to be characterized as a *rex Saturnalicius*. In the opinion of Holzberg 2002, 150, Nerva is a "Saturnalienprinz".

25 On the 'Saturnalian' characterization of Book XI, see Citroni 1989, 215 (in the context of a wider discussion on the importance of the socio-cultural model of Saturnalia in the epigrams of Martial); according to Holzberg 2002, 148–150, such a characterization has to be envisaged within the compositional strategies of Martial's fourth 'triad' (Books X–XII) as a whole. On the emperor Nerva in Book XI, in connection with Saturnalian issues, see also Lorenz 2002, 210–219; Nauta 2002, 437–440.

26 Morelli 2008b, especially 111–130; see also Hinds 2007, 118–123 and 130.

dog, nor cup. Yet you aim, Nestor, at being called, and seeming, a poor man, and look to having a place among the people. You are a fraud, and flatter yourself with an empty honour. It is not poverty, Nestor, to have nothing at all.

There is a strong Catullan flavour in this part of the book. Mart. 11.31 is dedicated to an eccentric host who always serves to his guests just *cucurbitae*, presented in various ways, and (l. 20) *hoc lautum vocat, hoc putat venustum* ('this he calls elegant, this he thinks charming'). Critical attention has centered on the adjective *venustus*, which Martial does not use elsewhere (the adjective had a neoteric flavour, but it is difficult to imagine that it was still alive in common use at the time). It is a typical Catullan lexeme (see 3.2; 13.6, in an invitation to dinner; 22.2; 31.12; 89.2, 97.9; and 35.17, *venustē*; and 86.3, the noun *venustas*), but the whole sentence in Martial actually recalls Catullus: see 12.4 *hoc salsum esse putas?* ('do you think this funny?'; the poem is addressed to Marrucinus who steals handkerchiefs of the guests and thinks it is amusing; see also ll. 4f.: *fugit te, inepte, / quamvis sordida res et invenusta est*, 'you are mistaken, you silly fellow; it is ever so ill-bred, and in the worst taste'); and 97.9 *hic futuit multas et se facit esse venustum*. The reference to Catullan banquets is also evident shortly thereafter, in 11.34.4 *cenabit belle, non habitabit Aper* ('Aper will dine, but not lodge nicely'), where the allusion to Catul. 13 is confirmed a little later by the almost identical opening motto of Mart. 11.52 *cenabis belle Iuli Cerealis apud me.*[27]

In Mart. 11.32 the imitation of Catul. 23 is clear from the *incipit*, which reproduces the persistent anaphora of negative particles. The catalogue continues for about half the poem; allocution addressed to the dedicatee Nestor is located just in l. 5 (according to a pattern, which is not unusual in Martial). All items in this 'list of poverty' are identical to those present in Catul. 23 or in Mart. 1.92: they are cleverly 'reused' by alternating essential *brevitas* (see the rapid allusion at l. 1 *nec toga nec focus*) and larger syntactic structures (l. 2) or accumulation (the Catullan *nec servus* expands to take up all the l. 3 *nec puer aut senior, nulla est ancilla*

---

27 See Merli 2008. 11.34 blends the two themes of the 'small' or 'uncomfortable estate' and the invitation to dinner. Aper (a speaking name, which combines the two themes: his estate is so wild that even a *noctua* would not dwell there) has bought his poor estate not to live there, but for dining with the *nitidus Maro* (the name Aper returns in more than one epigram on the theme of dinner, intended for easy pun). Scherf 2001, 49 f., cleverly analyses the sequence of poems focused on the dinner theme in Book XI: 31, 34 and 35 are against bad guests or hosts, as well as, in the second part of the liber, 65, 66 and 77 (dominated by the image of a crowded but very poor banquet). In the middle, poem 52 (on Cerealis' dinner) and 57 provide a contrasting positive paradigm.

nec infans, 'there is no boy slave or an older one or a maidservant or a baby').[28]
We have to be careful in considering the existence of self-allusive devices among
different books of Martial (instead of 'mechanical' reuse of *iuncturae* and themes
extracted from the immense repository of the author); nevertheless, the recovery
of the singsong rhythm with emphatic alliteration in l. 4 (*nec sera nec clavis nec
canis atque calix*) does seem self-allusive. In the second hemistich, Martial exactly highlights both innovating items, which were already present in 1.92.6 and 10
(the *canis* and especially the *calix*; Nestor 'exceeds' even Mamurianus' model,
because the latter at least had a *lacerna*, and maybe a dog). The erotic element
seems to be absent: attention is focused on the description of Nestor's extreme
poverty. Nestor arrogates to himself the title (the *honos*) of *pauper*, but he is actually a destitute; and there is a substantial difference between a *pauper* (who is
still a member of the *populus*) and a destitute (hence the final pun). The 'Catullan' micro-context (Mart. 11.31, 11.34) already makes it easy for the *lector* to recognize the allusions to Catul. 23, but a close imitation of the same poem follows
at no great distance, at the beginning of the second half of the *liber* (a little after
11.52, with which we already dealt): Mart. 11.56.

> Quod nimium mortem, Chaeremon Stoice, laudas,
>   vis animum mirer suspiciamque tuum?
> Hanc tibi virtutem fracta facit urceus ansa,
>   et tristis nullo qui tepet igne focus,
> et teges et cimex et nudi sponda grabati,   5
>   et brevis atque eadem nocte dieque toga.
> O quam magnus homo es, qui faece rubentis aceti
>   et stipula et nigro pane carere potes!
> Leuconicis agedum tumeat tibi culcita lanis
>   constringatque tuos purpura pexa toros,   10
> dormiat et tecum, qui cum modo Caecuba miscet
>   convivas roseo torserat ore puer:
> o quam tu cupies ter vivere <u>Nestoris</u> annos
>   et nihil ex ulla perdere luce voles!
> Rebus in angustis facile est contemnere vitam: 15
>   fortiter ille facit, qui miser esse potest.

Because you, Stoic Chaeremon, so much praise death, do you want me to admire and look
up to your mind? 'Tis a jug with a broken handle that creates this virtue of yours, and a
melancholy hearth chill with no fire, and a beggar's rug, and bugs and the framework of
a bare truckle-bed, and a short toga, your one covering night and day alike. Oh, what a
great man you are, who can do without dregs of red vinegar and straw and black bread!

---

28 Kay 1985, 141–143, analyzes the rich literary background of this satire against poverty, not
only in Catullus and epigrammatic poetry, but also in comedy and the genre of satire.

Come, imagine your pillow swells with Leuconian wool, and that close-napped purple binds your couches, and a boy waits upon you who, while he mixed the Caecuban yesterday, distracted your guests with his rosy lips! Oh, how you will long to live Nestor's years thrice over, and wish to lose no moment of any day! In narrow means 'tis easy to despise life: he acts the strong man who is wretched and can endure.

Chaeremon is a wise 'cynical-stoic', a typical character in Martial's poetry who often mocks such falsely severe *contemptores vitae.* The poem is perfectly divided into two mirror-patterned halves: 1–2 + 3–8 + 9–14 + 15–16.[29] The usual 'catalogue of miseries' at ll. 3–8 reproduces many themes and *iuncturae* we have already enucleated: the *urceus* with *fracta ansa* seems to be a kind of substitute of the *curtus calyx* at 1.92 (see also 11.32); after the inevitable *ignis* at l. 4, we once again meet with the *teges* (see 11.32.2) and the omnipresent *cimex*; at l. 5 the final idiom is almost identical to the second hemistich of 1.92.5 (*et nudi sponda grabati*);[30] the *toga brevis* is also present, as in 1.92.7–8. Original features are the *faex* at l. 7 and the *panis niger,* not so attractive a meal for Chaeremon (it is noteworthy that, in the opinion of some commentators, Catul. 23.4 alludes to the *panis lapidosus*).[31]

Links between 11.32 and 11.56 are manifest to Martial's reader, and the name itself of the *miser* in 11.32 (Nestor) cannot be random. In Book XI this name is present only in 32 and 56. In 11.32 it is magnificently incongruous: it is the name of a king adopted by someone homeless.[32] In 11.56 it returns as an antonomasia of longevity (and this is the most common use of the name in Martial),[33] but the reader cannot but think of the Nestor of 11.32, given the strong link that exists between these two poems.[34] The characters of Nestor and Chaeremon are closely related. They suggest two models of 'sobriety' which are, so to speak, shown to be mocked and 'discarded', in the network of cultural, literary, and moral paradigms presented to the reader in book XI. The impression is that

---

29 See Lorenz 2002, 19 n. 67.

30 The term *grabatus* (a popular Graecism which occurs in poetry only in satire and epigram, see Lucil. 251 Marx; Fur. Bib. 5 Mor.= Blänsd. = Courtn.; Catul. 10.22, cf. Ernout / Meillet 1959⁴, 279) appears in Martial only in 1.92.5, 11.56.5, 12.32.11 (imitations of Catul. 23) as well as in 6.39.4 and in 4.53.5 (this last poem, as 11.56, deals with the motif of the ragged 'cynical' wise).

31 See Ellis 1889², 60 f.

32 See Kay 1985 *ad loc.:* "The point is that the name (i. e. Nestor) evokes a king, not a beggar"; see also Marsilio 2008, 923.

33 See Vallat 2008, 281 f.

34 As concerns the name of Chaeremon, Kay 1985 *ad loc.* argues that it is connected *kat'antiphrasin* to *chairein*, but see Vallat, 2008, 120. An allusion to Chaeremon, teacher of Nero, is also problematic: see, after Friedländer 1886 II, 195, Kay 1985, 192.

the destitute, miserable Nestor and the philosopher, the *Graeculus* Chaeremon, work as a kind of counterparts of the great Roman Emperor, Nerva. The latter is praised at 11.5, at the beginning of the book:

> Tanta tibi est recti reverentia, Caesar, et aequi,
>   quanta Numae fuerat: sed Numa pauper erat.
> Ardua res haec est, opibus non tradere mores
>   et, cum tot Croesos viceris, esse Numam.
> Si redeant veteres, ingentia nomina, patres,   5
>   Elysium liceat si vacuare nemus:
> te colet invictus pro libertate Camillus,
>   aurum Fabricius, te tribuente, volet;
> te duce gaudebit Brutus, tibi Sulla cruentus
>   imperium tradet, cum positurus erit;   10
> et te privato cum Caesare Magnus amabit,
>   donabit totas et tibi Crassus opes.
> Ipse quoque infernis revocatus Ditis ab umbris
>   si Cato reddatur, Caesarianus erit.

As great is thy reverence for right and justice, Caesar, as was Numa's, but Numa was poor. 'Tis a hard task this, not to sacrifice manners to wealth, and, though thou hast surpassed many a Croesus, to be a Numa. Were our sires of old, mighty names, to return, were it allowed to empty the Elysian grove, to thee Camillus, liberty's unconquered champion, will pay his court, gold at thy giving will Fabricius accept, in thee as captain will Brutus be glad, to thee bloody Sulla will resign his power when he shall seek to lay it down; and thee the Great Captain, allied with Caesar, only a private citizen, will love, and Crassus will bestow on thee all his wealth. Cato, too, himself, were he called back to return from the nether shades of Dis, will be Caesar's partizan.

Nerva is endowed with the same virtues of Numa: but Numa was a *pauper*, while Nerva is so wise that he manages to have severe *mores* while enjoying the *opes* of many Croesuses (ll. 3–4). The wisdom of Nerva is the exact opposite of that of Chaeremon: it is not the ostentation of a ragged misery that pretends to despise comforts; it is rather a way to exploit wealth and power so as not to undermine virtue, sense of justice, and sobriety. There is a kind of antithesis (at a significant remove within Book XI) between the two gnomic sentences that characterize Nerva and Chaeremon: 11.5.3 f. *ardua res haec est, opibus non tradere mores* / *et, cum tot Croesos viceris, esse Numam*; 11.56.15 f. *rebus in angustis facile est contemnere vitam:* / *fortiter ille facit, qui miser esse potest.*[35] Nerva's virtue, unlike

---

35 The idiom *ardua res haec est* is nearly identical in 7.28.9 (see Kay 1985, 69). In 11.5.3 the *gravitas* is still sober: celebratory tones rise with the double antonomasia in the next verse. On the other hand, 11.56.14 *rebus in angustis* eqs. seems to propose a malicious reading of Hor. *Carm.* 2.10.21 f. *rebus angustis animosus atque* / *fortis adpare* (see also Kay 1985, 194).

that of Chaeremon, has much to do with Roman *mores*, as indicated by the long series of exempla drawn from history at ll. 5–14.[36] The model that comes out, on the other hand, has nothing to do with the miserable 'pauperism' of Nestor, who wants to be part of the Roman *populus* without having the basic requirement: *paupertas*. Numa, at least, was poor, something that Nestor cannot possibly be while arrogating to himself this right (cf. 11.32.5f. *adfectas, Nestor, dici atque videri / pauper*). Affectation, a feature that connects Chaeremon and Nestor, is opposed to *simplicitas*, 'sincerity', and the *libertas* which allows the sensual joy of the Saturnalia, which Nerva represents in another 'programmatic' epigram, 11.2.5f.: *clamant ecce mei 'Io Saturnalia' versus: / et licet et sub te praeside, Nerva, libet*, 'Look, my verses shout "Hurrah for the Saturnalia!" Under your rule, Nerva, it's allowed, and it's our pleasure'.[37]

11.15 is even more significant, for its references to 11.5:

> Sunt chartae mihi, quas Catonis uxor
> et quas horribiles legant Sabinae:
> hic totus volo rideat libellus
> et sit nequior omnibus libellis.
> Qui vino madeat nec erubescat   5
> pingui sordidus esse Cosmiano,
> ludat cum pueris, amet puellas,
> nec per circuitus loquatur illam,
> ex qua nascimur, omnium parentem,
> quam sanctus Numa mentulam vocabat.   10
> Versus hos tamen esse tu memento
> Saturnalicios, Apollinaris:
> mores non habet hic meos libellus.

I have writings that Cato's wife and that grim Sabine dames might read; I wish this little book to laugh from end to end, and be naughtier than all my little books. Let it be drenched in wine and not ashamed to be stained with rich Cosmian unguents; let it play with the boys, love the girls, and in no roundabout phrase speak of that wherefrom we are born, the parent of all, which hallowed Numa called by its own name. Yet remember that

---

36 Kay 1985, 68, correctly argues that the general tone of the poem is strongly influenced by the 'Republican' ideals and imagery that dominated in the first times of the reign of Nerva and Traianus. Further information on this topic is to be found in Leberl 2004, 351f. On the paradox of *Cato Caesarianus*, see Rosati 2006, 51.

37 Saturnalian themes and Catullan allusions are also present in 11.6, a much discussed poem, particularly with regard to the idiom *passerem Catulli*: see, after Kay 1985, 71–76, at least Swann 1998, 55f.; Obermayer 1998, 72f.; Williams 2002, 166–168; Hinds 2007, 114f. (123 about Mart. 11.2). In general, on the importance of the Catullan theme of *basia* in Martial, see also Grewing 1996, 341–354.

these verses are of the Saturnalia, Apollinaris: this little book does not express my own morals.

Numa 'the wise', the model for Nerva's *sapientia* at 11.5, used to call the *mentula* by its name. Cato's wife and Sabine ladies may not read the new *libellus* (we have to recall that Cato is another model of austere *Romanitas*, present both in 11.2.1 and in 11.5.14): other *chartae* of Martial are more suitable for them (but, regarding this feminine modesty, the same malice of another poem by Martial, 3.68, seems intended here).[38] At the end of 11.5, the *sphragis* is given by one of the many allusions (like Mart. 1.35) to Catul. 16.5 f. *nam castum esse decet pium poetam | ipsum, versiculos nihil necesse est.*[39] In short, the pattern traced by the initial epigrams of Book XI seems quite consistent in all its elements:[40] genuine sincerity is found in both Nerva and in his *alter ego* Numa; spiciness and *lusus Saturnalicius* are the most authentic legacy of the Roman world (see also 11.20, with full citation of a biting epigram of Augustus).[41] Scattered over the course of the *liber* (11.32 and 11.56), there comprise two counter-exempla of negative 'poverty', whose paradox is to be, in both cases, ridiculous and ostentatious. On the other hand (once again paradoxically), Nerva, the Saturnalia which he presides, and Martial's *libellus* itself (which goes around *pingui sordidus ... Cosmiano*, 11.15.6) are honest and truthful, rich and pleasure-seeking, but not in contradiction with the eternal pattern of Roman *mores*: the compliance of Cato and Numa (11.5 and 11.15) with the *princeps* and with the frivolous opulence of the Saturnalia unmasks the mock severity of Chaeremon in 11.56. In order to conjure this complex web of intratextual references, the Catullan paradigm is constantly taken into consideration: in particular, the 'parallel' imitations of Catul. 23 in Mart. 11.32 and 11.56 help to 'build' the book, providing the reader with important landmarks for creating a path throughout the *liber*. In perfect consistency with these literary strategies, two new human *typi* are added to the 'vicious' characters depicted in Mart. 1.32 and 1.77: the destitute who boasts of being a *pauper*, and the disdainful philosopher *à la grecque*.

---

38 On Mart. 11.15 and the programmatic 'return of *mentula*' in Book XI, see, after Kay 1985, 98–100, at least Williams 2002, 165 f.; Hinds 2007, 123.
39 See now Morelli forthcoming a and forthcoming b.
40 In general, the initial sequence of the poems (from 11,1 to 21) and the importance of Saturnalian issues are well analyzed by Citroni 1988, 29–31; Merli 1993, 252f. and 1998, 154; Scherf 2001, 56–58.
41 Mattiacci 2016.

The last essay of this large production of literary types, based on the imitation of the same Catullan model, is given by Mart. 12.32:[42]

O Iuliarum dedecus Kalendarum,
vidi, Vacerra, sarcinas tuas, vidi;
quas non retentas pensione pro bima
portabat uxor rufa crinibus septem
et cum sorore cana mater ingenti.   5
Furias putavi nocte Ditis emersas.
Has tu priores frigore et fame siccus
et non recenti pallidus magis buxo
Irus tuorum temporum sequebaris.
Migrare clivom crederes Aricinum.   10
Ibat tripes grabatus et bipes mensa,
et cum lucerna corneoque cratere
matella curto rupta latere meiebat;
foco virenti suberat amphorae cervix;
fuisse gerres aut inutiles maenas   15
odor inpudicus urcei fatebatur,
qualis marinae vix sit aura piscinae.
Nec quadra derat casei Tolosatis,
quadrima nigri nec corona pulei
calvaeque restes alioque cepisque,   20
nec plena turpi matris olla resina,
Summemmianae qua pilantur uxores.
Quid quaeris aedes vilicosque derides,
habitare gratis, o Vacerra, cum possis?
Haec sarcinarum pompa convenit ponti.   25

O you disgrace of July's Kalends, I have seen your traps, Vacerra, I have seen them, the lot that was not distrained upon for two years' rent, and which your wife carried, red-headed with her seven curls, and your white-headed mother, together with your hulking sister. Furies were they, methought, emerged from the night of Dis! These two ladies in front, you, parched with cold and hunger, and paler than faded boxwood, the Irus of your day, followed: you would have thought Aricia's hill was shifting! There went along a three-legged truckle-bed and a two-legged table, and, alongside a lantern and bowl of cornel, a cracked chamberpot was making water through its broken side; the neck of a flagon was lying under a brazier green with verdigris; that there were salted gudgeons, too, or worthless

42 On the relationship between Mart. 12.32 and Catul. 23, see now Marsilio 2008, who makes interesting remarks (see also below, n. 48 and 52), although it is probably too much to say that there is a 'rivalry' between Martial's *ego* and Vacerra exactly as it happens between Furius and Catullus in Catul. 23 (it seems unnecessary to suppose that Vacerra is attacked as lacking in literary skill or because *invenustus* in literary tastes, see Marsilio 2008, 923 and 929; in addition, in Martial's poem another key motif is totally missing, viz. the erotic rivalry between *Catullus* and Furius).

sprats, the obscene stench of a jug confessed – such a stench as a whiff of a marine fish-pond would scarcely equal. Nor was there wanting a section of Tolosan cheese, nor a four-year-old chaplet of black pennyroyal, and ropes shorn of their garlic and onions, nor your mother's pot full of foul resin, the depilatory of dames under the walls. Why do you look for a house and scoff at rent-collectors when you can lodge for nothing, o Vacerra? This procession of your traps befits Beggars' bridge.

The theme is that of the paradoxical *pompa* of the poor. Vacerra spreads out his meager possessions, accompanied in a sad procession by the disheveled women of his family (*uxor, soror* and *mater*). The constant reference to Catul. 23 is revealed by several localized details (Vacerra brings his family with him, he is *frigore et fame siccus*, l. 7, as Furius is in Catul. 23.12–14;[43] he carries a poor stove for his *focus*, l. 14).[44] Compared to Catullus, Martial's poem plays in antiphrasis. Vacerra, as opposed to Furius, is pale and not in good health (there is probably also a reference to the typical color of the Gauls)[45] in Mart. 12.32.8: the *iunctura* is similar to Ov. *Met.* 4.134 f. *oraque buxo / pallidiora gerens* (Thisbe looks at the blood-stained soil and pales terrified before discovering the tragic destiny of her beloved Pyramus; see also *Met.* 11.417 f., about Alcyone, and then *Priap.* 32.2; see also Apul *Met.* 1.19; 9.30), but perhaps there is also the influence of some Catullan characters such as the dude from Pisaurum, in all probability a penniless starving like Furius, who courts Iuventius (Catul. 81.4 *inaurata pallidior statua*).[46] In general, it is the issue of extreme indigence, not that of the 'health paradox', that has most deeply interested Martial: after the first book, he never again sets in relation the two themes (not even 'at a distance', within the same *liber*). Martial clearly favored the thematic axis (as in Book XI) which better fits the compositional strategies of his book.[47] The poet follows suggestions, imagery, and vocabulary he has himself gradually built up and consolidated in the treatment of the topic: now this set of features is superimposed on the original Catullan

---

43 See already Friedländer 1886 II, 237.

44 In this regard cf. Watson 2004, 315 f. and n. 15.

45 See Watson / Watson 2003 *ad loc.*, and Watson 2004, 321. The 'Gallic' characterization of Vacerra and his family is given by the *cognomen* (see Watson 2004, 320, although an Etruscan origin is also possible: Ernout / Meillet 1959⁴, 710; on the name Vacerra see also Vallat 2008, 503 f.) and by some typical somatic features: the wife is *rufa* (v. 4), the sister is *ingens* (v. 5).

46 On the 'whiteness' of the lover in Catullus, cf. Morelli 2007, 539.

47 This difference seems a little neglected in Marsilio 2008, especially 929 f. In Book XI as well as in Book XII, though in different ways, Martial insists on the distinction between poverty (with dignity, freed from need) and indigence. The Catullan, mocking *makarismos* of the 'dry constitution' loses its motive, and the thinness of arid Vacerra regains its proper meaning (this is also a 'challenge' for the reader: he has to recall the Catullan background and to appreciate the different treatment of the motif in Martial).

model and seems to be almost one and the same thing with it. We meet once again with the *grabatus* (l. 11) and the *curtus* tableware (in this case, the humble *matella*, l. 13).[48] The pattern is shaped in such a way as to become a parody. Vacerra's *pompa* (l. 25) is not what the word suggests: there is nothing of Martial's sacred processions (see e. g. 8.78.2; however, the women-*Furiae* give the scene lugubrious *colores*) and the miserable parade is far from the noisy pomp of the rich landowner who goes from the city to the country (a theme which is comically dealt with by in Mart. 3.47).[49] The term *pompa* occurs inside the book only here and at 62.9, and the contrast could not be more marked. In 12.62.9 (*Ausonio similis tibi pompa macello*, 'an array like an Ausonian market') there is the opulent pomp of Priscus, a powerful Romanized patron who came back to Spain; in 12.32.25, there is the miserable 'procession' of Vacerra, probably a stranger in Rome.[50] In general, Priscus brings with him to Spain a wealth and an affluence that are worthy of Rome.

In 12.32, on the other hand, even items that can recall the topic of the simple, rural, *parva casa*, are treated with a clear intent to insult.[51] This epigram manages to display the overall tension which permeates the whole book, involving urban, rural and 'Spanish' themes. What in the country might be considered a sign of an ancient and respectable *simplicitas*, in Rome becomes a sign of humiliating lack of resources (and Vacerra is forced to brag with the *vilicus* renting townhouses, l. 23, as if he had resources enough to live in the city). Especially if one accepts the interpretation of Lindsay Watson, who argues that Vacerra is a Celtic immigrant living on the margins of Rome's urban life, there are some interesting resonances between 12.32 and the context in which it is inserted.[52] Also in Book XII the biting mockery on indigence finds its space: but the

---

[48] The focus is on the poverty of the groceries that Vacerra brings with him (ll. 15–20: see Bowie 1988, 170 f.): Marsilio 2008, 927 is right in observing that the list of food recalls *in opponendo* many scenes of Martial's banquets, in particular those related to the theme of the poor but decent dinner, cheered by friends (see once again 11.52).

[49] See Morelli 2008a, 36 f. The paradox of the situation is that it might be believed that Vacerra is migrating to Rome from the most miserable country (even from the *clivus Aricinus* of the beggars, see l. 10), while he was evicted from an urban home: it is almost an exile in Rome... On Vacerra as a hypostasis of the beggar Irus, see Vallat 2008, 202 f.

[50] See Watson 2004, above, in the text.

[51] See Watson / Watson 2003 *ad loc.*; Watson 2004, 317.

[52] Watson 2004, 323, identifies a contrast with the previous 12.31, the famous epigram of Martial on his Spanish *buen retiro* (and certainly the condition of the *ego* in this poem, a happy Roman *Hispaniensis* in the quiet Spanish province, could not be more different from that of Vacerra, a Gallus transplanted in the *Urbs* and forced to the margins of society: on this subject, see also Marsilio 2008, 926). Anyway, more generally 12.32 fully fits into the dynamics 'Rome/rural

topic is set in a dynamic relationship with other issues and it finds a new sense throughout the *liber*. There is a redefinition of wealth and poverty, which are relative values, established in constant confrontation among different geographic and social 'spaces': center and margins, *Urbs*, *rus*, Spain. The ancient motif of rustic simplicity is recalled in the course of the book just to draw a sharp contrast between urban, uppish poverty and non-showy richness in the *rus*, and often in Spain.

We should probably better reconsider the problem of the 'authorial' arrangement of Book XII,[53] which – like its *fratres* – is built on sophisticated structural strategies. The author makes reference to motifs and vocabulary he himself has imposed in the Roman cultural space, appealing to a shared literary memory (self-allusive practices are highly probable, as he is now a consolidated *auctor*) and to the strength of an epigrammatic model, Catullus 23: Mart.12.32 is the last 'verification' of its large productivity.

---

world/Spain' that characterizes the entire book: after Merli 2006b, 341–344, interesting ideas in this regard are in Rimell 2008, 193–199. Just think of the contrast between the squalor of belongings and furnishings available to Vacerra and the opulent sloppiness that characterizes rural residence and the Spanish *ego* in 12.18 (see in particular l. 18).

53 I limit myself to referring to the recent *status quaestionis* in Craca 2011.

IV Occasional Poetry and Literary Genres

Elena Merli

The *festinatio* in Flavian poetry: a clarification

1 Introduction

In the occasional and celebratory poetry of the Flavian age a frequent motif is that of the *festinatio*: the rapid drafting of a text that is *Zeitgedicht*, required to respond quickly to the expectations or requests of patrons and the promptings of particular events. The poet claims to have composed a single poem or an entire book with great rapidity, infringing upon a principle rooted in Callimachean and Horatian tradition: the slow, laborious process of *emendatio*.

As it often appears in Statius' prefaces, the *festinatio* 'of the poets' (a necessary qualification, in that the motif can also be found in prose genres, where its value is wholly or partly different)[1] has often been identified with the examples of it in the *Silvae*: nevertheless, this is a significant and distinctive variant, and it would be reductive to describe all of the facets of this phenomenon in 'Statian' terms. It is actually much more varied, as it is, so to speak, a modern *topos*, which is unburdened by a rigid, normative tradition.[2] Therefore, this paper includes examples from Ovid's poetry of exile and the epigrams of Antipater and, above all, Martial.

This study starts from Ovid's elegy from Tomis, where the *festinatio* is closely linked to the epistolary genre; then, its presence in epigrams will be analysed in

---

This work follows up and takes further some suggestions in Merli 2013, on the contrasting complementary motif of *lima* and *emendatio* in Flavian poetry. My thanks to Maria Luisa Catoni, Mario Citroni, Franca Ela Consolino and Gianpiero Rosati for their careful reading and detailed comments.

1 Particularly in the epistolary genre, of which we shall see some examples, and in genres aiming at synthesis and the *utile*, such as treatises (see Sen. *Nat.* 3 *praef.* 4; Plin. *Nat.* 3.42), the biography and historiography of Cornelius Nepos (*vit. praef.* 8) and Velleius Paterculus (1.16.1; 2.41.1; 108.2; 124.1). The role of *festinatio* in Velleius is much discussed: see, among others, Woodman 1975 and Lobur 2007.

2 On the *festinatio* in the *Silvae* see Rosati 2015. For many useful comments in studies on Statius' *praefationes*, see Johannsen 2006 (especially 245–248; 263 and 267; 316–322); Newlands 2008; Pagán 2010. On the poetics of the improvisation and *celeritas* in the *praefatio* to the first book, see also Hardie 1983, 78–85. Laurens 1965, 325 recognizes the *topos* as common to Statius, Martial and Greek epigram.

https://doi.org/10.1515/9783110534436-008

order to trace a specific relation with the professional writers of panegyric poetry; Statius' text, particularly the preface to the first book of the *Silvae*, will cast light on the complexity of the *topos*, which varies according to whether it has a private setting or is written for a wider public; finally, one original version of it can be seen in Martial's last books. My overall aim is to remove the interpretation of the *festinatio* from the usual alternatives of seeing it either as a rhetorical gesture of *deminutio* similar to Catullus' *sprezzatura*, or the fearful concern at how an inadequately polished text will be received; instead, I shall try to analyze it in the context of celebratory poetry in the Flavian age and its specific 'imperial' features, bearing in mind the aspects that the *topos* takes on in individual authors and in the different situations of communication and diffusion of literary texts.

2 Ovid and the epistolary *festinatio*

The strongly communicative orientation in Ovid's late elegies introduces into Latin poetry innovative features that derive from the contingent situation (though they are not limited to that). One of these is the *festinatio*. In a literature that is also *officium*, a celebratory poem is less effective if it arrives too late for the event it eulogizes. For example, by the time Ovid's panegyric verses reached Rome, even though they were *carmina properata* (*Pont.* 3.4.59),[3] Tiberius' triumph over Illyricum would already have been celebrated for some time: a poem would attract little attention and have limited success without the ingredient of *novitas* (*Pont.* 3.4.51f.). The text uses for openly encomiastic purposes a typical feature of letter-writing: the writer articulates cognizance of his own distance, of space and of time, in relation to the recipient. Thus, Cicero, at the outset of *Fam.* 2.7, congratulates Curio on being elected tribune of the *plebs*: inevitably, his congratulations arrive late, but the writer seems unworried, as *sera gratulatio reprehendi non solet … longe enim absum, audio sero* ('it is not usual to find fault with a tardy congratulation … for I am far off, and news reaches me slowly'). In writing to someone of the same social level, untimeliness does not particularly bother the speaker (although he thematizes it), unlike the elegy of exile, where the motif takes on urgency and assumes a clearly adulatory orientation.

The problem of *tempestivitas* is not only raised in relation to public ceremonies and members of the Augustan house. In *Pont.* 4.11 the poet offers Gallio his

---

3 In the same way, in *Pont.* 4.8, begging Germanicus to mitigate the conditions of his *relegatio*, Ovid presents as an argument in his favor the fact that, if he is transferred closer to Rome, he will be able to celebrate the deeds of his patron *quam minima mora* (v. 88).

condolences on losing his wife, but, rather than eulogizing the deceased, expresses embarrassment for his delay in writing, which nullifies the desired function of a *consolatio*. Only now, in fact, has Ovid received news of the loss his friend has suffered, and his reply can only reach Rome about a year later. The risks inherent in the operation are obvious: a *consolatio intempestiva* may reawaken, rather than attenuate, a grief that had since been assuaged (ll. 17–20). But this consideration, which we also find in Statius' reflections,[4] is combined with another: the recipient might have remarried in the meantime, and a poem of consolation regarding the previous spouse might seem somewhat out of place. On this cheerful note the epistle ends (ll. 21f.):

> Adde, quod – atque utinam verum mihi venerit omen! –
> coniugio felix iam potes esse novo.

> Moreover – and may the omen I speak become true –
> you may already be happy through a new marriage! (transl. Wheeler, slightly modified)

Significantly, it is the only consolatory text to be found in the collection, and is also the shortest of the *epistulae* from Pontus (11 distichs): the *brevitas*, which is typical of the epistolary *festinatio* and often referred to by Cicero,[5] is here also due to the specific choice not to develop *topoi* that might be inappropriate, and to foreground the difficulty of identifying the subject of the poem. The epistle closes with an unexpected and insouciant twist that is almost double-faced, as if anticipating a possible development in events that has taken place in the meantime.[6]

In other letters from Pontus, the *festinatio* is inflected as a 'pure' adherence to epistolary modes: these poems are extraneous to the celebration of a specific event and embody haste on the author's part to re-establish or revive contact with a distant friend and with the Roman public. For example, the end of *Tr.* 1.1, ll. 123f., is directed to the *liber* that is about to head for the capital:

> plura quidem mandare tibi, si quaeris, habebam,
> sed vereor tardae causa fuisse viae.

---

4 Affinities between *Pont.* 4.11 and Statius' *consolationes* are noted by Lechi 1978, 14; for Statius see *infra* n. 20.

5 See, for example, Cic. *Fam.* 12.22a.2 *plura scripsissem nisi tui festinarent*; 15.18.1f. *longior epistula fuisset ... sed flagitat tabellarius*; *Att.* 5.17.2 *nunc propero, perscribam ad te paucis diebus omnia.*

6 For Claassen 1999, 24 and 121, it is a jocular reference to Augustus' measures against those who remarried too soon.

> more directions for you, if you ask me, I have been keeping,
>   but I fear to be the cause of lingering delay. (transl. Wheeler)

There is a similar opening to *Tr.* 3.7.1 f., *vade salutatum subito perarata Perillae / littera*, and *Pont.* 2.11.1 f., which sends Rufus a *brevi properatum tempore ... opus* (this certainly refers to a single epistle, but its placing at the end of the book as a kind of farewell may also suggest the book as a whole). These three cases do not refer to a *kairos*, where timing is essential; nonetheless, the suggestion is given that the text was written quickly so as to reach the recipient as soon as possible.

What we have seen so far is enough to show the limitations of explaining *festinatio* or *celeritas* in Ovid in terms of *sprezzatura*, a dissimulated elegance, which would ultimately go back to the reassuring (and awkward) shadow of Callimachus.[7] We should instead bear in mind that it was the specific, innovative situation of the distance from Rome that introduced the motif of *festinatio* to Latin poetry; in some cases it was due to the very nature of letter-writing, fictitiously recreated (the need for haste, often without *plura mandare*, so as to shorten the time of long-distance communication), in others to the need for celebratory pieces not to arrive too late for the occasion, if they are to obtain the desired appreciation and effect.

3 The epigram: Antipater of Thessalonica

A few decades later, the conventions of long-distance writing (a mixture of intensity and prudence) developed by the banished poet would be transferred to long-distance writing for reasons of deference and convention, as part of the social hierarchy and its literary representations. The poetry of the Flavian age written in Rome produced more examples of the panegyric *festinatio*, linked to a specific *kairos*, than epistolary ones (of which there are traces in the twelfth Book of Martial, composed in Bilbilis, from where it was sent to Rome), and it became an expression of the professional poet's pride to be able to compose quickly fine poems of a certain length. We should therefore separate the two concepts of *festinatio* and *brevitas*, so often brought together in letter-writing (and also in the

---

7 See, for example, Helzle 2003 *ad Pont.* 2.11.1 f., where the scholar adds: "vor Martial halte ich dieses Motiv für affektiert, denn schnelle Komposition wurde v. a. von der kallimacheischen Dichtungstheorie verworfen". This fails to take into account letter-writing conventions (identified in the texts from Pontus since Froesch 1968, 158 f.) and can be taken as an example of what Denis Feeney acutely describes as a "pan-Callimachean tendency" in modern criticism (Feeney 2002, 245 n. 28).

consolatio to Gallio), and recognize that something like the opposite is the case: a poet's *festinatio*, to be worthy of mention, has to be applied to sufficiently long texts, for the speed of composition to be regarded as displaying virtuosity. In short, if in letters the *festinatio* conditions the formal aspects of the text, particularly by determining their brevity, in panegyric poetry it is a mode of composition that should not leave a trace on the finished work, and of which we would know nothing if it were not explicitly referred to by the author.

In various cases the fact is introduced without any external reason, almost like a free variant: that is to say, the *kairos* that is the subject of the text is predictable and expected, and the poet could well have written the verses celebrating it unhurriedly. One example is offered by a Greek epigram from the late Augustan age: the note with which Antipater of Thessalonica sends L. Calpurnius Piso Frugi a birthday present of a small book that he has laboriously produced in a single night (presumably, though it is not certain, the one before the happy day), asking him to appreciate the humble gift (*AP* 9.93.1 f. = *GPh* 31.1 f.):

Ἀντίπατρος Πείσωνι γενέθλιον ὤπασε βίβλον
    μικρὴν ἐν δὲ μιῆι νυκτὶ πονησάμενος.

Antipater has given Piso a book for his birthday,
    a little one, the labour of a single night. (transl. Gow-Page)

What would today sound like a *gaffe* if attributed to a book of poetry was clearly welcome to Piso, and it added something to the value of the gift. The speed with which a work is produced is neither a potential source of stylistic faults nor a sign of negligence, but demonstrates technical competence in the service of the eulogy. The concentration in the pentameter of concepts like *agrypnia*, *ponos* and *mikra rhesis* guarantees the quality of the collection, even by Callimachean standards, but it is a level that is paradoxically reached through an effort that is concentrated in time.[8] This text is typical of Greek epigram in Rome, whose authors were urgently aware of the problem of their relation with the previous Hellenistic poets, and is part of the internal dynamics of the dialogue between the two *Garlands*;[9] but it is also useful in various ways for understanding

---

8 It is not clear if we have to understand that he actually composed all the texts in a single night or simply put the book together in that time, using at least in part epigrams already available: in the first case it must have been a rather short collection, in the second it may have been more extensive (see Nauta 2002, 106). The occasional and timely nature of the composition in the *Garland of Philip* is brought out by Argentieri 2007, 161.
9 The poetics of the *Garland of Philip* has yet to be satisfactorily explored. The insistent and original contrast with Hellenistic epigram may explain the choice of *oligostichia*, announced in the proem (*AP* 4.2.5 f. = Philip 1.5 f. *GPh*, with Lausberg 1982, 37–42), and the polemical attitude to

the motif in Latin literature: the *festinatio* is part of a new poetry that can achieve excellence without following the principle of *lima*; it has a role in both poetics and social relations, as part of a homage and a dialogue that is not between equals; it has positive connotations, to the point that it is thematized even when it would be possible not to do so; those using it are professionals of the panegyric and the *Zeitgedicht*, which requires a text of a certain length and substance (in this case it is a book, although a 'small' one); the general reference to haste that we find in letter-writing is sometimes replaced by a precise time reference (here 'just one night', from a few hours to one or two days in the case of Statius' pieces, as we shall see). This last feature serves to overturn the principle of 'length of time' characteristic of *labor limae* (one need only think of the nine years of Cinna's *Zmyrna* in Catul. 95), arousing the reader's admiration.[10]

This leads to a significant corollary: *festinatio* is not identical with improvisation. They are similar, in that both are linked to the figure and technical experience of the professional poet, but they are not wholly overlapping:[11] improvising on a subject that has just been suggested or on an ongoing event is different from composing a text quickly but in the course of a few hours or days. Another difference between the two lies in the fact that, while even amateurs tried to impress by composing a few lines on the spot (there is, for example, Trimalchio's epigram in Petron. 55.2–4), the *festinatio*, which is found in texts of a certain length, was for the professional poet alone.[12]

---

the slavish admirers of Callimachus (called 'Supercallimachi' by Phil. *AP* 11.347 = 61 *GPh*; see, too, *AP* 11.321 = Phil. 60 *GPh* and *AP* 11.322 = Antiphanes 9 *GPh*).

10 We can use these factors to clarify the substantial difference between *festinatio* in celebratory poetry and the motif of haste in Catul. 50, where the language of *festinatio* is absent and the original variation of *agrypnia* and the rapid composition of the poem are not part af a dialogue between two *amici inaequales*; in addition, in the case of Catullus it is a single poem, whereas in Antipater and Martial they are whole books, fairly hefty texts that show their author's professional capacity.

11 For improvisation as part of a professional poet's equipment, see Hardie 1983, 22; 76–85 and 145. The subtle distinction between improvisation and *festinatio* is noted by Nauta 2002, 251. There is a similar distinction in rhetoric: Quintilian appreciates a poet's capacity to improvise and recommends it as an example to orators (10.7.19), but disapproves of haste in writing the text, as, even if the first version is revised and corrected, *manet in rebus temere congestis quae fuit levitas* (10.3.17).

12 It is worth mentioning briefly that we can also establish a difference between the performance of professionals and amateurs in the case of improvisation. We need only recall the virtuoso nature of Archias' verbal acrobatics (Cic. *Arch.* 18 *quotiens ego hunc Archiam vidi ... cum litteram scripsisset nullam, magnum numerum optimorum versuum de eis ipsis rebus, quae tum agerentur, dicere ex tempore! quotiens revocatum eandem rem dicere commutatis verbis atque sententiis!*, 'how often have I seen this man, Archias ... when he had not written a single word, re-

Thus, while pretty well anyone felt able to improvise or toss off a few distichs, a whole book, however short, or a long piece well over a hundred lines, required a skilled poet: Martial himself reminded his readers of this, putting in his place the author of a few well-turned epigrams with the words *facile est epigrammata belle / scribere, sed librum scribere difficile est*, 'it's easy to write epigrams prettily, but to write a book is hard' (7.85.3f.). On this, Alex Hardie reminds us that, in a period of widespread literary dabbling, the professionals needed strategies to distinguish themselves from amateurs to mark out the value of their 'product'.[13] This is indirectly confirmed by the fact that there is no trace of the *topos* in Pliny's letters, where the problem of finding the time to give to poetry has different connotations, being linked, as we know, to the question of the ruling class's *otium*.[14]

4 The epigram: Martial

The inclusion of the motif as a free variant is also to be found in Martial. The last epigram of the *Xenia* gives Domitian crowns of roses (13.127):

> Dat festinatas, Caesar, tibi bruma coronas:
>   quondam veris erat, nunc tua facta rosa est.

> Winter gives you hurried garlands, Caesar.
>   The rose used to be spring's, now it has become yours.
>   (transl. Shackleton Bailey, slightly modified)

The locution *festinatas coronas* indicates crowns of blooming roses on the eve of the Saturnalia, the festival during which the *Xenia* are explicitly placed (see 13.1):

---

peat extempore a great number of admirable verses on the very events which were passing at the moment! how often have I seen him go back, and describe the same thing over again with an entire change of language and ideas!'), or Antipater of Sidon (Cic. *de Orat.* 3.194), or the case of the boy prodigy Sulpicius Maximus, as illustrated by Hardie 1983, 83f., as part of an account of professional poets who provided these kinds of firework displays; there are some thoughtful suggestions on the manner and dignity of 'professional' improvisations in Rome in Gentili 1985, writing about the phenomenon in eighteenth-century Italy.

13 Hardie 1983, 49.

14 The most significant passage is *Ep.* 4.14, on the subject of hendecasyllabes, *quibus in vehiculo, in balineo, inter cenam oblectamus otium temporis* ('with which I pass my leisure hours pleasantly when driving, or in the bath, or at dinner'). The attitude towards poetry-writing is typical of the upper class: note, for example, that, among Pliny's poetry-writing friends, only Caninius Rufus was an epic poet, writing in a demanding, large-scale genre that could not be produced in one's spare time.

in honour of the emperor, the roses have bloomed without awaiting the spring. *Festinatas coronas* has often been seen as containing a meta-literary sugges-tion:[15] although poetological interpretations, taken to excess, can easily become banal – we must resign ourselves to the fact that a drop of water is sometimes a drop of water, and a rose is a rose – in this case I am inclined to go down this road, mainly because the couplet comes at the end of the book, a prominent po-sition that Martial often used to include declarations and cues for poetics and dialogue with his readers. In this particular distich the motif is not linked to pos-sible defects in the *libellus* due to its being rushed, but is a guarantee of quality: just as the rose, although it has blossomed out of season, has no faults, so Mar-tial's collection of poems, though prepared in haste, shows no signs of weak-ness; on the contrary, the *festinatio* increases the value of both objects.[16]

As another example, in epigram 2.91,[17] Martial begs Domitian to renew his *ius trium liberorum* conceded by Titus, and reminds the emperor, as a sign of merit, that he has often dedicated and donated books of epigrams in the past; they were probably collections now lost containing nothing but panegyrics, such as the *Liber de spectaculis* (also a *festinata* collection, see the epigram 31 [35])[18] or the *libellus* on the game of hares and lions, which later became part of the first collection of varied epigrams (see 1.6 with Citroni 1975 *ad loc.*). Here below I quote the beginning of Mart. 2.91 (ll. 1–4):

> Rerum certa salus, terrarum gloria, Caesar,
> sospite quo magnos credimus esse deos,

---

15 See Fowler 1995, 55 and also Barchiesi 2005b, 325, who links him to the "hasty" poetics of Martial's books of epigrams.

16 Flowering out of season is a mark of distinction and value much appreciated in the Flavian age, as is shown by Fabbrini 2007, 253–255. By contrast, for Leary 2001 *ad loc.* "The word [*fes-tinatas*] has, nonetheless, also to refer negatively to M's book, allegedly rushed to be in time for the *Saturnalia*". An interesting possible comparison is offered by Crinagoras, *AP* 6.346 = 6 GPh, where, sending winter roses to a beautiful lady (Antonia Minor?), the poet notes in the final dis-tich that the flowers could not wait (*mimnein*) for the spring sun: they were in a hurry.

17 The passage is debated: as well as the survey of interpretations in Williams 2004 *ad loc.*, see also Holzberg 2004, 251 and Hinds 2007. The dating is fixed by Daube 1976, followed by Nauta 2002, 336f., in the year 82, when, on coming to the throne, Domitian confirmed all the honours distributed by his brother Titus, including the concession of the *ius trium liberorum* to Martial.

18 It may be a fragment, or the final epigram in the collection. Coleman 2006 *ad loc.* sums up the discussion; see also Weinreich 1928, 24–28 (who suggests it is the conclusion of the final epi-gram).

si festinatis totiens tibi lecta libellis[19]
    detinuere oculos carmina nostra tuos...

Caesar, the world's sure salvation, glory of the earth,
    whose safety is our assurance that the great gods exist,
if my poems, so often read by you in hurried little volumes,
    have detained your eyes... (transl. Shackleton Bailey, slightly modified)

In a lofty, formal context Martial calls his booklets *festinati:* this means it was a characteristic invulnerable to criticism and rooted in strategies of eulogy that were part of a dialogue between two *inaequales*. A nuance of modesty can certainly be noted in the passages analysed, but to me it seems linked more to the poetics of the epigram, a minor genre *par excellence*, than to the hasty composition. Indeed, this last feature has the function of increasing the merit of the humble poetic object and underlining both the author's virtuosity and his solicitude for its powerful recipient.

5 Statius' *Silvae*

In Statius the concept appears in a more complex form. The references to the *celeritas* of his father as a poet confirm that it was a merit and ability of professionals. Statius' *pater* had completed a piece on the destruction of the Capitol before the fire was wholly put out, more quickly than the flames themselves, *multum facibus velocior ipsis* (*Silv.* 5.3.201). That *tempestivitas*, considered a value for the panegyric and occasional poetry, emerges clearly also from Statius' rebuke to Julius Menecrates for failing to inform him of the birth of his son: Statius came to hear of the happy event *vulgari fama* instead of in a letter sent *protinus*, meaning that, inevitably, his celebration of it is now both late and ineffec-

---

19 The reading found in all the manuscripts, *tibi lecta*, went unquestioned till Shackleton Bailey 1978, who suggested *collecta*, a conjecture later included in his editions for Teubner and Loeb. His main argument is that *tibi lecta* would be a repetition of *detinuere oculos* in the following line. Citroni 1988, 5, followed by Williams 2004 *ad loc.*, defends the original text while admitting that the suggested correction is attractive: *lecta* and *detinuere oculos* would be a climax, in that the second expression indicates the reader's intense attention. But a difficulty remains: cautious expressions as *contigeris si ... libellos* (1.4.1) and *tu tantum accipias: ego te legisse putabo* (5.1.9), used in offering the book to Domitian, make it a little doubtful that *totiens tibi lecta* captures the right tone. The solution of the problem may be linked to the difference between the gift to the emperor of an essentially celebratory private book and that of a wide-ranging collection of epigrams marked by *varietas* and humour.

tive, *tardus inersque* (*Silv.* 4.8.32–42); we might also recall the reflections on the delicate question of the best timing of a *consolatio*.[20]

However, *celeritas* seems ambivalent in the text in which it is presented most extensively and systematically – the *praefatio* to the first book of the *Silvae*. Statius' evident pride at composing hundreds of lines in a very short time (*biduo*; *singulis diebus*; *uno die*; *intra moram cenae*), his claim that many will not believe him, and his invitation to some of the patrons eulogised (Stella, Vopiscus, Etruscus) to bear witness in his favour, have a corrective function in the fear that the hurried lines might have traces of the absence of *lima* (*Silv.* 1 *praef.* 1–7 and 11–15):

> Diu multumque dubitavi, Stella, iuvenis optime [...] an hos libellos, qui mihi subito calore et quadam festinandi voluptate fluxerunt [...] congregatos ipse dimitterem. quid enim ⟨opus eo tempore hos⟩ quoque auctoritate editionis onerari, quo adhuc pro Thebaide mea, quamvis me reliquerit, timeo? [...] sed apud ceteros necesse est multum illis pereat ex venia, cum amiserint quam solam habuerunt gratiam celeritatis. nullum enim ex illis biduo longius tractum, quaedam et in singulis diebus effusa. quam timeo ne verum istuc versus quoque ipsi de se probent!

> Much and long have I hesitated, my excellent Stella [...] whether I should assemble these little pieces, which streamed from my pen in the heat of the moment [...] For why ⟨should they too⟩ be burdened with the authority of publication ⟨at a time⟩ when I am still anxious for my *Thebaid*, although it has left my hands? [...] But with the general public they must necessarily forfeit much of its indulgence since they have lost their only commendation, that of celerity. For none of them took longer then a couple of days to compose, some were turned out in a single day. How I fear that the verses themselves will testify on their own behalf to the truth of what I say! (transl. Shackleton Bailey)

This clear contrast between ostentation of one's capacities and fear of negative criticism (which has no exact parallel in the *festinatio* of Ovid, Antipater and Martial) has been seen variously as a *topos* of modesty, a proud declaration, and an ambiguous hovering between self-promotion and anxiety.[21] Actually,

---

20 *Silv.* 2 *praef.* 7–9 and 1.1–8 presents the question of the *festinatio* in the case of a consolatory text, underlining its potentially counterproductive results (v. 8: *intempesta cano*), but observing at the same time *cum paene supervacua sint tarda solacia* (*praef.* 11 f.); by contrast, the *consolatio* to Abascantus on the death of his wife Priscilla (*Silv.* 5.1) arrived after a year, when his grief was no longer so strong as to inhibit the function of a poetic gift, but still sufficiently alive to give it a meaning (ll. 16–32, with Gibson 2006 *ad loc.*).

21 Hence the reasonable but partial judgments of Newlands 2002, 33 f. (affinity between Statius' *celeritas* and Catullus' *sprezzatura*) and Rühl 2006, 111 (expression of pride); Johannsen 2006, especially 246–248 and 254 sees an alternation and ambivalence between pride and concern, the latter caused by the lack of *lima*. Previously Dams 1970, 152 had claimed: "das lyrische Gedicht ist nicht mehr die Frucht durchgearbeiteter Nächte, sondern wird mehr oder weniger

these contrasting views can be united and the ambiguity clarified if we bear in mind the two stages in the diffusion of the *Silvae*: first, immediate, private circulation through performance or the gift of individual pieces to the recipient of each, and, later, publication in a larger collection of poems intended for the generic reader.

The question is part of the larger one of whether and how much it is appropriate to collect and publish texts, which were originally dedicated to a patron and linked to a specific occasion; that is, whether a poem that is by its very nature ephemeral and rushed has enough prestige and dignity to be a worthy item of a *Gedichtbuch* that is written to last.[22] Statius was proud of his virtuosity as a celebratory poet, but he displayed great caution towards the later, not obvious, channel of circulation for those texts: after all, the further removed they are from both the event that suggested them and their original context, the less effective is the *gratia celeritatis* and the text as *Zeitgedicht*. On this point the poet expects negative criticism, to which he replies brusquely in the preface to the fourth book (the first in which the motif of the *festinatio* does not appear explicitly).[23] Pliny was faced with a somewhat similar problem a few years later, in hoping that his letters when collected for publication would gain the interest of readers *quamvis iam gratiam novitatis exuerint* (*Ep.* 1.2.6).

Celeritas allows the immediate, effective celebration of an event and therefore arouses wonder and admiration in the context of performance, but it raises a basic question when the hurried pieces are part of a *Gedichtbuch*. A collection of poems which aspires to the condition of literature and not just brilliant *divertissement* should not usually be rushed; on the contrary, one would expect it to be clearly connected with the poetics of *labor limae*.[24] Pliny once again provides

---

nachlässig hingeworfen": but the *festinatio* does not seem to me to contain a significant degree of *Nachlässigkeit*.

22 Less than a century earlier Ovid has handled these cases quite differently, not including in the books for the general public the *epicedium* for Messalla and the *epithalamium* for Fabius Maximus. He himself tells us of these works in *Pont.* 1.7.29 f.; 1.2.129–132, i.e. in a period of his career when public and private were no longer clearly distinguished (see Citroni 1995, 459–463).

23 Statius makes a point of fearing the public's judgment in the preface to the first book of the *Silvae*, while he ostentatiously ignores it in the preface to the fourth book. The relation between the two texts is dealt with by Johannsen 2006, 294–296; on the dual readership of the *Silvae* see Rosati 2015.

24 A stimulating account is offered by Gentili 1985: a propos of eighteenth-century improvisations, the scholar notes the absurdity of judging this kind of poetry by parameters that are normally used for evaluating written poetry (384). However, these parameters are perfectly legitimate when, as in Statius' *Silvae*, the text of the performance becomes part of a *Gedichtbuch*.

a partial comparison when he claims to have chosen for publication the letters written with the most care (*Ep.* 1.1.1 ... *epistulas, si quas paulo curatius scripsissem*).

The motif of *celeritas* in Statius' first *praefatio* therefore performs various functions: it promotes the work, displays the author's technical mastery, and acts as a 'lightning conductor' for the decision to publish the items in the book.[25] Insisting on the hasty character of many *silvae* and specifying the details of the time of composition, Statius tells the generic reader something he would otherwise be unaware of, displays his technical talent, and safeguards himself from any criticism either of the operation in itself or of lack of a proper revision of the text.

Finally, let us note that the poet insists on the lack of a long *emendatio* as being due to the essential conditions of a piece of homage and a deliberate choice to follow them, and not to any incapacity or idleness on his part. When pieces composed in accordance with the dictates of *celeritas* are published in volume form, he does not fail to recall that he is the author of epic poems composed with *labor limae*, and, from the very first *praefatio*, emphasizes the *Thebaid* as his most authentic and committed work. More generally, there are frequent references both to the *Thebaid* and the *Achilleid* in the course of the *Silvae*:[26] in a poetry which does not require, and by nature barely tolerates, corrections, Statius contrives to present himself as a careful craftsman, as the author of epic poems contrasting with or complementing the *Silvae*, the significance of the *festinatio* in his work overall being limited.

Comparison with Martial yields further elements, if we accept the equation by which one of his booklets (from the hypothetical one dedicated to the game of hares and lions – about sixty lines in all – to the single-theme collections of *Xenia* or *De spectaculis* – between 200 and 300 lines) corresponds, in length and partly in function, to a single *silva*, and, similarly, a book of various epigrams corresponds to a book of *Silvae*. Here I draw on an important study by Mario Citroni: up to a certain point in his career Martial kept the two spheres of homage and entertainment separate while, from the first book of epigrams of various nature onwards, he mixed tones and themes, speaking above all to

---

Rühl 2006, 128–135 has some good observations on the distance between a 'spoken' and a 'written' text.

25 These functions are recognized by Gérard Genette to the "préface originale" (Genette 1987, 183–194). Johannsen 2006 verifies the applicability of the concept of 'paratext' to Statius prefatory epistles; on the "Roman paratext" see Jansen 2014.

26 See *Silv.* 4.4.87–100; 7.7 f. and 21–24; 5.5.36 f.; to the *Achilleid* alone in *Silv.* 5.2.163, and to the *Thebaid* in *Silv.* 5.3.233 f. Some useful points are in Johannsen 2006, 307–313 and Newlands 2009.

the generic reader.[27] Now, the first three cases of *festinatio* in Martial (the probable conclusion of the *De spectaculis*, that of the *Xenia* and the reference to the *libelli* in 2.91) are all addressed to a *princeps* and appear in, or refer to, single-themed collections. Of these, the *De spectaculis* and the *libelli* for Domitian are eulogistic, while the *Xenia* are part of the occasional poetry dedicated to the Saturnalia and all things concerning them (games, food and diversion). From the first book of epigrams of various nature onwards, the motif of the author's haste or impatience in writing the work as part of a homage disappears, while an attitude partly similar is attributed, in different circumstances and for different reasons, to the book itself (which in 1.3 is raring to be put on the market, taking as a model Horace's *liber-puer*, *Ep.* 1.20) or to the *librarius* (whose *properare* causes errors in the text put on sale, see 2.8). In short, the time in question is no longer that of writing but of publishing (*haec una peragit librarius hora*, 2.1.5; 8.4) a volume destined to face the public (1.3; 2.1). If a *libellus* like the *De spectaculis* could be composed quickly, its *festinatio* even giving it a sort of added value, the later choice of publishing larger collections intended for different kinds of readers indicates that Martial was explicitly laying claim to the lofty, dignified literary character of his poetry, which was now removed from the practical, ephemeral dimension of the *Zeitgedicht* and, therefore, from the need to write in haste or to display that fact. In Martial, then, the motif of the *festinatio* emerges very clearly indeed before the poet's artistic advance in the books of various epigrams, in which he took his texts out of the exclusive ambit of occasional and 'entertainment' poetry.

   Both Martial and Statius claim to be able to write in haste, in accordance with a modern, useful and even necessary principle whose aim is to manage to communicate with friends who are *inaequales* and powerful; both, however, employ a strategy aimed at not reducing the representation of their talents and literary commitments to a superficially impressive gift. Their works are sharply divided into two categories, Martial's essentially diachronically (in the context of a 'career' devoted to the genre of the epigram yet also with fairly distinct phases), Statius synchronically, his poetry being divided into two literary genres at the antipodes from each other (following a lofty model, traced back in the first *praefatio* to Homer and Virgil, no less). In this way each author circumscribes the place of the hurried elements in his poetry, displaying his capacity for that kind of writing while at the same time identifying it as only one aspect of his literary commitment.

------

27 Citroni 1988, 5 f. For the *Xenia* see the contribution on the literature for the Saturnalia by Citroni 1992.

6 Martial again

On the margins of the general picture are the two cases in which Martial again takes the motif as his subject at the end of his career, in a collection of varied epigrams for the generic public: the second edition of the tenth book and the twelfth book. And so, to conclude, let us look at these (apparent) exceptions to the tendency that links the *festinatio* to private or occasional verses. Epigram 10.2 is the proem to the second edition of the book, which was published in 99, probably with the principal aim of expunging and replacing the items in honour of Domitian that abounded in the first edition of 95. It therefore documents a delicate transition in the poet's career (ll. 1–4):

> Festinata prius, decimi mihi cura libelli
>   elapsum manibus nunc revocavit opus.
> Nota leges quaedam sed lima rasa recenti;
>   pars nova maior erit: lector, utrique fave...

> In composing my tenth little book, too hastily issued earlier,
>   I have now recalled the work that then slipped from my hands.
> Some of the pieces you will read are alread known, but polished with a recent file,
>   the greater part will be new. Reader, wish well to both... (transl. Shackleton Bailey)

This is the only instance in which the *festinatio* is found in a text aimed directly at the generic reader, disengaged from the function of homage; and it is the only one in which it is presented as negative, requiring later correction. What made the *cura* of the previous edition so hasty is not clarified: the image of the book slipping from his hands is presented as accidental rather than as a deliberate choice of the poet's, giving a curiously reduced impression of Martial's control over his work and his responsibility for it. If we accept the conjecture that the first edition of the tenth book was strongly marked by court eulogy, it is fairly easy to read between the lines (as has been suggested)[28] the idea of a *festinatio* deriving from the desire to please the emperor: *festinata cura* would allude to his adulation of Domitian, a characteristic that could be noted as needing revision, particularly with the advent of Trajan. Martial refers the *festinatio*, here for the first time, to a book of varied epigrams, but with the aim of denying its appropriateness in that context.

It is worth dwelling longer on the introductory epistle to the twelfth book, written after Martial's return to Spain. After complaining about the boredom of

---

28 See Citroni 1988, 6; Buongiovanni 2009, 520 f. I have dealt at greater length with this text in Merli 2013, 176–178.

provincial life, the author claims to have prepared the collection *paucissimis die-bus* as a welcoming gift to his patron Terentius Priscus; the text ends with a request to the recipient to *diligenter aestimare et excutere* the epigrams so as to send to Rome a book originating in Spain (*Hispaniensis*) but not of Spanish race (*Hispanus*), and so worthy of the demanding readers of the capital.

This text has a place to itself in our survey as it takes up the motifs of 'writing from afar' and nostalgia for Rome, typical of the Ovid of Tomis. The *festinatio* is introduced in relation to a patron and a private occasion (the arrival of Priscus), but is grafted onto the opening of a collection for a wider public (the end of the epistle, like that of epigram 2, leaves no doubt as to that):[29] the personal gesture, an expression of affection and private homage, is inextricably linked to the long-distance dialogue with the Roman public. It is the only case in which the motif has no negative connotations in a collection of varied epigrams, creating an original and specific variant that combines and synthesizes aspects of the epistolary *festinatio* and panegyric poetry.

In this case the *festinatio* is partly connected with the Roman reader. It certainly suggests a private communication to Terentius Priscus, hastening to meet his requests, but Martial also succeeds at last in sending a new book to the Roman public (it is not clear whether by exploiting his patron's return or through some other means). In addition, linked as it is to the figure of the professional, able to respond to the promptings of the *kairos*, the *festinatio* indicates here that the poet can still do his job despite the rather unstimulating cultural context in which he lives:[30] in short, the motif reassures both Priscus and Roman readers who had had no news of Martial for three years. This is very unlike both the *topos* of modesty and the fear that haste has made the verses weak: note that in the request for corrections, any defects in the *liber* would not derive from the *festinatio*, but from the dull Spanish environment (a provincial book is by nature inferior to one originating in Rome, as Martial had already declared in the

---

29 A vexed question in Martial philology is whether the *libellus* for Terentius Priscus substantially coincides with the book designed for publication in Rome: the general tendency for some years has been in favour of the idea, see Nauta 2002, 115 f. and 125 f.; Lorenz 2002, 234–238; Johannsen 2006, 107 f.; however, the thorny question remains open as to whether the *liber* is identical with the twelfth book in the form is has reached us or whether some epigrams were added by a publisher after Martial's death (as conjectured first by Lehmann 1931, 48–52).

30 It is not, then, a motif that indicates "potentielle Qualitätsmängel" of the book, or a "stereotype Herabsetzung des eigenen Werkes" on Martial's part (see Johannsen 2006, 189), but rather the "typical boast of a professional author" (Bowie 1988, 27). Martial does not seem really worried that the book might be poorly received, but is confident that a few verses will be enough for readers to recognize it as his own: *versus duos tresve legantur, / clamabunt omnes te, liber, esse meum* (12.2.17 f.).

proem to the third book, composed in Cisalpine Gaul). Ovid similarly down-played the texts from Pontus as weak or inferior to his previous ones, not be-cause they were written in haste, but because they were uprooted from the cul-tural and intellectual *humus* of the capital (see, e. g., the declarations in *Tr.* 3.14 and 4.1, and in *Pont.* 1.5).

More generally, while Titus and Domitian were the recipients of the *festinatio* in early Martial, in the last two books of various epigrams the *festinatio* itself is placed, directly or indirectly, in relation to the anonymous 'devoted reader': in the tenth book the *amicus lector* and in the twelfth, through Priscus, the demand-ing Roman public, which, in the prefatory epistle, takes on the personal charac-ter of a distant and much-missed friend in whom we must recognize the real re-cipient of the Spanish collection. Martial uses the motif freely, no longer fearing that his work may be confused with ephemeral poetry, but trusting his capacity and his readers' affection.

7 Conclusions

The earliest examples of the *festinatio* 'of the poets' in Latin are in the Ovid of Tomis, where it is grafted onto real geographical distance and the conventions of epistolography; the motif is then transferred to texts composed in Rome as a communication between *inaequales*. Without exception they are fairly extend-ed pieces: no longer single letters, but *libelli* of epigrams or poems in hexameters of several hundred lines. Sometimes the time of writing is specified, with a dis-play of the author's virtuosity: he is able to compose good verse in defiance of the principle of *labor limae*. Yet technical pride is not enough to neutralize the sense of the restrictions of a celebratory poem or a *divertissement*: significantly, in Martial's epigram the *topos* refers to single-theme *libelli* and is abandoned with the first book of various epigrams. Statius' decision to publish overtly *fes-tinati* pieces, which he had already used in a private context, in books for the generic reader seems a daring innovation. He was the first to thematize the *topos* in large collections for the Roman public, and the ambiguity and uncer-tainty of the concept in his work derive from this peculiar situation.

We are faced with a specific, characteristic feature of imperial celebratory poetry. This feature, by contrasting with *labor limae* but not to be subsumed in actual improvisation, both a compliment to the recipient and a demonstration of skill by authors who refused to be merely professional virtuosi, was a delicate and awkward choice, in that pieces written in haste were unlikely to be granted the full dignity of art. Both Martial and Statius practised – sometimes ostenta-tiously – the *festinatio* in their writing, yet at the same time brought other strategies into play to distinguish themselves and their poetry from this fashion, which could only be one of the features of their artistry and their ambition to become future classics.

Alessia Bonadeo

Scattered remarks about the 'non-genre' of Statius' *Silvae*. The construction of a minor canon?

First of all I want to clear up my classification of the *Silvae* as 'non-genre'. Far from being a provocation, this label highlights how Statius' occasional poetry eludes, if not resists, precise identifications in terms of genre. With their *varietas* and *polyeideia*, the *Silvae* (the single poems as well as the whole collection) display a marked propensity to the crossing and diffraction of modules and models of genre, whose codes are disassembled and reassembled in new ways each time according to the *kairos*.

As is well known – and this prevents me from giving the *status quaestionis*[1] in detail – it is almost impossible to draw the exact generic framework of the *Silvae*, or to imagine a single genetic matrix for them, whether based on modern categories of genre or on the classifications of ancient rhetorical handbooks. The complex semantics of the title does not help settle the issue. I do not want to go into this *vexata quaestio*[2] because, whatever solution is accepted, it does not seem possible to infer any specific indication from what is only a title,[3] and not a label of genre loaded with precise poetological connotations.

Even the *praefationes* to the single books, despite their strong metaliterary character, do not display a greater awareness of a generic identity. The lexical range employed by Statius, when referring both to single poems and the collection as a whole, is heterogeneous and non-specific: *libellus, libelli quasi epigrammatis loco scripti, opusculum, carmen, egloga, sermo*.[4] Such labels are not to be interpreted in a technical sense, according to current categorizations; they instead testify to a certain instability in terminology and classification that characterizes the lexicon of a genre still under construction. An example of the same attitude is represented by Plin. *Ep.* 4.14.8 f., a passage which establishes the in-

---

1 Bonadeo 2010, 129 ff. with a bibliographical survey.
2 See again Bonadeo 2010, 151 ff. and now Malaspina 2013.
3 *Sic* Frère / Izaac 1944, xxviii.
4 *Libellus* (1 *praef.* 18; 30; 3 *praef.* 12; 24) is employed also in the plural (1 *praef.* 3; 3 *praef.* 3) to indicate all the poems collected in a *liber*, while in 2 *praef.* 16 f. the phrasing *libelli quasi epigrammatis loco scripti* alludes to a group of poems sharing an analogous *stili facilitas*. As for the other terms: *opusculum* (4 *praef.* 23; the plural in 2 *praef.* 3 is referred to the poems of a whole *liber*, in 4 *praef.* 3 to a set of *libri*), *carmen* (2 *praef.* 11), *egloga* (3 *praef.* 21; 4 *praef.* 20), *sermo* (3 *praef.* 23).

https://doi.org/10.1515/9783110534436-009

terchangeability of terms such as *epigrammata*, *idyllia*, *eclogas* and *poematia*.[5] The result is the convergence of these classifications towards a general characterization of occasional poetry as *minor*, in contradistinction to the implicit benchmark of those *eidē* traditionally ranked as high order.

A negative definition of the *Silvae* in relation to epic poetry appears already in the prefatory epistle to the first book of the collection: here the *Silvae* are characterized as an experiment, whose right to be published seems even more uncertain since Statius is still anxious about his recently published *Thebaid*, a masterpiece that meets the requirements of traditional aesthetic canons (Stat. *Silv.* 1 *praef.* 1–15):

> Diu multumque dubitavi, Stella, iuvenis optime et in studiis nostris eminentissime, qua parte voluisti, an hos libellos, qui mihi subito calore et quadam festinandi voluptate fluxerunt, cum singuli de sinu meo profugissent, congregatos ipse dimitterem. <u>Quid enim oportebat hos quoque auctoritate editionis onerari, quando adhuc pro *Thebaide* mea, quamvis me reliquerit, timeo? Sed et *Culicem* legimus et *Batrachomachiam* etiam agnoscimus, nec quisquam est inlustrium poetarum qui non aliquid operibus suis stilo remissiore praeluserit.</u> Quid quod haec serum erat continere, cum illa vos certe, quorum honori data sunt, haberetis? Sed apud ceteros necesse est multum illis pereat ex venia, cum amiserint quam solam habuerunt gratiam celeritatis. Nullum enim ex illis biduo longius tractum, quaedam et in singulis diebus effusa. Quam timeo ne verum istuc versus quoque ipsi de se probent!

> Long and hard, Stella, excellent young man, very brilliant in our studies, for that area you chose to cultivate, I was in doubt whether I should collect these small pieces, that, sprung out of my mind one by one, flowed for a sudden inspiration and a kind of pleasure of haste, and bring them out myself. <u>What was the need, in fact, to burden them with the weight of publication since I am still anxious for my *Thebaid* though it has left me? Yet we read the *Culex* and also keep on reading the *Batrachomachia* and there is none of the distinguished poets who did not precede his works with some divertissement in a minor key.</u> What about the fact that it was too late to keep them back since you and the others, in whose honour they were conceived, had them already in your hands? But they cannot but lose much of the indulgence among other people because they have lost the only quality they had: immediacy. None of them, in fact, had a gestation period of more than two days, and some were also produced in a single day. How I fear that the verses themselves will show that what I say is true!

---

5 *Unum illud praedicendum videtur, cogitare me has meas nugas ita inscribere 'hendecasyllabi', qui titulus sola metri lege constringitur. Proinde, sive epigrammata sive idyllia sive eclogas sive, ut multi, poematia seu quod aliud vocare malueris, licebit voces; ego tantum hendecasyllabos praesto* ('Only this – it seems – must be stated beforehand: I think I'll name these trifles of mine 'hendecasyllables', a title responding merely to a metrical principle. So you can call them epigrams or idylls or eclogues or, as many do, little pieces or anyhow you prefer; however, I suggest only 'hendecasyllables''). Translations of Latin passages are my own.

Despite a certain initial understatement, Statius' intentions are clear. On one hand, he aims to play the role of *vates* and ties this aspiration to epic verse. At the same time, he is also aware that his prestige depends on a product of greater social marketability (i.e. occasional poetry) and, for that reason, he tries to find a theoretical justification for the pragmatic bipartition of his work. On the other hand, as Gianpiero Rosati has shown,[6] when the publication of the collection extends the circle of recipients from an *entourage* of clients/addressees to a wider audience of intellectuals, the poet aims at forestalling criticism of the extemporaneous character of his own texts, which is marked by a poetics – or, at least, a *cliché* – of *impromptu* and/or *festinatio*. These trends could be exhibited to a new generation of patrons interested in popular (or 'consumer') literature, but were destined to receive a cold reception by educated readers anchored to traditional parameters of aesthetic evaluation. Within such a horizon of expectation, the lack of *mora* and *labor limae* could penalize poems that *celeritas* had legitimized in relation to the *kairos*. Safer, on the contrary, was now in reality the favourable reception of the *Thebaid*, which was 'for twelve years the object of wakeful toil' by the poet (*Theb.* 12.811 *bissenos multum vigilata per annos*). This famous *explicit*, not so distant in time from the *praefatio* of *Silvae* Book 1, shows the apparent paradox of a *poema longum* which, thanks to its multi-year gestation, has undergone the poet's patient and wakeful chisel work, the Callimachean and neoteric *labor limae*.

In this perspective, Statius' strategy of preventive defence aims at gaining him credit as an epic *auctor* composing in a minor key; in order to secure a favourable reception to his *Silvae*, he exhibits by way of 'safe-conduct' the authorship of the epic poem (*Thebais mea*) in relation to which occasional poetry is presented as a *praelusio*.

This is a puzzling definition, whose etymological meaning collides both with Statius' statement about the *Thebaid*'s priority over the *Silvae* and with the date of the single poems, which cannot precede the composition of the epic poem. Giuseppe Aricò[7] has proposed a radical solution to this problem, which leaves aside the welter of hypotheses trying to explain the term and make it plausible on the chronological level.[8] According to him *prae-* is endowed with an axiological (not chronological) meaning: as a consequence, *praelusio* establishes an ascending taxonomy of the *Silvae* and the epos on a value scale.

---

6 Rosati 2015.
7 Aricò 1972, 4 ff. and Aricò 2008, 1 ff.
8 Cf. van Dam 1984, 3; Newlands 2008, 236 f.; Newlands 2011, 4.

Be it primary or not, the aesthetic-ideological aspect in the use of *praeludere* seems to me undeniable. This is confirmed by the contiguous determinative syntagm *stilo remissiore* ('in a minor key') and by the other etymological component of the term: *ludere*. The note of relaxation inherent in the concept of *lusus* cannot but confirm the subordinate position and the nature of *minora* attributed to the *Silvae* that are thus placed in the rank of poetic *otium* in comparison with what is configured as the *negotium* of epic in a real life where poetry is the only activity, totalizing and all-encompassing.[9]

A contribution to the definition of the *Silvae* in relation to *epos* is given also by the pairing of the *Culex* with the *Batrachomachia*. These are *praelusiones*, juvenile experiments in a minor key; nevertheless, the approval they enjoy is sanctioned by their ongoing diffusion. *Sed et* Culicem *legimus et* Batrachomachiam *etiam agnoscimus*, Statius says, which I would translate 'Yet we read the *Culex* and also keep on reading the *Batrachomachia*'. In the light of Statius' bilingualism, I believe that the parallel with the Greek ἀναγιγνώσκω proves essential for understanding the semantics of *agnosco* in context.[10] The verb is sometimes interpreted in the estimative sense of *probare, adprobare*,[11] and sometimes in the sense of 'recognizing, recognizing as authentic', with a possible allusion to the dubious Homeric authorship of the text.[12] However, the resemblance in sound, the homology of the verbal roots, and the often indifferent value of the prefix allow the activation of a semantic calque that transfers to *agnosco* the proper meaning of ἀναγιγνώσκω ('to know well, know again' and also 'to read'). The result is the creation of a semantic neologism or, probably, a *hapax* alluding to the persistence of a good knowledge of the poem, supported by a practice of reading or, perhaps, also of reading and rereading for the purpose of learning.[13] This *transfert* could also have been favoured by the intention of finding a Greek-sounding counterpart to the previous *legere* in order to outline a sequence 'Latin verb + Latin title / Greek title + Greek verb'. The hyper-connotation, then, in an evaluative/eulogistic sense of both the lexemes (not only of *agnosco*) can be deduced implicitly from the sanction of a work's prestige implied, as I mentioned just now, by its being read and reread over time.

---

9 For Statius' revising the categories of *otium* and *negotium* cf. Bonadeo 2012, 128 ff.
10 For this opinion cf. also Lieberman 2010 *ad loc.*, who mentions the presence in the *Silvae* of other bold calques from Greek.
11 Cf. *ThlL* I 1360.
12 E.g. Rostagni 1961², 91 and n. 43; Traglia / Aricò 1980 *ad l.*; Canali 2000 *ad l.*
13 The hypothesis of a school use of the *Batrachomachia* from the imperial age onwards is fostered e.g. by Fusillo 1988, 43.

Conversely, I am not much comfortable with the hypothesis of Statius' inter-vention in the debate about the Homeric authenticity of the *Batrachomachia*. However I do not intend to go into the thorny question of Statius' knowledge of the authorship of the poem. My considerations instead are focused on the tex-ture of the *praefatio*; here, even the alleged hypothesis of the non-authenticity of the two short poems would spoil the logic of the argumentation: indeed, Statius is legitimizing *minora* by a principle of *auctoritas*. It is not their intrinsic artistic quality that provides the *Culex* and the *Batrachomachia* with literary dignity, and validates their attribution to the two great poets: after all, they are *praelusiones stilo remissiore*. On the contrary, precisely their belonging to the same forge of the *Iliad*, the *Odyssey* and the *Aeneid* ensures them a value and the right of cir-culation. Likewise, as poems which *solam habuerunt gratiam celeritatis*, the *Sil-vae* owe their 'right to be printed' to the circumstance of coming from the same 'factory' of the *Thebaid*, as Statius reminds us from the outset of the *praefatio*, introducing and crediting himself as the author of the major poem.

This 'legitimating strategy' rests on the assumption that those who excel in the *genus grande* cannot but excel in the production of 'humble level poetry' as well. But there is something more, perhaps. One gets almost the impression that epos is identified as a sort of *Urgattung* or hyper-genre, containing the matrices of all poetic forms.[14] This is a concept that Statius seems to affirm again in the opening words of *Silv.* 4.2, where, on the point of celebrating the banquet offered by Domitian, he individuates its literary precedent in the symposial scenes of epic poems like the *Odyssey* and the *Aeneid*. Similarly, Quintilian (*Inst.* 10.1.46) compares Homer to the Ocean, from which all rivers and springs originate, be-cause his work provided the source for all the genres of eloquence. The archetype of this belief, however, which was evidently widespread,[15] seems to date back to Aristotle's *Poetics* (1448b 34 ff.), where the Homeric poems are represented as the seed of both tragedy (the *Iliad* and the *Odyssey*) and comedy (the *Margite*).

Again according to Aristotle (1448b 20 ff.), the *Margite* is the prototype of the γελοῖον, and its protagonist, who bears in his name the sign of his stupidity, rep-resents the category of the φαῦλοι: so, for obvious reasons of convenience, it could not provide the model for a celebratory 'production on demand' like the *Silvae*. The *Batrachomachia*, on the contrary, could prove more suitable, both for the absence in it of ideological subversion of heroic ethics, and for its being easily comparable to a 'minor' Latin counterpart like the *Culex* attributed to Virgil. The pairing of the two *libelli* may have been encouraged by their similar

---

14 Cf. Bonadeo 2013, esp. 40.
15 On Homer's fortune in Latin criticism cf. Mazzoli 1970, 160 ff. and 228 n. 35.

animal theme, clearly expressed in their *tituli*. The development of that theme in a heroic format, which discloses a variety of potential literary implications, is likely to be one of the features for which Statius has identified the two poems as a precedent for the *Silvae:* that is, the intersection of codes and registers belonging to different genres. Many other points of contact between the two texts are highlighted by critics, who sometimes interpret them as evidence of an analogous way of reproducing a poetic manner with pseudo-epigraphic intentions.[16] However, from Statius' point of view, if we take for granted the authenticity of the two short poems, the factor that unites them and brings them closer to the *Silvae* is precisely their nature of pseudo-epic, or epic in a minor key. This implies the mastery of the epic code and style, as well as a gap between form and content which produces a comic effect: this consists in confirming *per iocum* a high term of reference, whose *gravitas* is dissolved, but not desecrated, in *lusus*; and this while the tension between large and small, humble and high, turns into hyperbole and leads to heroizing what is not heroic.

In the mention of the *Culex* and the *Batrachomachia*, however, it is perhaps possible to grasp something more than a strategy of legitimating one's own art on the basis of illustrious predecessors. This is due to the fact that the two short poems, which are not referred to anywhere else in all Latinity, are mentioned (in pairs with their epic counterparts) by Martial, not long before the drafting of Statius' *praefatio*.

The texts in question are four epigrams (183–186) of Book 14,[17] which open a larger section of poems intended to accompany the gift of books (14.183–196). The list of the presents is inaugurated by Homer's *Batrachomachia*, followed by the *Iliad* and *Odyssey* combined into a single manuscript, and continues with Virgil's *Culex*, followed by the *Aeneid*.

CLXXXIII Homeri *Batrachomachia*
Perlege Maeonio cantatas carmine ranas
  Et frontem nugis solvere disce meis.

CLXXXIV Homerus in pugillaribus membraneis
Ilias et Priami regnis inimicus Ulixes
  Multiplici pariter condita pelle latent.

CLXXXV Vergili *Culex*
Accipe facundi *Culicem*, studiose, Maronis,
  Ne nucibus positis arma virumque legas.

CLXXXVI Vergilius in membranis
Quam brevis inmensum cepit membrana Maronem!
  Ipsius vultus prima tabella gerit.

CLXXXIII Homer's *Batrachomachia*
Read and keep on reading the frogs sung in Maeonian verse
  and learn to smooth your brow with my trifles.

CLXXXIV Homer on parchment tablets
The *Iliad* and Ulysses hostile to Priam's kingdom are hidden
  stored together in many-folded skins.

CLXXXV Virgil's *Culex*
Receive, studious reader, the *Culex* of the eloquent Maro
  To avoid reading, set aside nuts, '*Arma virumque*'.

CLXXXVI Virgil on parchment
How small a parchment has comprised the mighty Maro!
  The first leaf bears the image of his face.

Immediately perspicuous is the intention of creating an alternation between a light text and a more serious one, between an *opusculum* and the *opus magnum* of the same author. The light tone of the two minor poems is revealed, in one case (183), by the use of expressions such as *nugis* and *frontem solvere* and, in the other (185), by the sanction of the greater adequacy of the *Culex*, compared to the *Aeneid*, both to the atmosphere of the *Saturnalia*, which is evoked by the game of nuts, and to the expectations of a *lector studiosus*, especially if the epithet *studiosus* is to be understood as "ironically antiphrastic".[18] Let us focus now on 183. A metapoetic reading of this epigram is suggested by Licia Pini,[19] who interprets the whole sequence 183–196 as a cycle with a prologue and an epilogue, marked by the presence of poetic statements. The initial epigram would have an apologetic and programmatic tone: Martial would confirm his option for light poetry, defending himself from his detractors and finding an endorsement to his practice in the presence of a light work even in the production of the great Homer.

This interpretation is based on the assumption that *nugis ... meis* at 14.183.2 has a self-referential meaning and alludes to Martial's epigrams. Such an as-

---

18 I quote Leary 1996 *ad l.*
19 Pini 2006, esp. 476 ff.

sumption, however, is by no means obvious, because it collides with the principle of anonymity that should govern the *Apopohoreta:* these are, in fact, intended to be a sort of collection of notes to be reused *ad libitum* by readers to accompany their gifts.[20] The thesis of Martial's personal intervention is defended by Pini with persuasive arguments, which there is no need to repeat here. I would only like to emphasize that – even if we suppose *ab absurdo* that *nugis … meis* is an allusion to an anonymous *auctor* of light poetry, and therefore exploitable by an infinite number of users of the epigram – the crucial point is that Homer's minor work is individuated as a reference model for this kind of production. Then, the similarity of its role with Virgil's minor work seems guaranteed by the peculiar *status* of 183–186: a rather well-isolated group of poems within the section devoted to the gift of books.

Thus, Statius and Martial refer to the *Culex* and the *Batrachomachia* as cultural mentors for a kind of poetry that, though varied and highly differentiated, is included as a whole in the general category of *minora*, a 'super' or 'extra-generic' category. It would be rather simplistic to consider such references as fortuitous. Instead, it is likely that the two short poems were fashionable at the time and enjoyed renown and diffusion both in publishing and, perhaps, in school practice, where they could represent a first, lighter and captivating approach to the style of epos. But these are only assumptions and pre-conditions for the individuation of the two poems as literary models, while perhaps the roots and purpose of this choice are more specific.

Mario Citroni[21] has demonstrated that, in the first century of the Empire, there is a hyper-restricted and integrated Greek-Latin canon that consecrates Homer and Virgil as the supreme excellencies in the field of epic. Our main witness for this is represented by Quintilian (*Inst.* 10.1.85 f.),[22] who considers Virgil to be the best Latin epic poet, as well as the closest one to the greatness of Homer: he recalls a judgment he heard in his youth from Domitius Afer, who established a taxonomy in which Virgil stood as the second after Homer, but in a

---

20 On the *Apophoreta* and *Xenia* as practical repertoires cf. Citroni 1989, 206 ff.

21 Citroni 2005a, 26.

22 *Itaque ut apud illos Homerus, sic apud nos Vergilius auspicatissimus dederit exordium, omnium eius generis poetarum Graecorum nostrorumque haud dubie proximus. Utar enim verbis isdem, quae ex Afro Domitio iuvenis excepi: qui mihi interroganti quem Homero crederet maxime accedere, "secundus, inquit, est Vergilius, propior tamen primo quam tertio".* ('Therefore, as Homer among them [*scil.* the Greeks], so Virgil among us provided the most auspicious commencement, Virgil who is undoubtedly the closest to Homer of all the poets of this genre, both Greek and Latin. I will use, in fact, the same words I heard in my youth from Domitius Afer that, when I asked him who, according to him, came nearest to Homer, said: "Virgil is second, but closer to the first than to the third"').

position closer to the first than to the third. Although not always so explicitly oriented in an axiological sense, traces of a shared judgement about the poetic superiority of the pair Homer-Virgil, in a kind of Greek-Latin *koinē*, are evident also in Statius and Martial.[23]

Therefore I think that, when situating their verses under the 'patronage' of the *Batrachomachia* and the *Culex*, the two poets reveal the purpose of constructing a canon of *minora* modelled on the well-known and shared canon that identifies Homer and Virgil as the *auctoritates* of epic, or, indeed – according to the aforementioned principle of inclusion of the *genus humile* in the *genus grande* – as the reference models of poetry *tout court*, and the depositaries of that 'hypercode' deputed to regulate every literary phenomenon.

This is an important cultural operation: it means not only to provide an artistic 'pass' for a poetic production usually considered as second-rank, gratifying its sponsors at the same time. It also means to codify that production, and, ultimately, to give it an identity (even if not corresponding to a precise category of genre), and this by means of its inclusion in a consolidated system of literary classifications, although via a 'negative' comparison with the well-defined pole of epic.

Moreover, I would only remind that the canonizing value of this choice seems to be sanctioned also by its continual revival by authors from different ages and cultural backgrounds, professing minor genres and attempting to legit-

---

23 Mart. 5.10.7 f. (Homer and Virgil are mentioned as archetypal examples of artistic excellencies whom glory smiled upon only *post-mortem*, since the Maeonides was an object of derision by his contemporaries, and, when Maro was alive, the Romans still continued to read Ennius); Mart. 14.57 (the names of Homer and Virgil are an antonomasia for dactylic poetry, whose rhythm a word like *myrobalanum* does not fit); Stat. *Silv.* 1.3.81 ff. (the scenario of the stories of Odysseus and Aeneas is a touchstone for the beauty of the site of Manilius Vopiscus' villa); Stat. *Silv.* 2.7.33 ff. (in a laudatory hyperbole, Smyrna and Mantua are defined as less noble, and even unworthy of competing with the region of the Betis that is the home of Lucan, now dead and celebrated on the occasion of his birthday); Stat. *Silv.* 4.2.1 ff. (the legendary banquets of Alcinous and Dido are a paradigm for the magnificent banquet offered by Domitian, while Statius asserts his inability to celebrate the imperial symposium, even if Smyrna and Mantua together intertwined their fragrant wreaths over his head); Stat. *Silv.* 5.3.61 ff. (in composing a lament for his father Papinius, Statius says that, if fate had allowed him to honour the memory of his parent with a monument higher than the walls of the Cyclopes or the Pyramids, in an ideal ceremony that would see him singing, as a *sacerdos*, his father's deeds, paternal devotion would not have ranked him second to Homer and, indeed, would tend to match him with Virgil).

imate their art: from Erasmus of Rotterdam to Lope de Vega, from Edward Guilpin to Thomas Nashe.[24]

Finally, let us return to antiquity. This construction of a minor canon by Statius and Martial is not only indicative of the debate and the cultural needs which characterize the circles of the two poets. In fact, it also represents the nth excerpt of a mute dialogue between two authors who, although writing for the same occasions and clients, systematically ignore each other.

Personally, I cannot think of Statius as being unaware of the precedent offered by Martial's *Apophoreta*. On the contrary, it seems plausible to me that Statius knew and remembered it quite well: when coining the Graecism *agnoscimus*, he is perhaps alluding to the analogous compound verb (*perlege*, with intensive prefix) that we read in Mart. 14.183. This would be an oblique allusion to which, however, the use of a Greek *sphragis* adds personal colour. Apart from the interlinguistic pun, this appropriation involves the level of content. Statius keeps up the pair of excellencies identified by Martial, and thus contributes to sanctioning its canonical validity. At the same time, he adapts the same couple of authorities to his own portrait as a poet. When opening the collection of the *Apophoreta*, the epigrammatist expresses a programmatic refusal to write about *Thebas, Troiamve malasve Mycenas* ('Thebes, Troy or evil Mycenae', 14.1.11), repudiating the high genres with their mythological apparatus and pomposity of style, and contrasting them to the sphere of *lusus* (l. 12). Statius seems almost to reply and react to that orientation, when he presents himself as the author of an epic poem (the *Thebaid*) who chooses to make concessions to ludic poetry. That is to say, he asserts and legitimizes the inclusion, within the all-encompassing notion of *lusus* (and under the aegis of 'classics' such as Homer's *Batrachomachia* and Virgil's *Culex*), of a different kind of poetry that, though aware of its 'minor *status*', dares to relate itself to epic, as a reproduction of it on a different scale, and not by way of opposition.

---

24 In this regard cf. e.g. Broich 1967 and Fusillo 1988, 20; 48 ff., to be consulted for detailed quotations.

Carole E. Newlands
The early reception of the *Silvae*: from Statius to Sidonius

The reception of Statius' *Silvae* begins with Statius himself. But although the *Silvae* heavily inform the poetry of late antiquity, there is virtual silence in our literary sources until the fifth century poet Sidonius Apollinaris explicitly mentions them.[1] Nonetheless, as I shall discuss in this article, both poets prove important commentators on these new experiments in occasional poetry. In particular, the comments of Statius and Sidonius suggest a method of reading the *Silvae* that can help us appreciate a significant aspect of all the works of this ambitious Flavian poet, namely its interrelatedness.[2] Although in today's classroom the *Silvae* are often read separately from the epics or simply ignored, Statius and Sidonius suggest that they are closely connected with the *Thebaid* and shaped by it through contrasting and overlapping themes. Thus not only do the *Silvae* pay testimony to the new Flavian elite culture of luxury and leisure, as Rosati has demonstrated, but they also provide an interpretive commentary to the *Thebaid*.[3] Moreover, the comments of Sidonius in particular steer us away from the tropes of belatedness and decline commonly associated with Statius.[4] Writing in parlous times when the former certainties of the Roman world were crashing down around him, Sidonius champions Statius' *Silvae* as a supreme literary representative not only of Flavian culture but of the classical heritage itself. Improvisation is not a defining feature of the genre of *silvae* for Sidonius, but rather a rich diversity of themes and knowledge. This method of reading the *Silvae* as a symbolic 'treasure house' of antiquity is best demonstrated by Sidonius' *Carm.* 22, a poetic ecphrasis of a villa that engages in creative interplay with both the *Thebaid* and *Silvae*; it is framed, moreover, by a prose epistle promoting

I would like to thank my Italian colleagues again for their superb hospitality in Turin and for their generosity in sharing their recent work.

1 It is possible that Quintilian's reference at *Inst.* 10.3.17 f. to what he calls the fashion for composing *silvae*, hastily composed, heated compositions, may nod to Statius. The *Silvae* were virtually ignored by the late Antique grammarians; see the important study of Kaufmann 2015.
2 Discussion of the *Achilleid* lies outside the scope of this paper which focuses on the relationship between the *Silvae* and Statius' prior work, the *Thebaid*. However, the second epic's exploration of the fluidity of gender and genre associates it retrospectively with the *Silvae*.
3 Rosati 2006.
4 See Hinds 1998, 83–97.

https://doi.org/10.1515/9783110534436-010

the aesthetic virtues of Statius' *Silvae*. While Sidonius is an astute commentator on the *Silvae*, he also anticipates the later development of the genre in the Renaissance, beginning with the *Silvae* of Poliziano.[5] But first I will look at how Statius himself lays the ground for Sidonius' later comments about the *Silvae*.

In his epistolary prefaces to the *Silvae* Statius defines and defends his new work, and necessarily so, for the new, untraditional *Silvae* were surely not at all what his readers would have expected from the epic poet of the *Thebaid* which had appeared just a year previously in 92 CE. In the *Silvae* Statius relocates in Flavian Rome the occasional themes of Hellenistic epigram such as descriptions of works of art, dedications of monuments, laments and consolations, developing them into much longer hexameter poems with a self-conscious style that is both improvisational and elevated.[6] As Bonadeo has argued, following Henri Frère, the *Silvae* are a mélange of improvisations.[7] The *Silvae* experiment with new aesthetic principles of 'sudden heat and the pleasure of haste' (*subito calore et quadam festinandi voluptate*, 1 *praef.* 3), key elements of an improvisational style suited for poetry written for public and social occasions that requires the semblance, at any rate, of speed of composition and intense emotion but also sophisticated learning, given the cultured recipients. The hybridity of the genre is displayed in the mixture of the poems' themes, ranging from praise of the new colossal statue of Domitian to praise of friend's villas and private baths. Statius' use of Greek terms for individual poems – for instance in the preface to Book 2 he names the first an *epicedion* and the last a *genethliacon* – suggests that the *Silvae* are sophisticated experiments with various genres, particularly elegy and epigram. Statius also gives the names of the recipients of these poems. Thus an essential facet of this new genre is the high status of its swiftly composed poems as gifts, part of a system of a culture of exchange between a wealthy, culture-seeking patron, often upwardly mobile, and a poet who has just made his name with the *Thebaid*.[8] But not everyone was Statius' friend.

Statius defends his new literary turn in the epistolary preface to Book 1 of the *Silvae*, addressed and dedicated to his poet friend Stella, presenting himself as a great epic poet in the lineage of Homer and Virgil (1 *praef.* 5–9):

---

5 On the character of Poliziano's *Silvae* see Fantazzi 2004, viii–xi.
6 On the relationship between Statius' *Silvae* and Hellenistic epigram see the fundamental work of Hardie 1983.
7 Bonadeo 2010, 151–153.
8 Zeiner 2005.

quid enim [ ] quoque auctoritate editionis onerari, quo adhuc pro Thebaide mea, quamvis me reliquerit, timeo? Sed et Culicem legimus, et Batrachomachiam etiam agnoscimus, nec quisquam est inlustrium poetarum qui non aliquid operibus suis stilo remissiore praeluserit.

For why (should I burden myself) with the responsibility of publication when I am still on edge over my *Thebaid*, although it has left me? But we read the *Culex* and we still know the *Batrachomachia*, and there is no famous poet who has not made some prelude to his works in a more relaxed vein.

By arguing that he follows Homer and Virgil in composing works that are literary 'play', Statius boldly inserts himself into the company of the greatest epic poets of antiquity. He does not name Ovid and Lucan, and thus promotes himself as the final member of an illustrious epic triad.[9] Indeed his *Silvae*, unlike the minor works of Homer and Virgil, were written after his first epic poem; he thus suggests that they are works of literary maturity.

As Johannsen argues, one purpose of the epistolary *praefationes* used by Statius (and also Martial) at the start of their poetry books is to mediate the reader's response to the work that they introduce.[10] Thus Statius attempts in the prefaces to the *Silvae* to forestall expected criticism, which a great poet like the author of the *Thebaid* might attract when he surprisingly changes literary direction. He elaborates a theoretical framework to justify his choice of a new genre and a style that is *remissior*, 'more relaxed' and thus, however, open to the criticism of lacking polish and substance.

In the preface to Book 2 of the *Silvae*, for example, Statius justifies the improvisational style in the case of his poem of consolation on the untimely death of Atedius Melior's young foster son Glaucias (2 *praef.* 7–12):

huius missi recens vulnus, ut scis, epicedio prosecutus sum adeo festinanter ut excusandam habuerim adfectibus tuis celeritatem. nec nunc eam apud te iacto qui nosti, sed et ceteris indico, ne quis asperiore lima carmen examinet et a confuso scriptum et dolenti datum, cum paene supervacua sint tarda solacia.

I tackled the fresh wound of his loss, as you know, with an epicedium written so hastily that I considered the speed would be justified by your feelings. For I don't make an issue of my speed with you, who are in the know, but I point it out to others so that nobody will examine with too critical a file a poem written by a troubled writer and given to a grieving recipient, when late consolations are almost superfluous.

---

9 Vacca's *Life of Lucan* ascribed to the Neronian poet a variety of works apart from the *De Bello Civili*, including ten books of *Silvae* which Statius, however, does not mention, even in *Silvae* 2.7, his tribute to Lucan. See Newlands 2011, on *Silv.* 2.7.54–72.

10 Johannsen 2006 analyses the function of this textual space as a "paratext" (esp. 38–45); cf. the earlier discussion of Newlands 2002, 32–36; also Newlands 2011, 57 f.

The key words *festinanter* and *celeritatem* define the improvisational style, justified here by the occasion: his poem reflects the immediacy of grief that the
poet shares with the bereaved; delay in writing the consolation would have
been counterproductive. Nauta has observed that true improvisation would involve actual writing of a poem on the spot; he suggests that we should, strictly
speaking, talk rather of quick or hasty composition.[11] Nonetheless, Statius clearly wants to give the impression of writing in the heat of the moment, and our
term "improvisational" works well for that purpose. What matters in his poem
on the death of young Glaucias is that the poet's grief is also fresh and he can
thus write with deep feeling and sympathy to his friend. However, since the *epicedium* was published in a collection probably two years after its publication,
Statius here articulates a rhetoric of 'occasionality'.[12] Improvisation is thus offset
by the care taken with the arrangement and collection of the poems for publication. Like neoteric poets' frequent declarations of modesty, 'occasionality' is a
trope that draws attention to the poet's artistic virtuosity.[13]

Statius raises the prospect of unsympathetic criticism with the phrase *asperiore lima* (2 *praef.* 10). For Augustan poets the *limae labor* ('work of the file', Hor.
Ars 291) was a metaphor for the necessary emendation and polish that they applied to their work before publication; thus Ovid in exile laments that he left behind a *Metamorphoses* that lacked *ultima lima*, 'the final file' (*Tr.* 1.7.30). In post-
Augustan poetry, however, the *lima* was often transferred by the author to an
amicus as a tribute to the friend's literary competence.[14] As Merli notes, Statius
is an exception. He dedicates his poems to his friends and requests in return for
his gift their support upon publication, but he does not ask them to critique his
work.[15] The poems of the *Silvae* are gifts of exchange; it would not have been appropriate for the recipients to alter or find fault with a gift. Moreover, as poetry
written in the heat of the moment, the *Silvae* had no ostensible need of a 'file'; by
contrast, the metaphor is used a second time in the *Silvae* of his *Thebaid*, an epic
work much labored over, *nostra | Thebais multa cruciata lima* ('our Thebaid, tor-
tured with many a file', *Silv.* 4.7.25 f.). In the preface to Book 2 an overly harsh
lima is ascribed therefore not to a helpful friend but to a potential, anonymous
reader-critic of Statius' new work.[16] Unlike this imagined critic, Statius' friend

---

11 Nauta 2002, 251.
12 See Newlands 2011, on 2 *praef.* 11, and 11 f.
13 See Newlands 2011, 3 f.
14 See Coleman 1988, on *Silv.* 4.7.26.
15 See the important discussion in Merli 2013, 177–190, of Statius' use of *lima* and related terms.
16 On the contrasting 'care' and 'labour' involved in the composition of the *Thebaid* cf. also *Silvae* 3.3.142 f.; 3.5.33–35; Newlands 2009, 398–400; Merli 2013, 187–189.

Atedius Melior understands the poet's new aesthetics (*apud te ... qui nosti*); the anonymous *quis* represents the potentially hostile, outside literary-critical world.

In the preface to Book 4 of the *Silvae*, published two years after the publication of Books 1 through 3 as a set,[17] we find out how this new poetry was actually received: Statius admits that the *Silvae* have indeed met with a hostile reception from some critics (4 *praef.* 24–26, 29–31):

> quare ergo plura in quarto Silvarum quam in prioribus? Ne se putent aliquid egisse qui reprehenderunt, ut audio, quod hoc stili genus edidissem ... exerceri autem ioco non licet? 'secreto' inquit. Sed et sphaeromachia spectantes et palaris lusio admittit.

> Why are there then more poems in the fourth book of Silvae than in the previous ones? So that those who have criticized me, so I hear, because I had published a genre of this type, may not think they have accomplished anything ... but isn't it allowed to exercise for fun? 'In private,' he says. But the sphaeromachia and the trial fencing allow spectators.[18]

Statius is not very specific, but it seems that critics objected that the *Silvae* lacked the *gravitas* that was expected of the great interpreter of Theban *nefas*. Occasional poetry written as 'play' was perhaps better suited to the informal, 'private' readings to which Pliny the Younger refers; friends circulated the poems they had composed through epistolary correspondence or evenings together (*secreto*).[19] The imagery of 'training exercises' suggests that Statius' innovative poetry is seen to lack the final refinement of serious work. But that imagery is somewhat disingenuous. The preface to Book 1 has already blown Statius' modest cover in regard to playful style. For Homer and Virgil 'played' before they wrote their master epics, not after; with the *Silvae* Statius has upset the traditional career model of generic ascent and shows his originality and boldness. Moreover he has applied Callimachean principles of the 'final file' to his epic poem (*Silv.* 4.7.25 f.), not to his short, occasional poetry. He is a poet eager to experiment with and challenge literary conventions; his swift compositions expose their author's virtuosity.

To return now to the preface to Book 1 of the *Silvae*, the very mention of the *Thebaid* there (1 *praef.* 6) can be interpreted, I suggest, as a programmatic demonstration of the significance of the *Thebaid* as a shaping force upon the *Silvae*; in turn, the *Silvae* can shed light on the generic fluidity of the epic. For while Statius in the *Silvae* defines his epic poem and his new occasional poetry in anti-

---

17 On the probable publication of Books 1–3 as a set see Coleman 1988, xvi–xx.

18 The meaning of *sphaeromachia* is uncertain. See Coleman 1988, ad loc., who suggests that it involves some kind of trainee fighting with foils.

19 Myers 2005; Newlands 2012, 17–20.

thetical stylistic terms – the one crafted and polished over twelve years (*Theb.* 12.811 f.), the other composed in two days or less (*Silv.* 1 *praef.* 13–15) – the chronological proximity of the two works, his prevalent use of hexameter, and his frequent references to the *Thebaid* (and later to the *Achilleid*) do not let the reader forget that the author of the *Silvae* is also a prestigious epic poet. As Bonadeo comments, "oggi e domani continua e continuerà ad essere maestro seppure in una veste nuova".[20] Recent scholarship has started to pay attention to the meanings generated by thematic and generic interplay between these two works, which have for so long been treated separately.[21] As Bessone argues, "c'è continuità tra *Tebaide* e *Silvae*", especially with regards to the language of poetry and power; *Silvae* 1.1, for instance, constructs a heroic image of the emperor in an ambitious attempt to develop an epicising language of public panegyric.[22] I will add briefly to the particularities of this discussion on the interchange between the *Thebaid* and the *Silvae* by turning to an important image in Statius' poetry, as Merli has recently shown: namely the river, a traditional symbol of poetic inspiration.[23] I will begin with the *Thebaid*.

In the catalogue of Argive heroes in *Thebaid* 4, the river Achelous is introduced, apparently gratuitously, as he is only a bystander (103–109):

> fletaque cognatis avibus Meleagria Pleuron
> et praeceps Calydon et quae Iove provocat Iden
> Olenos Ioniis et fluctibus hospita portu
> Chalcis et Herculea turpatus gymnade vultus
> amnis; adhuc imis vix truncam attollere frontem
> ausus aquis glaucoque caput summersus in antro
> maeret, anhelantes aegrescunt pulvere ripae.

> ... and Pleuron of Meleager wept for by kindred birds and steep Calydon and Olenos who challenges Ida with her Jupiter and Chalcis which by its port affords hospitality to Ionian waves, and the river whose face was disfigured by his wrestling with Hercules; still he scarcely dares to lift his maimed brow from the waters' depths and grieves with his head sunk in his blue-green cave while his panting banks sicken with dust. (transl. with minor revision by Parkes)

---

20 Bonadeo 2012, 114.
21 On Statius' use of references to the *Thebaid* in individual poems of the *Silvae*, see Newlands 2009; also Newlands 2012. See also Bonadeo 2012; Bessone 2011, 30–74 on the political as well as the poetic dimension; Merli 2013, 178–191
22 Bessone 2011, 37.
23 Merli 2013, esp. 63–141.

The mutilated forehead of the god, *truncam ... frontem*, is explained by Ovid's description of the same river god, *truncae ... frontis* (*Met.* 9.1f.); *lacerum cornu ... caput* (*Met.* 9.97).[24] As Micozzi has shown, Statius' mutilated Achelous bears the visible mark of his encounter with Ovidian myth-making.[25] At *Met.* 8.879–9.97 Ovid's river god explains that he lost his horn in a fight with Hercules; this story concludes an extensive story-telling session with Theseus and his companions which draws on Callimachean poetic models.[26] In the *Thebaid*, the intrusion of the river god Achelous into the catalogue, that most stalwart of epic conventions, programmatically demonstrates the debt that Statius owes to Ovid's *Metamorphoses*, a poem that is at its most genre-bending in the Achelous episode.

There is a further debt owed to Ovid here. At line 103 Statius lists 'Meleager's Pleuron' as one of the grieving towns; Statius alludes here to another Ovidian myth, that of Meleager, which occupies the midpoint of the *Metamorphoses* (8.445–546), a terrible tale of double family murders, revenge, and suicide, ending with the metamorphosis of Meleager's grieving sisters into guinea-fowl, *meleagrides* (*Met.* 8.544–550):[27]

> ... natis in corpore pennis
> allevat et longas per bracchia porrigit alas
> corneaque ora facit versasque per aera mittit.
> interea Theseus sociati parte laboris
> functus Erectheas Tritonidos ibat ad arces.
> clausit iter fecitque moras Achelous eunti
> imbre tumens.   550

(Diana) lightens them with the growth of wings on their body, stretches out long wings over their arms, gives them horny beaks and sends them, transformed, into the sky. Meanwhile Theseus, having performed his part in his allies' hunt, was heading for the citadel of Athens. Achelous blocked his path and, swollen with rain, created delay.

Ovidian myth thus introduces the highly relevant theme of fatal, tragic family conflict into Statius' epic catalogue.[28] The allusion is perhaps strengthened by line imitation: in both the *Metamorphoses* and the *Thebaid* the end of the story of Meleager's sisters is followed three lines later by the introduction of Achelous (*Met.* 8.546, 549f.; *Theb.* 4.103, 106).

---

24 See Parkes 2012 on *Theb.* 4.107.
25 Micozzi 2007, on *Theb.* 4.106f.
26 See Barchiesi 1989, 57–64.
27 On the centrality of this myth in the *Metamorphoses* see Hinds 1985, 21f.
28 Pleuron was the birth city of Meleager's mother; see Parkes on *Theb.* 4.103.

Since Virgil imitated Callimachus' line placement of the Euphrates, rivers can often be seen to have programmatic significance.[29] The complex allusion in the *Thebaid* to Ovid's *Metamorphoses*, I suggest, draws attention with Hellenistic-style finesse to the precedent Ovid's epic offered in terms not only of generic fluidity but also of multiple perspectives, including a tragic vision. Through Ovid Statius introduces doubt and ominous foreshadowing to a deeply conventional topos, the catalogue of heroes, providing a 'sub-narrative' that condemns the war as the Argives march past. Programmatically, Statius' Achelous embodies the generic fluidity of Statius' poem – but also the central paradox of its theme, the endless recycling of violence and suffering. In the *Metamorphoses* the horn wrenched from the river god's forehead is transformed into the abundant cornucopia, overflowing with fruit, of which the river god himself partakes (*Met.* 9.87–97). But Statius gives us a river god for whom still nothing has changed, *adhuc truncam frontem* (*Theb.* 4.107), for he bears the ineradicable sign of suffering and loss on his physical body. In Statius' *Thebaid* the Ovidian river incorporates the aesthetics and politics of the Theban story, endless repetition of pain and suffering through a recursive history.[30]

Statius seems to allude to this passage in *Silvae* 1.3, Statius' first villa poem on Vopiscus' estate at Tibur (*Silv.* 1.3.43–46):

> an quae graminea suscepta crepidine fumant
> balnea et impositum ripis algentibus ignem,
> quaque vaporiferis iunctus fornacibus amnis   45
> ridet anhelantes vicino flumine nymphas?

> (or shall I tell) of the baths which smoke, placed high on a grassy ridge, and the fire imposed on the cool banks, where the river, joined to steaming furnaces, laughs at the nymphs gasping in its nearby waters?

The river Anio, celebrated by Horace in his poems on Tibur (*Carm.* 1.7, 4.3) as a naturally turbulent stream (*Carm.* 1.7.13 *praeceps Anio*), has been temporarily controlled to provide water for the villa's baths.[31] The river god laughs at the

---

29 Virgil, following Callimachus, placed the Euphrates river six lines from the end of *G.* 1 (509), *G.* 4 (561), and *A.* 8 (726). Virgil also politicized his debt to Hellenistic poetics by using the imitation to chart a narrative of progress from chaos to triumph, from Octavian to Augustus. Ovid imitated Virgil in the *Ars Amatoria* by placing the Euphrates six lines before the end of the Gaius Caesar episode (1.223). See Scodel / Thomas 1985.

30 On the notion of the recursive history of the *Thebaid* see Patterson 1991, esp. 132. Cf. however Bessone 2011, 186–199, who argues that repetition in the *Thebaid* can include the notion of progress (if we accept that Theseus is a positive force in the poem who demonstrates *clementia*).

31 On the relationship between Horace and Statius in *Silvae* 1.3 see Newlands 1988a.

nymphs gasping from the heat – and in wonder.[32] *Ridet anhelantes* (46) occupies the same metrical space as *maeret anhelantes* in the *Thebaid*, where the river grieves that its banks are drying up and parched (109). The contrast between *ridet* and *maeret* gives us the differences between the *Silvae* and the *Thebaid* in a nutshell: in the aftermath of violence the epic river of the *Thebaid* has all the *gravitas* of grief, and the indelible memory of his mutilation is forever branded on his forehead; conversely, the river of the *Silvae* shows the *levitas* of joy and pride in technological improvements.[33] Later the poet imagines the river god bathing in his own delightfully placid and warm stream (70–75).

But the contrast is not absolute. By losing one of its horns, the Achelous of the *Thebaid* has been partially emasculated, deprived of its physical, fertile powers; as a direct result, its banks are drying up. The power of the Anio has likewise been tamed, but with beneficial results. However, the Anio is subdued only when it flows through Vopiscus' estate where it creates a privileged, separate space for Vopiscus' poetic pursuits (*Silv.* 1.3.20–24):

> ipse Anien (miranda fides), infraque superque
> spumeus, hic tumidam rabiem saxosaque ponit
> murmura, ceu placidi veritus turbare Vopisci
> Pieriosque dies et habentes carmina somnos.

> The Anio itself (a wonder to be believed), in spate above and below the estate, here sets aside its swollen wrath and harsh roar, as if afraid to disturb the Pierian days of peaceful Vopiscus and his poetry-filled dreams.

The tamed river of the *Silvae*, panting with beneficial heat, nonetheless derives its positive value in part from the maimed and angry rivers of literary tradition, not least the *Thebaid*. Foaming and swollen with wrath above and below Vopiscus' estate (20 f.), the river frames this ideal landscape with reminders of its epic force and destructive power. Indeed, Statius' frequent allusions in the *Silvae* to the world of gods and myth, the involvement of the gods with humans in the contemporary present, and his almost constant use of the hexameter keep the epic world frequently in mind. As Bonadeo argues, moreover, *doctrina* and an interest in vivid description are common features of all Statius' poetry.[34] In *Silvae* 1.3 the temporary change in the Anio's flow and force also highlights the contin-

---

32 In *Silvae* 1.3 Statius plays on the double meaning of *nymphas* as 'nymphs' or 'currents of water'.
33 On this distinction between the two works see the valuable insights of Bessone 2011, 33–57, esp. 33–37.
34 Bonadeo 2012, 126 f.

gent nature of peaceful order, and of the leisured conditions for poetic composition. Water is one of the most unstable substances, and joy and grief can be but two sides of the same coin.

As Merli points out, rivers and streams in the *Silvae* are often associated with the divine inspiration of the patron himself.[35] For Horace, by contrast, Tibur is the site where he himself finds inspiration (*Carm.* 4.2 and 4.3). Statius appropriates Horace's Tibur only vicariously through his poetry, since Vopiscus now owns Horace's land. The expected poetic succession of Statius to Horace is thus diverted to the patron, adding, however, value to the poem's status as a special gift for Vopiscus. Moreover, by drawing fulsomely on a range of poetic sources, including epic – 'why should I praise the gardens of Alcinous?' Statius asks at line 81 – our poet draws attention not only to the marvels of his patron's villa but also to the virtue of his own innovative poem about the villa and the transformative power of his art over domestic life.[36] If Vopiscus' villa is more marvelous than the palace of the legendary Phaeacian king, then Statius is an Odysseus-like figure. He too is only a temporary visitor to the marvelous estate, but he possesses epic eloquence. Thus, in their complementary use of programmatic rivers and river gods, the *Thebaid* and the *Silvae* show a certain fluidity of genre even as they stake out their generic parameters; their imaginative and aesthetic worlds are never very far apart.

Let us turn now to Sidonius. Although there are many allusions to the *Silvae* in late antique poetry, there is no explicit reference to these poems until the works of this fifth century man of letters from Gaul, Sidonius.[37] There is no commentary tradition for the *Silvae* as there was by the fifth century for the *Thebaid*.[38] In a recent article Kaufmann suggests that the neglect of the *Silvae* by late Antique grammarians may have contributed to their loss until the fifteenth century.[39] All the more important then are the explicit references to the *Silvae* by the fifth century writer-bishop Sidonius Apollinaris. Moreover, he put into practice his interpretation of the *Silvae* particularly in *Carm.* 22, the description of a friend's villa, where he demonstrates both his admiration for Statius (*Papinius tuus meusque*, 226) and a new concept of the genre of *silva*.

---

35 Merli 2013, 73–96.
36 Rosati 2006.
37 See for instance the close parallels between Ausonius' *Mosella* and *Silvae* 1.3 discussed by Kenney 1984, 192–196; Newlands 1988b.
38 By the fifth century, the *Thebaid* had the commentary of Lactantius Placidus; see Sweeney 1997; Kaufmann 2015.
39 Kaufmann 2015.

Sidonius lived between 430 and 489 CE. He was a prominent member of the Gallo-Roman elite, and his collected letters and poems provide a valuable window onto the waning of late Antique Roman culture. For the last twenty years of his life he was the bishop of Clermont.[40] His two direct references to Statius' *Silvae* occur in his 'occasional' poems which seem to have been written in the decade before he became bishop, a period of acute political and social change in Gaul with the progressive barbarian takeover of key regions and towns.

Sidonius admires Statius' *Silvae* particularly for their vivid, descriptive qualities. At *Carm.* 9.229, after commending Statius for his epic, Theban *furor* (226 f.), he describes Statius as a poet who 'paints the jeweled meadows of his charming woods' (*pingit gemmea prata silvularum*). Sidonius here modifies the key arboreal metaphor of the *Silvae* with the metaphorical addition of *gemmea prata*, 'jeweled meadows'. The phrase suggests not only an obvious relation to what Roberts calls the "jeweled style" characteristic of a significant branch of late Antique aesthetics but also, paradoxically, both luxuriant description and containment, that is, the creation of a privileged poetics from mixed woods – a late antique desire for order, perhaps, as well as for "bling".[41] 'Jeweled meadows' suggests a precious space tamed, adorned and protected by fences, hedges or walls, an aesthetic image that also reflects the contemporary need for safety and preservation in the face of barbarian *furor*. The idea of cultivation and preservation implicit in the metaphor of 'jeweled meadows' sidesteps the issue of improvisation, a key feature of Statius' definition of the *Silvae*.[42]

Strikingly then, improvisation and the attendant qualities of heat and haste are not features of the fuller definition of the *Silvae* offered in the prose epilogue to *Carm.* 22, Sidonius' lavishly descriptive poem on the villa of Pontius Leontius. The villa ecphrasis is framed by a letter to this aristocratic friend from the region of Aquitaine (6):[43]

> si quis autem carmen prolixius eatenus duxerit esse culpandum, quod epigrammatis excesserit paucitatem, istum liquido patet neque balneas Etrusci neque Herculem Surrentinum

---

40 Harries 1994, 3–10, dates the publication of Sidonius' collected poems to 469 CE, the year he became bishop, thus marking a clear break in Sidonius' life as a writer; the collected letters were published in 477 CE. On Sidonius' life and dating of his works see also Delhey 1993, 1–12; also for an introduction to Sidonius' poetry see the excellent Loeb edition of Anderson 1936, 1965.
41 Roberts 1989.
42 On the widely discussed meaning of the term *Silvae* cf. Coleman 1988, xxii–xxiv; Nauta 2002, 252–254; Wray 2007; Bonadeo 2010, 151–153 (with ample bibliography).
43 Delhey 1993, 9–12 dates this poem to between 461 and 466 CE, after the take-over by the western Goths of Narbonne, where the poem was written; cf. Sidonius, *praef.* 1.1 f. On Narbonne see also Harries 1994, 125–130.

neque comas Flavii Earini neque Tibur Vopisci neque omnino quicquam de Papinii nostri silvulis lectitasse; quas omnes descriptiones uir ille praeiudicatissimus non distichorum aut tetrastichorum stringit angustiis, sed potius, ut lyricus Flaccus in artis poeticae volumine praecipit, multis isdemque purpureis locorum communium pannis semel inchoatas materias decenter extendit.

If anyone thought my rather long poem should be faulted on the grounds that it exceeded the brevity of epigram, he, it is quite clear, has not read the baths of Etruscus or Hercules of Sorrento or the locks of Flavius Earinus or Vopiscus' Tibur or anything at all from the *Silvae* of our Papinius; that man of exquisite judgement does not confine his verse within the parameters of distichs or four-line stanzas but rather, as the lyric poet Horace teaches in his book on the art of poetry, once he has introduced his theme, he decorously extends it by the frequent use of purple patches to embroider common themes.

Sidonius here addresses two potential criticisms of his villa poem: it is too prolix (*prolixius*) – at 235 lines long it is about twice the length of Statius' villa poems *Silvae* 1.3 and 2.2 –; and, if we take 'prolix' also in its related sense of 'copious', it is too luxuriant in style (*OLD* 1d). Sidonius uses the model of Statius' *Silvae* in rebuttal. He selects as precedent the poems of architectural description that are an innovative feature of the *Silvae:* specifically *Silvae* 1.5 on the baths of Claudius Etruscus, *Silvae* 3.1 on the temple of Hercules on the estate of Pollius Felix, and *Silvae* 1.3 on Vopiscus' villa at Tibur, Statius' first villa poem.[44] The poem on Earinus' hair, *Silvae* 3.4, might seem an anomaly, for while it is a praise poem, it is not an architectural ecphrasis, but it uses myth and vivid description in inventive ways that are also characteristic of the architectural poems.

In this passage Sidonius appeals also to Horace for support for the intricately descriptive style of his villa poem. The passage Sidonius has in mind occurs at the start of Horace's *Ars Poetica* (Hor. *Ars* 14–19):

inceptis gravibus plerumque et magna professis
purpureus, late qui splendeat, unus et alter   15
adsuitur pannus, cum lucus et ara Dianae
et properantis aquae per amoenos ambitus agros,
aut flumen Rhenum aut pluvius describitur arcus.
sed nunc non erat hic locus.

Works nobly begun and professing great things often have one or two purple patches sewn on so as to glitter far and wide, for instance when there is a description of Diana's grove and altar, the course of water hurrying through pleasant fields, the river Rhine, or a rainbow. But now is not the place for this discussion.

---

44 On the villa poem as a particular innovation of Statius in the *Silvae* see Newlands 2002, 119–121.

Sidonius interprets the Augustan poet rather freely for his purposes. For whereas Horace urges sparing use of the 'purple patch', Sidonius by contrast changes Horace's *unus et alter ... / pannus* ('one or two patches', 15 f.) to *multis ... purpureis ... pannis* ('many purple patches').[45] In citing Horace, Sidonius perhaps recognised the close debt Statius' *Silvae* had to Horace's poetry.[46] According to Brink, Horace is counseling against "virtuoso pieces unrelated to the larger poetic aim", whereas Sidonius seems to be arguing for such pieces.[47] Yet probably this is not a wilful misinterpretation of Horace on Sidonius' part but rather a modification, for he also acknowledges the Horatian principle of *decorum* when he writes that elaboration must be done *decenter*, that is, with a sense of proportion and dignity.[48] The description of Statius as *praeiudicatissimus* implies too that Sidonius regards the Flavian poet as highly discriminating in his use of description and digressions. He does not 'bind' (*stringit*) his verse in too tight a metrical form, but his elaboration observes *decorum*. In his praise of the experimental aesthetics of Statius' *Silvae*, Sidonius thus modifies Horace's counsel. The framing of *Carm.* 22 by an epistle shows that Sidonius followed Statius in his innovation and play with generic boundaries, but he caps Statius' poems not only with the greater length of his villa poem, *Carm.* 22 at 235 lines,[49] but also with the framing of the poem by *two* prose epistles to his patron, a dedicatory preface and an epistolary epilogue; Statius' *Silvae* use a single prose epistle to introduce each separate poetry book.

What is absent from Sidonius' discussion of the *Silvae* here is again acknowledgement of their improvisational character. The reason may lie in the nature of Sidonius' late antique reception of Statius' poetry, which is shaped by an acute awareness that the traditions and values represented by the Roman villa and its poetry were under serious threat. Sidonius lived through a time of radical social and cultural change, experiencing first-hand the ravages of towns and countryside inflicted by the Visigoths. Thus he begins his preface to *Carm.* 22 with these words: 'I am writing this at leisure at Narbonne, once named after Mars and now recently made *martial* in reality' (*apud Narbonem quondam Martium dictum, sed nuper factum moras necto*), a reference to the siege of Narbonne by the Visigoths

---

45 See Brink 1971, on Hor. *Ars* 15 f. He explains *pannus* as referring in this context to a type of adornment sewn onto clothing, equivalent to the *segmenta*, the trimmings of purple and gold that Ovid refers to for instance at *Ars* 3.169.

46 See Hardie 1983, 155–171.

47 Brink 1971, on Hor. *Ars* 18.

48 Delhey 1993, 209 suggests that Sidonius relies not on Horace directly but on the commentary of the pseudo-Acron. But, as he notes, the idea behind *extendit* seems to be Sidonius' own.

49 Statius' villa poems *Silvae* 1.3, 2.2, and 3.1, are respectively 110, 155, and 186 lines in length.

in 437 that left the city in ruins, and its subsequent occupation by Theoderic in 462, probably shortly before *Carm.* 22 was written.[50] Sidonius himself owned a villa, described at length in the prose epistle to Domitius (*Ep.* 2.2).[51] But this prose description of Sidonius' villa is modest in language and style compared to *Carm.* 22, his gift poem for Pontius Leontius. When Sidonius wished to soar in style and imagination and to mythologise contemporary domestic life in praise of a friend, he turned to Statius' poetry, the *Thebaid* as well as the *Silvae*. The 'jeweled meadows' of the *Silvae* are particularly precious as enduring fragments of the rich tradition of Graeco-Roman antiquity. The poetic villa description of *Carm.* 22 represents an escape from the present day realities of the uncertainties of war – so powerfully evoked in the *Thebaid* – and a temporary turn to gorgeous architecture, wonderful works of art, richly expressive language, the enduring bonds between patron/friends, as well as vivid memorialisation of a vanishing way of life.

Moreover, improvisation does not suit the leisurely character of Sidonius' villa poem (*moras necto*). Indeed, as I shall now argue in the final part of this essay, although Sidonius takes the *Silvae* as a central model for his description of the villa of his friend Pontius Leontius, the *Thebaid* provides both the framework and the cause for his description. Sidonius thus incorporates the continuity he recognized between Statius' epic and the *Silvae* into his villa poem, thereby acknowledging and preserving the memory of both bodies of work.

First, for example, the villa description is embedded in a complex mythological frame. Sidonius invokes the Muse Erato (12–21) to tell the origins of the villa; her inset narrative encloses another inset narrative, for it is the god Apollo who actually describes the villa in conversation with his brother Bacchus (101–230). It is an ambitious nesting narrative scheme worthy of Ovid's *Metamorphoses*; or we can think too of Statius' bold generic innovation in the *Thebaid* of inserting Hypispyle's speech and indeed another epic, a condensed *Argonautica*, into the centre of his *Thebaid* (5.48–498).

Key allusions also indicate the importance of the *Thebaid* as a narrative framework for Sidonius' villa poem. At its start, Bacchus is on his way to Thebes after his victory over India when Apollo intercepts him and tells him to head to Leontius' villa instead (64–66):

---

50 See above note 44. See also Harries 1994, 131–133, who notes that villa culture in the fifth century was, with few exceptions, in serious decline.
51 See Gibson 2013b on the influence of Pliny's *Epistles* on Sidonius.

iamque iter ad Thebas per magnum victor agebat
aera et ad summas erexerat orgia nubes, 65
cum videt Aonia venientem Delion arce.

And now the victor was making his way through the mighty sky to Thebes and had raised
his revelling procession to the tops of the clouds, when he sees the Delian god coming from
the Aonian citadel.

As Delhey points out, the phrase *iter ad Thebas* (64) describing Bacchus' journey
alludes to the start of Statius' Theban narrative, when Oedipus summons the
Fury Tisiphone from Hell: *notum iter ad Thebas* (*Theb.* 1.101). Bacchus' triumphal
return from victory over foreign peoples also evokes the episode in *Thebaid* 4
where Bacchus is making his way to Thebes after his victory over northern tribes
(652–663) and tarries at Nemea, creating drought. Here, as in Sidonius' poem,
Apollo plays a major role, for Statius invokes Apollo to tell Bacchus' story at
Nemea (*Theb.* 4.649–651), and he significantly helps Bacchus delay the Argives
(*Theb.* 4.689–691);[52] likewise in *Carm.* 22 Apollo tells the story of his encounter
with Bacchus (86–230).

A particularly complex allusion to Statius occurs when Sidonius' Apollo dis-
suades Bacchus from continuing on to Thebes (86 f.), *num forte nocentes, / Bac-
che, petis Thebas?* He here echoes Tydeus' call for arms against *Thebasque nocentes* (3.354).[53] The expression 'harmful Thebes' also evokes the opening of
Silvae 1.5 on the baths of Claudius Etruscus (one of the poems in Sidonius' list
in the epistolary epilogue), where Statius invokes Thebes in his call for a
pause in epic composition for architectural description (8 f.): *paulum arma no-
centia, Thebae, / ponite* ('set aside your harmful weapons for a little, Thebes').
Sidonius' cross-referential use of the phrase *nocentes ... Thebas* thus prepares
us for a shift from an epic narrative to villa ecphrasis, a particular innovation
of Statius in the *Silvae*. Thus the geographical turn of Bacchus away from Thebes
to Gaul and the villa of Leontius represents too a generic shift from epic to *Silvae*,
and from martial narrative to villa description.

Bacchus' diversion from Thebes also represents a moral shift for the patron
deity of Thebes, an escape from a sinful city, *nocentes Thebas*, permanently
marked by the sacrilege of Agave, Niobe, and Oedipus (*Carm.* 22.88–100). Instead, Bacchus will share the patronage of Leontius' villa in Gaul with Apollo
(220–230), thereby providing an antitype to the Theban archetype of civil war
and to his own involvement in antiquity's tragic city of recursive, violent history.
Apollo's injunction at 220, *iam divide sedem*, invokes the possibility of peaceful

---

52 See Parkes 2012, on *Theb.* 4.649–651.
53 The same phrase is used by Tisiphone to Pietas at *Theb.* 11.486.

'division' between brothers. Significantly, Bacchus and Apollo, partners in crime in the *Thebaid*, are also frequently invoked together in the *Silvae* as inspiring deities.[54]

The poetics of the *Thebaid* and of the *Silvae* remain intertwined in Sidonius' poem, for Theban myth not only provides the motivation for the poem, namely Bacchus' return from a triumph and his encounter with Apollo, but the *Thebaid* also articulates at this point what we can identify as a 'poetics of delay' that influences Sidonius' conception of the genre of *silva*. Bacchus' return in the *Thebaid* motivates the most experimental, extended 'purple patch' of all, the dramatically long narrative delay of the Hypsipyle episode that does indeed temporarily halt the war by significantly hindering the onward march of the Argive army into Theban territory. In *Carm.* 22 Bacchus' triumphant return from war motivates an extended villa ecphrasis that far outdoes Statius' villa poems in length.

At the start of his epistolary preface, Sidonius identifies his poetic ecphrasis as a 'weaving of delay', *moras necto* (*praef.* 1). He here alludes to Bacchus' words at *Thebaid* 4.677, *nectam fraude moras*, in which he announces the drought that will hinder the advance of the Argive army and occasion the Hypsipyle episode, with consequences that extend over four books of the epic (*Theb.* 4.646–7.104). *Mora* is a quasi-technical term for an extended 'digression', and *necto* is a common metaphor for literary narration (*OLD* 10); Hypsipyle, for instance, uses *necto* of her speech at *Theb.* 5.36, *quid longa malis exordia necto?* ('why do I weave a long preamble to an evil tale?'). Ovid uses *mora* of the river Achelous who, by preventing the onward journey of Theseus and his men in Book 8 of the *Metamorphoses*, creates a 'delay' for storytelling and exuberant generic transgressions, 549: *clausit iter fecitque moras Achelous* ('Achelous closed off the way and created delay').

Sidonius, I suggest, was a bold innovator. By making epic 'delay' a defining characteristic of the villa poem, Sidonius recognised the generic fluidity of the *Thebaid*; but he also drastically altered the defining characteristic of Statius' *Silvae*, improvisatory speed of composition. The reason for this change was surely not simply a rhetorical interest in prolixity. Lobato has shown that a frequent theme of Sidonius' poetry is the impossibility of writing poetry in a barbarian world (with, among other calamities, an educated audience in decline).[55] The villa poem, with its celebration of friendship, leisure, ancient culture, its dense knowledge of the classical past and mythology, represents a temporary

---

54 Cf. *Silvae* 1.2.17–19, 1.2.220, 1.4.19–21, 1.5.3, 2.7.7 f., 5.1.26, 5.3.6 with 12 f. See Gibson 2006b, on *Silvae* 5.3.6.
55 Lobato 2010.

stopping of time, a delay against the encroachment of the new 'Thebans' who were irrevocably altering Sidonius' Roman world. Indeed, Sidonius imagines Pontius reading his poem at a banquet; that is, like the *Silvae*, these poems were meant for times of leisure. The cups from which Pontius and his friends drink are said to be particularly capacious, *pateris capacioribus* (5), a suggestion that the ample draughts of wine will be complemented by the ample, leisurely presentation of Sidonius' version of Statius' *Silvae*.

Sidonius seems conscious that this version, like the original, is shaped by the politics of cultural exchange. Leontius is honoured by his inclusion with the cultured men praised by Statius and named in Sidonius' epistolary epilogue (5) – Etruscus, Earinus, and Vopiscus. Sidonius understood the important role that the descriptive praise poem played in the Roman patronal system of gift exchange and acquisition of cultural capital; but the recording of names had particular urgency and pathos in the straitened circumstances in which Sidonius wrote. Improvisation with its connotations of transience as well as fluency is understandably not a defining feature of his *silva*. Rather, *mora* for Sidonius represents an attempt to make a space for memory by slowing down time, at the end of Roman time.

Sidonius knew that there was always a *Thebaid* present in the *Silvae*. Certainly he has often been derided for his difficult and indeed 'prolix style', despite his defence in *Carm.* 22.[56] On the other hand, Auerbach felt keenly Sidonius' importance as the last, brilliant expression of Roman culture:

> The great model for epideictic description was Sidonius … the gaudy peacock, as Alan of Lille called him. Actually it is unfair to Sidonius to regard him solely as a rhetorical mannerist; and if we take the trouble to read our way into his letters and poems, we find great wit and charm … The many figures and the difficult order, which combines profusion with condensed syntax, are often, though not always, well adapted to the content; and what he has to say is worth reading, for he provides the last picture of ancient society and its life.[57]

Whatever we may decide about his poetry, Sidonius, writing at the end of Roman time, was surely Roman antiquity's most important interpreter of the *Thebaid* and the *Silvae*. He poignantly – and creatively – took advantage of the fluidity of genre that characterizes both works and paid tribute to Statius' *Silvae* as being among the finest representatives of Roman culture. Van Waarden's remarks also seem apposite here: "formalised literature is not a genre of decline; it flow-

---

56 On recent attempts to rehabilitate Sidonius as both a bishop and an artist see, for instance, Harries 1994, van Waarden 2010.
57 Auerbach 1965, 196.

ers wherever the socially unifying function of art is preferred to its individual heuristic potential".[58] Indeed, does not the oxymoronic metaphor of 'jeweled meadows' describe *Carm.* 22 as well as Statius' *Silvae?* For it suggests not only a brilliant culture preserved as if in amber, but also the possibility, at any rate, of continuing innovation and growth in a space of common delight.

---

58 Van Waarden 2010, 65.

Jacqueline Fabre-Serris

The *Argonautica* of Valerius Flaccus and the Latin tradition on the beginning and end of history (Catullus, Virgil, Seneca)

In a 1995 article entitled 'Figure dell'intertestualità nell'epica romana', Alessandro Barchiesi flagged, as sites in the epic genre likely to admit intertextual references, certain modalities of discourse associated with ideas of transmission and interpretation, such as "il fato, la fama, la memoria e la profezia".[1] Such discursive strategies we find in one of the texts which is in the background of the *Argonautica* of Valerius Flaccus: Catullus' *carmen* 64. This epyllion had considerable influence on Roman literature because of the way in which its author connected *fama* and *fatum*. He presents the crossing of the sea ventured by the sailors of the Argo as a daring act performed by sons of gods, whose exceptional *fama* he salutes,[2] and he places their expedition at the centre of his reflections on *fatum*, not only that of the members of the crew, but of humanity as a whole. In his view, the history of mankind had truly begun at the end of the Golden Age, the turning point at which he locates this first military venture between Europe and Asia, which would inaugurate the Age of Heroes. Without treating in detail his rewriting of the Hesiodic myth of the Ages, I only recall that Catullus highlights, by using *ekphrasis* and prophecy, the dark underbelly of the exploits of other heroes, namely Theseus and Achilles (breach of faith, vengeance, death, grief, and familial ruin). At the end of his text, Catullus gives a negative description of the present state of humanity which alludes to the contemporary situation at Rome. Abandoned by the gods because of their *impietas*, mortals are engaged on a path of self-destruction which Catullus depicts in the colours of the Iron Age.[3] A century later, the influence of Catullus is perceptible in the work of Seneca: the chorus of the *Medea* puts forward an equally negative reading of the evolution of human history.[4] It was impossible for Valerius Flaccus, when he chose to write an epic on the *Argonautica*, not to situate

---

1 Barchiesi 1995, 51.
2 Catul. 64.22–24: *O nimis optato saeclorum tempore nati / heroes, salvete, deum genus, o bona matrum / progenies, salvete iterum...* ('O you who were born at a time in the ages so much desired, heroes, hail! Race of the gods, o great progeny of your mothers, hail a second time!').
3 On *carmen* 64, see Desbordes 1979, Biondi 1980, Thomas 1982, Cairns 1984, Zetzel 1983, Syndikus 1990, Fabre-Serris 2008, 167–179.
4 See Fabre-Serris 2008, 191–204.

https://doi.org/10.1515/9783110534436-011

himself in relation to these two Roman predecessors, even though he had made a different generic choice: his linking of *fama* and *fatum* is inspired by Virgil, a poet, like him, writing epic.[5] In the *Aeneid*, Virgil associates the *fama* of Aeneas and his companions with the exploits accomplished at Troy, during their voyage and on their arrival, and with the role that their enterprise of returning to Italy plays in the general frame of the *fatum* planned by Jupiter for mortals and for Rome. This *fatum*, which is positive (the result will be to secure mankind's happiness thanks to the return of the Golden Age), is set out by the god in book 1 and book 12, but is also evoked through the vision of the history of Rome given in the prophetic speech of Anchises and the *ekphrasis* of the shield of Aeneas.[6] A similar scheme is found in Valerius Flaccus: the epic exploits which bring about the *fama* of the members of the Argonautic expedition are redeployed in the context of a globally positive *fatum* which concerns humanity as a whole. This *fatum* is foretold, by means of various narrative strategies including prophecies, in book 1 and book 4.

In this paper, I would like to try to disentangle the threads which weave the choices made by Valerius Flaccus into these two more or less antagonistic Roman traditions, one represented by Catullus and Seneca, the other by Virgil. In fact, it seems to me that the complexity of Valerius Flaccus' position can be clarified by this dialogue with his predecessors, in the course of which he was particularly sensitive to the fact that they used myths as instruments of reflection on the origins and changes of the world order.

What did the achievement of the Argonauts consist of, according to Valerius Flaccus? In Apollonius the answer is twofold: winning the Golden Fleece and undergoing trials on the outward voyage and return.[7] The Roman poet affirms, for his part, that Pelias' request had only been a pretext for imposing on Jason the crossing of the sea, and that this had been his true test (V. Fl. 1.64–66; 71; 73–76):

> Mox taciti patuere doli nec vellera curae
> esse viro sed sese odiis immania cogi
> in freta [...]
>
> Heu quid agat? [...]

---

5 That is, so far as it appears from a comparison of the texts which have been transmitted to us *in toto*, since the fragments of the text of Varro Atacinus do not allow a profitable comparison.
6 As Barchiesi 1995, 52 underlines: "L'*Eneide* tende così a produrre una storia in cui la tradizione, rielaborata dal narratore, si risolve in 'fato'."
7 A.R. 1.440–442: 'Your destiny and the will of the gods is that you return with the fleece, but on the way there and the way back you will suffer great hardships'.

> an socia Iunone et Pallade fretus
> armisona speret magis et freta iussa capessat,
> siqua operis tanti domito consurgere ponto
> fama queat?[8]

Soon the secret trick appears clearly to him: as to the fleece, this man cares not for it, but it is because of his hatred that he must himself confront the savagery of the waves [...]

Alas, what should he do? [...]

... or else, with the backing of Juno and Pallas resounding with arms, to have more hope and (try to) master the waves which have been assigned to him, if from such a great feat, the conquest of the sea, glory can arise?

Valerius Flaccus situates himself here in line with *carmen* 64, from which he takes up the idea that the Argo had been the first ship to sail on the vast sea, and which is centred, moreover, on this exploit. But he chooses to adopt the point of view of Jason, whose state of mind he describes at the moment when Pelias assigns him the task. It is, then, through the doubts and apprehensions of the future hero that an enterprise is evoked whose boldness Catullus had valorized without restriction.

At the moment of departure, the task assigned by Pelias is recalled anew from Jason's point of view. This time, it is not the hero's thoughts that are related, but his speech. As he makes a libation to the sea god, the leader of the expedition implores the help of the gods (V. Fl. 1.194–201):

> O qui spumantia nutu
> regna quatis terrasque salo complecteris omnes,   195
> da veniam. Scio me cunctis e gentibus unum
> inlicitas temptare vias hiememque mereri:
> sed non sponte feror nec nunc mihi iungere montes
> mens tamen aut summo deposcere fulmen Olympo.
> Ne Peliae te vota trahant: ille aspera iussa   200
> repperit et Colchos in me luctumque meorum.

O you who shake with a nod your kingdoms covered with foam and clasp all the lands from the depths of the sea, grant me your favour/your forgiveness! I know that I alone, amongst all nations, try forbidden routes, and that I deserve a storm. But my departure is not due to personal impulse, and, in any case, I do not intend now to join the mountains or demand lightning from the peak of Olympus. May the wishes of Pelias not lead you astray: it is he who devised this harsh order, to draw up the people of Colchis against me and plunge my family into mourning.

---

8 Valerius' text is that established by Liberman 1997.

The idea that Jason ought not to have embarked on this enterprise, but that it was imposed upon him by Pelias, is an echo of Seneca. It is for this reason that the chorus asks the gods to spare the hero after his return, in other words, to save him from the vengeance of Medea: *iam satis, divi, mare vindicastis: / parcite iusso* ('now you have avenged the sea sufficiently, gods; spare one who acted under orders', Sen. *Med.* 668 f.). The expressions *inlicitas temptare vias* and *non sponte feror* are calqued on two passages of the *Aeneid: Iuvenes, quae causa subegit / ignotas temptare vias* (Verg. *A.* 8.112 f.) and *Italiam non sponte sequor* (4.361). The comparison with Aeneas suggested by these two references to Virgil[9] contributes also to reducing Jason's responsibility. It is clear, in fact, in both of these Virgilian contexts that Aeneas is acting under the influence of a divine force: in book 8 he obeys the injunctions of Tiber, and in book 4 the orders of Mercury. In Valerius Flaccus the prayer of the leader of the expedition receives the immediate response of the gods in the form of two prophecies delivered by the seers of the expedition, Mopsus and Idmon. They speak in turn, and propose (to the reader) two different readings of the destiny of the Argonauts, one rather negative, the other rather positive. In fact, as scholars have underlined,[10] they combine to give a rather complex picture of the future. If we confine ourselves to Latin authors,[11] Valerius Flaccus therefore opted not to choose between the points of view of his predecessors. He presents tragic and epic views of the expedition as equally valid, even if the order in which he has the two seers speak implies a preference, inasmuch as the reassuring words of the second counterbalance, in a way, the menacing elements in the prophecy of the first. Mopsus describes what he sees in the sacrificial flame, which rises in the air at the moment when Jason makes his libation. Neptune convenes a council of the gods of the sea, who all call upon him to defend his law (*legem*, 213), but Juno and Minerva intervene and finally the gods accept (*cessere*, 216) the departure of the Argo to sea. As Andrew Zissos has noted,[12] the key terms of this passage (*legem, cessere*) recall Seneca, but by inverting his point of view. The remainder of the prophecy, which corresponds to the second part of the expedition, and at the same time to the second part of the text of Valerius Flaccus, is more disordered, although it is clearly marked by a tragic perspective. Mopsus relates visions whose meaning he does not understand, as shown by the use of interrogative adverbs: *quid* or *unde*. The reader here deciphers the death of Hylas,

---

9 Zissos 2008, 184 f.
10 See Feeney 1991, 316 f.; Hershkowitz 1998, 26 f.; Zissos 2004a, 319.
11 For links with Apollonius, see Zissos 2004a, 319.
12 Zissos 2004a, 320 n. 34. See Seneca's *Medea*, where *leges* is used in verse 319 and coupled with *cessere* in verses 364 f.: *nunc iam cessit pontus et omnes / patitur leges...*

the fight of Pollux against Amycos, the fire-breathing bulls, the warriors born from the earth, all armed, the murder of the sons of Jason, the fire in Corinth and the departure of Medea in a chariot. These enigmas terrify those who hear them. It is then that the other seer, Idmon, intervenes, *plenus fatis Phoeboque quieto* ('full of the fates with which a peaceful Apollo inspires him'). Idmon sets out a general perspective, which is epic (V. Fl. 1.234–236):[13]

> Quantum augur Apollo
> flamma*que prima docet, prae*duri* plena *labori*s
> cerno equidem, patiens sed quae ratis *omnia vin*cet.
>
> Regarding the lessons of augur Apollo and of the first flame, for my part I see events full of very hard labour, but all liable to be overcome by this skiff.

This passage has received commentary in abundance. In these remarks, whose aim is compensatory, several of the words chosen recall the *Georgics*, and particularly the way in which Virgil presents the end of the Golden Age and the beginning of a new period for humanity, harsher but wanted by Jupiter: *Labor omnia vicit / improbus et duris urgens in rebus egestas* ('hard work conquers all, and urgency of need when the situation is difficult', Verg. *G.* 1.145 f.).[14] That Valerius Flaccus intended here to correct a negative view is indicated also by the presence of the word *ratis*, here used positively, whereas Horace in *Carm.* 1.3 (11) and Seneca in the *Medea* (302), the first serving as a model for the second, employ it in passages which condemn the invention of sailing, judged impious by both.[15] In the *Georgics*, Virgil means by *labor* that which is inherent in the invention of agriculture. It is ingenious to present an invention on the sea as equivalent to an invention on land. But the reference to the Virgilian text allows Valerius Flaccus, above all, to valorize the exploit of the Argonauts as the first act initiating a new period in the life of mankind, which corresponds to the beginning of the destiny determined by the supreme god. It is from the *Georgics*, therefore, that Valerius Flaccus borrows the version of the end of the Golden Age that he substitutes for both that developed by Catullus in *carmen* 64, and the one proposed by Seneca in the second choral ode of his *Medea*. It should be recalled

---

13 I refer, for what he calls "epic and tragic sensibilities", to the analysis of the two prophecies by Zissos 2004a, 323.

14 See Schubert 1984, 22–25; Feeney 1991, 330 f.; Wacht 1991, 5–8.

15 *Illi robur et aes triplex / circa pectus erat, qui* fragilem *truci / commisit pelago* ratem / primus...*, 'he had oak and a triple row of bronze around his heart, the one who first risked a frail skiff on the wild sea' (Hor. *Carm.* 1.3.9–11); *Audax nimium qui freta* primus / rate *tam* fragili *perfida rupit...*, 'Too bold was he who first, in a frail skiff, broke the treacherous waters' (Sen. *Med.* 301 f.).

further that the latter describes the Golden Age, which the expedition of the Argo ended, with traits borrowed from the description of it that Virgil had given in his fourth *Bucolic:* namely, the non-existence of deceit (*fraus*) and the absence of voyages, to which Seneca adds a limitation of resources (*opes*) to those produced by the cultivation of the paternal land (*Med.* 329–334).

Valerius Flaccus makes his choice of the point of view developed in *Georgics* 1 even more explicit by referring again to Virgil in the words that Jason then adds (V. Fl. 1.244–247):

> Non mihi Thessalici pietas culpanda tyranni
> suspective doli; deus haec, deus omine dextro
> imperat; ipse suo voluit commercia mundo
> Iuppiter et tantos hominum miscere labores.

> I should not blame the piety of the Thessalian tyrant by suspecting a ruse; it is a god, a god, who gives us an order with a favourable omen; he himself wanted for the world, which is his own, for there to be commerce between men, and to set in motion such great trials.

Indeed, we find here echoes of the way in which Virgil commented on the invention of agriculture (*G.* 1.121 f.): *Pater ipse colendi / haud facilem esse viam*[16] *voluit*, 'the father of the gods himself desired that the path of agriculture should not be easy'. If he is still conscious of the difficulties inherent in the task which awaits him, Jason no longer interprets the test which is imposed on him as the effect of a tyrant's machinations. The wording leaves a question open: is this for the good of mankind? Valerius Flaccus uses the word *commercia* (246). It is a recollection of Seneca,[17] who had used it with a negative valence concerning navigation, as confirmed by Valerius' use of the verb *miscere* (247), drawn from the same Senecan text. Valerius Flaccus is indeed referring to a remark in the *Naturales Quaestiones*, formulated as a rhetorical question: *Quid quod omnibus inter se populis commercium dedit et gentes dissipatas locis miscuit?* ('and what about the fact that it (the wind) created trade between all peoples and mingled races geographically dispersed?', Sen. *Nat.* 5.18.4). According to Seneca, the winds, devised by

---

16 On the reference to Virgil, see Feeney 1991, 330f. This image of the *via*, a metaphor for human life, is steeped in a double tradition, poetic and philosophical, which goes back to Hesiod's *Works and Days* ('before virtue the immortal gods placed sweat. It is a long, steep path which leads to it, and harsh at its beginning ...', 289–291), and passes through the sophistic tale of the two paths between which the man of *labores*, Hercules, had to choose.

17 On the reference to Seneca, see also Feeney 1991, 331, in particular as regards the use of the word *discrimina* (V. Fl. 1.217), thus commented upon: "The Argonauts are going to produce the civilized world of Jupiter's new order by travelling right through *discrimina rerum* (1.217), right through the sea, in other words, the thing that keeps the parts of the world separate."

the god who arranged the world (*dispositor ille mundi deus*), allowed for sailing, but what ought to have been a benefit turned out to be destructive because of the 'madness of the human race' (*humani generis dementia, Nat.* 5.18.4). It is for a moral reason, then, that Seneca condemns sailing (*Nat.* 5.18.4):

> Non eadem est his et illis causa solvendi sed iusta nulli. Diversis enim irritamentis ad temp-tandum mare impellimur: utique alicui vitio navigatur.

> Men do not all have the same reasons for casting off, but nobody has a just reason. For even if the motives that impel us to confront the sea are different, whatever the case it is under the influence of some vice that people set sail.

Considered from this angle, to what vice was the expedition of the Argonauts owed? Because of the golden fleece, one would expect the answer to be: *cupidi-tas*. In fact, this is a motive which is not put forward by any of the Roman authors who wrote about the Argonauts. Catullus extols the sailors of the Argo by empha-sizing that they constituted the elite of the Greek youth, which has the effect of minimizing the fixed goal 'to take back from the people of Colchis the golden fleece' (*auratam optantes Colchis avertere pellem,* Catul. 64.5). Seneca displaces the question of the origin of the first sea voyage to a discussion of its results: *Quod fuit huius | pretium cursus? Aurea pellis | maiusque mari Medea malum, | merces prima digna carina* ('What was the price of this journey? The golden fleece and Medea, an evil greater than the sea, a wage worthy of the first ship', Sen. *Med.* 360–362). In his tragedy, more than the golden fleece taken from the Colchian people, Medea is the symbol of *commercia* between peoples instituted by the invention of sailing. Seneca makes the woman taken to Greece by the Argonauts into an incarnation of passions which, starting in the Age of Heroes, eventually caused the ruin of human relations in families and states. This is an idea which had been initiated in the ending of *carmen* 64 by Catullus, who represents human madness as responsible for the degradation and deprav-ity of the morals of present-day society: *omnia fanda nefanda malo permixta fu-rore | iustificam nobis mentem avertere deorum* ('the fact that all things, both those permitted and those forbidden, have been mingled by evil rage has turned the just spirit of the gods away from us', Catul. 64.405 f.). Seneca gives *furor* the face and the name of a woman, because he judges women totally incapable of controlling their passions, and for this reason, but also because of what is diffi-cult not to regard as hateful impulses towards them, he assigns them a negative social role within families and states. A remark in the *Phaedra* on the rupture of the primordial pact with nature (which brought it about that man lived according to nature's laws) is particularly illuminating on this subject, insofar as Seneca seems to draw these conclusions from his reading of the story of the Argonauts as the episode initiating the negative evolution of human relations at the end of the Golden Age: *rupere foedus impius lucri furor / et ira praeceps quaeque succensas agit / libido mentes...* ('this pact [with nature] was broken by an impious madness for profit, anger that rushes headlong, and all the passions/desires that cause agitation by inflaming minds', Sen. *Phaed.* 540–542). It is even more tempting to relate, in this list of *vitia*, 'the madness for profit' to the search for the golden fleece, and anger and desire to the behaviour of Medea, because her name is mentioned in the following verses. Seneca here develops an apocalyptic vision of life in the cities, inspired by the end of Catullus' *carmen* 64, but where all the victims in families are exclusively male. He concludes with the *dux malorum:* woman, a 'deadly race', for which he proposes Medea as an emblematic name: *sileantur aliae: sola coniunx Aegei / Medea reddet feminas, dirum genus* ('silence for the others; one alone, the wife of Aegeus, Medea, will account for women, a deadly race', Sen. *Phaed.* 563 f.).

I have made this long excursus on Seneca[18] because the contrast between his negative vision of the *commercia* between men, which sailing has brought about, and the way Valerius Flaccus presents these same *commercia* can illuminate, I think, Valerius' perspective on the effects that the opening up of the sea have had on human life. Seneca's position is that of a philosophical mythographer. He reads the story of the Argonauts as an allegorical tale on the evolution of humanity after the Golden Age, and this provides him with a conceptual model for thinking about the evolution of the individual, starting from the emergence of passions in a (supposedly original) state in which one would spontaneously obey the (natural) voice of reason. In Valerius Flaccus, on the other hand, there is no direct moral characterization of these *commercia*. The word is used to designate relationships which are deliberately not described. The poet adds the word *labores*, specifying that these *labores* will be shared by all those engaged in this *commercia*. But this is a term to which he has previously given positive connotations, by recalling book 1 of the *Georgics*. For Virgil, thanks to the various *artes* they invented and to their *labor*, men improved their lives according to the plan laid out for them by Jupiter (*G.* 1.125–146).[19] It is likely that here Valerius Flaccus is responding also to Lucan, to whom, as has been noted,[20] *commercia*

---

18 Fabre-Serris 2008, 191–204.

19 One might remark that Valerius Flaccus here responds to Seneca by using, in conjunction with *labor*, a word valorized by the Stoics, and by Seneca in particular. Stover 2012, 56 is right to refer it back to *De Providentia* 2.2; however, I do not think that there is a convergence of views here, but rather a sort of use of Seneca against himself, since Valerius Flaccus is not in total agreement with Seneca's interpretation of the myth of the Argonauts.

20 Kleywegt 2005, 150; Galli 2007, 158; Stover 2012, 54.

mundo refers. The juncture is found in book 9 of the *Bellum civile*, in a verse, inspired by Seneca, which condemns another consequence of sailing: the pillage resulting from shipwrecks (*sic cum toto* commercia mundo / *naufragiis Nasamones habent*, 'it is thus because of shipwrecks that the Nasamonians have dealings with the whole world', Luc. 9.443f.). The reference is to shipwrecks caused by the Syrtes; in other words, to *commercia* which are not owed to any *labor*.

After confirming that the *labores* which await them have been wanted by Jupiter, Jason encourages his men to have confidence in their ability to triumph over them: *Ite, viri, mecum dubiisque evincite rebus* ('go, heroes, and triumph with me over doubtful circumstances', V. Fl. 1.248). This exhortation to believe in the success of the enterprise, because it forms part of a divine plan for the world, is reinforced by the version that Valerius Flaccus gives of an epic motif which serves, precisely, to make known the divine will at work in human history: discussion in the council of the gods. In the *Argonautica*, this discussion takes place at the moment when the gods are watching, from heaven, the departure of the ship. It is set in motion by *Sol*, who is worried about the fate of his son, the king of Colchis, who once benevolently hosted Phrixos and gave him his daughter in marriage. Mars takes his side; Pallas and Juno oppose him. It is then Jupiter who takes the floor to reveal that all these events have been accomplished and fulfilled according to an order fixed since the beginning of time (V. Fl. 1.531–533). In hearing Jupiter, the reader learns that the expedition of the Argonauts put in motion the beginning of the true history of humanity, which Valerius Flaccus understands in the sense of relations between different peoples (*commercia*). The supreme god adduces an important clarification. He reveals that each step of this history will be characterized by the domination of one continent, or one people, by another. Jupiter explains that, in the present phase, the region which extends from the places where Eurus blows to the Hellespont and to Tanais is all-powerful, but that, in the wake of the relationships set in motion by the sailing of the Argo, Asia will soon yield its dominance to Greece (V. Fl. 1.542f.):

> Accelerat sed summa dies Asiamque labantem
> linquimus et poscunt iam me sua tempora Grai

> But the last day is rapidly approaching; we are deserting Asia, which is faltering; already the Greeks demand from me the era which is theirs.

As has been remarked,[21] the expression *summa dies* recalls book 2 of the *Aeneid*, where it is employed by Panthus in the context of the fall of Troy and the transfer of its power to Greece (Verg. *A.* 2.324–327):

---

21 Schetter 1959, 302 n. 1; Wacht 1991, 9 n. 31; Stover 2012, 31f.

Venit summa dies et ineluctabile tempus
Dardaniae. Fuimus Troes, fuit Ilium et ingens
gloria Teucrorum; ferus omnia Iuppiter Argos
transtulit

The last day has come, and with it the inevitable hour for Dardania. The Trojans are no
more, Ilion is no more, no more is the immense glory of Troy; cruel Jupiter has transferred
everything to Argos.

Tim Stover concludes that, with the reuse of *summa dies*, the revival of Troy in
Italy emerges. Panthus speaks only of the transfer of Troy's power to Greece,
but the reader of the *Aeneid*, who has read the speech of Jupiter in book 1,
knows that this is only one part of his plan.[22] Panthus' pessimistic wording
(*summa dies*) is later counterbalanced in line 145 of *Aeneid* 7: *advenisse diem
quo debita moenia condant* ('the time has come to found the promised city').
This does not seem to me a sound line of reasoning. If the reader of the *Aeneid*
is supposed to read Virgil's text continuously, this is not the case for the reader of
the *Argonautica*, since the technique of reference does not imply that the *entire
source text* is recalled in the background, but only the *immediate passage* from
which the borrowed expression is drawn. If Valerius had wanted to set one passage against another (the speech of Jupiter against what Panthus understood as
the plans of the supreme god), he would have inserted an allusion to *Aeneid* 1: it
is by means of the technique of "double reference" that an author renders this
kind of intention explicit. The expression *summa dies* can only, then, to my
mind, refer to the reflections of Panthus, and not to those of the reader of the
Aeneid who, when he reads this passage, can effectively compare it to all the
other verses on the same theme in the poem. One of the peculiarities of Virgil,
well shown by Gian Biagio Conte,[23] is his multiplication of points of view.
With this reference, Valerius Flaccus chooses to restrict himself only to the
point of view of Panthus, which, as it happens, is recalled precisely so as *not*
to evoke the Roman empire. What follows is equally significant. Lines 546–551
carry the mark of the practice of mythographers, who highlight the shared se-
quences in mythical events when they put them in order:

---

22 For Stover 2012, 32 "By having Jupiter himself employ the phrase *summa dies* during his
prophecy, Valerius at once recalls the fall of Troy in *Aeneid* 2 and Jupiter's revelation that
'Troy' will rise again in *Aeneid* 1".
23 Conte 1984, 67: "ad una verità che non è più unica viene a corrispondere una struttura di
relazioni plurime – una verità che ha punti di vista relativi, che si irradia secondo un'ottica va-
riabile [...] Virgilio introduce la pluralità dei punti di vista".

> ... Nec vellera tantum
> indignanda manent propiorque ex virgine rapta
> ille dolor, sed – nulla magis sententia menti
> fixa meae – veniet Phrygia iam pastor ab Ida
> qui gemitus irasque pares et mutua Grais   550
> dona ferat

Not only do they continue to be indignant about the Fleece and especially to resent the rape of a young girl, but – no decision is more fixed in my mind – soon, a shepherd from Phrygian Ida will come, who will bring to the Greeks, by way of reciprocal gifts, similar grounds for groans and anger.

The scheme proposed here goes back to a more complex precedent: the sequence constituted by the rapes of Io, Europa, Medea, and Helen, established by Herodotus in his preface to book 1. In this series, the historian makes the abduction of Medea not only the direct cause of that of Helen, but the indirect cause of the Trojan War, the Greeks having decided to destroy in turn the power of Priam (Hdt. *praef.* 3f.). By this reference to Herodotus, Valerius Flaccus characterizes negatively, this time, the *commercia* mentioned earlier by Jupiter. The rape of women will be at the origin of *conflictual* relations between peoples, the resolution of these conflicts being up to Jupiter alone – for reasons not explained, except the suggestion that there is a sort of correspondence between the reasons for his action on earth (outrage towards immoral *commercia*, which in turn contributes to retaliatory actions) and a prior plan of the supreme god.

Jupiter merely indicates that he did not act out of nepotism: *neque enim terris tum sanguis in ullis / noster erat cum fata darem* ('there was nobody of my blood on earth when I fixed the destinies', V. Fl. 1.533f.). This statement is presented as a response to the request of *Sol* on behalf of his son Aeetes. Since he was not guided by the motivations of kinship, Jupiter – Valerius Flaccus underlines – has been just: 534f. *iustique facultas / hinc mihi cum varios struerem per saecula reges* ('this being the case, I had the opportunity to be just when I set up various kings through the ages'). Should we see here also a stance taken relative to Virgil? In book 1 of the *Aeneid*, Venus intervenes in favour of the Trojans, side by side with Jupiter, precisely *as the mother of Aeneas*.

Valerius Flaccus' Jupiter does not give any reason for the various fluctuations of dominion which will occur in the world after the age of Greek supremacy (V. Fl. 1.555–557):

> ... gentesque fovebo
> mox alias. Pateant montes silvaeque lacusque
> cunctaque claustra²⁴ maris; spes et metus omnibus esto.

> Soon, I will favour other peoples. Let mountains lie open, forests, bodies of water, all the
> barriers of the sea; let there be hope and fear for all.

He concludes his speech by insisting on the idea that nothing is fixed in what
appears as a contest of which he will be *arbitrator* (558), which in fact contra-
venes the very idea of destiny. Is this to say that what is planned is simply a competition between peoples? And that the result will depend on the will of Jupiter,
which will be another form of destiny? The god specifies, however, that his
choice will be made on the basis of experiment, but without indicating any of
the criteria which will guide him (V. Fl. 1.558–560):

> Arbiter ipse locos terraeque summa movendo
> experiar quaenam populis longissima cunctis
> regna velim linquamque datas ubi certus habenas.

> For my part, I shall arbitrate: by changing the places and lands which have domination, I
> shall experiment to find out to which reign over all people I wish to assign the longest du-
> ration, and where I shall leave the reins fixedly.

It is difficult to distinguish oneself more emphatically from Virgil, whose Jupiter
knows the details of destiny since its beginnings and proclaims that the *imperium* of the world will be up to Rome. The narrative of the great feat of the Argonauts, the crossing of the Symplegades, in book 4 confirms that Valerius Flaccus
wanted to place emphasis, not on the end of human history, as is the case in the
Aeneid (with the return of the Golden Age in book 6, or the image of a stabilized
imperium in book 8), but on its beginning, marked by the opening up of the seas
(V. Fl. 4.711–713):

> Tum freta quae longis fuerant impervia saeclis
> ad subitam stupuere ratem Pontique iacentis
> omne solum regesque patent gentesque repostae.

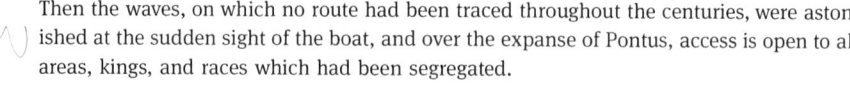

> Then the waves, on which no route had been traced throughout the centuries, were aston-
> ished at the sudden sight of the boat, and over the expanse of Pontus, access is open to all
> areas, kings, and races which had been segregated.

---

24 The word is an echo of Seneca: *claustra profundi* (*Med.* 342).

He also chose to underline that this opening of the seas is still ongoing at the time when he is writing his epic. It is for these kinds of exploits that he celebrates Vespasian in the first verses of his text (V. Fl. 1.7–9): *tuque o pelagi cui maior aperti / fama, Caledonius postquam tua carbasa vexit / Oceanus Phrygios prius indignatus Iulos* ('o you whose opening of the seas has increased your glory, ever since Caledonian Ocean carried your sails, which previously had not judged worthy the Phrygian descendents of Iulus'). The mention of the 'Phrygian descendents of Iulus' looks evidently towards Virgil and implicitly underlines the exaggeration of his praise of Augustus, who is celebrated in book 6 of the *Aeneid* for his extension of the empire to the limits of the world (795–797). By continuing this extension towards the West, Vespasian follows in the footsteps of Jason, at the same time heading towards the completion of his heroic enterprise – the very first one in which human beings engaged.[25]

Conclusion

When he makes the expedition of the Argonauts the true beginning of human history, seeing in it the origin of *commercia*, Valerius Flaccus situates himself in the tradition of a symbolic reading of the mythic voyage, inaugurated by Catullus. However, he differentiates himself from the author of *carmen 64*, as well as from Seneca and Virgil, in that he does not envisage the completion of the cycle of conflicts and successive dominations initiated by the first traversal of the sea: he does not include in the poem's horizon that distant point of arrival, whether in the form of the destruction of humanity, or of the permanent domination of one people over all others. And this, to my mind, is because he refuses to adopt, or finally abandons (after taking it up), a moral perspective.

His Medea is presented in a very negative fashion in the passage in book 5 which initiates the second part of the epic (219 f.): *Ventum ad furias infandaque natae / foedera et horrenda trepidam sub virgine puppem* ('we have come to furies, an abominable pact concluded with a girl, and a ship trembling at the power of a terrifying maiden'). One would believe, in reading *infanda* or *horrenda*, that these verse were written by Catullus, or Seneca. But, as has been noted, what stands out in the second part of the text is the image of a young girl, driven against her will by a passion which tears her away from her family and homeland, leaving her dependent on a man in whom (as she understands in the

---

25 Stover 2012, 63 uses an expression which I find apt, in speaking about Vespasian as "a latter-day Argonaut".

end) she cannot invest her trust. The moral blurring which operates throughout the latter books of the *Argonautica* impairs irretrievably the *fama* of Jason and his companions, preventing at the same time all clear-cut characterization of the *fatum* of men: Valerius does not connote human fate in general terms, either in the negative sense proposed by Catullus and Seneca, with their idea of an irremediable moral degradation which touches all of humanity, or in the positive sense proposed by Virgil's epic, with its confident vision in Augustan politics as an instrument of salvation and moral renewal.

Andrew Zissos

Generic Attire: Hypsipyle's Cloaks in Valerius Flaccus and Apollonius Rhodius

One of the noteworthy features of Valerius Flaccus' *Argonautica* is its fresh delineation of many of the figures associated with the Argonautic myth that he had inherited from Apollonius Rhodius, his principal narrative model. In a number of respects the figure of Hypsipyle stands out in this regard. Valerius elevates her to an extraordinary level of epic dignity, while investing her with paradigmatic force. At the same time, he subjects the Lemnian queen to a thoroughgoing 'Romanization'. For Hershkowitz, Valerius' Hypsipyle episode features "the most explicit instance of 'Romanization' in the poem".[1]

Hypsipyle is cast as a figure of surpassing familial *pietas*. She is the only Lemnian woman *not* to succumb to the powerful and malignant influence of the goddess Venus, the only one *not* to participate in the extermination of the island's menfolk. Indeed, Hypsipyle not only abstains from this nocturnal slaughter, but also delivers her father Thoas from impending peril. This deliverance "is not just the salvation of the father, but also the salvation of the very figure who, as king, is the emblem of patriarchal society".[2] The rescue is achieved through a daring subterfuge: Hypsipyle disguises Thoas in the likeness of his father Bacchus as part of a religious procession – a detail unique to Valerius' version.[3] The god himself – the father's father – is said to assist the daring enterprise (2.277 f.). In this way Hypsipyle spirits her parent out of the city, then leads him stealthily to the shore, where she places him in a small boat, and entrusts him to the waves. Valerius' account of Hypsipyle's harrowing father-saving heroics span more than 60 verses (2.242–305), a noteworthy escalation of the five matter-of-fact lines that Apollonius devotes to the exploit (A.R. 1.620–624).[4] In the Flavian epic, as Vessey observes, "Hypsipyle, unmarried, is an *exemplum pietatis* in respect to Thoas as *paterfamilias*".[5]

---

1 Hershkowitz 1998, 136.
2 Burkert 1983, 191, not referring specifically to Valerius' version.
3 Garson 1964, 274 points out that Hypsipyle's ruse to rescue Thoas bears a suggestive resemblance to that used *against* Thoas in Euripides' *Iphigenia in Tauris*.
4 Arico 1991, 204 speaks of Hypsipyle's 'aristeia'.
5 Vessey 1985, 335. The absence of any mention of the mother (likewise omitted from Apollonius' account; Schol. A.R. 1.601 identifies Thoas' wife as Myrine) allows Valerius to accentuate this quality.

https://doi.org/10.1515/9783110534436-012

Valerius' treatment of Hypsipyle entails a reconception of the inherited figure that is at once cultural and literary. In this reconception, as is often the case, the *Aeneid* stands as a crucial intermediary between the two Argonautic epics. While Valerius' diverse and mutually implicated intertextual modalities resist facile generalizations, it is certainly true that a favored strategy of his is to refashion elements of the Argonautic narrative along essentially Virgilian lines. The Flavian poet's well-known tendency to graft onto the narrative body of Apollonius' epic the poetic language and thematic concerns of the *Aeneid* is very much in evidence in the Hypsipyle episode. That Valerius' Hypsipyle owes much to Virgil's Dido is well known – and not altogether surprising from the perspective of the broader literary tradition, inasmuch as Virgil's delineation of Dido owed much to Apollonius' Hypsipyle. Hershkowitz has aptly discussed Valerius' Hypsipyle as a kind of inverted intertextual replay of Virgil's Dido; she concludes as follows:[6]

> The interplay between all three figures (*scil.* Valerius' Hypsipyle, Apollonius' Hypsipyle, and Virgil's Dido) is important, but Dido is more central to the representation of Valerius' Hypsipyle than is Apollonius' Hypsipyle, both by providing an intermediate Roman epic reading of Apollonius' Hypsipyle, and by serving as a negative model for Valerius' version of the Lemnian queen.

The situational parallels between the Lemnian and Carthaginian queen on the one hand and their itinerant lovers Jason and Aeneas on the other are clear enough and hardly need elaboration here. But Hershkowitz' term "negative model" points to Valerius' ameliorative recasting: the Flavian Hypsipyle is an *improved* version of Virgil's Dido. Valerius, moreover, ambitiously expands beyond this 'natural' point of Virgilian contact. Most strikingly, he recasts the initial account of the Lemnian massacre, whereby the island's womenfolk murder its entire male population, along the lines of the Virgilian narrative of the fall of Troy in *Aeneid* 2.[7] In this scheme, Hypsipyle's rescue of her aged and ailing father Thoas by spiriting him out of the doomed city (*patriae ... ruentis*, 2.343) replays Aeneas' rescue of Anchises from the butchery of Troy's final night. In an iconic Virgilian gesture Hypsipyle takes up the physical burden of her father's ailing body (*excipit artus*, 2.253) and bears him to safety – and she does so with 'pious hands' (*pias manus*, 2. 249). This assimilation of the courageous, pious – and evidently physically robust – Hypsipyle to the eponymous hero of the *Aeneid* is a gesture of obvious significance.

---

6 Hershkowitz 1998, 136–146; quotation at 145 f.
7 Hershkowitz 1998, 137.

Part of Hypsipyle's 'improvement' over Dido, then, derives from her intertextual convergence with Virgilian characters other than the Carthaginian queen, characters found in more 'heroic' passages of the *Aeneid* than those of its fourth book. In a grand gesture, as the narrative switches from the horrors of the massacre to the singular *pietas* and brave exploits of Hypsipyle, Valerius apostrophizes his heroine and casts her as the *laus una* of her tottering fatherland. In this apostrophe, the Flavian poet makes a full commitment to epic commemoration, making the propagation of Hypsipyle's fame a Roman cultural endeavor, and promising not merely enduring renown, but renown coextensive with the Roman empire itself (V. Fl. 2.242–246):[8]

> sed tibi nunc quae digna tuis ingentibus ausis
> orsa feram, decus et patriae laus una ruentis
> Hyspipyle? non ulla meo te carmine dictam
> abstulerint, durent Latiis modo saecula fastis   245
> Iliacique lares tantique palatia regni.

> But now, what words can I bring worthy of your immense courage, Hypsipyle, splendor and lone glory of your collapsing fatherland? No age shall cast aside your story told in my song, so long as the centuries are marked by the Latian calendar (*fasti*), and the homes (*lares*) founded from (the fall of) Ilium and the palace of our mighty empire still stand.

This address to Hypsipyle amounts to a composite intertextual construction drawn from Virgil's Nisus and Euryalus episode in *Aeneid* 9. The first part of the apostrophe echoes Ascanius' addresses to the two Trojan heroes (Verg. *A.* 9.252f. and 296):

> quae vobis, quae digna, viri, pro laudibus istis
> praemia posse rear solvi?

> What reward shall I deem may be given you, men, what recompense for these noble deeds?

> sponde digna tuis ingentibus omnia coeptis.

> Assure yourself of all that is due to your mighty undertaking.

The rest of the address draws upon Virgil's culminating authorial apostrophe to Nisus and Euryalus, whereby the two Trojan heroes are promised eternal fame (Verg. *A.* 9.446–449):

---

8 On the apostrophe and its importance, see Poortvliet 1991, 148–150; Hershkowitz 1998, 136f.; Bernstein 2008, 31.

> ... si quid mea carmina possunt,
> nulla dies umquam memori vos eximet aevo,
> dum domus Aeneae Capitoli immobile saxum
> accolet imperiumque pater Romanus habebit.

> If my songs have any power, the day shall never dawn that wipes you from the memory of
> the ages, not while the house of Aeneas stands by the Capitoline's steadfast stone, not
> while the Roman father holds sovereignty.

Rather strikingly, Valerius has followed Virgil in associating heroic memorialization with the cultural institutions and chronological span of the Roman Empire itself. He makes "religious continuity with the mythical (and epic) past, as well as monumental markers of Roman wealth and power, the guarantors of poetic immortality".[9] Hypsipyle and her fame are pointedly linked to Roman forms of commemoration, to *Latiis ... fastis*, that is, the list of Roman magistrates whose names were used to mark the years. The association is more striking in the case of Valerius' Greek heroine than in that of Virgil's pair of Trojan warriors on campaign in Italy, whose deeds contribute to the founding of the Roman Empire.

As the systematic Virgilian evocation makes clear, Valerius has invested Hypsipyle with a new heroic status, a fresh epic vigor. The Lemnian queen "is set up in this introduction as an exemplum of heroic female behavior, and one with a strong Roman dimension."[10] This striking cultural appropriation is part of a broader generic aggrandizement of the inherited Apollonian figure. In the Flavian *Argonautica*, as we shall see, Hypsipyle's deeds are ecphrastically reiterated at the conclusion of the Lemnian episode. This is a unique occurrence in the poem, a device of emphasis that closes Hypsipyle's narrative as it began it, with a gesture towards the commemoration of the Lemnian queen.

From the outset, then, the Flavian poet signals Hypsipyle's importance and heightened generic stature. What is perhaps less well recognized by modern critics is the paradigmatic importance of the Lemnian queen for Valerius' subsequent narrative, the way in which she and her story continue to resonate in later episodes. For Apollonius this is not the case: the Lemnian episode resonates intermittently at best and does not exert a significant 'carry over' effect.

---

9 Lovatt 2013, 363.

10 Hershkowitz 1998, 136. Bernstein 2008, 31 argues for an implicit "correction to the *Aeneid*'s economy of praise", but his characterization of the exploit of Nisus and Euryalus as "foolhardy" seems to go too far. Lovatt 2013, 363 takes a dimmer view, seeing Valerius as "confusing all this Virgilian material by applying it to a woman" – and (worse still) a woman who is "always already a tragic heroine".

In a recent article I have discussed Hypsipyle's importance as a paradigm for Medea in the second half of Valerius' poem.[11] The Flavian *Argonautica* marks an important shift in epic modes of heroism. A number of Valerius' characters demonstrate their heroic nature, their *virtus* and *pietas*, through inaction as much as through action – so, for example, Aeson in Book 1 opts *not* to incite civil war in response to Pelias' death sentence. Hypsipyle's shunning of participation in the Lemnian massacre, her surmounting of the *furor* that grips the other Lemnian women, offers an internal prototype for Medea's 'passive heroics' in the epic's later books. Indeed, Valerius achieves a partial assimilation of the Colchian princess to her exemplary Lemnian counterpart. The parallelism between two figures often treated as polar opposites in the literary tradition is a striking innovation on Valerius' part. He presents both Hypsipyle and Medea as models of filial devotion who become, whether sooner or later, father-saviors and exiles.[12] Both are victimized by Venus, who manifests a fury-like nature as she incites *furor*. In each case the goddess assumes a mortal disguise and intervenes directly, driven by hatred of a particular nation (2.101f., 6.467f.). Above all, of course, both women are lovers of Jason (and both are ultimately abandoned by him). Here Valerius underlines the parallelism with Medea's declaration *ne crede, pater, non carior ille est / quem sequimur* ('do not believe, father, that he whom I follow is dearer to me', 8.12f.). This devaluation of her affection for Jason vis-à-vis her father recalls, with inversion, Hypsipyle's earlier address to Jason as *carius o mihi patre caput* ('o dearer one to me than my father', 2.404). Here Medea, as it were, 'outdoes' Hypsipyle in filial sentiment – even if she, unlike Hypsipyle, will ultimately be unable to resist Venus' baneful influence.

In this paper I want to consider the importance of Hypsipyle and her story for the first half of the poem, and in particular the Cyzicus episode in Book 3. In the Flavian *Argonautica* the two episodes are mutually informing in ways that constitute a noteworthy departure from Apollonius' treatment. The connections that Valerius establishes between them have received little attention in scholarship to date. In addition to schematic similarities, I want to look at how Hypsipylean artifacts contribute to the creation of links between the two episodes. The artifacts in question are items of clothing: more specifically, they are cloaks made by Hypsipyle and given as gifts to her departing lover Jason. It is unclear whether she gives one or two such cloaks in the Flavian *Argonautica*, just as it is in the Hellenistic model. In each epic the decorations on one of

---

11 Zissos 2012, 107.

12 V. Fl. 5.683–687 anticipates Medea's future role as father savior, as discussed at Zissos 2012, 96f.

the cloaks are made the subject of an ecphrasis. My aim is to demonstrate that Valerius' treatment of Hypsipyle's sartorial gift giving participates importantly in both her own generic elevation and the continuing resonance of the Lemnian episode. The strategic repositioning of the cloak passages in question – Valerius locates them in the first half of the poem, whereas Apollonius had them in the second – likewise contributes to the effect. This all plays out as a characteristically subtle dialectic of imitation and difference vis-à-vis the Hellenistic model, a dialectic that helps to foreground Valerius' innovative elements. As will be seen, these innovative elements draw upon the *Aeneid*, and serve, *inter alia*, to nuance the intertextual connection between Valerius' Hypsipyle and Virgil's Dido.

The gift of a magnificent cloak is, of course, a familiar motif in ancient epic.[13] And an intricately decorated cloak is a favored object for ecphrastic elaboration. Valerius has already so treated the cloaks of the Dioscuri briefly in the catalogue of Argonauts in the first book (1.427–432). Likewise Apollonius has an elaborate description of a cloak, the gift of Athena, worn by Jason as he makes his eye-catching entrance in Lemnos (1.721–767); this is prior to the mention of cloaks given him by Hypsipyle, which feature in the penultimate and final books of the Hellenistic *Argonautica*.

In the hyper-masculine, often violent world of ancient epic, cloaks are frequently objects of particular interest. Like other textile products, they naturally have strong associations with the feminine.[14] As intricate artifacts of the domestic realm, and objects frequently circulated in the epic gift exchange economy, they also have broad associations with aristocratic – which is to say, heroic – culture. In Apollonius, the cloaks in question are very strongly linked to the erotic realm, as well as to deception and betrayal.[15] These associations call to mind the often harmful role of women's sartorial gifts in Greek tragedy. What is striking in Valerius' treatment is his determined and purposeful reversal of his Hellenistic model, his use of these objects to exalt 'upright' human behavior and to bolster the patriarchal values that underwrite much of Roman epic.

---

13 Poortvliet 1991, 223, adducing, in addition to the precedents in Apollonius Rhodius, Verg. *A.* 3.483 f. (a *chlamys*), 8.166 f. (a *chlamys* and weapons); Ov. *Met.* 13.679–681 (a *chlamys* and other items).
14 See, e. g., Lovatt 2013, 182.
15 Krevans 2002–2003, 181; similarly Rose 1985, 35, noting further that in Jason's case, "details of dress emblematize [his] erotic effect on others", and pointing to Medea's fascination with his attire in her reverie at A.R. 3.454.

1 Hypsipyle's Cloak(s) in Apollonius Rhodius

In order to contextualize Valerius' treatment, it will be useful to begin with the *Argonautica* of Apollonius Rhodius, for the idea of Hypsipyle giving Jason sartorial gifts undoubtedly comes from the Hellenistic *Argonautica* in the first instance. Whether or not Apollonius was Valerius' code model, he was certainly his exemplary model. The Lemnian episode occurs in the middle of Apollonius' opening book (1.601–914). There is no mention of any cloak given to Jason by Hypsipyle there, but much later in the narrative there are two references to cloaks given by the Lemnian queen to her Thessalian lover.[16] The first is a 'dark cloak' (φᾶρος ... κυάνεον) that Jason wears to his meeting with Medea (to carry out the rites of Hecate) the night before the contest with the fire-breathing bulls (A.R. 3.1204–1206):

> ... ἀμφὶ δὲ φᾶρος
> ἕσσατο κυάνεον, τό ῥά οἱ πάρος ἐγγυάλιξεν
> Λημνιὰς Ὑψιπύλη ἀδινῆς μνημήιον εὐνῆς.

> (Jason) ... drew around his body a dark cloak that Lemnian Hypsipyle had given him, a memento of their frequent lovemaking. (transl. Seaton)

The characterization of the cloak as a "memento of their frequent lovemaking" (εὐνῆς, 'bed', is clearly metonymic) is quite risqué by the standards of ancient epic. The adjective ἀδινῆς probably has the sense 'frequent' (so Seaton) or perhaps even 'intense'.[17] In his commentary, Hunter observes that we are probably meant to gather that Jason and Hypsipyle had had sex "on or under this robe."[18]

The second Hypsipylean cloak is a 'crimson' (πορφύρεον) garment of divine manufacture, which features in one of the most notorious passages of the Hellenistic epic. This beautiful cloak, given to Jason by his erstwhile Lemnian lover Hypsipyle, is chief among the gifts used by Jason and Medea to entice the latter's brother Absyrtus to his doom (A.R. 4. 421–434):

> Ὣς τώγε ξυμβάντε μέγαν δόλον ἠρτύναντο
> Ἀψύρτῳ, καὶ πολλὰ πόρον ξεινήια δῶρα·
> οἷς μέτα καὶ πέπλον δόσαν ἱερὸν Ὑψιπυλείης

---

16 Similarly there is retrospective mention of a φᾶρος ... ξεινήιον given to Pollux by his Lemnian lover at A.R. 2.30f. The most prominent cloak of Apollonius' epic is that given to Jason, along with a spear, by the goddess Athena (1.721–767), discussed below, n. 34.
17 As advocated by Krevans 2002–2003, 180.
18 Hunter 1989, 230.

πορφύρεον. τὸν μέν ῥα Διωνύσῳ κάμον αὐταί
Δίῃ ἐν ἀμφιάλῳ Χάριτες θεαί, αὐτὰρ ὁ παιδί
δῶκε Θόαντι μεταῦτις, ὁ δ' αὖ λίπεν Ὑψιπυλείῃ,
ἡ δ' ἔπορ' Αἰσονίδῃ πολέσιν μετὰ καὶ τὸ φέρεσθαι
γλήνεσιν εὐεργὲς ξεινήιον. οὔ μιν ἀφάσσων
οὔτε κεν εἰσορόων γλυκὺν ἵμερον ἐμπλήσειας·
τοῦ δὲ καὶ ἀμβροσίη ὀδμὴ πέλεν ἐξέτι κείνου
ἐξ οὗ ἄναξ αὐτὸς Νυσήιος ἐγκατέλεκτο
ἀκροχάλιξ οἴνῳ καὶ νέκταρι, καλὰ μεμαρπώς
στήθεα παρθενικῆς Μινωίδος, ἥν ποτε Θησεύς
Κνωσσόθεν ἑσπομένην Δίῃ ἔνι κάλλιπε νήσῳ.

So they two (*scil.* Jason and Medea) agreed, and prepared a great web of guile for Absyrtus, and provided many gifts such as are due to guests, and among them gave a sacred robe of Hypsipyle, of crimson hue. The Graces with their own hands had wrought it for Dionysus in sea-girt Dia, and he gave it to his son Thoas thereafter, and Thoas left it to Hypsipyle, and she gave that fair-wrought guest-gift with many another marvel for Aeson's son (*scil.* Jason) to wear. Never could you satisfy your sweet desire by touching it or gazing upon it. And from it a divine fragrance breathed from the time when the king of Nysa (*scil.* Dionysus) himself laid to rest thereon, flushed with wine and nectar as he clasped the beauteous breast of the maiden-daughter of Minos (*scil.* Ariadne), whom once Theseus forsook on the island of Dia, when she had followed him from Cnossus. (transl. Seaton)

That Apollonius uses the term πέπλος here, a rather more vague designation than φᾶρος, used at 3.1204–1206, tells us very little. This could very well be the same cloak mentioned in the earlier passage; the insistence of Shapiro that this must be the case is, however, unjustified.[19] Krevans, for one, sees the two cloaks as distinct, which she sees as appropriate generosity for a royal host.[20] More important for present purposes is the narrative context in which this cloak appears: namely, the murder of Medea's brother Absyrtus. This murder takes place on one of the Brygian Islands, where the Argonauts find themselves blockaded by a Colchian fleet under the command of Absyrtus. In this difficult situation, Jason and Medea hatch a plot to ambush and kill Absyrtus, reckoning that the loss of their commander will confuse and weaken the Colchian forces. The murderous scheme is set in motion by Medea contacting her brother on

---

19 Shapiro 1980, 271.

20 Krevans 2002–2003, 179, seeing two cloaks as more consistent with Apollonius' emphasis elsewhere on the generosity towards the Argonauts of Hypsipyle and the other Lemnian women (1.657 f., 846, 2.30 f.). Krevans additionally points out that Hypsipyle has a prior mythographic connection to gifts of clothing: one of the most persistent traditions about Lemnos in pre-Apollonian sources is that the Argonauts competed in athletic games there, judged by Hypsipyle, with clothing as prizes (Pi. *O.* 4.17–27, *P.* 4.251–254; Simon. *PMG* 547).

the pretense of arranging a secret meeting by a temple of Artemis. The message is accompanied by guest gifts as a pledge of good faith, most alluring among them being the magnificent cloak of Hypsipyle. In Apollonius' account, then, Hypsipyle's cloak is an integral part of a treacherous scheme to lure Absyrtus into a deadly ambush – a scheme jointly concocted and executed by Jason and Medea.

Critics have often identified the murder of Absyrtus as "the central crisis of the voyage of the Argo".[21] As a murder achieved by stealth it constitutes a gross violation of heroic norms.[22] Jason's amputation of the extremities (hands and feet) from the body and his sucking in and spitting out of Absyrtus' blood is a rather gruesome supplementary action that does nothing to restore epic decorum. The narrator's observation that this mutilation is a customary (θέμις, 4.479) ritual for 'murders by treachery' (δολοκτασίας, 4.479) is, as Goldhill observes, laced with irony.[23]

Apollonius' unsettling treatment implicates both Medea *and* Jason in a base and deceitful murder.[24] Jason's ambush of Absyrtus and subsequent mutilation of his corpse (albeit in an expiatory rite) constitute a singularly unsavory moment in his rather problematic heroic career. Lawall has observed that this slaying of an unsuspecting and defenseless adversary entails an abandonment of all heroic values, as well as a transgression of Phineus' advice to be guided by piety.[25] Moreover, as Fränkel points out, neither the Argonauts' survival nor the success of their mission are at stake here: all that is at risk is the love affair of Medea and Jason – an affair that will prove disastrous for everyone it touches.[26] Inasmuch as it demonstrates Medea's propensity for kin murder, this episode participates in Apollonius' anticipation of the tragic (Euripidean) fallout of the love affair. It also contributes to the souring of that love affair: Hutchinson for one sees the killing as the initial source of deterioration in Jason and Medea's relationship.[27]

---

21 Mori 2008, 187 f., with additional references.
22 Wilamowitz (apud Rose 1985) suggests that Apollonius' model may have been a tragic play. Mori 2008, 187 notes that the ambush "raises questions about the representation of Jason and Medea, the central characters of a poem that is in many ways patterned on Homeric epic and is often responsive to the expectations generated by it. Although the relative prominence of Jason and Medea makes them comparable to figures like Achilles, Odysseus, or Penelope, they are, unlike their Homeric counterparts, involved in the treacherous murder of a family member".
23 Goldhill 1991, 331 f.
24 Well discussed in Hunter 1987, 131, which I follow here.
25 Lawall 1966, 167.
26 Fränkel 1968, 494.
27 Hutchinson 1988, 128.

So Absyrtus is lured to his death by the gift of this scintillating garment, a garment that had once belonged to the god Dionysus. It is an object of divine manufacture, the handiwork of the Graces, and has a divine fragrance arising from its use as bedding during Dionysus' sexual encounter with Ariadne (A.R. 4.430). The god had subsequently given it to Hypsipyle's father Thoas, and from him it was passed on to his daughter Hypsipyle. Here it should be borne in mind that, according to the genealogy followed by Apollonius, Hypsipyle is the granddaughter of Dionysus and Ariadne, the Cretan princess who had been abandoned on Naxos by Theseus, and was subsequently rescued and made the consort of that god. The description of the cloak closes with an emphatic reference not to Ariadne as the blissful bride of Dionysus, but rather to 'the maiden-daughter of Minos, whom once Theseus forsook on the island of Dia when she had followed him from Cnossos' (4.433 f.).[28]

As is well known, Apollonius makes Theseus' relationship with Ariadne, in which the Greek hero makes use of the smitten girl's aide only to cast her aside later on, an often ironic paradigm for Jason's relationship with Medea. Indeed, the cloak is doubly paradigmatic because Jason's treatment of Hypsipyle herself fits the same scheme. In Apollonius, as Hunter observes, Hypsipyle-Jason, Ariadne-Theseus, and Medea-Jason, "are all seen to be part of the same pattern, and thus mutually illustrative".[29]

Apollonius' Hypsipyle, then, as Krevans observes, "is consistently associated with gifts of textiles, and those gifts are in turn associated with love-making and betrayal".[30] In the final analysis, Hypsipyle's cloaks draw attention to Jason's philandering and the exploitative side of his conduct. Although the source of the gifts, Hypsipyle is not afforded particular prominence by them, nor is her character afforded delineation. She merely registers as one of Jason's sexual conquests, subject to the same archetypal pattern of 'love them and leave them' characteristic of Greek heroes like Theseus. Not by accident is Apollonius' Jason identified by Beye as a 'sexual hero'; the same critic finds in the imagery of the various cloaks associated with Jason the alternating rhythm of love and hate that permeates the epic.[31]

---

28 Krevans 2002–2003, 181.
29 Hunter 1989, 208.
30 Krevans 2002–2003, 181; cf. Lovatt 2013, 182: Hypsipyle's cloaks in the Hellenistic *Argonautica* are "first given by Hypsipyle to Jason (who abandons her) and then by Jason and Medea to Absyrtus, to entice him into their ambush, an episode both immoral and unepic."
31 Beye 1969, 51 f.

2 Hypsipyle's Cloak(s) in the Flavian *Argonautica*

In Valerius' epic as we have it, the poet twice mentions a cloak given to Jason by Hypsipyle, with the earlier of the two passages accompanied by an ecphrasis. This corresponds quantitatively to the Apollonian schema; but the passages themselves are very different in nature and occur much earlier in the narrative. Valerius has made a double alteration and a double transposition: one might think of Apollonius' Hypsipyle ecphrasis-gift complex as cancelled out in its original location, resituated and transformed.[32]

2.1 The Cloak Ecphrasis in Book 2

The first passage occurs at the conclusion of the Lemnian episode itself. Upon learning of the Argonauts' impending departure, a tearful Hypsipyle utters a sad but dignified farewell to Jason and gives him, as a parting gift, a cloak (*chlamys*) that she herself has made (V. Fl. 2.408 f.):

> ... dixit lacrimans haesuraque caro
> dona duci promit chlamydem textosque labores.

---

32 Despite the incompleteness of the Flavian *Argonautica*, we can be confident that this is indeed a case of transposition, that Valerius did not intend directly to duplicate Apollonius' Hypsipylean cloak passages. The first Apollonian passage, (A.R. 3.1204 f.) featuring the cloak worn by Jason when meeting Medea on the eve of his trials in Colchis, falls within the narrative compass of Valerius' poem as extant and there is no mention in the corresponding passage (7.389–538) of any cloak worn by Jason, let alone one given him by Hypsipyle. The second cloak passage (A.R. 4.421–434) is more problematic, since the episode in which it occurs, that of the death of Absyrtus, occurs just beyond the point at which Valerius' text breaks off. The Flavian poet nonetheless provides clear indications that he would not have followed Apollonius' account of Absyrtus' death in which the cloak figures. The murder scheme in the Hellenistic epic is premised on the willingness of the Colchians to enter into negotiation. It is true that Valerius' Argonauts, like their Apollonian counterparts, are minded to return Medea to the Colchians in exchange for free passage (V. Fl. 8.385–399); but Absyrtus has already declared that the return of Medea would not satisfy him and that he will consider no pact whatsoever with the Argonauts (8.270–272). Absyrtus' bellicosity, his specific ruling out of negotiations with the Greek heroes, leaves no scope for the initial diplomatic contacts and subsequent meetings that lead to his death in the Hellenistic *Argonautica*. In other words, the Argonauts' proposal to exchange Medea for free passage amounts to wishful thinking in Valerius' account, and would have proven to be an instance of what I have elsewhere referred to as 'negative allusion' – that is, an embedded reference to a version of the myth that the poet has chosen *not* to follow; see Zissos 1999.

> She spoke through her tears, and brought forth a gift to abide with the leader she so loved, a cloak of woven handiwork.

The embroidered images are then elaborated in a brief ecphrasis (2.410–417). As a garment given to Jason by Hypsipyle and described at some length, this cloak corresponds to and constitutes a notional substitution for Hypsipyle's cloak in the fourth book of the Hellenistic *Argonautica* (A.R. 4.421–434), discussed above.[33] As already noted, this repositioning effectively cancels out the debased narrative context of the ecphrasis of Hypsipyle's cloak in the earlier epic. There is an obvious 'contextual' elevation vis-à-vis Apollonius' cloak of Hypsipyle, which, as discussed above, has a twofold association with deception. And there is an equally obvious poignancy that accrues from the transposition. Rather than being mentioned retrospectively, the garment features at the emotionally wrought moment in which Hypsipyle gives it to her departing beloved. Poortvliet notes the affective charge of *haesura* (2.408): Hypsipyle wants the cloak to abide with Jason as a treasured possession, to 'cling' to him. This is evidently a very personal gift, and it speaks to Hypsipyle's deep and abiding love for Jason.[34] If the cloak featured here is the same item that Jason parts with in the following book then *haesura* will come to be freighted with retrospective irony, pointing to an asymmetry in emotional commitment that proves to be all too characteristic of Jason's relationships.

One aspect of the *chlamys* that makes it a deeply personal object is the fact that it was made by Hypsipyle herself. This is an important difference from the Hellenistic *Argonautica*, where the corresponding garment is a product of divine

---

33 The intertextual engagement is actually more complex, involving a characteristic distillation of inherited Apollonian elements on Valerius' part. Prior to mentioning the Hypsipylean cloaks, Apollonius has Jason, as he walks to his initial meeting with Hypsipyle, sport a dazzling cloak, whose multiple scenes are made the subject of an ecphrasis (A.R. 1.721–767; Lovatt 2013, 182 speaks of this passage as the 'code model' for subsequent cloak ecphraseis). This eye-catching cloak was given to Jason by Athena, along with a spear. As Valerius has no such cloak, Hypsipyle's gift to Jason of an image-laden cloak along a weapon (a sword) clearly stands in for it. Valerius thus enacts a concentration of Apollonius' treatment: as numerous scholars have recognized, his cloak of Hypsipyle at 2.408–417 corresponds to *both* the cloak given to Jason by Hypsipyle, and ecphrastically elaborated in Apollonius' fourth book *and* the cloak given to Jason by Athena, and ecphrastically elaborated in Apollonius' first book. See e.g. Hershkowitz 1998, 142f.; Carderi 2008, 219–221. The latter speaks of *contaminatio* and notes important reversals, including the fact that whereas Apollonius uses the cloak ecphrasis in his first book as a prelude to the erotic relationship, creating a sense of expectation, Valerius uses his cloak ecphrasis in Book 2 to conclude the same relationship.
34 Poortvliet 1991, 224.

manufacture, and has a complex history of prior ownership and (sexual) usage. By having Hypsipyle make the garment herself, Valerius puts exemplary feminine industry on display – and does so in a particularly significant context. The Lemnian tale constitutes one of the most stark and sustained reversals of gendered expectation in all of ancient myth. The gender reversal includes not just the homicidal rampage that eradicates the island's male population, but also the women's subsequent assumption of all vacated male offices and functions – most strikingly in political and military spheres. Hypsipyle, who is made queen of Lemnos in the aftermath of the slaughter, has thus far been defined largely in terms of masculine heroics and masculine political roles. Against this backdrop, her weaving marks a reversion to a quintessentially virtuous female activity that serves to reaffirm the familiar, asymmetrical gender organization underpinning virtually all ancient societies. To be sure, Valerius' initial account of the Lemnian massacre and the subsequent establishment of a fully functional female society on the island seems to hint at the arbitrary and contingent character of the patriarchal order. Playing a role thrust upon her by circumstances, Hypsipyle has evidently proven to be a just and competent ruler of a fully functional all-female society. Once a male presence is reestablished, however, she seems to revert to more 'gender-appropriate' activity.

Hypsipyle has, moreover, decorated the garment with a pair of graphic compositions, that depict, first, her earlier rescue of her father during the Lemnian massacre, and, second, the abduction of Ganymede by Jupiter's eagle. These images are ecphrastically elaborated over eight verses (2.408–417). Limitations of space restrict discussion to the first representation.[35] This pictorial narrative, by depicting Hypsipyle's deliverance of Thoas, personalizes the garment, while adding a sense of epic elevation (V. Fl. 2.410–413):

illic servati genitoris conscia sacra
pressit acu currusque pios: stant saeva paventum
agmina dantque locum; viridi circum horrida tela
silva tremit; mediis refugit pater anxius umbris.

On it (*scil.* the garment) she had depicted with her needle the rites that were the means of her father's deliverance, and the pious vehicle (*scil.* that conveyed him); there the savage multitude (*scil.* of Lemnian women) stands in fear and makes way. All around sways the wild forest, woven in green thread; her anxious father seeks refuge in the midst of the shade.

---

35 With regard to the second scene, suffice it to observe here that the Ganymede scene amounts to a virtual 'continuation' of the Virgilian ecphrasis at *A.* 5.250–257 (images on the cloak awarded to Cloanthus during the funeral games for Anchises), so that Valerius leaves a conspicuous intertextual marker as he reworks the Apollonian model.

In the earlier account Hypsipyle first hid her father in the temple of Bacchus (2.247–260), and then led him, disguised in the likeness of the god, to the sea by chariot (2.261–278). The ecphrasis captures the second stage of this exploit, putting on display Hypsipyle's daring act of filial piety (*pios*, 2.411). It is significant that Valerius here offers a pictorial recapitulation of an earlier part of his narrative. As noted earlier, this is a unique device of emphasis, a kind of 'ecphrastic closure' that monumentalizes Hypsipyle's heroic *pietas* while underscoring the importance of Hypsipyle and her story in the Flavian *Argonautica*.[36]

In intertextual terms, Valerius achieves a subtle generic recoding vis-à-vis Apollonius, as erotic passion is displaced by filial devotion – a substitutional scheme that is also evident with Medea in the second half of the poem.[37] A more subtle substitutional dynamic plays out with regard to the god Bacchus/Dionysus. Instead of the Dionysian erotics associated with the cloak in Apollonius' ecphrasis – the god had used the garment as bedding during a sexual encounter with Ariadne, and this had endowed the cloak with a lingering 'divine fragrance' (ἀμβροσίη ὀδμὴ, 4.430) – Hypsipyle's embroidery depicts purification rites for Bacchus, her ancestral deity, in the wake of the Lemnian massacre, used as a subterfuge for saving her father Thoas.

The fashioning of cloaks, robes, and similar garments by mortal women in ancient epic is often, as Mueller has well discussed, a vehicle for their own renown: epic women are, to use that critic's phrase, "weaving for *kleos*".[38] But that *kleos* normally derives solely from their skill as manufacturers, not from the commemoration as such: women in ancient epic rarely tell their own stories, whether through this or any other medium. Hypsipyle thus achieves a highly unusual articulation of the 'voice of the shuttle' – one in which she is able to affirm her own renown as both manufacturer and subject of a graphic composition.[39]

---

36 Cf. Garson 1964, 273: "This is the aspect of Hypsipyle of which the poet chooses to remind his reader just before she fades from the narrative."

37 Zissos 2012.

38 Mueller 2010.

39 Hypsipyle will become an even more striking exception to the rule in Book 5 of Statius' *Thebaid*. By using a visual medium for narration, Valerius' Hypsipyle becomes a kind of 'patriarchal' version of Ovid's Philomela, whose autobiographical work of weaving (*vestes*) is used to communicate her terrible experiences to her sister Procne (*Met.* 6. 412–674). A connection with Ovid's Philomela is suggested by Poortvliet 1991, 225, noting the relevance of the Ovidian episode as a precedent for "the use of embroidery to convey a message". A further interesting parallel is the use of Bacchic rites as a subterfuge to rescue Philomela in Ovid and Thoas in Valerius. There are some interesting differences as well: Hypsipyle herself conceals her story from the public view (and will eventually suffer by its propagation), whereas Philomela's story is suppressed by others (and she will be delivered by its propagation).

Hypsipyle's cloak is an object whose significance clearly exceeds its use value; it is also an apt gift for the moment. Just before giving the cloak to Jason, Hypsipyle declares a love for him that surpasses that for her father (*carius o mihi patre caput*, 2.404). This, as Poortvliet observes with arresting understatement, "is no small compliment when coming from Hypsipyle".[40] Carderi is surely right to connect the declaration to the image on the cloak of Hypsipyle's deliverance of her father.[41]

In addition to its broader commemorative function, the garment has a power and significance arising from its psychological implications of its autobiographical tale. In having Hypsipyle produce a 'graphic song' of her own past, one specifically intended for Jason's eyes, Valerius enacts a crucial shift in characterization vis-à-vis Apollonius. As Poortvliet reasonably concludes, the cloak embroidery seems to be meant "to convey a message" to Jason.[42] By recording her own brave actions during the Lemnian massacre, Hypsipyle is disclosing a past that was carefully concealed from Jason and his comrades in the earlier epic. Just as the success of Hypsipyle's heroic exploit depended upon its concealment from the other Lemnian women, so the successful coupling of the Lemnian women with the Argonauts depended upon concealment of their recent nocturnal rampage. In the Hellenistic *Argonautica* Hypsipyle creates a false backstory (A.R. 1.793–826), concealing the truth of the massacre through the use of 'crafty words' (μύθοισι ... αἱμυλίοισιν, A.R. 1.792); as Hunter observes, "the narrator's highly judgmental account is set in counterpoint to Hypsipyle's account to Jason of the same events".[43] Valerius, by contrast, aligns Hypsipyle's pictorial disclosure with the narrative voice. This constitutes an important improvement upon Apollonius' Hypsipyle, who is a persistent dissembler in her interactions with Jason (1.793–833). In Apollonius, as Lovatt rightly observes, Jason is in a sense used and deceived by Hypsipyle, just as she is used and ultimately abandoned by him.[44] In place of her dissembling in the Hellenistic *Argonautica*, Valerius' Hypsipyle opts for honesty, in an evident attempt to remove the barrier

---

40 Poortvliet 1991, 222.
41 Carderi 2008, 220, though perhaps pressing the point too far.
42 Poortvliet 1991, 225, followed by Caviglia 1999, 29 and Carderi 2008, 220. This view is misguidedly rejected by Spaltenstein 2002, 421, who bluntly declares "Il ne s'agit pas d'un message détourné d'Hypsipyle á Jason (et quelle raison aurait-elle de le faire?)".
43 Hunter 1993, 111.
44 Lovatt 2013, 183.

to genuine intimacy which falsehood and evasion inevitably erect.[45] Again the 'contextual' elevation vis-à-vis Apollonius' treatment, where Hypsipyle's cloak has a twofold association with deception, is a crucial feature.

At first glance, Hypsipyle's presentation of a cloak as a parting gift to Jason seems to sound a rather Homeric note. For in the *Odyssey*, when a guest is ready to depart, "the standard protocol is for female hosts to offer gifts that represent their own role within the domestic sphere".[46] But outcome should not be confused with initial intent: it is unlikely that Hypsipyle originally intended the garment as a parting gift. In ancient epic, cloaks and similar products of weaving represent a substantial investment of time and labor. In the *Odyssey* Penelope is able to hold the suitors at bay for a full three years under the (evidently plausible) pretext that she was weaving a shroud for her father-in-law Laertes. It seems safe to assume that Hypsipyle worked on this cloak for a lengthy period. The cloak had no doubt long been intended for Jason, but only became a parting gift after his abrupt decision to quit the island. In suddenly ordering departure, Jason was reacting to the sharp rebuke of Hercules, who had scathingly accused him of being minded to take up residency on Lemnos ('*si sedet Aegaei scopulos habitare profundis ...*', 2.383). After Hypsipyle's parting words to Jason, in which she mentions being pregnant by him and urges him to return to Lemnos on his way back from Colchis, Jason is referred to (by the narrating voice) as her 'Thessalian husband' (*Haemonii ... mariti*, 2.425). The focalization is uncertain and the designation no doubt ironic, but the expression unquestionably speaks to Jason's comportment to that point, which, in keeping with the overarching intertextual paradigm, has been reminiscent of that of Aeneas in *Aeneid* 4.[47] Two verses later, the term *coniunx* is used of the Lemnian lovers of other Argonauts (2.426 f.).[48] All this suggests that Hypsipyle, much like the Virgilian Dido, had been hoping and perhaps even expecting that her relationship with Jason would become permanent. In the context of such expectation, the pictorial disclosure on Hypsipyle's cloak has even deeper emotional significance.

---

45 In the wake of the ecphrasis Valerius provides no indication of an act of internal reception on Jason's part, and it cannot be taken for granted that he 'gets the message' in an epic that repeatedly thematizes the failure of verbal and visual communication.
46 Mueller 2010, 6.
47 Well discussed by Garson 1964, 273.
48 This, of course, recalls the ambiguity that prevails in the Virgilian model, with Dido referring to her relationship with Aeneas as *coniugium* (*Aen.* 4.171), and speaking of *conubia* and *inceptos hymenaeos* (316), before coming to the devastating realization that he is not *coniunx* but merely *hospes* (323 f.).

Along with the cloak, Hypsipyle gives Jason a second gift that affords the sequence a more overtly patriarchal thrust, the sword of her father Thoas (V. Fl. 2.418–421):

> tunc ensem notumque ferens insigne Thoantis
> 'accipe,' ait 'bellis mediaeque ut pulvere pugnae
> sim comes, Aetnaei genitor quae flammea gessit
> dona dei, nunc digna tuis adiungier armis.

> Next she brings the sword of Thoas, with the emblem she knows so well: 'take it', she says, 'so that I may be by your side in wartime and in the dust of battle, the shimmering gift of Aetna's god (*scil.* Vulcan) that my father bore, worthy now to be added to your weaponry'.

A sword is, to be sure, a conventional epic gift.[49] But this is a personal object inasmuch as it belonged to her father Thoas; there is an affective charge to *notum*, used of the sword's emblem, which Hypsipyle "knows so well".[50] Indeed, her emotional identification with it is so strong that she imagines Jason's use of it in combat as allowing her to 'accompany' him onto the battlefield (*ut pulvere pugnae sim comes*); again the sense of deeply personal gifts that 'cling' to their recipients is at the fore. This sword is an object of divine origin, but its manufacture by Vulcan means in effect that it originated on the island (the location of that god's underground forges). It was evidently meant to descend through the male line of the royal house of Lemnos. In the absence of a male heir to Thoas, its bestowal by Hypsipyle implies an offer – and surely not the first – of the throne to Jason through marriage as Thoas' successor.[51] The Lemnian specificity of the gift is meant to remind Jason of Hypsipyle's homeland – and, in a sense, to summon him back to it, a point reinforced by the mention of her pregnancy, which she anticipates yielding a male and potential heir (V. Fl. 2.422–424):[52]

> 'i, memor i terrae, quae vos amplexa quieto
> prima sinu, refer et domitis a Colchidos oris
> vela per hunc utero quem linquis Iasona nostro.'

---

49 Poortvliet 1991, 223–4, additionally pointing out that "the cloak and sword [given by Hypsipyle] correspond to Jason's cloak and spear, gifts from Pallas Athena and Atalanta respectively, as described at A.R. 1.721 ff. and 769 ff".

50 As Poortvliet 1991, 228 observes, the sense of *notumque ... ensem* is "the emblem she knew so well", rather than "renowned emblem" (Mozley).

51 Apollonius' Hypsipyle explicitly offers Jason her father's throne when they first meet (1.827–829) and again as Jason departs (1.890–892).

52 Hypsipyle's reference to a second 'Jason' in her womb recalls and inverts Dido's lament that she does not have a *parvulus ... Aeneas* (*Aen.* 4.328 f.) to console her after Aeneas' departure.

'Go, go now, but forget not the land that first embraced you to its breast, and from Colchis' conquered shores direct your sails back here, I pray you, by this Jason that you leave in my womb'.

That such appeals elicit no consequential response on Jason's part points to his shortcomings in terms of family relations, an impression reinforced by a subtle elision vis-à-vis Apollonius' account. Hypsipyle's certainty regarding her pregnancy is a departure from the Hellenistic *Argonautica*, where she remains in doubt at the end of the episode. During their final moment together, Apollonius' Hypsipyle asks Jason for instructions *in case* she is pregnant. He replies that, should he die on his quest for the golden fleece and should she bear him a son, then upon reaching maturity that son is to be sent to Iolcus to protect Jason's parents from the tyrant Pelias (A.R. 1.904–909). This touching and thoughtful moment has no counterpart in the Flavian *Argonautica* – a suggestive omission, given that Hypsipyle has declared herself pregnant and anticipates bearing a son.

In Virgilian terms, this second gift involves an ameliorative recasting of the Dido-Aeneas tragedy. Hypsipyle's exemplary self-control is once again evident in her emotionally restrained response to Jason's departure: there are no histrionics, no thoughts of (let alone attempts at) suicide. As Hershkowitz observes, "the second gift, the sword which belonged to Thoas (2.418), displays Hypsipyle's dedication to her father as much as to her lover, and is even more significantly Dido-esque [*scil.* than the cloak], taking the place of the sword given by Aeneas to Dido, with which she commits suicide (*Aen.* 4.645–647). By giving a sword to Jason rather than receiving one from him, Hypsipyle demonstrates that she will not follow the same path as Dido".[53]

2.2 The Cloak Retrospective in Book 3

In the wake of the Lemnian episode, the reader does not have long to wait before reencountering Hypsipyle – or, more precisely, a garment fashioned by her. This garment appears in the very next book, in the course of the Cyzicus episode (2.634–3.458). The Cyzicus episode is afforded considerable prominence by Valerius, who devotes almost three times more space to it than Apollonius. The essential details are, nonetheless, taken from his Greek predecessor. The Argonauts put to shore on an isthmus inhabited by the Doliones, and are graciously received there by the young king Cyzicus. After enjoying a few days of hospitality

---

53 Hershkowitz 1998, 143.

they set sail, but their erratic course accidentally leads them back to their point of departure, where they make landfall at night. In the darkness they fail to realize their navigational error, and the Doliones, thinking that they are under attack by their hostile neighbors, the Pelasgians, engage them in battle. A fierce conflict ensues in which the Doliones suffer a great many casualties, and Cyzicus himself is slain by Jason. When dawn finally breaks the awful mistake is revealed, suspending the fighting and precipitating anguished lamentation on both sides.

It is worth briefly pointing out that, as with the Lemnian massacre, so here in Valerius' account of the Dolionian slaughter there are suggestive evocations of the Virgilian fall of Troy. So, for example, "there can be no doubt that *hostis habet portus* (3.45), the cry of one of the Doliones, [...] harks back to Hector's admission of defeat to Aeneas, *hostis habet muros* (*Aen.* 2.290), or that *concretos sanguine crines*, applied both to the dead Cyzicus (3.286) and to Hector in Aeneas' dream (*Aen.* 2.277), is transferred intentionally from Troy in its utter destruction".[54]

Of more immediate interest for present purposes is the fact that, in the aftermath of the calamity, during Cyzicus' funeral rites, Jason places on the king's pyre a garment that had been given him by Hypsipyle, a cloak that she had hastily snatched from her loom, and given to Jason just before his departure from Lemnos (V. Fl. 3.340–342):

> dat pictas auro atque ardentes murice vestes
> quas rapuit telis festina vocantibus Austris
> Hypsipyle.

> He makes gift of a garment embroidered with gold and glowing with crimson dye, which Hypsipyle tore in haste from her loom when the south winds were calling.

As already noted, this second, retrospective mention of a Hypsipylean cloak notionally corresponds to the first such scene in the Hellenistic *Argonautica* (A.R. 3.1204–1206, cited and discussed above), thereby completing the transposed 'replay' of Apollonius' two passages. A question arises as to whether this garment is the same cloak given to Jason by Hypsipyle in the earlier passage. Critics are divided: of recent scholars, Poortvliet understands two references to a single cloak, whereas Spaltenstein insists they are different.[55] The question does not admit certainty, and it is not impossible that Valerius has deliberately replicated the ambiguity hovering over Apollonius' two cloak passages, as discussed earlier.

---

54 Garson 1964, 271.
55 Spaltenstein 2004, 106 f.; Poortvliet 1991, 224.

That said, the balance of the evidence seems to incline towards understanding two references to a single garment, which will be my operating assumption in what follows. The relative clause *quas rapuit telis festina … Hypsipyle* (3.341f.) speaks to the suddenness of the Argonauts' departure, which, as already noted, took the Lemnian women by surprise (2.393–396). The striking synchrony of the two gift-giving reports makes it difficult to imagine two virtually identical items being given at precisely the same moment. Regardless of how one answers the question, there is a clear evocation here of the Hypsipyle episode, and so a corresponding emotional 'carry-forward' from its final scene. Even more intriguingly, there is also a 'carry-back': Jason's gesture has retrospective implications for the earlier scene.

Hypsipyle clearly regarded her gifts as personal objects freighted with emotional significance, and so outside the 'economy' of gift exchange. The cloak in particular is a highly personal object that was meant to help him *not* to forget Hypsipyle, which she had meant for him to retain and keep close at hand. Her wish that Jason would retain her gifts as treasured and enduring keepsakes (expressed in the formulation *haesura … dona*, 2.408f.) is promptly dashed by his act of consigning the garment to the flames. For Jason the gifts are evidently just so many high-value items, freely to be circulated in the reciprocal regime of aristocratic gift exchange that pervades ancient epic. As part of this economy Jason had earlier presented Cyzicus with a cup and a Thessalian bridle (3.9–14); he now presents him with one final gift, Hypsipyle's cloak, to honor him in death. The fact that it is a splendid object made by royal hands adds to the prestige of the gesture, and that appears to be the extent of the matter for Jason. The alacrity with which he has re-circulated this particular gift – he received it some days earlier – underscores the conspicuous dashing of Hypsipyle's emotional aspirations. Worse still – this cloak is not even destined for ongoing circulation: it is consumed by the flames, along with the body of the slain king. The short life and prompt obliteration of the cloak seems emblematic of Jason's short-lived and superficial commitment to Hypsipyle and her memory. This is one of the jarring consequences of Valerius' proximate placement of his second Hypsipylean cloak passage. Jason's erotic career involves a series of relationships with women who seem to be interchangeable, and thus expendable, sexual partners. This is given symbolic expression in the aftermath of the first such relationship, when Jason consigns the cloak to the flames, a cloak that probably contains important biographical information about Hypsipyle, and so stood as an eloquent emblem of the woman herself.

There is, of course, a crucial intermediate model exerting its influence here: Jason's funereal gesture, his transforming, as it were, of Hypsipyle's cloak into Cyzicus' shroud strikes a resoundingly Virgilian note. As scholars have long recognized, the cloak placed on the corpse of Cyzicus recalls the cloak given by Dido to Aeneas, mentioned retrospectively, which Aeneas lay upon the corpse of Pallas, before returning it to Pallas' father Evander (Verg. *A.* 11.72–77):[56]

> tum geminas vestis auroque ostroque rigentis
> extulit Aeneas, quas illi laeta laborum
> ipsa suis quondam manibus Sidonia Dido
> fecerat et tenui telas discreverat auro.   75
> harum unam iuveni supremum maestus honorem
> induit arsurasque comas obnubit amictu.

> Then he (*scil.* Aeneas) brought forth two purple garments stiff with gold, that Sidonian Dido, happy over their work, had made for him, and shot the warp with delicate gold. One of these he sadly folds around him (*scil.* Pallas), a final honor, and veils with the cloak the hair about to burn.

The Virgilian 'replay' exemplifies Valerius' filtering of his Apollonian subject matter through the *Aeneid*, and, in broader terms, his fondness for the simultaneous use of multiple, mutually-intertwined intertextual models. More importantly for present purposes, the Virgilian evocation recalls Aeneas' two great interpersonal catastrophes: Dido and Pallas. The first catastrophe arises when he leaves Carthage and Dido, abandoned and childless, commits suicide. The second catastrophe, the battlefield death of his young charge Pallas, leaves an ally and friend, the elderly widower Evander, bereft of his only son. These are perhaps the two most devastating instances in the *Aeneid* of the 'collateral damage' caused by its protagonist carrying out his divinely ordained mission. And Aeneas' gesture of placing Dido's cloak on the corpse of Pallas creates a symbolic connection between the two victims of Trojan destiny.

The intertextual mapping is quite sophisticated here, involving systematic parallelism covering a range of passages in multiple episodes of two triads. By creating a linkage between Hypsipyle and Cyzicus through the cloak motif, Valerius is able to construct a sustained equivalence between his three characters Jason – Hypsipyle – Cyzicus and the Virgilian trio Aeneas – Dido – Pallas. The mapping culminates in a moment of profound grief caused by the wrenching battlefield death of a young man. Here Valerius' repeated emphasis on Cyzicus' youth helps to reinforce the parallelism, and the associative device registers more grimly than in the model, inasmuch as Jason has killed Cyzicus with his own hands.

---

56 Hershkowitz 1998, 142f.; similarly, e.g., Poortvliet 1991, 226f.; Spaltenstein 2004, 107; Carderi 2008, 219.

As we have seen, Hypsipyle is cast as an 'improved' Dido, and part of that improvement comes from her assimilation to the father-preserving Aeneas. Jason on the other hand, here evokes Virgil's Aeneas in his greatest lapse – and this as he probably destroys the very image of Hypsipyle's Aeneas-like heroics. Even the assimilation to the lapsed Aeneas does not occur without slippage that further throws into relief Jason's shortcomings. To begin with, Aeneas has two identical cloaks from Dido – Reed has suggested that Dido initially intended that she and Aeneas would each wear one on the twin thrones of Carthage.[57] Whatever the intended purpose, the Trojan hero clearly loses little in destroying one of two identical items. More importantly, there is a considerable difference in the interval of time and lived experience between Aeneas' and Jason's respective acts of receiving, and then parting with, the cloaks. In the Virgilian interval Aeneas has learned of Dido's death, encountered her shade in the underworld, and been irrevocably rejected by it: the relationship had been terminated in every conceivable sense. Aeneas' gift may be "ill omened inasmuch as it evoked the collapse of his reciprocal relationship with Dido",[58] but that collapse has already been acted out in full, making the consignment of the cloak to the funeral pyre an appropriate gesture in all respects. Jason, on the other hand, left Hypsipyle just days ago, and his relationship with her is still very much alive – at least from the point of view of Hypsipyle who, it will be recalled, is pregnant with Jason's child, and eagerly awaiting his return.

In the *Aeneid*, Aeneas' mission is consistently framed in patriarchal terms. Aeneas draws both from his father Anchises and his son Ascanius the motivation to persevere in the face of adversity. The passing of dynastic power from father to son is an intrinsic thematic element.[59] Pallas, of course, represents a failure of this process, and his Valerian counterpart, Cyzicus, embodies the same failure. The termination of his dynastic line is made emphatic by a gloomy rite that Valerius adds to his account. Immediately following the provision of Hypsipyle's cloak, Cyzicus' royal scepter is placed with his corpse, to burn along with it (V. Fl. 3.343–346):

> ... ille suum vultus conversus ad urbem
> sceptra manu veterum retinet gestamen avorum.
> nam quia nec proles alius nec denique sanguis,
> ipse decus regnique refert insigne parenti.

---

57 Reed 2009, 82.
58 Coffee 2010, 26.
59 Moskalew 1982, 179.

He (*scil.* the dead Cyzicus) with his face turned towards the city holds in his hand the scepter that his forefathers bore before him. For since no offspring nor any of his blood survives him, he bears back to his father the splendid emblem of his realm.

This bleak detail, which underscores the connection between Cyzicus and his city, is unique to Valerius' version. The royal and paternal emblem on the scepter (*insigne*, 3.346) recalls that on Thoas's sword (*insigne*, 2.418), which has of course been alienated from its rightful realm and has presumably participated in the terminated transmission of its Dolionian counterpart.

3 Broken Families

Through the structural device of Hypsipyle's cloak, then, Valerius' Lemnos and Cyzicus episodes are drawn into contact and made mutually informing. This is by no means an isolated effect: a number of additional elements draw the two episodes together. In this regard the figure of Cyzicus' young wife Clite is of particular interest. In Apollonius she is a non-speaking figure, whose grief-stricken suicide is reported almost as an afterthought.[60] In the Flavian *Argonautica*, by contrast, she features prominently, being afforded a lengthy speech of lament (3.316–329), as she clings (*haerentem*, 331) to her husband's dead body.[61] Clite mourns not just Cyzicus' death, but the fact that she has no children by him, which adds to her sense of desolation (V. Fl. 3.317–319):[62]

> '... necdum suboles nec gaudia de te
> ulla mihi, quis maesta tuos nunc, optime, casus
> perpeterer tenui luctum solamine fallens.'

> '... no progeny, no joy have I had from you by which I might, though sad, endure your fate, cheating my grief with that slight solace.'

Clite's bitter lament over the lack of progeny, which alone might have afforded consolation for the loss of Cyzicus, recalls the complaint by Virgil's Dido of

---

60 For this departure from Apollonius, see Manuwald 1999, 92 f.

61 Valerius' use of *haerentem* is perhaps not coincidental here: just a moment before Jason 're-places' Clite's embrace of Cyzicus' body with that of Hypsipyle's cloak, which was supposed to cling to him (*haesura*, 2.408, discussed above).

62 Valerius follows A.R. 1.973 in having the couple still childless at Cyzicus' death, but the Flavian poet makes much more of this detail; Hyg. *Fab.* 16 reports a rival version in which the couple had sons, whom Jason confirmed in power as their father's successors.

her own childless condition (*A.* 4.327–330).[63] As has been observed, Hypsipyle's earlier delineation depends upon Dido as a *negative* model, and nowhere is the inversion more striking than in her reproductive success: she is pregnant by Jason, and, indeed, is destined to bear twin sons. With the childless and bereft Clite, Dido is once again evoked, but the paradigm now plays out in all its Virgilian misery.[64] The two Valerian figures might be said to be connected by coordinated and complementary allusions to Virgil's Dido, invoked as an inverted or negative model in the first instance and a more direct model in the second.

Additional intertextual shadings in Clite's speech participate in the broader pattern of allusions to the fall of Troy in the two episodes. It was noted earlier that Valerius' account of the ill-fated battle between the Argonauts and Doliones, much like that of the Lemnian massacre, includes evocations of the Virgilian fall of Troy; Clite's speech now expands the frame of reference by evoking the *Homeric* fall of Troy. Her address to her dead husband suggestively recapitulates two wifely addresses by the Iliadic Andromache: her moving plea to the living Hector in *Iliad* 6, and her lament over his dead body in *Iliad* 24.[65] In the first instance, Clite declares that, because she had lost all members of her original family, Cyzicus had embodied all family relations for her – not just a husband, but a brother and a parent as well (V. Fl. 3.323–325):

> 'tu, mihi qui coniunx pariter fraterque parensque
> solus et a prima fueras spes una iuventa,
> deseris heu ...'

> 'You alone were my husband and brother and parent, and now you abandon me, my one hope from earliest maidenhood.'

This is clearly modeled on Andromache's speech at *Il.* 6.407–439, in which she anticipates Hector's death and the devastating impact it will have upon her. Like Clite, Andromache catalogues the obliteration of her original family – mostly slain by Achilles – and concludes that Hector now fulfills the roles of all those family relations (Hom. *Il.* 6.429 f.):

> Ἕκτορ ἀτὰρ σύ μοί ἐσσι πατὴρ καὶ πότνια μήτηρ
> ἠδὲ κασίγνητος, σὺ δέ μοι θαλερὸς παρακοίτης.

---

63 See, e.g., Garson 1964, 271; Poortvliet 1991, 230; Manuwald 1999, 93 f.
64 Except, of course, for Dido's suicide; Valerius does not follow Apollonius in reporting a grief-stricken by Clite. He does, however, create a secondary parallelism between Cyzicus and Dido, so that the couple constitutes a kind of intertextual 'composite', with the delusive conduct and death of Cyzicus 'rounding out' the replay of the Virgilian Dido: see Garson 1964, 270 f.
65 Garson 1964, 271; Hershkowitz 1998, 94.

'You, Hector, are father to me, and queenly mother, you are my brother and my stalwart husband.'

No less striking are the echoes of Andromache's lament over Hector's corpse in the final book of the *Iliad*. Her declaration *primis coniunx mihi ereptus in annis* (3.316, 'husband, taken from me in your prime') echoes *Il.* 24.725 ἄνερ ἀπ' αἰῶνος νέος ὤλεο ('husband, you perished young'). Likewise Clite's complaint (V. Fl. 3.326–328):

> ast ego non media te saltem, Cyzice, vidi
> tendentem mihi morte manus aut ulla monentis
> verba tuli.

> But I did not even see you. Cyzicus, reaching out to me in the midst of death or carry away any word of advice.

recapitulates that of the Homeric Andromache (Hom. *Il.* 24.743–745):

> οὐ γάρ μοι θνήσκων λεχέων ἐκ χεῖρας ὄρεξας,
> οὐδέ τί μοι εἶπες πυκινὸν ἔπος, οὗ τέ κεν αἰεὶ
> μεμνήμην νύκτάς τε καὶ ἤματα δάκρυ χέουσα.

> For you did not die in bed, raising your hands to me, nor did you say any wise words to me, which I could always remember, shedding tears for you night and day.

Hector is the preeminent Homeric instance of a warrior who leaves behind a widow, and it is through his death, the most important of the *Iliad*, that Homer adumbrates the fall of Troy, an event that he never directly narrates. Valerius here draws upon the deep Iliadic sympathy for Hector, and in so doing implicitly assimilates Jason to the family destroying Achilles.[66] This places Jason on the wrong side of the paradigm – and the opposite side from Hypsipyle.

Indeed, Hypsipyle is a particularly apt figure for throwing Jason's shortcomings into relief. Whereas Hypsipyle's disposition and activity are consistently directed towards unification and preservation of the family, Jason's are directed, however unwittingly, towards fragmentation and destruction. As Hutchinson well observes, "the moral contrast between the dutiful Hypsipyle and the forgetful Jason is related to her literary immortalization and his grim fate".[67] The Lemnian episode "associates intrafamilial violence with a wider inversion of social

---

66 Knight 1995, 89 detects this Iliadic connection in Apollonius' Cyzicus episode, so that Valerius is here drawing upon his Hellenistic predecessor.
67 Hutchinson 2014, 173.

norms".[68] Against this narrative backdrop, Hypsipyle's rescue of her father assumes overpowering importance as the epic's outstanding exemplum of familial *pietas*. The authorial apostrophe by which she is introduced (2.242–246, cited above) underscores the centrality of familial *pietas* in Valerius' epic. And it is precisely here that Jason falls short.

By the end of Book 3, Jason has directly or indirectly caused the fragmentation or destruction of four different families: his original family and that of the tyrant Pelias in Thessaly, his nascent family with Hypsipyle, and that of Cyzicus. This is a substantial accumulation of 'collateral damage'. Here we should recall that Valerius deviates from Apollonius and the entire poetic tradition in having Jason's father Aeson die at the end of Book 1, forced to commit suicide by the tyrant Pelias' death sentence. Along with Aeson, his wife Alcimede commits suicide, and Jason's younger brother is callously executed by Pelias' henchmen. This eradication of Jason's nuclear family is the direct result of his vindictive recruitment of Pelias' innocent son Acastus, an act of aggression against Pelias' family, to which the tyrant responds by ordering the execution of Jason's father (1.709–725). Jason's rash act is disastrously compounded by negligence in not providing for the security of his family prior to departing (1.693–698).[69] In this sequence, as one critic notes, "Jason is allowed to appear stupid, or at least grossly improvident".[70] As I have argued elsewhere, "in neglecting to provide for his father and family Jason emerges as something of an Aeneas manqué".[71]

Aeson, who, unbeknownst to Jason, took his own life shortly after Argo's departure, is subtly integrated into the familial calculus of the Cyzicus episode through a pair of references that 'frame' the battle narrative itself. Before unwittingly taking up arms against his former host, Jason addresses his absent father (3.81), invoking him on the eve of a battle that will leave Cyzicus' family as devastated as his own. This provides, at the start of Jason's latest interpersonal calamity, an ironic reminder that Aeson is dead as a result of Jason's prior reckless conduct. The second reference to Aeson comes when Jason, in his lament over

---

68 Bernstein 2008, 31, with a useful discussion.

69 A noteworthy departure from Apollonius's account, in which Acastus joins the expedition of his own accord (1.321–323), with no consequences for Jason's family: see Zissos 2008, 167 and 172–173.

70 Gossage 1969, 93.

71 Zissos 2008, 367. Again, we might compare Apollonius' Jason's concerns to provide for his family's protection, as seen in his instructions to Hypsipyle (1.904–909, discussed above). It should also be noted that, in opting for this version, Valerius has preempted Jason's one celebrated gesture of filial *pietas* in the earlier tradition: his request, after his homecoming, that Medea magically transfer years from his own lifespan to that of his ailing father (Ov. *Met.* 7.164–168; characterized as *pietas* at 169).

the death of Cyzicus, mentions that his father's impending death had been prophesied to him before Argo set sail (3.302). This disclosure, which underscores his thoughtlessness in not providing for his family's defense, once again brings the latest instance of familial destruction into contact with its predecessor. At their parting Jason and Cyzicus had not only cemented their relationship through a formal gift exchange, but had also joined hands in a symbolic union of their two families: *minibus ... datis iunxere penates* ('they clasped hands and made their houses one', 3.14).[72] As it turned out, this symbolic union of the two families guaranteed their mutual devastation.

4 Conclusion

This essay began by identifying Valerius' transposition and reconception of the Hypsipylean cloak passages as a characteristic reworking of Apollonius' treatment, and then considered its broader implications for the thematic economy of the poem. As I have observed elsewhere, whereas the Hellenistic poem unfolds according to a guiding aesthetic that privileges miniaturization, digression and episodic juxtaposition, the Flavian *Argonautica* consistently strives to create strong thematic and figural connections between different parts of his epic. Valerius integrates Apollonius' disparate episodes through robust narrative structures, created by studied use of symmetry, parallelism and internal echo.[73] The linkage achieved by Valerius' ingenious reconception and repositioning of the Apollonian references to Hypsipylean cloaks is a case in point. As has been shown, this inherited device, filtered through Virgil's *Aeneid*, participates in a broader web of connections between the Lemnos and Cyzicus episodes. Valerius' inventive reshaping of the contours of the two episodes further contributes to the effect. So, for example, in motivating the two episodes the Flavian poet has generated the shared motif of an offended female deity overcome by 'epic anger' at a human affront: Venus is outraged at her lack of worship on Lemnos; Cybele at Cyzicus' unwitting slaying of one of her lions. In the latter case, Valerius has invented this 'back story' to motivate through divine affront what Apollonius simply attributed to human accident and a vague notion of destiny. Both goddesses satisfy their wrath by engineering a mass slaughter – and both massacres are emphatically nocturnal. Apollonius, by contrast, as Venini points out, does

---

72 On the 'created kinship' so formed, see Bernstein 2008, 52.
73 Zissos 2008, xxviii.

not specify that the Lemnian slaughter took place at night (A.R. 1.609–626).[74] By accentuating the grizzly nocturnal element in the Lemnian episode (2.171f., 196f., 291f., 396) Valerius has aligned it with the Cyzicus episode – and of course the fall of Troy.[75] The respective deities' callous indifference to the many innocent victims their actions cause is another shared feature of the two divine revenge schemes, as is the fact that the victims are all male.[76] Indeed, Valerius' strategy of episodic convergence is evident in his invocation of what might be called the 'Lemnian scenario' in the later episode. That is to say, Jupiter eventually intervenes to halt the battlefield carnage because, had it continued, the entire male population would have been lost and the ability to self-propagate along with it (V. Fl. 3.246–248):

> quod si tanta lues seros durasset in ortus,
> exstinctum genus et solas per moenia matres
> vidisset stratamque dies in litore gentem.

> If such slaughter had lasted until dawn broke at length, then that day would have seen the race extinguished, nothing but mothers upon the walls, and a nation lying dead upon the shore.

The parallel drawn here is striking precisely because it is not really valid. Even if all the combatants had been slain, male children and adolescents would have survived, as well as older men. But this notionally replicates the demographic threat to Lemnos faced by the island's all-female population after the massacre. Such straining for parallelism underscores Valerius' overarching strategy of episodic convergence, a convergence that, as we have seen, maintains contact with Hypsipyle and her story, thereby affirming its importance for the subsequent narrative.

---

74 Venini 1972, 16f., pointing out Valerius' broader preference for nocturnal scenes, which bring out elements of horror; for the nocturnal slaughter motif, see also Gärtner 1998, 209.
75 As Burck 1971, 173ff. points out, the Argonauts' battle with the Doliones is one of the very few night battles in ancient epic.
76 Bernstein 2008, 52.

VI War and Generic Tensions

Helen Lovatt

The beautiful face of war: Refreshing epic and reworking Homer in Flavian poetry

"War is beautiful because it establishes man's dominion over the subjugated machinery by means of gas masks, terrifying megaphones, flame throwers, and small tanks. War is beautiful because it initiates the dreamt-of metalization of the human body. War is beautiful because it enriches a flowering meadow with the fiery orchids of machine guns. War is beautiful because it combines the gunfire, the cannonades, the cease-fire, the scents, and the stench of putrefaction into a symphony. War is beautiful because it creates new architecture, like that of the big tanks, the geometrical formation flights, the smoke spirals from burning villages, and many others …".

Filippo Tommaso Marinetti, quoted by Walter Benjamin.[1]

1 Introduction

When Statius narrates the first full day of warfare, the real beginning, the march-out of the *Thebaid* in book 8, he points out the beauty of war (Stat. *Theb.* 8.402–405):

pulcher adhuc belli vultus: stant vertice coni,
plena armenta viris, nulli sine praeside currus,
arma loco, splendent clipei pharetraeque decorae
cingulaque et nondum deforme cruoribus aurum.   405

Beautiful still is the face of war: the helmet-peaks stand straight, the horses are complete with men, no chariot is without a guide, arms are in their place, shields shine, quivers and belts are fine, and gold is not yet dulled by blood.

He was not the only observer in the ancient world to see this beauty, as Sappho fr. 16 shows:

ο]ἰ μὲν ἰππήων στρότον, οἰ δὲ πέσδων,
οἰ δὲ νάων φαῖσ' ἐπ[ὶ] γᾶν μέλαι[ν]αν
ἔμμεναι κάλλιστον, ἔγω δὲ κῆν' ὄτ-
    τω τις ἔραται·

Some say thronging cavalry, some say foot soldiers,
others call a fleet the most beautiful of

---

1 Marinetti 1912 quoted by Benjamin 1969, 241 f.

https://doi.org/10.1515/9783110534436-013

sights the dark earth offers, but I say it's whatever you love best.

Sappho is making an argument about different types of beauty: we all have our own opinions, whether about erotic beauty, or different types of military beauty, or the relationship between the two. This argument must be generic as well as gendered: Sappho has chosen not to write about the glory of military success, but about erotic desire. The workings of Sappho's argument, the use of Helen as an example, and the nature of her erotic desire, have all received a good deal of attention; the idea of cavalry, foot soldiers and fleets as beautiful has received much less.[2] Similarly, when people are interested in the aesthetics of war, they usually think about the aesthetics of violence, which is not exactly the same thing.[3] The horror of war is never entirely absent, as we will see, but there is a beauty of order, power and potential which exists primarily at the beginning of war and is intensified by its impending horror.[4] The aftermath of battles and the horrors of 'thanatotourism' have received some attention, with a focus on viewing battlefields.[5] What of the other end of war, namely its beginning, as an encapsulation of the strength, potential and power of individuals and societies? My recent book explores the active beauty of the hero, especially when he is compared to a horse as he enthusiastically gallops to war.[6] Faces are important, of course, but there is an impersonal beauty to the march-out as well, seen from the perspective of a distant viewer. This distance, as in Lucretius 2.5–6, where the philosophical viewer of another's troubles is compared to someone watching a war unfold from a high mountain-top, evokes the sublimity of shifts in perspective. The sublime is another key concept when thinking about the aesthetics of war (and the aesthetics of epic battle in particular):[7] positive and negative, beauty and destruction, overwhelming force and terror, all contribute to

---

2 See for instance Pelliccia 1992; Fredricksmeyer 2001; Zellner 2007.

3 Chariotis 2005, 189–213. His chapter "Aesthetics of War" is primarily about the Hellenistic aesthetic and how it relates to representations of war in art and historiography, especially realism, violence and sudden reversals of fortune.

4 My colleague Richard Rawles suggests an analogy with ballet: a lifetime of physical training, a large number of people working together, discipline and physical beauty.

5 Lovatt 1999, Pagán 2000, Manolaraki 2005.

6 Lovatt 2013.

7 Epic as sublime genre: "In generic terms, the totalising, panoptic aspirations of epic exhibit affinities with the sublime's superhuman impulses" (Day 2013, 13).

the fundamental ambivalence of the sublime.[8] But the beauty of war is not reducible to the sublime.

Many questions underlie this chapter: to what extent is the beauty of war a generic construct? Does epic treat war more as a spectacle than, say, historiography? How and why is war beautiful? What is it about war that makes it beautiful? These questions are much more effectively addressed at the beginning of war than in its complex and muddied aftermath. This paper tackles the question of genre by, on the one hand, going back to the code model of epic, the *Iliad*, and, on the other, comparing Flavian epic with other Flavian literature. It focuses on three main areas: first, how does Statius refresh the idea of epic by going back to Homer?[9] Secondly, how does Statius' approach to the topos of the march-out compare to the approaches of Valerius and Silius? Thirdly, how does the image of fresh, new, beautiful war compare with images of war in other genres, particularly in the Flavian period? In the end, this chapter aims to enrich our appreciation of the ways in which ancient writers approached the idea of war as beautiful.

2 Homer and the march-out

A topos of epic poetry (and, more recently, epic film) is the march-out scene. As the two armies prepare to join battle, each army musters and marches out to the battlefield, ready to fight and as yet undamaged. The *Iliad* is foundational for defining this "theme of armies marching out to battle".[10] There are three main passages that contribute to the Iliadic march-out, spread across books two to four: at 2.445–487 the troops muster; Athene inspires the Achaeans; in a series of similes the troops are compared to a forest fire, a flock of birds, a meadow full of flowers, a swarm of insects, a herd of goats; Agamemnon orders them, himself compared to an ox; the poet calls on the Muse and the catalogue of ships begins. At 3.1–14 the catalogue is over and the two armies face each other. The noise of

---

8 My reading of the sublime is indebted to Day 2013, which is an excellent introduction to theories of the sublime, and focuses on epic as a genre.

9 On Statius and Homer, see Juhnke 1972, who gathered much data; Smolenaars 1991 has many excellent observations on Statian intertextuality; McNelis 2007 (and 2004) has argued that Statius sets a Callimachean tendency against a non-Callimachean aesthetic, along the way pointing out the depth and detail of Statius' engagement with Homer, for instance in the catalogue of book 7. I have discussed elsewhere (in Lovatt 2005) the games of *Thebaid* 6. I am inspired by Frisby 2013, which examines the *Thebaid* as a rich reading of Homer and argues that Statius takes the epic figure of substitution to such an extreme that it becomes a comment on the nature of epic itself. On Statius and Greek literature see Augoustakis 2014.

10 Kirk 1985, 380.

the Trojans is compared to the clamour of cranes, in contrast to the silence of the Achaeans. The dust raised by their feet is compared to mist on the mountain. Finally at 4.422–455 the armies clash and the actual battle begins: the Danaans' feet sound like waves crashing onto the shore, while the Trojans bleat like a flock of sheep; gods and personifications drive them on, culminating with the figure of Eris who grows enormous, into the sky; the clash of shields and spears creates a huge sound; the shock of meeting is like the shock of two rivers in flood crashing into each other. These three passages work together to create a powerful image of the enormity of the conflict in the *Iliad*.[11]

These passages have long been seen as powerful and memorable:[12] but what gives them such a strong impact? The density of imagery is one factor: the cluster of seven images leading up to the catalogue, along with the catalogue itself, constitutes the most powerful and detailed description of the greatness of both the Achaean army and the *Iliad* itself.[13] Scott argues that the similes used here all evoke more intense versions in the same simile families and that the main impression is of the weak leadership of Agamemnon.[14] According to Scott, the imagery "presents a consistent poetic background of the more lyrical and peaceful qualities of nature": I am not convinced that pastoral implies weakness. These similes function as a prelude to later more intense images. Further, the imagery of agriculture creates a strong contrast between ordered productivity and the destruction to come. Several images evoke the natural sublime, the awe-inspiring power of natural forces, which overwhelms the viewer and creates a strong sense of smallness in the face of the universe: the forest fire, mountain mist, crashing waves and clashing floods all invoke in different ways Kant's "dynamical sub-

---

11 Kirk 1985, 264 points out the close connection between this passage and the beginning of book 3: "The repetitions and overlapping imagery serve to link the elaborate scenes of preparation with the actual advance of each army". Similarly, he points to the striking correspondence with the "first elaborate march-out" at 4.422–456. See Kirk 1985, 376–385 on this section.

12 From the scholiasts onwards these passages have made a great impression: Kirk (1985, 163) points out that "AbT rightly drew attention to the grandeur of conception and language" in the passage of book 2. Of the book 4 images, and the whole sequence, he says: "The effect of these repeated images of the noise and surge of waves and torrents is to give an unforgettable impression of the size and power and serried ranks of the Achaeans in particular, almost like a force of nature itself; and incidentally to suggest how earlier scenes […] lead in the end to the vast clash of arms which is now to follow".

13 "Never again will the power of the largest expeditionary force in Greek legend be made so explicit with the names of heroes from all parts of the Greek world joined in the panoramic display […] a moment of order from which the maelstrom of the *Iliad* will be generated" (Scott 2005, 28).

14 Scott 2005.

lime".[15] The forest fire image is particularly interesting because it uses a negative and terrifying image to describe a positive visual glory (Hom. *Il.* 2.455–458):

> Ἠΰτε πῦρ ἀΐδηλον ἐπιφλέγει ἄσπετον ὕλην   455
> οὔρεος ἐν κορυφῇς, ἔκαθεν δέ τε φαίνεται αὐγή,
> ὣς τῶν ἐρχομένων ἀπὸ χαλκοῦ θεσπεσίοιο
> αἴγλη παμφανόωσα δι' αἰθέρος οὐρανὸν ἷκε.

As obliterating fire lights up a vast forest along the crests of a mountain, and the flare shows far off, so as they marched from the magnificent bronze the gleam went dazzling all about through the upper air to the heaven. (transl. Lattimore)

The fire is destructive, distant, and associated with mountain peaks. Its brightness is like the gleam of the weapons shining upwards to heaven. Similarly, the awe-inspiring destructive power of the sea is harnessed through waves which build and repeatedly strike the shore to describe the beat of an enormous number of feet (Hom. *Il.* 4.422–428). Other images fit into the category of Kant's "mathematical sublime":[16] the numbers are too great for the mind to grasp. The sky full of migrating birds, fields full of leaves and flowers, and insects swarming, all evoke uncountable numbers. Herds of goats and sheep further imply prosperity, and the tone of these images evokes natural order and the order of prosperous human endeavour. Agamemnon's wealth and power are also awe-inspiring. In effect, these scenes are what epic is all about: size, power and force. The force of the multitudes constitutes the force of epic poetry. The beauty of the march-out scene, then, lies in the gigantic number of people, ordered, equipped and facing imminent destruction.

The epigraph from Marinetti is interesting partly because it seems to pick up on some of the Homeric images: war "enriches a flowering meadow with the fiery orchids of machine guns" which refers to fire and flowers; "geometrical formation flights" might apply to migrating birds as well as fighter planes; the technology of the day takes its place with gleaming bronze in place of tanks and guns, farming in place of factories; sounds (waves, fire) and smells (flowers, goats) as well as distant views. The Homeric poems already possess a keen sense of the paradoxical beauty of war.

---

15 Day 2013, 52–55 on the Kantian sublime.
16 Day 2013, 54.

3 Statius and Homer

The main focus of this paper is a passage in book 8 of the *Thebaid* in which Statius offers a new 're-beginning' of his poem. At *Thebaid* 8.342–427 the second day of fighting begins. On the previous day and in the previous book, the Argive army had finally arrived at Thebes; Jocasta's desperate attempt to stop the fighting was interrupted and overwhelmed by the infuriation of the tigers of Bacchus. Book 8 begins with the aftermath of Amphiaraus' living *katabasis*. Finally there is a sequence which represents the first formal joining of battle in the poem: each side marches out, the Thebans from the seven gates, all named (353–357), the Argives led by Thiodamas and still lamenting Amphiaraus. Statius signals a new beginning with a new invocation.

Our passage has much in common with the Homeric march-out sequence, both in structure and detail. It begins with an invocation, in which Statius asks Apollo for a greater lyre, signifying a more epic (and, I would argue, more Homeric) mode (Stat. *Theb.* 8.373 f.):

> sed iam bella vocant: alias nova suggere vires,
> Calliope, maiorque chelyn mihi tendat Apollo.
>
> But now wars call: pile up other strength for new things, Calliope, and may a greater Apollo make taut my lyre for me.

Our first Homeric passage (*Il.* 2.445–487) begins with Athena inspiring troops with the aegis and driving them to war; later at *Il.* 4.439–445 Ares and various personifications, culminating with Eris, continue Athena's work. Statius' passage is fundamentally based on the book four passage, but includes elements from the passages in books two and three. The personifications Death, the Furies and the Fates take over the battlefield, leading to Mars, who expels from the mind reasons for holding back in battle. Homer's series of similes lurks in metaphorical form: at 390 the horses burn (*flammantur*) to attack (cf. image of forest fire at *Il.* 2.455–458); the dust/weather connection at *Il.* 3.10–14 operates in 391 *niveoque rigant sola putria nimbo* ('they spatter the dusty soil with a snowy cloud'). The clash at 398 f.:

> iam clipeus clipeis, umbone repellitur umbo,
> ense minax ensis, pede pes et cuspide cuspis...
>
> Now shield on shield, boss pushes against boss, sword threatens sword, foot against foot, spear against spear...

with its emphasis on shield and boss draws on (among other passages) Hom. *Il.* 4.446–449:

Οἳ δ' ὅτε δή ῥ' ἐς χῶρον ἕνα ξυνιόντες ἵκοντο,
σύν ῥ' ἔβαλον ῥινούς, σὺν δ' ἔγχεα καὶ μένε' ἀνδρῶν
χαλκεοθωρήκων· ἀτὰρ ἀσπίδες ὀμφαλόεσσαι
ἔπληντ' ἀλλήλῃσι, πολὺς δ' ὀρυμαγδὸς ὀρώρει.

> Now as these advancing came to one place and encountered, they clashed their shields to-
> gether and their spears, and the strength of armoured men in bronze, and the shields mas-
> sive in the middle clashed against each other, and the sound grew huge of the fighting.

This, the most Statian of mannered passages, with its heavily patterned and re-petitive polyptota, is in fact the most Homeric part, which suggests that stylistic oppositions between the "primitive and original best" and the "mannered late-comer" are artificial. The emphasis on shining at 401 (*nitent*) and 404 (*splendent*) recalls the gleam reaching to the heavens at Hom. *Il.* 2.457 f. and the shining ar-mour at 4.431 f. The passage in *Iliad* 4 finishes with the huge sound arising from battle, which is compared to the clash of two torrents. In a series of weather im-ages, Statius compares the *fragor* of battle with the crash of a snowstorm on Rho-dope, the boom of Jupiter's thunder and noise of hail on the Syrtes (407–411). The mass of missiles (javelins, rocks, arrows) at 412–421 continues the storm theme (*nubila*, 413; *pluunt*, *fulgura* 417), which comes to a climax at 413–417 with a re-working of the Homeric image of the two rivers in flood crashing into each other as two winds clashing (*alterno turbine*, 424), although the surprise ending on *se-reno* (417) changes this into a battle between storm and calm.

Resonances of other Homeric material underline the Homeric connections in this section of the *Thebaid*. Juhnke points out the similarity between Tisiphone at 8.344–347 inspiring the Thebans with the trumpet and Eris at *Iliad* 11.5–14, in which her cry stimulates desire for battle, including a repetition of 2.453 f. at 11.13 f.[17] He also notes the detailed echo in the highly mannered lines 398 f. of *Iliad* 13.130–135:

φράξαντες δόρυ δουρί, σάκος σάκεϊ προθελύμνῳ	130
ἀσπὶς ἄρ' ἀσπίδ' ἔρειδε, κόρυς κόρυν, ἀνέρα δ' ἀνήρ·	
ψαῦον δ' ἱππόκομοι κόρυθες λαμπροῖσι φάλοισι	
νευόντων, ὡς πυκνοὶ ἐφέστασαν ἀλλήλοισιν·	
ἔγχεα δ' ἐπτύσσοντο θρασειάων ἀπὸ χειρῶν	
σειόμεν'· οἳ δ' ἰθὺς φρόνεον, μέμασαν δὲ μάχεσθαι.	135

---

17 Juhnke 1972, 126.

locking spear by spear, shield against shield at the base, so buckler leaned on buckler, helmet on helmet, man against man, and the horse-hair crests along the horns of their shining helmets touched as they bent their heads, so dense were they formed on each other, and the spears shaken from their daring hands made a jagged battle line.

Juhnke meticulously compares the lines in Statius with other imitations of the Homeric lines in Ennius, Furius, *Aeneid* 10 and Silius 4 and 9; Statius and Homer have more elements in common than any of the other versions have with either.[18] The density of the engagement is also a key theme in the Statian passage.

There are, of course, many differences of tone and emphasis. There is a darker tone in the *Thebaid*. The image of Death flying over the battlefield and causing a sort of night to fall, made psychological as Mars removes the love of light from the fighters, and literal as the densely packed weapons obscure the sun, can be contrasted with the predominance of light in the Homeric passages. In Homer there is clear differentiation between the bleating Trojans and the glittering Achaeans, while in Statius all the fighters are, as is appropriate in this more than civil war, one undifferentiated mass. However, there is a real sense that Statius is going back to the *Iliad* here to make a claim for his own battle as the most epic of Roman literature.

Let us come back to the four lines with which we started and the 'beautiful face of war' (Stat. *Theb.* 8.402–405):

> pulcher adhuc belli vultus: stant vertice coni,
> plena armenta viris, nulli sine praeside currus,
> arma loco, splendent clipei pharetraeque decorae
> cingulaque et nondum deforme cruoribus aurum.   405

Beautiful still is the face of war: the helmet-peaks stand straight, the horses are complete with men, no chariot is without a guide, arms are in their place, shields shine, quivers and belts are fine, and gold is not yet dulled by blood.

Statius seems to use the explicit articulation of the beauty of war to offset the darkness. The descriptions of the different aspects of troops begin positively,

---

18 Enn. *Ann.* 584 Sk.; Bib. *poet.* 10 Morel; Verg. *A.* 10.361; Sil. 4.352 f.; 9.322–325 (see below). Statius and Homer are the only texts to include a spear, and to use two different shield-related pairs (σάκος and ἀσπίς; *clipeus* and *umbo*). *Pes pede* enters the tradition with Ennius, perhaps inspired by Tyrt. 8.31 (καὶ πόδα πὰρ ποδὶ θεὶς καὶ ἐπ' ἀσπίδος ἀσπίδ' ἐρείσας) and *viro vir* with Furius Bibaculus (picking up on Hom. *Il.* 16.215 ἀσπὶς ἄρ' ἀσπίδ' ἔρειδε, κόρυς κόρυν, ἀνέρα δ'ἀνήρ); these are the two that are repeated in Verg. *A.* 10. *Mucro mucrone* in Furius seems likely to have inspired *ense ensis* in Statius, which is in turn echoed by Silius (or vice versa).

but soon betray a negative evocation of the destruction that will soon occur. The double negative in *nulli sine praeside currus* ('no chariot without its guide', 403) brings out the double vision here: the beauty of war is a veneer through which we can already see the imminent chaos, disorder and death. As the forest fire encapsulates both brilliance and destruction, so the splendour of the shields (and their honour: *decorae*, 404) quickly changes into *nondum deforme cruoribus aurum* ('gold not yet deformed by gore', 405).

We can see this when we compare Statius' build-up to war with those of the *Aeneid* and other Flavian epicists. Valerius, Statius and Silius all mix Homer with Virgil, and Lucan is another important influence. By examining various passages in the *Aeneid*, Lucan book 7 (the battle of Pharsalus), Valerius Flaccus book 6 (the war between Perses and Aeetes, inserted into the Argonautic narrative) and Silius Italicus book 9 (the battle of Cannae), I explore how these various marches and clashes compare to those in Homer and Statius.

4 Virgilian and Homeric beginnings

There is no equivalent scene depicting the march-out and joining of formal battle in Virgil, but elements of the march-out persist in the framing of the catalogue in book 7. When the Italians respond to the death of Silvia's stag (7.511–530), Allecto blows a pastoral horn, and the farmers and the Trojans flock for an 'unagricultural struggle' (523 *non certamine agresti*). Virgil reflects on the pastoral tone of the imagery in Homer's mustering by making it literally pastoral and underlining the point of departure between normal farming life and war (Verg. *A.* 7.523–530):

> derexere acies. non iam certamine agresti
> stipitibus duris agitur sudibusue praeustis,
> sed ferro ancipiti decernunt atraque late   525
> horrescit strictis seges ensibus, aeraque fulgent
> sole lacessita et lucem sub nubila iactant:
> fluctus uti primo coepit cum albescere vento,
> paulatim sese tollit mare et altius undas
> erigit, inde imo consurgit ad aethera fundo.   530

The lines are drawn; this is no country battle with sturdy clubs or burned-out firebrands; they fight with two-edged steel, a horrid harvest of unsheathed swords that bristle far and wide, and arms of brass that glisten when the sun strikes and they fling their light beneath the clouds: as when a wave, beneath the wind's first breath, begins to whiten; slow by slow, the sea will lift its combers higher until, at last, it climbs to heaven from its lowest depths. (transl. Mandelbaum)

Here pastoral imagery creeps into the battle (*seges*), but otherwise it bears a strong resemblance to the Homeric material. The shining bronze which challenges the sun and throws its light up to the clouds re-works *Il.* 2.457 f., while the simile takes a different line on the waves at 4.422–426. The emphasis is not on the power of the army, but on the power of the war itself, as emotions and momentum build. But this is emphatically not a march-out, a formal joining of battle: Latinus resists. Against his will the allies gather for the catalogue. The invocation (Verg. *A.* 7.641–646) evokes other Homeric moments:

> Pandite nunc Helicona, deae, cantusque movete,
> qui bello exciti reges, quae quemque secutae
> *complerint campos acies, quibus Itala iam tum*
> *floruerint terra alma viris, quibus arserit armis.*
> et meministis enim, divae, et memorare potestis;   645
> ad nos vix tenuis famae perlabitur aura.

> O goddesses, now open Helicon and guide my song: what kings were spurred to war; what squadrons filled the plains behind each chieftain; what men graced lovely Italy even then; what arms set her ablaze. For goddesses, you can remember and retell; the slender breath of that fame can scarcely reach to us. (transl. Mandelbaum)

The metaphors of the Italian earth, first flowering with men then burning with arms, evoke two of the Homeric similes from the cluster that introduces the catalogue. When Evander's troops leave Pallanteum with Pallas in their midst, there is something of a march-out, with dust, shining armour and the beautiful face of Pallas. But Aeneas' absence in book 8 means that formal battle cannot be joined: book 9 consists of siege, sortie, and Turnus' single-handed invasion of the walls. Only in book 10, with the arrival of Aeneas, and his fiery shield at 10.260–275, is there a sense of battle properly begun: but the fact of Aeneas' arrival by boat completely changes the dynamics of the battle. Instead of a charge there is a disembarkation. Even in book 11 the next day of battle begins with the ambush planned by Turnus and Camilla, while battle in book 12 is again unplanned, sparked off in response to the breaking of the truce (reworking *Iliad* 4, but without the formal context of battle). It is as if Virgil holds back from committing himself to a fully Iliadic confrontation, even as he reworks the initiatory gestures of the *Iliad* into his own climax.

In *Thebaid* 7, Statius comments on, and arguably corrects, Virgil's re-working of Homer. Bacchus' tigers are clearly modelled on Silvia's stag, but Tisiphone enrages the tigers, who are responsible for their own deaths. Statius inverts the structures of violator and violated: the tame becomes wild, and the invading force is unjustly attacked. When the Argive forces respond, breaking up Tydeus' impassioned call to war, which in itself inverts Diomedes' response to Agamemnon in the Epipolesis, they respond in manifest disorder (Stat. *Theb.* 7.615–631):

> ... saevus iam clamor et irae 615
> hinc atque inde calent; nullo venit ordine bellum,
> confusique duces vulgo, et neglecta regentum
> imperia; una equites mixti peditumque catervae
> et rapidi currus; premit indigesta ruentes
> copia, nec sese vacat ostentare nec hostem 620
> noscere. sic subitis Thebana Argivaque pubes
> conflixere globis; retro vexilla tubaeque
> post tergum et litui bellum invenere secuti.
> tantus ab exiguo crudescit sanguine Mavors!
> ventus uti primas struit intra nubila vires, 625
> lenis adhuc, frondesque et aperta cacumina gestat,
> mox rapuit nemus et montes patefecit opacos.
> nunc age, Pieriae, non vos longinqua, sorores,
> consulimus, vestras acies vestramque referte
> Aoniam; vidistis enim, dum Marte propinquo 630
> horrent Tyrrhenos Heliconia plectra tumultus.

Now there is a savage shouting and angers here and there grow hot; war comes in no order, the leaders are mixed with the herd, and the commands of those in charge are ignored; the cavalry are mixed together with squadrons of footsoldiers and swift chariots; the heaped up supply of men itself presses them in as they rush, neither is there space to show themselves nor to recognise the enemy. So the Theban and Argive youth clashed in sudden clumps; the banners and the trumpets are behind their backs and the war-horns following them find war. How great a war grows red with blood from such a small beginning! Just as a wind builds its first strength within the clouds, still gentle, and carries along the leaves and open treetops, soon it has seized the grove and laid open the dark mountains. Now come, Pierian sisters, we consult you not about distant deeds, tell of your own columns and your own Aonia; for you have seen it, while with war too close the Heliconian lyre shudders at Tyrrhenian tumult.

Juhnke considers 615–627 as an inversion of Verg. *A.* 7.505–530. While Virgil has taken the imagery of the Homeric march-out and destabilised it by making it part of the plan of the forces of chaos, Statius separates the two parts again. His Virgilian beginning of war puts the emphasis on disorder in book 7, culminating in Hades' *pereant agedum discrimina rerum* ('let all the distinctions of matter perish', *Theb.* 8.37). Smolenaars suggests that the choice of the relatively rare *indigesta* in *premit indigesta ruentes / copia* (619 f.) may echo Ovid's description of chaos at *Metamorphoses* 1.7 (*chaos, rudis indigestaque moles*), lending weight to the cosmic implications of the military disorder in this passage. Order is at least superficially restored with our second beginning, this time an Iliadic beginning, a march-out with its sponsoring deities, and glittering armour.

I explore this response to Virgil's use of Homer further through the way Statius has reworked the image at 7.625–627 from *A.* 7.528–530, which itself transforms *Il.* 4.422–428. In the *Iliad* this image forms the climax of the march-out: the army appears as waves crashing repetitively onto the shore, with the noise explicitly compared to the beat of marching feet. In the *Aeneid* this becomes a single wave gradually growing up to heaven under the impetus of the wind, like the figure of Eris, a symbol of the war gradually taking hold. Statius moves the focus from wave to wind, from sea to land; the storm is now in the trees, not at sea, so the Homeric aspects of the Virgilian simile have been effaced.[19] This movement from sea to land or land to sea is a feature of Virgil's engagement with Homer: his chariot race becomes a ship race, his march-out a disembarkation. With his chariot race, Statius presents himself as going back to Homer: and the race is strongly evoked in the passage of book 8 which I have identified as his Homeric beginning. The horses at *Theb.* 8.393–398, desperate for battle, evoke the horses desperate to race at 6.392–401:

> ... stant uno margine clausi,
> spesque audaxque una metus et fiducia pallens.
> nil fixum cordi: pugnant exire paventque,
> concurrit summos animosum frigus in artus.   395
> qui dominis, idem ardor equis; face lumina surgunt,
> ora sonant morsu, spumisque et sanguine ferrum
> uritur, impulsi nequeunt obsistere postes
> claustraque, compressae transfumat anhelitus irae.
> stare adeo miserum est, pereunt vestigia mille   400
> ante fugam, absentemque ferit gravis ungula campum.

> ... They stand shut in by one line,
> hope and bold fear together with pale confidence.
> Nothing is fixed in their hearts: they fight to get out and they panic,
> a spirited shiver runs down from the top through their limbs.
> The same fire surges through masters and horses; eyes flash with fire,
> mouths sound with bits, and the iron burns with blood and
> foam, the battered posts are unable to stand in the way
> and the bolts, the gasp of anger held in check smokes across.
> To stand is so wretched that a thousand steps perish
> before the flight, and the heavy hoof strikes the absent field.

Theb. 6.401 and 7.392 both echo the famous dactylic line from Virgil's mini-march-out in *Aeneid* book 8: *quadrupedante putrem sonitu quatit ungula campum* ('the hoof shakes the dusty field with four-footed sound', 8.596). Both passages

---

comment on the tension between narrative momentum and delay: the foreshadowing and holding back of the war, the starting and the re-starting, the imitating and re-imitating. Intensity is generated by desire to begin, the desire to be Homer again. Statius' two beginnings, in book 7 and book 8, can thus be seen as a Virgilian beginning and a Homeric beginning. The poem goes gradually deeper, towards the roots of epic, eventually trumping the *Aeneid* with the *Iliad*.

5 A Lucanian flavour

Homer is not the only predecessor at play in our central passage from *Thebaid* book 8: if Statius competes with Virgil to appropriate Homer, the main text which leads Statius away from Homer is Lucan. We have mentioned Juhnke's analysis of 398 f. as fundamentally Homeric: but might they not also evoke lines 6 f. of Lucan's proem?

> ... infestisque obvia signis
> signa, pares aquilas et pila minantia pilis. (Luc. 1.6–7)

> ... standards meet hostile
> standards, matched eagles and javelins threatening javelins.

It is a key moment for the definition of civil war as national suicide, battle between like things, through the figure of polyptoton, emphasising similarity in difference. As Caesar and Pompey's troops approach for the battle of Pharsalus, they glitter hyperbolically (Luc. 7.214 f.):

> miles, ut adverso Phoebi radiatus ab ictu
> descendens totos perfudit lumine colles

> The soldier descending, struck by the opposite rays
> of the sun pours light through all the hills.

Theb. 8.395–397, in which Statius' armies rush forward and he focuses on the space between them, might evoke Luc. 7.460–466:

> ut rapido cursu fati suprema morantem   460
> consumpsere locum, parva tellure dirempti,
> quo sua pila cadant aut quam sibi fata minentur
> inde manum, spectant. vultus, quo noscere possent
> facturi quae monstra forent, videre parentum
> frontibus adversis fraternaque comminus arma,   465
> nec libuit mutare locum.

When they had consumed the ground which was delaying the final moment of fate with a swift run, and were kept apart by a small space, each was watching to see where his own javelin would fall and which hand from there the fates threatened for him. Faces, through which they could know what horrors they were about to commit, of parents they saw with brows opposing and brotherly arms close at hand, but they did not want to shift their ground.

This passage links our Statian moments in books 7 and 8: in book 7 there is no space to recognise the enemy (621 *noscere*); in book 8 they advance and watch the space shrink, leading into the spectacle of equal weapons matched against one another. Madness and *vitae prodiga virtus* ('Courage wasteful of life', 406) start the battle, and the ensuing *fragor* ('crash') is like the *fragor* which echoes around the mountains surrounding Pharsalus in gigantomachic hyperbole (Luc. 7.477–484):

> ... tunc aethera tendit
> extremique fragor convexa inrumpit Olympi,
> unde procul nubes, quo nulla tonitrua durant.
> excepit resonis clamorem vallibus Haemus   480
> Peliacisque dedit rursus geminare cavernis;
> Pindus agit fremitus, Pangaeaque saxa resultant,
> Oetaeaeque gemunt rupes, vocesque furoris
> expavere sui tota tellure relatas.

> then the uproar mounted skyward and assailed the dome of farthest Olympus – Olympus, from which the clouds keep far away, and whither no thunders reach. The Balkan took up the noise in its echoing valleys and gave it to the caves of Pelium to repeat; Pindus roared, the Pangaean rocks echoed, and the cliffs of Oeta bellowed, till the armies were terrified by the sound of their own madness repeated from all the earth. (transl. Duff)

Following this come the missiles, which are javelins controlled by Fortuna. In Statius: *casus agit virtutis opus* ('chance does virtue's work', 421); in Lucan: *rapit omnia casus, / atque incerta facit quos volt fortuna nocentes* ('chance seizes all things, and uncertain fortune makes guilty those she wants to', 7.487 f.). Statius' weapons go one step further than Lucan's. Lucan's create night; those of Statius create night and do not leave enough room for themselves:

> ... ferro subtexitur aether
> noxque super campos telis conserta pependit. (Luc. 7.519 f.)

> ... The aether is covered by iron
> and night made by interlacing weapons hangs over the fields

exclusere diem telis, stant ferrea caelo
nubila, nec iaculis artatus sufficit aer. (Stat.*Theb.* 8.412 f.)

They shut out the day with weapons, iron clouds stand
in the sky, nor is the narrowed air sufficient for the javelins.

None of these echoes are close, their similarities more situational than verbal:
but cumulatively it seems probable to me that Statius was imparting a Lucanian
flavour to his Homeric re-start. Lucan has very little that is Homeric, but we can
see how Statius is melding the two together.

6 Valerius Flaccus and Silius Italicus: the battle to be epic?

A different approach can be seen in Valerius Flaccus, who does have a march-out
in his mini-*Iliad* of book 6. After the invocation of 33–41, the catalogue of the out-
landish barbarian forces of Perses at 42–170 culminates with the key Iliadic simile (V. Fl. 6.163–170):

nec tot ab extremo fluctus agit aequore nec sic
fratribus adversa Boreas respondet ab unda,
aut is apud fluvios clamor volucrum, aethera quantus   165
tunc lituum concentus adit lymphataque miscet
milia, quot foliis, quot floribus incipit annus.
ipse rotis gemit ictus ager tremibundaque pulsu
nutat humus, quatit ut saevo cum fulmine Phlegram
Iuppiter atque imis Typhona reverberat arvis.   170

Boreas drives not so many billows from the ocean's bounds, nor so answers his brothers
from opposing waves: not so loud is the clamour of birds about the rivers, as is then the
blare of trumpets that ascends to heaven, filling with frenzy the mingled myriads, numerous as leaves or flowers in the opening year. The plain itself groans beneath the beat of
wheels, and the ground trembles and quakes at the shock, as when Jupiter strikes Phlegra
with his angry brand and hurls back Typhon to the deepest recesses of the earth. (transl.
Mozley)

Here the wave simile begins this tour de force of miniature recapitulation, followed by other elements from the initial cluster in *Iliad* 2: clamour of birds,
sound ascending to heaven, multitudinous troops like leaves or flowers, topped
off with Jupiter's gigantomachic thunder. This passage may also have been in
Statius' mind: he too includes Boreas, and finishes our passage with the figure
of Jupiter starting a storm, doubly appropriate since Jupiter has generated Sta-

tius' war in order to destroy humanity.[20] Statius and Valerius have focused on different parts of the Homeric imagery. This seems likely to be a deliberate strategy of avoidance on the part of the later author. It is also interesting that Valerius avoids the beautiful face of war: his troops do not glitter, and they move straight into death, blood and arms destroyed on the battlefield. Instead, we see the beauty of war through Medea's fascination with the beautiful figure of Jason, as she watches this mini-*Iliad* which has been put on by Juno particularly for her benefit. While Statius gradually moves towards the Iliadic climax of battle, Valerius' interpolated war must get straight down to business.

Silius has many more opportunities for march-out scenes, but the structure of his poem often follows historiography rather than epic. Ticinus and Trasimene avoid the Homeric tropes; at Trebia, the Carthaginians are in historical mode, while the Romans are more epic (Sil. 4.514–524):

> erumpunt, cunctisque prior volat aggere aperto
> degener haud Gracchis consul. quatit aura comantis   515
> cassidis Auruncae cristas, umeroque refulget
> sanguinei patrium saguli decus. agmina magno
> respectans clamore vocat, quaque obvia densos
> artat turba globos rumpens iter aequore fertur,
> ut torrens celsi praeceps e vertice Pindi   520
> cum sonitu ruit in campos magnoque fragore
> avulsum montis volvit latus: obvia passim
> armenta immanesque ferae silvaeque trahuntur,
> spumea saxosis clamat convallibus unda.

They burst out, and the consul flies before all when the rampart lay open, no unworthy heir of the Gracchi. The breeze shakes the horse-hair crest of his Auruncan helmet, and glory shines back from the blood-red cloak of his fathers on his shoulder. Looking back on the ranks, he summons them with a great shout, wherever a densely packed mass narrows his way in a crowd and breaks it, he is borne on the plain, just as a torrent rushes headlong from the peak of high Pindus with a roar into the plains and tearing away the side of the mountain rolls it down with a great crash: everywhere the cattle in its path are dragged away and the huge beasts and the woods, and the foamy water sounds in the rocky valleys.

Note that the Homeric resonances have been transferred from the armies as a whole onto the figure of the single heroic commander.

---

20 Arguably it is even more appropriate in the other direction, since Valerius' reference to earthquake might evoke the earthquake which has just happened in *Thebaid* 7; particularly replacing the beat of feet with the beat of wheels – Amphiaraus is famous for his chariot-racing and driving. But that would call for a much later dating of Valerius – possible, but very much against the grain of current orthodoxy which sees Valerius as Vespasianic. See Stover 2008.

In the build up to Cannae, as Silius prepares for his catalogue, the magnitude of the army is emphasised, but with no Homeric similes (Sil. 8.352 f.):

> non alias maiore virum, maiore sub armis
> agmine cornipedum concussa est Itala tellus.

> Never was the soil of Italy trampled by a greater concourse of men or by a larger body of cavalry in arms.

Later there is an explicit comparison to the Trojan war, but it is set before a passage of omens rather than a reflection on the grandeur of the massed troops (Sil. 8.617–621):

> Ignosset quamvis avido committere pugnam
> Varroni, quicumque simul tot tela videret.
> tantis agminibus Rhoeteo litore quondam
> fervere, cum magnae Troiam invasere Mycenae,   620
> mille rates vidit Leandrius Hellespontus.

> Any man who had seen so great an army mustered might have pardoned Varro's eagerness to fight a battle. In ancient times when great Mycenae attacked Troy, Leander's Hellespont saw a thousand ships swarm with as huge a host on the shore of Rhoeteum.

Finally when the two sides meet, Silius pulls out all the epic stops (Sil. 9.278–286):

> Iamque propinquabant acies, agilique virorum
> discursu mixtoque simul calefacta per ora
> cornipedum hinnitu et multum strepitantibus armis   280
> errabat caecum turbata per agmina murmur.
> sic, ubi prima movent pelago certamina venti,
> inclusam rabiem ac sparsuras astra procellas
> parturit unda freti fundoque emota minacis
> expirat per saxa sonos atque acta cavernis   285
> torquet anhelantem spumanti vertice pontum.

> And now the two armies closed; and the rapid movement of men, together with the neighing of hot-breathing horses and the loud clashing of weapons, sent a dull roaring noise through the moving ranks. So, when the winds begin a battle on the deep, the sea is big with pent-up fury and storms that will soon drench the stars; then, churned up from the bottom, it breathes out sounds of menace through the rocks; and, driven from its caves, torments the restless water with its foaming eddies.

The hot-breathed horses recall Statius' chariot race moment and the storm winds the climax of the Statian passage (*Theb.* 8.423–427). This passage evokes Statius rather than Homer. At 9.304–325 the description of the beginning of battle con-

tinues in similarity to Statius: at 9.304, the shouts going up to heaven are as loud
as Jupiter demanding fresh thunderbolts during the gigantomachy (cf. the importance of Jupiter at *Thebaid* 8.409 f.). The cloud of missiles (*nimbus telorum*, 310 f.)
evokes Statius' iron cloud (*stant ferrea caelo / nubila*, 412 f.). The densely packed
fighting at 315 f. recalls the densely packed weapons at *Thebaid* 8.419 f. All this
culminates in an expanded version of Statius' clash of polyptota (8.398 f.) including the sequence shield-sword-foot (Sil. 9.322–325):

> ... galea horrida flictu
> adversae ardescit galeae, clipeusque fatiscit
> impulsu clipei, atque ensis contunditur ense.
> pes pede, virque viro teritur

> Helmet, clashing fiercely against helmet of a foe, flashed fire; shield striking shield fell to
> pieces; and sword broke against sword. Foot pressed against foot, and man against man.

Silius expands each phrase with vivid verbs (*ardescit, fatiscit, contunditur, teri-
tur*), literally surpassing Statius. In neither Valerius nor Silius is there any mention of the beauty of war, and Statius' close engagement with the Homeric sublimity of enormous armies is not repeated.

7 Tacitean spectacles

To what extent are these march-out scenes purely epic? Comparison with historiography and with Tacitus in particular, as a partly Flavian author, reveals some
similarities. There is something of the idea of the beautiful face of war in the introduction to the battle of Mons Graupius at Tacitus *Agricola* 29–35. The muster
of the British forces is described before Calgacus' famous speech (Tac. *Agr.* 29.3–
5):

> nam Britanni nihil fracti pugnae prioris eventu et ultionem et servitium expectantes, tan-
> demque docti commune periculum concordia propulsandum, legationibus et foederibus
> omnium civitatium vires exciverant. iamque super triginta milia armatorum aspiciebantur,
> et adhuc adfluebat omnis iuventus et quibus cruda ac viridis senectus, clari bello et sua
> quisque decora gestantes...

> For the Britons, not at all broken by the outcome of the previous battle and waiting only for
> revenge and slavery, at last having learnt that a common danger must be pushed away with
> the help of agreement, had gathered together through embassies and treaties the strength
> of all their states. And now over thirty thousand armed men were on display, and moreover
> all the raw youth and those in a green old age were flowing towards battle, men famous in
> war and each wearing their own decorations...

The vast force is put on display and the emphasis is on the variety of ages involved. Further, at the end of the speech we have the motifs of shouting and glittering, though the former is marked as a barbarian trait (Tac. *Agr.* 33.1):

> Excepere orationem alacres, ut barbaris moris, fremitu cantuque et clamoribus dissonis. iamque agmina et armorum fulgores audentissimi cuiusque procursu...

> They received the speech keenly, as is the barbarian custom, with raging, song and cacophonous shouting. And now the columns and the glittering of arms and the boldest men in their dash forward...

These brief panoramic overviews do form a sort of muster and march-out, but they are dwarfed in comparison with the enormous speeches that they introduce (Calgacus from 30–32; Agricola from 33 f.).[21] The description of forces at the siege of Placentia (*Hist.* 2.22) includes the glittering of weapons (*fulgentes armis virisque campi*, 'the fields glittering with arms and men'). However, the use of the tag *armis virisque* may well evoke epic.[22] There is much more research to be done on this, but the fact that Lucan avoids the trope of the march-out and Silius reserves it for the epic sublimity of Cannae suggests that there is something fundamentally epic in its generic associations.

8 Faces and the beautiful face of war

Sappho fr. 16 sets military beauty against human beauty in the face of Anaktoria. It is therefore no surprise that actual faces play an important role in constructing the beautiful face of war. Lucan emphasises the theme of recognising the faces of the enemy (Luc. 7.463). For Statius this ties into the idea of the universal destructiveness of war, embodied by the beautiful face of Parthenopaeus, whose death is emblematic of the whole poem, as we see in the repetition of *Arcada, Arcada, Arcada* at *Thebaid* 12.805–807. In Statius' catalogue Parthenopaeus is described by his face, most beautiful in the entire army (Stat. *Theb.* 4.251 f. and 265):

> pulchrior haud ulli triste ad discrimen ituro
> vultus et egregiae tanta indulgentia formae [...]
>
> igneus ante omnes auro micat, igneus ostro...

---

21 The battle between Pharasmenes and Orodes at 6.34 f. is exemplary and spectacular according to Ash 1999, but the drama of the different opposing types of fighters and different ethnicities is displayed in battle rather than in a march-out. See also Ash 2002.
22 Ash 2002, 269 f.

Not more beautiful is the face of any man about to go out
to the grim struggle and there is such sympathy inspired by outstanding beauty [...]

fiery with gold before all he flashes, fiery with purple...

Similarly, in Virgil's mini-march-out, the focus is squarely on Pallas, as beloved, beautiful, object of the gaze (Verg. *A.* 8.587–596):

> ... ipse agmine Pallas
> it medio chlamyde et pictis conspectus in armis,
> qualis ubi Oceani perfusus Lucifer unda,
> quem Venus ante alios astrorum diligit ignis,   590
> extulit os sacrum caelo tenebrasque resolvit.
> stant pavidae in muris matres oculisque sequuntur
> pulveream nubem et fulgentis aere catervas.
> olli per dumos, qua proxima meta viarum,
> armati tendunt; it clamor, et agmine facto   595
> quadrupedante putrem sonitu quatit ungula campum.

> ... Pallas himself goes
> in the middle of the column, conspicuous in cloak and painted weapons,
> just as when Lucifer drenched by the waves of Ocean,
> whom Venus loves before all other fires of the stars,
> raises his sacred face to the sky and undoes the shadows.
> The mothers stand terrified on the walls and follow with their eyes
> the dusty cloud and the squadrons gleaming with bronze.
> The armed men head through the thickets, where the road
> turns nearest; a shout goes up, a column is made,
> and the hooves shake the crumbling plain with a four-footed sound.

Pallas is not just an erotic object, in the comparison to the morning star, but also has a face that blazes and goes up to heaven; dust, shout and gleaming bronze recapitulate Homeric imagery, and instead of conveying the beat of feet in an image, Virgil uses the dactylic rhythm to its full extent. Here the beautiful face of war is segregated from the destruction to come, except in the minds of the terrified mothers.

9 Conclusions

The beautiful face of war in Latin epic is summed up in the physical beauty of the hero. We can see how important this topos is in the reception of epic in Flavian personal poetry. Parthenopaeus is used as an emblem of Latin epic at Martial 10.4. At 9.56 he is used in a parody of the beautiful epic boy:[23] Spendophoros is going to war, but he is too beautiful for it. His wounds should rather be the wounds of love. His naked face, helmet removed, becomes the ultimate vision of heroic nudity; his beautiful face and body sum up a version of war so glamourous as to be entirely unrealistic (Mart. 9.56):

> Spendophoros Libycas domini petit armiger urbis:
>   quae puero dones tela, Cupido, para,
> illa quibus iuvenes figis mollesque puellas:
>   sit tamen in tenera levis et hasta manu,
> loricam clypeumque tibi galeamque remitto;   5
>   tutus ut invadat proelia, nudus eat:
> *non iaculo, non ense fuit laesusve sagitta,*
>   *casside dum liber Parthenopaeus erat.*
> quisquis ab hoc fuerit fixus morietur amore.
>   O felix, si quem tam bona fata manent!   10
> dum puer es, redeas, dum vultu lubricus, et te
>   non Libye faciat, sed tua Roma virum.

Spendophoros is going to Libya's cities as his lord's armour-bearer: Cupid, prepare shafts to give the boy, those with which you pierce youths and soft girls: But make sure there is also a smooth spear in his tender hand. Never mind about a breast-plate, shield, and helmet; and so that he will enter the battlefield safe, let him be nude: Parthenopaeus was not wounded by a javelin, a sword, or an arrow, as long as he was free of a metal helmet. Whoever is pierced by this one, will die of love. O happy one, who has such a good fate in store! Return while you are a boy, while your face is smooth; and do not let Libya, but your Roma make you a man.

Martial's *reductio ad absurdum* shows how crucial this moment is in the reception of the *Thebaid*. Despite the grimness of Statius' war narratives, it is the aestheticisation of the hero which steals the show. The beautiful face of war is at the centre of contemporary images of Statius' epic.

What does this exploration of the beautiful face of war tell us about genre in the Flavian period? The epics of this period have often been read as epic successors of Virgil. But Homer is very important in Statius' conception of what epic battle should be like, and Homeric grandeur has connotations of an originary glory of epic, before it was tarnished by contamination from tragedy, by the Roman obsession with civil war, even if Statius deliberately mixes Homer with Lucan to tarnish it even as he uses it. The double-edged nature of sublimity is already pres-

---

23 Statius is the only source who mentions Parthenopaeus with a spear, so "it seems probable he has influenced Martial in this respect" (Henriksén 1999, 35).

ent in the *Iliad*, glory interwoven with terror. Statius is particularly interested in this Homeric paradox, which is used in one miniature recapitulation by Valerius Flaccus, but does not feature in Silius, where Statius himself seems to form the touchstone. Statius uses multiple beginnings just as he uses multiple epic endings. It is striking that the beginnings occur in roughly reverse chronology: Lucan in the first word of the proem, Ovid's Theban history in the paths not taken elsewhere in the proem; Virgil's beginning of war in book 7; the *Iliad*'s march-out in book 8. The *Thebaid* is gradually going back into the serious territory of Homeric epic (just as the *Aeneid* sets *Odyssey* and Apollonius before *Iliad*). The extreme repetitions of epic are thematised by weapons pitched against weapons; yet the Homeric material gives impetus and energy to the epic battle, a noise going up to the stars, sublime in its magnitude.

R. Joy Littlewood

Epic on the edge: generic instability at the pivotal centre of Silius' *Punica* (10.336–371)

1 Introduction

When night fell on the field of Cannae, almost 50,000 Romans lay dead[1] and 19,300 had been taken prisoner,[2] losses more than three times as great as those of the British on the first day of the Somme.[3] With the annihilation of the largest army Rome had ever fielded, the survivors scattered in shock, and with Rome sparsely defended, could anything halt Hannibal's advance on Rome? At this point in his narrative, Livy relates how after the battle Maharbal, a cavalry commander, boldly promises Hannibal a victory feast in the Capitol within 5 days.[4] Delighted by the daring idea, Hannibal nevertheless responds cautiously, provoking Maharbal to retort that his commander knows how to win a battle, but not how to use a victory. Although it is improbable that the city, 250 miles away, would have fallen within five days, and although Hannibal could not easily sustain a protracted siege,[5] Livy tells this (possibly apocryphal) story to support a widespread contemporary view that Hannibal had made a fateful mistake in deciding not to follow up his victory at Cannae by a swift attack on Rome before the traumatized Romans could regroup.[6] Some 300 years after the event the anecdote would provide Silius with a graphic focus on which to build the turning point of his epic.

The aim of this paper is to demonstrate that within the fluid boundaries of Silius' epic narrative of Cannae, broadly regarded as the centre of the *Punica*, Hannibal's uncharacteristic moment of hesitation and missed opportunity after the battle marks a pivotal point of transition in conjunction with Hannibal's

---

1 Liv. 22.49.15 estimates 45,500 infantry and 2,700 cavalry, a more conservative estimate than Plb. 3.117.6.

2 Liv. 22.49.13 and 18.

3 See Lazenby 1996, 47 n. 56.

4 Liv. 22.51.1–4.

5 These points are convincingly argued by Lazenby 1978, 85 f. and 1996, 41–46.

6 Plb. 3.118 concludes his narrative of Cannae by observing that, since the Romans had now lost control of southern Italy, the Carthaginians were well placed to end the war by capturing Rome. Cf. 117.5–12, Liv. 22.50. 1–3, 51.1–6.

https://doi.org/10.1515/9783110534436-014

dream (Sil. 10.335–371).[7] I would suggest that the poet creates an illusion of generic instability for dramatic purposes. From the moment when Juno intervenes to impose her control over Hannibal, he is deprived of his military advantage fairly won and becomes a vulnerable individual caught under the wheels of Rome's destiny. This slippage from the national arena of historical epic to the tragic fate of individuals manipulated by the gods, predominant in Ovid's *Metamorphoses,* suggests, too, a transfer of focalization from the Roman narrator's denigration of Hannibal's barbarity in victory to the vulnerable Carthaginian, victimized by destiny and too ashamed to confide in his brother. The episode provides an interstitial break in the epic narrative and a proleptic vision of an imminent change in the military fortunes of Rome and Carthage in what might be described as intra-generic tension from the two extremes of epic.[8]

Generic play in Flavian epic can hardly be described as transgressive. Rather, it plays an integral part in the narrative, where it has diverse literary aims and consequences. Valerius creates generic tension by blending the heroic voyage of the Argo with the love of Jason and Medea and by introducing into a narrative of heroic conquest elegiac themes and ambiguous imagery, diversely applicable to both genres.[9] Like Valerius, Silius, on several occasions,[10] uses generic tension or instability as a means to explore a fundamental theme in his epic. Rome's eternal dilemma, teleologically expounded by Jupiter, is a cyclic phenomenon in which Rome's determination to conquer and ultimately achieve world power is, at each new stage of conquest, undermined by the dangerously sybaritic rewards of empire.[11] The cyclic nature of the allegorical conflict between *Virtus* and *Voluptas* is underlined by the diachronic sequence of Silius' literary fantasies on this theme, all of which invite a high level of irony, metapoetic reflection

---

7 For a survey of theories concerning the *Makrostruktur* of Silius' *Punica* see Fröhlich 2000, 18–28; Tipping 2004, 362 n. 59, Gärtner 2008 and Augoustakis 2010c, 9f. For Cannae as the turning point in the epic see Niemann 1975, 30–36; Feeney 1982, 358–362, who specifies Book 9 as the centre; Ahl / Davis / Pomeroy 1986, 2505–2510; Küppers 1986, 182–192; Delarue 1992, 155–160; Braun 1993, 181–183; McGuire 1995) 111f. For *Punica* 12 as the epic's formal centre see von Albrecht 1964, 19.

8 Cf. Wilson 1993, 222: "Like Ovid in his *Metamorphoses* Silius is engaged in the work of transformation, the transformation not of things but of activities and events."

9 On Jason as Sirius (V. Fl 5.363) see Stover 2012, 201–209; 214f., and, more generally, 183–187 with n. 23.

10 Sil. 7.409–493, 11.385–482 and 15.18–127.

11 Sil. 3.580f. *blandoque veneno / desidiae virtus paulatim evicta senescit* ('their manliness is slowly sapped and weakened by the seductive poison of indolence').

and political innuendo.[12] Proteus prefixes his prophecy of Rome's ultimate victory with a morality tale from Rome's earliest origins, *evolvens repetita exordia*, in which Paris' reckless (mis)judgement results in the sack of Troy.[13] The consequences of Hannibal's emotional reaction to his dream in *Punica* 10 and his subsequent refusal to march on Rome will be exacerbated by his fateful winter in Capua where he falls victim to Venus' assault on his soldierly abstinence. These two misguided decisions, driven by instinct and emotion in *Punica* 7 and 10, pave the way for a contrast with Scipio's rational, Roman choice of *Virtus* over *Voluptas* in *Punica* 15. These *intermezzi* of generic instability, during which the poet offers an evaluative judgement wrapped up in a witty, metapoetic sketch to illustrate the position and mindset of his characters, may also provide a *mora belli*, a delay deferring the final outcome of the epic.[14] It might be suggested that by appending Proteus' prophecy of Rome's victory to his Judgement of Paris, with its message that imprudent decisions have spelt disaster from the earliest origins of heroic epic,[15] Silius initiates a literary dialogue with Lucan and Statius who defer the encroaching *nefas* of civil conflict or fratricide with scenes involving reluctantly extracted prophecies.[16]

Finally, by transferring the suggestion of Livy's Maharbal to Hannibal's fiery brother Mago, Silius heightens the emotional tension of a scene in which Mago's disagreement, anger and contempt are ominously dissonant with his hitherto unquestioning loyalty.[17] This focalization not only changes the dynamics of the exchange but allows the poet to conclude his dream sequence with sinister epic symbolism implicit in *fraternas acies*.[18] It will be seen that internal conflict, too, finds a natural focus in an epic middle.

---

12 On irony in passages of generic instability see Barchiesi 2001 and Merli 2000. See also Gibson 2006a, 174–183.

13 Sil. 7.409–493. On this see Littlewood 2013.

14 Cf. Verg. *A.* 4.50–54, where Anna's advice, *innecte causas morandi* (51), underlines the elegiac nature of Aeneas' *mora* in Carthage.

15 Sil. 7.435 f. *tunc sic, evolvens repetita exordia, retro / incipit ambiguus vates reseratque futura.*

16 Luc. 5. 67–211, Stat. *Theb.* 3.534–580. On Statius see Ganiban 2007, 156–159, Parkes 2012, xvii–xx.

17 Sil. 7.290–337.

18 Hannibal appears to blame divine interference for the hailstorm that prevents him from taking Rome in 215 BC (Liv. 26.11.1–6).

2 Constructing the middle of the *Punica*

Defining the middle of Statius' *Thebaid*, McNelis distinguishes the actual point of narrative transition from the evolution of the epic narrative across several books.[19] In Silius' *Punica* the catastrophe at Cannae, anticipated by portents,[20] prophecies[21] and open antagonism between the consuls,[22] evolves across Books 8–10. As in the epics of Virgil, Lucan and Statius, the middle of Silius' epic marks the initiation of a new military challenge signalled by dreams and portents or a new invocation[23] and a new catalogue of troops.[24]

Imposing upon the historical outcome the teleological determinism of Roman epic, Jupiter prophesies, as Hannibal reaches the summit of the Alps, that the coming conflict will prove Rome's capability to achieve world supremacy.[25] Like Oedipus' curse on his sons at the beginning of Statius' *Thebaid*, this prophecy must follow its designated course.[26] Juno may aid and further the progress of the Carthaginian leader only as far as his victory at Cannae.[27] It is significant that at the height of the battle, even as the Volturnus wind thwarts the Roman attack, Jupiter warns Juno plainly of Roman victory, the fall of Carthage and the eclipse of her favourite: *certatis fatis et spes extenditis aegras* (Sil. 9.543 'you strive against destiny and cherish unsound hopes'),[28] words which signal the reversal of Carthaginian and Roman fortunes. Jupiter's promise that, through their defeats, the Romans will regain their former zeal for conquest, is echoed by Hanno, who identifies the Romans' grim refusal to accept defeat, which Hannibal himself had recognized in the ferocious expressions of the Roman dead at Trasimene (11.574–577):

> vos ego, vos metuo, Cannae. submittite signa
> atque adeo temptate, agedum, ac deposcite pacem:
> non dabitur. parat ille dolor, mihi credite maius
> exitium accepto.

19 McNelis 2007, 97–99.
20 Sil. 8.622–655.
21 Sil. 8.656–676.
22 Sil. 8.332–340.
23 Sil. 9.340–353. Cf. Verg. *A.* 7.37–45, Luc. 7.1–200, Stat. *Theb.* 7.424–467.
24 Sil. 8.355–612. Cf. Verg. *A.* 7.641–817.
25 Sil. 3.537–590.
26 Silius' representation of Hannibal's manipulation by Jupiter and Juno has been analysed by Häussler 1978, 198–211, Laudizi 1989, 83–92, Delarue 1992, 155–160 and Marks 2013, 298–301.
27 Sil. 1.37–39, 22–38; 8.25–38; 10.42–71, 83–91.
28 Sil. 9.544–550. The plural address includes Pallas, earlier admonished in lines 473–478.

It is you that I fear, Cannae. Lower your standards and make strenuous efforts to beg for peace. It will not be granted. Believe me, Rome's agony at Cannae is incubating a greater catastrophe than the one she has suffered.[29]

The new phase in the epic narrative is indicated by two formal literary devices, the new invocation and the new catalogue, which are, necessarily, situated before the battle of Cannae begins. Both anticipate in different ways Rome's fight back from military annihilation at Cannae to ultimate victory. The invocation promises that Cannae will inspire continuity of Roman *virtus*, but even as the poet celebrates Rome's unsurpassed *constantia* in her darkest hour, he hints, in *secunda*, of the future threat of imperial prosperity (Sil. 9.346 f. and 350–352):[30]

verum utinam posthac animo, Romane, secunda,
quanto tunc adversa, feras! [...]

pone, precor, lacrimas et adora vulnera, laudes
perpetuas paritura tibi; nam tempore, Roma,
nullo maior eris.

If only, Roman, you would accept prosperity with the same strength of character as you endure hardship! [...]

Abandon your grief and be grateful for your wounds. They will earn you everlasting renown for you will never surpass the glory of those days.

The invocation which introduces Silius' Cannae narrative in Book 8 anticipates the epigram which concludes defeat and aftermath narratives in Book 10, establishing a link with the cyclic pattern of imperial conquest and imperial *luxuria* (Sil. 10.657 f.)[31]:

Haec tum Roma fuit; post te cui vertere mores
si stabat fatis, potius, Carthago, maneres.

29 See also Sil. 5.674–676 *vereor ne ... /... huic fata dicarint / imperium, atque ipsis devincat cladibus orbem*, 'it misgives me that this land ... may be destined to hold empire, and may, even by its lost battles, conquer the world'.
30 In line 344 Silius summons the Muses not to turn from his *magnis ... ausis* since he will suggest a Rome greater than she will ever be: *nam tempore, Roma, / nullo maior eris* (351 f.). Cf. Verg. *A.* 7.44 f. *maius rerum mihi nascitur ordo / maius opus moveo*.
31 Cf. Verg. *A.* 2.58 and 8.642–645. See Fowler 2000, 123–127 and Tipping 2007, 224–231; 2010b, 197.

> This was Rome then; if it was fated that the Roman character should alter with the fall of Carthage, it would be better that Carthage remain strong!

The word *maneres* (658) evokes the sinister figure of Mettus Fufetius, warning of a darker association with the cycle of Roman civil war, a theme which runs, recurrently, through the Cannae narrative.[32] Civil conflict is present, too, in Silius' catalogue of farmer-soldiers who march to Cannae in *Punica* 8. Such legendary names as Picus and Tarchon might seem oddly dissonant with commanders whose names evoke future civil conflicts – Nero, Curio, Piso, Galba, Cethegus, Brutus – if these were not also an essential part of Roman history, testifying to the dire consequences of violated *Fides,* loyalties abused since Romulus for the sake of power.[33] Anchises' pageant of future Romans also includes among his heroes initiators of civil discord: the Gracchi, Caesar and Pompey.[34] In contrast to Hannibal's foreign mercenaries and nomadic tribal contingents which are distinguished by their primitive weaponry and barbaric fighting methods,[35] the catalogue of Italian allies whom Rome rallies from their pastoral homes to repel the Carthaginian invaders features a roll call of emotive place names linked with illustrious Romans and ancient cult: Cybele, Juno of Lanuvium, Fortuna of Praeneste.[36] Rome's divine origins and earliest epic are simultaneously evoked by the opening word *Faunigenae,* the pregnant epithet which Silius attaches to the indigenous Rutulians.[37] Although the coming conflict will leave many from these communities dead on the field of Cannae, among them Umbrian Crista's family from Todi, Rome's teleological destiny demands that these monuments of Roman culture must survive the onslaught of the advancing African barbarians. Silius' catalogue of troops marks a generic shift from pastoral to historical epic which merges seamlessly into one of the central themes of his *Punica:* the defence of Italy. At the same time it provides an antiquarian *mora belli* serving a

---

32 See Marks 2010, 132–140.

33 On this see McGuire 1995,110–118; Mezzanotte 1995, 383–385; McGuire 1997, 61–63, 85, 136–144. Marks 2010. For Curio specifically Marks 2008.

34 Verg. *A.* 6.826–835. Anchises' concluding words, 851–853, describing the Roman imperial mission of imposing peace and stable government provide intertextual links to Sil. 9.346 and 10.658.

35 Sil. 3.214–405. Polybius (1.67.8–11) comments on the confusion and mistrust in Hannibal's multi-racial army.

36 Sil. 8.355–612.

37 Enn. *Ann.* fr. 206 f. Sk. *vorsibus quos olim Faunei vatesque canebant.* Cicero links their prophetic utterances with the outcome of battles, *Div.* 1.101, *saepe etiam in proeliis Fauni auditi ... esse dicuntur.* Cf. *Div.* 1.114 f., Var. *L.* 7. 5.

similar purpose to Virgil's Evander guiding Aeneas around the site of Rome.[38] It is monument to the antiquity and sanctity of Rome's culture that is threatened by the approaching conflict.

3 The pivotal passage of *Punica* 10

As the battle rages, the poet gives supernatural force to Livy's 'legendary Cannae', the accretion of myths which attenuate the Carthaginian victory – the power of the Volturnus wind which buffets and blinds the south-facing Roman ranks, the duplicitous 'surrender' of a band of 500 Numidians, a massive rock flung by an anonymous assailant which shatters Rome's heroic consul, Paulus. Sublimated by resonances from Homer, Virgil and Lucan, Silius' battle narrative progresses inexorably through images and thematic material which constitute the poetics of defeat: the divided command, grotesque omens, excessive carnage, the flight of one consul and the death of the other, and finally, the crumbling resistance of the headless army. In ending the battle at the exact centre of *Punica* 10, the poet signals the approach of an imminent catalyst for Carthage's change of Fortune.

Clearly demarcated from the rout of the Roman army by the introductory *at Poenus,* the emotional responses of the victor of Cannae are visualized from a Roman perspective as the poet highlights the insatiable bloodlust and barbarity of a conqueror, devoid of Greco-Roman magnanimity or Stoic peace of mind,[39] who passes the night in feverish exaltation mingled with restless dissatisfaction because he has not yet destroyed the enemy capital (Sil. 10.326–332):

> At Poenus per longa diem certamina saevis
> caedibus emensus, postquam eripuere furori
> insignem tenebrae lucem, tum denique Martem
> dimisit tandemque suis in caede pepercit.
> sed mens invigilat curis noctisque quietem   330
> ferre nequit. stimulat dona inter tanta deorum
> hoc tantum, nondum portas intrasse Quirini.

> During the long battle the Carthaginian had measured time by feats of savage carnage. When the onset of darkness deprived him of the day's glory, he finally stopped fighting and spared his men from further slaughter. But anxiety kept him awake and he resented the tranquillity of the night. This thought alone tormented him: that when the gods had showered him with gifts, he had not yet entered the gates of Rome.

---

38 Verg. *A.* 8.184–369.
39 See Cic. *Off.* 1.61–92, especially 72f.

Picturing his triumphal entry into the city, his soldiers' hands smeared with carnage on their drawn swords, the gates of Rome smashed, her ancient walls on fire, Hannibal allows himself to gloat over the realization of his ambition. Having destroyed the Roman army at Cannae, he will further humiliate them by a holocaust of Jupiter's Capitoline temple, the symbolic decapitation of Roman power.

Enter Juno. The intrusion of a woman into epic often signals a passage of generic instability or tension. Juno comes not as Juno Lacinia or Tanit, the great goddess defender of Carthage, instigating Hannibal to greater (*maiora*) acts of epic bellicosity, but as *coniunx Saturnia* anxious to sidetrack Hannibal's ambition to fire Jupiter's Capitoline temple because she knows it is teleologically unsound. Juno's intervention takes the form of a picturesque but powerful mythological interlude in a strangely lighter idiom which refocuses the reader's attention on the vulnerability and the subconscious anxieties of the Carthaginian victor.

From the opposite end of the epic spectrum, from *Iliad* 14 and *Metamorphoses* 11, Silius selects as his model two personal and domestic scenes, which have as their unifying component the power of Sleep, for his Juno plans to impose her control over the Carthaginian through a dream in which he will be humiliated by supernatural forces (Sil. 10.340–350):

... ciet inde quietis   340
regnantem tenebris Somnum, quo saepe ministro
edomita inviti componit lumina fratris,
atque huic arridens 'non te maioribus' inquit
'ausis, dive, voco nec posco, ut mollibus alis
des victum mihi, Somne, Iovem. non mille premendi   345
sunt oculi tibi nec spernens tua numina custos
Inachiae multa superandus nocte iuvencae.
ductori, precor, immittas nova somnia Poeno,
ne Romam et vetitos cupiat nunc visere muros,
quos intrare dabit numquam regnator Olympi'.   350

At once she summoned Sleep, who rules the peaceful night, by whose good offices she has the power to close her brother's eyes against his will. Smiling coquettishly she said: "I summon you, Sleep, for no great endeavour nor do I ask you with your soft wings to make Jupiter my captive. You need not close his thousand eyes nor plunge into oblivion the obstinately wakeful guardian of Inarchus' heifer-daughter. I pray you, send the Carthaginian leader strange dreams to deter him from wishing to gaze on Rome and her forbidden walls which the lord of Olympus will never permit him to enter.

It is evident from Juno's allusion to Somnus as 'the one who often closes her brother's eyes', and her promise of a lighter task than overpowering Jupiter, that Silius is alluding to the salacious comedy in *Iliad* 14 where Hera, gorgeously adorned for the sole purpose of seducing her husband, bribes Somnus to enfold Zeus in a deep sleep after their erotic encounter, so that Poseidon may be free to help the Greeks.[40] The model is apt because Silius' Juno also intends to obstruct Hannibal's immediate military intentions. Her seductive approach, *atque huic arridens* (344), mirrors, in words and *sedes*, Venus marshalling her *cupidines* for Hannibal's seduction in Capua.[41] Like Zeus at the mercy of Hera, or Hannibal enthralled by Venus in Capua, the conqueror is soon to be disarmed. Juno's elegiac approach is accompanied by metapoetic asides: *Somnus* is required not for some new epic endeavour, *non te maioribus ausis, dive, voco* (343 f.), but for his personal attributes, his gentle wings, *mollibus alis* (344). While *maiora* and *audere* are both associated with the challenge of epic, the adjective *mollis*, often linked with sleep, belongs to the language of elegy; it also, aptly here, implies elegance and refinement.[42] The goddess completes her *captatio benevolentiae* with a final illustration of *Somnus'* involvement in the liaisons of Jupiter, his outwitting the vigilance of Io's peacock guardian, Argus, by closing simultaneously his thousand watchful eyes.

Juno demands that *Somnus* should conjure up dreams so strange, *nova somnia,* that they will compel Hannibal to abandon his intention of entering Rome. This clear allusion to the first line of Ovid's *Metamorphoses* effectively achieves Silius' crucial transition to an epic significant for its generic multiplicity, where excessive passions deviant from heroic morality end in personal tragedy. This *Somnus* with his cornucopia of poppy juice, his wand soaked in the waters of Lethe and his record of erotic meddling has little affinity with Ovid's narcoleptic god, *quies rerum, placidissime deorum.*[43] The true model for the terrifying intensity of his response to Juno's command is Ovid's *Morpheus*, proactive agent of *Somnus*, who conjures up, in *Metamorphoses* 11, a horrifying apparition of the nude white corpse of drowned Ceyx, his hair and beard still dripping with sea water as he recounts his own death to his horrified wife Alcyone who has been dreading this very thing. Hannibal's nightmare mirrors Alcyone's in that

---

40 Hom. *Il.* 14.153–353. Cf. *Il.* 14.249 with Sil. 10.343 f. '*non te maioribus*' inquit, / '*ausis, dive, voco nec posco ut mollibus alis / des victum mihi, Somne, Iovem*' ('I do not summon you, divine Sleep, for a burdensome task, nor do I ask of your silken winds to overcome Jupiter and place him at my mercy').

41 Sil. 11.390 *tum pueris dulce arridens*. For menace hidden in a smile, see Sen. *Con.* 9.2.6 *misero meretrix arridet*. Cf. the more dangerous *subridere* in Verg. *A.* 10.742; 9.740.

42 Virg. *Ecl.* 7.45, *somno mollior herba*, *G.* 2.470, *molles ... somni*. Cf. Stat. *Silv.* 1.5.29 *carmine molli*; Sil. 11.439. See also Newlands 2002, 216 f.

43 Ov. *Met.* 11.623.

he sees in vivid detail the thing he dreads most, which he is doomed to experience as a future reality.[44] A helpless and speechless participant in the disfigurement of his most cherished ambition, to fling firebrands, as a conqueror, into Jupiter's Capitoline temple, he hears his defeat thundered from the heavens, humiliating words and images which he will never expunge from his memory: *nec lux terribili purgavit imagine mentem* (371). In the visceral horror and sublimity of this apparition there is absolute finality: there will be no return to hope or past happiness for Ovid's Alcyone nor for Silius' Hannibal. Silius has created a double impression of generic slippage, first in Juno's seductive banter with Somnus and her complicit allusions to their interference in Jupiter's liaisons, and secondly in reducing the Victor of Cannae, at the height of his belligerent triumphalism, to resemble one of Ovid's most vulnerable women.

Silius' Hannibal has an almost erotic fascination with Rome, evinced by his obsessive survey of her sacred places when he reaches the walls in *Punica* 12 and by sexual innuendo present in the *moenia* motif.[45] His inability to comprehend Rome's sacred power is an important dynamic of the *Punica*.[46] As the barbarian's impatience to pursue his campaign[47] prevents him from taking a scientific interest in the Atlantic tides or volcanic fumaroles in the Phlegraean Fields,[48] so he undervalues the natural grandeur of the Alps by ordering his men to imagine themselves scaling the walls of Rome and Jupiter's Capitoline hill, so obsessive is his drive to conquer Rome.[49]

Hannibal's decision to retract his earlier intention of marching to Rome is dramatized as the consequence of a personal crisis of confidence brought on by a dream. As *Somnus* takes control of Hannibal's stormy mind, *rabidam mentem* (Sil. 10.357), we may observe the shift in focalization, from the narrator of Cannae to Hannibal himself, as the barbarian leader becomes the 'interested character.' At the beginning of his dream he is confident in his now familiar role as conqueror of the Romans (Sil. 10.358 f.):[50]

---

44 Sil. 12.541–730.
45 Sil. 10.332;12.583 f.
46 See Fowler 2000, 86–107; Cowan 2010, 347–351.
47 Sil. 3.61 *haec propere spectata duci nam multa fatigant* ('the general viewed these things in haste; for he had much to trouble him'); 12.104 f. *sed enim ductor numerabat inertes / atque actos sine Marte dies* ('but the leader was counting up all the idle days that had passed without battle').
48 Sil. 3.46; 12.157. See also Manolaraki 2010.
49 Sil. 3.509 f.
50 On deviant focalisation see Fowler 2000, 86–90. On Hannibal as focalizer in the *Punica*, see Cowan 2010, 347–351.

iamque videbatur multo sibi milite Thybrim
cingere et insultans adstare ad moenia Romae.

And he dreamed that he was even now surrounding the Tiber with a great army and standing at the walls of Rome hurling mockery.

He is forced to watch his dominant *persona* disintegrate as his ambition to sack
Rome and destroy her most sacred temple is scornfully exposed as empty threats
by Jupiter himself (Sil. 10.360–371):

ipse refulgebat Tarpeiae culmine rupis	360
elata torquens flagrantia fulmina dextra	
Iuppiter, et late fumabant sulphure campi,	
ac gelidis Anien trepidabat caerulus undis,	
et densi ante oculos iterumque iterumque tremendum	
vibrabant ignes. tunc vox effusa per auras:	365
'sat magna, o iuvenis, prensa est tibi gloria Cannis.	
siste gradum. nec enim sacris irrumpere muris,	
Poene, magis dabitur, nostrum quam scindere caelum.'	
attonitum visis maioraque bella paventem	
post confecta Sopor Iunonia iussa relinquit,	370
nec lux terribili purgavit imagine mentem.	

Radiant on the summit of the Tarpeian rock was Jupiter himself, whirling incandescent
thunderbolts in his raised fist. Sulphurous mists arose from the surrounding fields and
blue waters of the Anio quivered in its chilly depths. Again and again lightning flashed ter-
ribly before his eyes. Then a voice floated through the air: "Enough for you, young man, is
the glory you won at Cannae. Go no further. For you, Carthaginian, to penetrate Rome's sacred walls will be no more attainable than to tear the heavens apart." Having obeyed Juno's
commands Sleep left him, appalled at what he had witnessed and dreading greater conflicts. Nor did the new day cleanse his mind of the ghastly vision.

Word order enhances the nightmarish menace of Silius' Jupiter. *Ipse*, Himself, is
instantly identified by his aggressive posture on the Tarpeian rock and the verb
refulgebat, familiar from epiphanies in Ovid's *Fasti*. In the subsequent line each
word in turn heightens the effect of divine wrath: the raised fist, *elata ... dextra*,
with which the weapon is encompassed, the slow, deliberate aim, *torquens*, emphasized by three opening spondees, then whirling faster with the alliterative
flagrantia fulmina. As Jupiter whirls thunderbolts from the Tarpeian rock and announces Hannibal's defeat in a loud voice, Silius maximizes the enormity of his
impious gigantomachy by a striking and unmistakeable allusion in lines 360–362
to Statius' sublime description of Capaneus, his own arch-enemy of the gods.[51]

---

[51] Stat. *Theb.* 10.907 f., 927 f. *ipse furentem / risit et incussa sanctarum mole comarum / ... / talia*

The opening word, *ipse*, signals Statius' description of a menacing Jupiter mocking the fury and the taunts of Capaneus as he prepares his gigantomachic assault. The divinely self-confident pause before Statius' Jupiter flings his thunderbolt with all his force, *toto Iove*, is mirrored in Silius' dramatic enjambement of *Iuppiter* with its subsequent sense pause.[52]

Enriched by intertextual allusion, Silius' sublime rendering of Hannibal's nightmare with its implication of violated boundaries might be likened to the violation of boundaries which generates catastrophe in Statius' *Thebaid*. In this passage, rather than the realized version of the dream in *Punica* 12, Silius matches the sublimity of Statius. His Capitoline hill rises out of a sea of sulphurous smoke which resonates ominously with Hannibal's visit to the Phlegraean Fields with his new allies, the Capuan leaders, who tell him of fumaroles defiantly exhaled by imprisoned giants. The Anio, a river ever sensitive to the literary requirements of Flavian epic, now quivers, *trepidabat*, either in awe of the god or because of earth tremors caused by Jupiter's storm. Lightning, epic phrasing – *iterumque iterumque* – and a dramatic enjambement (Sil. 10.364 f.) complete the drama of the god's epiphany and a voice is heard from the Tarpeian crag pronouncing in heavy spondees Jupiter's teleological injunction imposing a limit on Hannibal's conquests: '*sat magna, o iuvenis, prensa est tibi gloria Cannis*' (366, 'you have gained glory enough, young man, at Cannae'). By his subsequent Virgilian allusion, *siste gradum*, which echoes Aeneas' ineffectual attempt to convince Dido of the power of destiny, the poet hints that, as Dido is unimpressed by Rome's sacred destiny, so too her descendant may be temporarily halted in his tracks by the awesome majesty of Jupiter, but that he will, like Dido, continue to tread his chosen path.[53]

Dismissing Hannibal with the generic *Poene*, Jupiter ruthlessly exposes the sheer impossibility of his gigantomachic assault on his sacred space. The god's majestic scorn is aptly conveyed in the words *scindere caelum*, 'tear the heavens apart', as Jupiter likens to cosmic destruction Hannibal's attempt at the decapitation of Roman power. Arrested in his tracks by Jupiter's apparition with its horrifyingly graphic revelation of the obsession that has driven him over the Alps and across Italy to his conquest at Cannae, the superstitious barbarian is overcome by fears of war against supernatural powers: *maioraque bella*

---

dicentem toto Iove fulmen adactum / *corripuit* ('Jove himself laughed at the madman, and shaking the thick mass of sacred locks ... Even as he (*scil.* Capaneus) spoke, the thunderbolt struck him, hurled with the whole might of Jove').

52 On Statius' passage (and the puzzling *toto Iove* in particular), see Reitz in this volume.

53 Verg. *A.* 6.465.

paventem (369). He reveals his vulnerability in his emotional response and his superstitious terror in the face of the supernatural, *attonitum visis*.[54]

Within the symbolism of the dream, Hannibal's desire to destroy Jupiter's temple is represented by the political metaphors of emasculating Rome by penetration and decapitation. It is possible to extract from this a further, cultural, interpretation in line with the implication that Rome must defend her ancient cult and sacred monuments from the barbarians which is apparent in the invocation and catalogue which introduce Silius' Cannae narrative. The sanctity of ancient places with their associated cult prominent in the Augustan poets was maintained and variously transposed by the Flavian epicists.[55] Silius perpetuates the cultic significance of ancient legend by imposing heroic stature on elegiac figures drawn from Ovid's *Fasti*. Two striking examples of generic transformation are Anna Perenna and Claudia Quinta, who both have their place in the Roman cultic background of Silius' Cannae narrative. When Anna Perenna appears to Hannibal before Cannae, she has been transformed from Ovid's vulnerable serial victim[56] into a formidable Valkyrie who extinguishes Hannibal's doubts and rouses him to fiery belligerence. Silius chooses Anna Perenna to promote Rome's defeat in recognition of her potency as a most ancient cult figure from the cult centre of Aeneas Indiges, Rome's mother city of Lavinium. Claudia Quinta belongs to the final chapter of Hannibal's invasion of Italy, the arrival in Rome of the sacred cult statue of Cybele in 204 BC, which was brought expressly to rid the land of the invader: *hostis ut Ausoniis decederet advena terris*.[57] Her moment of glory comes when, ominously, Cybele's ship is grounded in the Tiber and the priest decrees that it may be dislodged only by the hands of a chaste woman. Stripped of her Ovidian *persona* as a witty socialite of doubtful virtue, Silius' Claudia has acquired the stature of an epic heroine[58] who signals the approaching end of the conflict by her vindication of traditional Roman morality.

4 The Shadow of Civil Strife

Replacing the cavalry commander Maharbal with Hannibal's brother Mago, in his reprise of Livy's anecdote, gives Silius the means to initiate a quarrel between

---

54 On shades of meaning in the word *attonitus* in Lucan's epic see Sacerdoti 2012, 90–97.
55 See especially Fucecchi 2013, but also Marks 2013.
56 Ov. *Fast.* 3.545–654.
57 Sil. 17.1. Cf. Ov. *Fast.* 4.291–348.
58 On the generic transformation of Claudia Quinta, see Von Albrecht 1999, 301–316.

the brothers which foreshadows the fulfilment of Jupiter's prophecy (Sil. 10.372–384):

> Quos inter motus somni vanosque tumultus
> dedita per noctem reliquo cum milite castra
> nuntiat et praedam pleno trahit agmine Mago.
> huic ductor laetas Tarpeio vertice mensas   375
> spondenti, cum quinta diem nox orbe tulisset,
> celatis superum monitis clausoque pavore
> vulnera et exhaustas saevo certamine vires
> ac nimium laetis excusat fidere rebus.
> tum spe deiectus iuvenis, ceu vertere ab ipsis   380
> terga iuberetur muris ac signa referre,
> 'tanta mole' inquit 'non Roma, ut creditur, ipsa,
> sed Varro est victus. quonam tam prospera Martis
> munera destituis fato patriamque moraris?'

Into the turmoil and unsubstantial terror of Hannibal's sleep came Mago to announce that the camp had surrendered during the night with the rest of the army and he brought with him booty in large quantities. When he promised that within five days the general would be feasting on the Tarpeian rock, Hannibal prevaricated, while concealing Jupiter's warning and suppressing his fears; he offered as excuses the soldiers' wounds and exhaustion after fierce fighting and being over-confident in the hour of triumph. Then young Mago exploded, as much downcast as if he had been ordered to withdraw his army from the very walls of Rome, "With such a mighty effort Rome herself has not been conquered, as people think, but only Varro. Through what quirk of fate do you walk away from such generous rewards of war and keep your country waiting?'

When Mago bursts in, promising dinner on the Capitol within five days, Hannibal is reeling under the influence of his terrifying nightmare: *inter motus somni vanosque tumultus* (372). Intratextual resonances sharpen the dramatic irony of Mago's words, *laetas Tarpeio vertice mensas*, which can only conjure up in his brother's mind the merciless figure on the Tarpeian rock: *refulgebat Tarpeiae culmine rupis ... Iuppiter,* (360, 362). Mago's boast differs only slightly from Hannibal's earlier intention of marching straight from Cannae and setting fire to the Capitoline temple (335 f.). Now, to Mago's horrified disbelief, their once shared conviction, that the capture of Rome would be the corollary of victory of Cannae, is opposed by Hannibal with procrastination and excuses. Infuriated, Mago pours contempt on his brother's weakness. His taunt that all the effort expended in defeating the Romans at Cannae has achieved only the conquest of Varro contains a harsh and unpalatable truth, one that Hannibal himself has already come close to admitting after Trasimene,[59] namely that the tenacious valour of the surviving Romans will save Rome for world empire. Mago's opening words, *tanta mole*, pregnant with Virgilian allusion,[60] imply that the hardships required to forge the Roman race will have to be surpassed by the effort necessary for its destruction. Significantly the poet reinforces his teleological message at the moment where disagreement within the high command passes from the Roman to the Carthaginian forces.

Civil war, or conflict with resonances of civil war, breaks out in a new and bolder form in the seventh book of the epics of Lucan, Statius and Virgil, having been clearly anticipated in the previous book.[61] Silius follows this pattern in his central Cannae narrative, where the theme of internal division concludes the pivotal passage of *Punica* 10 in the form of a new faultline: disagreement within the Carthaginian high command. There is a further Flavian literary parallel in the structure of Josephus' *Bellum Iudaicum*. Familiar with the Greek historians and Virgil, Josephus underlines the danger of internal divisions by making the centre of his history and the ultimate cause of the destruction of Jerusalem the murder of the chief priest of the temple by extremist Jews.[62]

5 Conclusion

Hannibal's triumphalism after Cannae and his hubristic desire to destroy his enemy's god invites nemesis and divine retribution. Juno's request for this to be achieved through *nova somnia* carries an ominous intertextual warning of the dangers of metamorphosis.[63] Imprisoned in a dream from which he is powerless to escape, Hannibal's metamorphosis from conqueror to victim equates him with Ovid's Alcyone, a woman made vulnerable, like Hannibal, by her fear of losing the object of her desires. At the centre of the dream is the revelation of Hannibal's destiny no less than Rome's, and the poet heightens the Carthaginian's terror and the teleological force of his vision through intra-generic tensions between historical and mythological epic from opposite ends of the epic spectrum. In contrast with the ironic meta-literary episodes in *Punica* 7 and 11

---

59 Sil. 5.669–677.
60 Verg. *A.* 1.33 *tantae molis erat Romanam condere gentem.*
61 Verg. *A.* 6.830–835.
62 J. *BJ* 4.304–325, especially 318 (Loeb transl.) 'I should not be wrong in saying that ... the downfall of the Jewish state dated from the day on which the Jews beheld their high priest, the captain of their salvation, butchered in the heart of Jerusalem'.
63 Cf. Ov. *Met.* 1.1 f. *in nova fert animus mutatas dicere formas / corpora.*

featuring the allegorical rivalry of *Virtus* and *Voluptas*, the central position and pivotal importance of Hannibal's dream sequence demands complex generic instability. Juno's overtures to *Somnus*, which seem at first to belong to the register of erotic elegy, conceal a menace incipient in its Homeric origins, which expands into a sublime generic shift to the tragic world of Ovid's *Metamorphoses*.

As the momentum of the Carthaginian invasion falters, the Romans are pulled sharply back from the abyss of defeat first by Scipio's ruthless repression of a mass desertion led by Metellus and then by Fabius' spirited defence of Rome.[64] Despite his aggressive posturing at the gates and his penetrating scrutiny of sacred places within the walls,[65] Hannibal's subsequent attack on Rome in *Punica* 12 is no longer the organized strategy of an advancing conqueror. Already undermined by his dissolute winter in Capua, he has suffered a series of humiliating military defeats in Campania. He marches on Rome out of bravado because he is unable to defend Capua from blockade by several Roman armies. His defiant boast that the fall of Capua will be a price worth paying for the conquest of Rome[66] is no less empty than his mutinous promise to return, after freakish thunderstorms have forced him to pull up his standards and withdraw his forces from Rome's city wall.[67] Far more unnerving than his vision, on that occasion, of a multiplicity of Roman gods, each guarding his own sacred space as they defend the ancient city,[68] is Hannibal's true moment of nemesis: his direct confrontation with Jupiter in *Punica* 10.

---

64 Sil. 10.426–448, 594–656.
65 Sil. 12.565 f. *clausas nunc cuspide pulsat / infesta portas*; 567–570 *intrat / urbem oculis discit-que locos*, 730 *remeaturumque minatur.*
66 Sil. 12.514–517.
67 Sil. 12.730. Conversely, in Tac. *Ann.* 13. 41. 3, a violent storm with lightning flashes was thought to indicate the gods' complicity in Corbulo's successful siege of the Armenian capital of Artaxerxa.
68 Cf. Verg. *A.* 2.622 f., where Aeneas concedes defeat in the face of hostile gods at Troy.

Raymond Marks

Silius, Sicily, and the poetics of generic conflict: Grosphus in *Punica* 14.208–217

At the beginning of *Punica* 14 Silius indicates that his narrative is going to take a martial direction (1–10). The tone is set straightaway by an allusion (1 f.): *flectite nunc vestros, Heliconis numina, cantus / Ortygiae pelagus Siculique ad litoris urbes* ('Now, goddesses of Helicon, turn your songs to the sea of Ortygia and to the cities on Sicily's shores'). The first line echoes a line that appears twice in Virgil's *Aeneid*, in each case in a military context, introducing a catalogue of troops, Turnus' allies (7.641) and Aeneas' Etruscan allies (10.163): *pandite nunc Helicona, deae, cantusque movete* ('Now, goddesses, open up Helicon and mobilize your songs').[1] In directing the Muses' attention to Sicily (2), the poet next anticipates the subject matter of the book, Marcellus' invasion of the island and siege of Syracuse. But this proem looks beyond book 14 as well, anticipating other theaters of war to which the narrative will turn in books 15–17: Italy, Macedonia, Greece, Spain, North Africa (3–8). As Thomas Gärtner has pointed out, the passage also recalls in several respects the *Aeneid*'s medial proem in which Virgil signals the beginning of the epic's Iliadic half (7.37–45).[2] From this point to the end of the epic, then, we expect an unremitting sequence of battles, and, so that there is no mistake about this, Silius concludes with a clear statement about the direction in which we are heading (14.9 f.): *sic poscit sparsis Mavors agitatus in oris. / ergo age, qua litui, qua ducunt bella, sequamur* ('So demands Mars, stirred up in far-flung lands. Come on, then. Let us follow where the war-trumpets, where wars lead').

The expectations raised by the proem are met in what follows in book 14. After an opening digression on the history, culture, and geography of Sicily (11–109), Silius focuses extensively on military affairs: Marcellus arrives in Sicily, takes Leontini, and marches to Syracuse (110–191); there are, then, two catalogues, one of Rome's Sicilian allies, the other of Carthage's Sicilian allies,

---

1 Spaltenstein 1990, *ad* Sil. 14.1.
2 Both proems contain invocations, follow underworld episodes in preceding books (Aeneas' *katabasis* in *Aeneid* 6, Scipio's *nekyia* in *Punica* 13), and anticipate sustained martial content in the remaining books of their respective epics; Gärtner 2010, 84–86. The Silian proem, however, does not have quite the same structural significance as the Virgilian one. For something closer to a medial proem in the epic (with allusions to Virgil's proem in *Aeneid* 7 as well), see Sil. 11.1–3 with Marks forthcoming.

https://doi.org/10.1515/9783110534436-015

and an account of Hippocrates' and Epicydes' demagoguery in Syracuse (192–291); this is followed by Marcellus' siege of Syracuse (292–352), a sea battle in its harbor (353–579), a plague (580–617), and, finally, Syracuse's fall (618–684). But even as this martial epic narrative takes its course, Silius makes extensive use of poetic traditions that espoused, or were felt by the Romans to espouse, a non- or anti-epic agenda, and a decidedly non- or anti-martial epic agenda at that. One hears, for example, echoes of Callimachus in the book's opening digression on Sicilian history.[3] There are several references to non-epic poets in the book – Stesichorus (232) is one example – and to stories, such as that of Acis and Galatea (221–226) or the rape of Persephone (238–247), which would have been most familiar to Silius' readers from non-epic genres or, if from epic, from Ovid's *carmen perpetuum et deductum*, the *Metamorphoses*.[4] Sicily's historical association with pastoral poetry is acknowledged too, most notably early on (28–32) and, later, in connection with Daphnis' death in the sea battle (462–476).[5] This is just a small sample.

This chapter aims to add to our growing appreciation of Silius' non-epic appropriations in *Punica* 14 by examining his portrait of Grosphus, a Roman ally from Agrigento, in the first troop catalogue (14.208–217). I focus on this passage not only because it offers many examples of the poet's use of such material, specifically Callimachus' *Aetia*, Horace *Carm.* 2.16, and Ovid's exilic poetry, but also because it concisely illustrates a major literary theme in the book, the conflict between epic and non-epic poetic traditions.[6] I argue that Silius' appropriation and 'epicization' of the aforementioned poets entail a perversion of their non-martial, non-epic literary programs and thus become a way for him to assert the authority of his own martial, epic program over the 'small' genres they represent. In the broader context of the war in Sicily, this gesture blurs the lines between the book's content and its form, between the Romans' invasion of Sicily and the epic itself, and thereby sets Silius' epic agenda in mimetic relation to the Romans' military agenda: just as they conquer the island and establish their rule over it, so Silius' epic tames and subdues, as it were, non-epic genres for its own martial ends. This reading of the Grosphus passage, I should note, owes much to a recent study of Antony Augoustakis, who makes a good case

---

3 See Gibson 2010, 60–64, who is more interested, though, in the possibility of Silius' use of prose sources.
4 Cf. Wilson 2004, 230.
5 See Martin 1980, Vinchesi 1999, and Augoustakis 2012.
6 Other than Gibson 2010, there is almost nothing on Silius' relation to Callimachus in the scholarship. Horace's influence on Silius has received little attention (Martin 1990; Cowan 2006), and Ovid's only slightly more (Bruère 1958 and 1959; Wilson 2004).

for reading Daphnis' death, later in the book, in similar terms.[7] I hope, nevertheless, to build on his work by showing that Roman imperialism is not the only legacy of Marcellus' victory to which Silius looks ahead at the end of *Punica* 14. As we shall see, the easing of hostilities between the Romans and the Syracusans after Syracuse's fall occasions, through a revisiting of Hor. *Carm.* 2.16, a rapprochement between epic and non-epic poetry. In this final metapoetic gesture Silius acknowledges the lasting influence of 'small' genres and, especially, the Callimachean-neoteric tradition on his own poetry, a thing to which his extensive use of such poetry in the book otherwise testifies.

Now, let us turn to Grosphus and his cavalry from Agrigento in the catalogue of Rome's Sicilian allies (Sil. 14.208–217):

> ... altus equorum
> mille rapit turmam atque hinnitibus aera flammat
> pulveream volvens Acragas ad moenia nubem.   210
> ductor Grosphus erat, cuius caelata gerebat
> taurum parma trucem, poenae monimenta vetustae.
> ille ubi torreret subiectis corpora flammis,
> mutabat gemitus mugitibus, actaque veras
> credere erat stabulis armenta effundere voces,   215
> haud impune quidem; nam dirae conditor artis
> ipse suo moriens immugit flebile tauro.

Lofty Agrigento brings a squadron of a thousand horses and fires the air with neighing as it kicks up a cloud of dust heading for the walls. Their leader was Grosphus, whose engraved shield bore the image of a savage bull, a reminder of an ancient punishment. When the bull roasted bodies, fires set beneath it, it changed groans into moos, and one might believe that a herd, driven from their stables, was really bellowing, and yet not with impunity; for the inventor of that cruel work himself mooed pitiably when he died in his own bull.

Language and phrasing evocative of martial epic are in evidence from the start. The clausula *altus equorum* (208), along with the nearby *turmam* (209), echoes its previous occurrence in the epic when the battlefield at the Ticinus is drenched with the blood of men and horses (4.162f. *altus equorum* / ... *turmae*). *Mille rapit* (209) appears three other times in Latin, each in epic, in the same metrical *sedes*, and in a martial context,[8] and the pairing of *pulverea* and *nubes* (210) is consistently used in literature to refer to clouds of dust kicked up by cavalry, whether in battle or on the march.[9] Another epic model, though its context is not

---

7 Augoustakis 2012.
8 Verg. *A.* 7.725, 10.178; Stat. *Theb.* 3.578.
9 Verg. *A.* 8.593; Sen. *Ag.* 599f.; Stat. *Theb.* 4.664, *Silv.* 5.1.132; Sil. 2.174.

martial, is Virgil's description of Agrigento, when Aeneas sails past the city after his encounter with Achaemenides in the *Aeneid: arduus inde Acragas ostentat maxima longe / moenia, magnanimum quondam generator equorum* (3.703 f.: 'Then lofty Agrigento shows its massive walls far off, once a producer of noble horses').[10]

But Silius shifts from epic to non-epic models when he turns his attention to Grosphus and his shield in lines 211 ff. This shift is immediately detectable in the name Grosphus itself, which calls to mind Horace's friend Pompeius Grosphus, a wealthy equestrian landowner from Sicily, and an ode dedicated to him, *Carm.* 2.16.[11] There are several allusions to this poem in the passage, which develop a contrast between the harsh context of war in Silius' epic and the peaceful context of the Sicilian countryside evoked in the Horatian ode.[12] The contrast is conveyed, in part, through echoes of things Horace views as threats to a calm and tranquil life. For example, the cavalry Grosphus brings (208 f. *equorum ... turmam*) recalls the cavalry that is hounded by *Cura* in Horace's sixth stanza (*Carm.* 2.16.22 *turmas equitum*), and the cloud of dust Grosphus' cavalry kicks up (210 *pulveream ... nubem*), otherwise a martial, epic detail, now seems to engage with the ode's opening lines, in which a sailor wishes for *otium* when he is beset by a storm that covers the moon with an *atra nubes* (*Carm.* 2.16.2). More pointed contrasts emerge from a shift in context: the mooing of Grosphus' cows, which roam the countryside in Horace's poem (*Carm.* 2.16.34 *mugiunt*), are turned into the sounds, imitative of moos, produced by those burned alive in Phalaris' bull, depicted on Grosphus' shield (214 *mugitibus*; 217 *immugit*); the neighing of Grosphus' mares, which roam around his Sicilian estates (*Carm.* 2.16.34 *hinnitum,*), is turned into the neighing of horses arriving for battle (209 *hinnitibus*); and Grosphus' hundred mooing cows (*Carm.* 2.16.33 *centum*) undergo epic expansion and become a thousand war-horses (209 *mille*).[13]

Silius, however, is not developing these contrasts without the complicity of Horace's own poem, which itself contrasts war and peace. In the ode's second

---

10 Spaltenstein 1990, ad Sil 14.208.

11 Grosphus is also mentioned in Hor. *Ep.* 1.12.22 f. The name is quite rare, however; other than Horace's Grosphus, we only hear of a Grospus, also from Sicily (Cic. *Ver.* 3.56), and two Grosphi, who were *duumviri* in Pompeii in 59 CE (*CIL* IV.3340.143).

12 Nisbet / Hubbard 1978, 253 briefly acknowledge Silius' debt to Horace: "both here [in the Silian passage] and in our poem [*Carm.* 2.16] there are references to cavalry squadrons, neighing horses, and cattle (real or bronze). Silius seems to have taken *hinnitibus* from Horace (34), and so perhaps his other material."

13 I follow Nisbet / Hubbard 1978, *ad* Hor. *Carm.* 2.16.33 in taking *greges* to refer to cattle (cf. 33 f. *Siculaeque ... vaccae*) rather than sheep.

stanza, we hear of bellicose Thrace (*Carm.*2.16.5 *bello furiosa Thrace*) and the warring Mede (6 *Medi pharetra decori*) seeking *otium* and of *Cura* following *turmas equitum* in stanza six (21), as was noted above.[14] Grosphus' own association with war is hinted at in several details too. There is, for one, his neighing mare, which is 'suited to the *quadriga*' (*Carm.* 2.16.35 *apta quadrigis equa*). Nisbet and Hubbard understand this to refer to horses raised for chariot-racing, but *quadriga* may also call to mind their use in triumphal processions or representations of them in commemoration of military victories.[15] Consider also the reference to wool dyed in purple, which immediately follows (*Carm.* 2.16.35–37): *te bis Afro / murice tinctae / vestiunt lanae*, 'wool, twice dyed in African purple, clothe you'. Most readers focus on the color's association with luxury and understand it in relation to Horace's rejection thereof. Nisbet and Hubbard go farther in proposing that it refers to the *angustus clavus* that Grosphus, as an equestrian, might wear or to "a commercial interest in luxury textiles". And yet, a military association, such as with the purple worn by a *triumphator*, is not out of the question, especially given the juxtaposition of this detail to that of the *quadriga*.[16] Finally, Grosphus' name is itself suggestive of war, as it means 'javelin' (γρόσφος) in Greek; in fact, Horace makes a pun on the name in stanza 5 (*Carm.* 2.16.17–18): *quid brevi fortes iaculamur aevo / multa?*, 'Why do we steadfastly aim at so many things during our short lives?'.[17] It is not entirely clear how these details should inform Horace's depiction of Grosphus in the ode. Does he have military hopes or aspirations? Do his commercial activities include dealings with the Roman army? Was he formerly a soldier or does he come from a line of military men?[18] Whatever the case, one thing is clear: Grosphus is a landowner living peacefully in Sicily, not a military man, and it is his wealth or, rather, the misguided notion that wealth may give him peace of mind that Horace criticizes;

---

14 *Aeratas ... navis* (*Carm.* 2.16.21) may refer to battleships (so, Davis 1991, 210 f.; Pöschl 1991², 124) and thus be another martial detail.

15 Nisbet / Hubbard 1978, *ad* Hor. *Carm.* 2.16.35.

16 Nisbet / Hubbard 1978, *ad* Hor. *Carm.* 2.16.35. Also, note that the color is mentioned earlier in the poem (*purpura*, 7) in a stanza describing the bellicosity of Thracians and Medes.

17 Nisbet / Hubbard 1978, *ad* Hor. *Carm.* 2.16.17. Cf. Davis 1991, 207: "the witty wordplay helps to situate Grosphus metaphorically in the camp of the militaristic 'other' – along with warlike nations such as Thracians and Persians."

18 Perhaps Horace is hinting at Grosphus' status as an equestrian by associating him with both war and horses; for the equestrian order had supplied the cavalry in the early Roman army. Grosphus' equestrian status, a detail otherwise known only from Porphyrio (*ad* Hor. *Carm.* 2.16), would thus be indicated in the poem. Also, see West 1998, 117, who considers the possibility of an allusion in lines 21 f. to the *transvectio equitum*, a parade of equestrians held annually on July 15.

his association with war is something grounded in the past, whether his own or his family's, or is something unrealized and potential. Silius, though, picks up on this association in Horace's poem and uses it as a basis for his invention of a Sicilian ancestor who fought on the Roman side in the Second Punic War. The difference between these two Grosphi neatly illustrates the difference between the poetic contexts in which they appear, lyric and epic.

But we are invited not simply to acknowledge this distinction, but to view lyric and epic as being in conflict with one another as well, and Horace's poem provides the template for this generic tension. The principal contrast around which *Carm.* 2.16 revolves is between the peace of mind Horace derives from his simple, frugal lifestyle and the anxieties that plague men involved in commerce, war, or politics. In steering Grosphus toward *otium* and away from *negotium*, he offers, to be sure, a kind of Epicurean paraenesis. But he also offers a defense of his own lyric agenda and in such a way as to set it apart from the very genre Silius engages in, epic.[19] Note the adjectives *parvus* and *tenuis* when Horace advocates the frugal life in stanza 4 (*Carm.* 2.16.13 f.): *vivitur parvo bene, cui paternum / splendet in mensa tenui salinum*, 'he whose father's salt-cellar shines on a modest table lives well on little'.[20] Such programmatic language, familiar from the Callimachean-neoteric tradition in Rome, aligns Horatian lyric or, rather, this instance of Horatian lyric with 'small' genres, such as epigram, elegy, or pastoral, all of which were regarded as alternatives to 'big' genres like epic. A still more explicit statement of this kind is found in the poem's final lines (*Carm.* 2.16.37–40): *mihi parva rura et / spiritum Graiae tenuem Camenae / Parca non mendax dedit et malignum / spernere vulgus*, 'Fate, which does not lie, has given me a small property and the delicate inspiration of the Greek Muse and to spurn the spiteful crowd'. Again, the adjectives *parvus* and *tenuis* play a part in conveying the point, but we also hear in the latter, given its connection with *Graiae Camenae*, an echo of Callimachus' Μοῦσαν λεπταλέην (*Aet.* 1.1.24 Pf.). Moreover, the phrase *spernere vulgus* calls to mind Callimachus' rejection of the 'cyclic poem' and commonplace themes in *Epigr.* 28.1 ff. (ἐχθαίρω τὸ ποίημα τὸ κυκλικόν ...) or Horace's formulation of that idea, as in *Carm.* 3.1.1 (*odi profanum vulgus et arceo*).[21] And so, as echoes activate our memory of *Carm.*

---

19 Studies of the poem tend to focus on its moral-philosophical dimension: e. g., Syndikus 1972, 439–454; Nisbet / Hubbard 1978, 253–255; Pöschl 1991², 122–142; West 1998, 112–119. Davis 1991, 205–215, differently, emphasizes how Horace "align[s] an ethical outlook with an aesthetic orientation" (205) in the poem.

20 See Canobbio in this volume.

21 On Horace's Callimacheanism here in *Carm.* 2.16, see Mette 1961, 138, Commager 1962, 37 f., and Davis 1991, 214 f. For Callimacheanism in Horace's poetry, more broadly, see Wehrli 1944,

2.16, we are reminded of the generic tensions in that poem and are invited to apply them to the Silian passage. We thus read Silius' epicization of Horace's lyric as a poetic response or challenge rather than a mere act of appropriation and feel that the Horatian intertext and its addressee Grosphus sit uncomfortably in their new environment, having been forcibly wrenched from their lyric moorings and thrust into the vast sea of martial epic poetry.

Silius' use of non-epic poetry is further evident in his *ekphrasis* of Grosphus' shield, and, again, one senses that there is something almost polemical about his engagement with this material. The shield depicts the bronze bull of Phalaris, an early tyrant of Agrigento. Phalaris would lock his victims in the hollow body of the bull, have a fire lit beneath it, and roast them alive; the torture device was fitted with pipes that would channel the screams and groans of its victims so as to produce the effect of mooing. The story predates Silius by many centuries – the earliest reference to it is in Pindar (*P.* 1.95–98) – and the cruelty of Phalaris, for his use of the device, was long proverbial in Roman writers.[22] But Silius includes in lines 216 f. an interesting addendum to the story, that the inventor of the bull was himself roasted alive in it. What is telling about this detail is that it first appears in the *Aetia* of Callimachus (2.45–46 Pf.), who, as noted above, came to represent for many Romans of the late Republican and Augustan periods a literary ethos alternative to, if not in direct conflict with, that of large-scale epic.[23] That we are meant to think of Callimachus here seems to me likely, not only because Silius alludes to him several times elsewhere in *Punica* 14, but because the Callimachean provenance of the Perillus story had been secured in Latin literature from its earliest attestations, first in Propertius, the self-styled "Roman Callimachus" (2.25.11 f.), then in Ovid's erotic and exilic poetry, including the avowedly Callimachean *Ibis*.[24]

Ovid's treatment of this Callimachean story, specifically, appears to be recalled in the *ekphrasis* as well. As Bruère and Spaltenstein note, the detail of the realistic mooing the bull produces (214 f. *mugitibus ... veras ... voces*) echoes *Tristia* 3.11.48, where Perillus explains to Phalaris this feature of the torture-device: *mugiet, et veri vox erit illa bovis*, 'he will moo, and it will be the sound of a real

---

Commager 1962, 31–49, and Thomas 2007, 50–56. On the Romans' appropriation of Callimachean terminology and the distinction between 'small' genres, like lyric or elegy, and the 'big' genre of epic, see Nauta 2006, who offers a clear, succinct discussion of the topic from a Flavian perspective.

22 For the Phalaris legend from Pindar to Roman writers, see Hinz 2001, 47–77.

23 The inventor, whose name is found in our sources as Perillus, Perillos, or Perilaos, is usually said to have been the bull's first victim.

24 Ov. *Ars.* 1.653–656; *Tr.* 3.11.39–54, 5.1.53 f., 5.12.47 f.; *Pont.* 2.9.44, 3.6.41 f.; *Ib.* 437–440.

cow'.[25] Another echo, though its connection with Perillus' story is less evident on first glance, is Silius' description of the bull's inventor, which recalls Ovid's description of himself in *Pont.* 2.11: *dirae conditor artis* (216) = *Naso, parum faustae conditor artis* (*Pont.* 2.11.2).[26] We might leave the parallel at that, were it not for the fact that Ovid compares himself with Perillus in his own poetry (*Tr.* 5.12.47 f.): *utque dedit iustas tauri fabricator aeni, / sic ego do poenas artibus ipse meis* 'and just as the designer of the bronze bull paid a just penalty, so do I for my arts'.[27] An allusive and less direct comparison is drawn in *Ibis* 5 f., where Ovid refers to his punishment, exile, which he brought upon himself by his poetry: *nec quemquam nostri nisi me laesere libelli, / artificis periit cum caput arte sua*, 'nor did my little books harm anyone except me, when the life of the artist perished by his own art'. Line 6 contains an echo of *Ars Amatoria* 1, where, after arguing that liars and deceivers deserve to be punished by their own designs, Ovid relates how Thrasius was killed by Busiris and Perillus by Phalaris and then concludes (655 f.): *neque enim lex aequior ulla est / quam necis artifices arte perire sua*, 'for no law is more just than that contrivers of death perish by their own art'.[28] As we can see, by alluding to *Pont.* 2.11.2 in *Pun.* 14.216 Silius identifies Ovid with Perillus in a way that is consistent with Ovid's own identification with the doomed inventor.

Ovid is, thus, appropriated for epic ends, just as Horace and Callimachus are in the passage, and we might sense that he sits uncomfortably, no less than they, in this epic environment. I say this not only because his corpus is predominantly elegiac and, hence, 'small' in generic terms, but because, even when it comes to the *Metamorphoses*, its neoteric poetics and focus on myth make it a rather different type of epic than the more traditional historical, martial epic of the *Punica*. Additionally, Silius chooses to recall Ovid at his most vulnerable, in his exile poetry, and with specific reference to the punishment he incurred for a literary choice. And as that choice was in all probability an elegiac work, the *Ars Amatoria* – note his allusion to the *Ars* and his use of the word *ars* in the passages cited above – and, further, as he compares his fate to that of Perillus as well, the Silian phrase *poenae monimenta vetustae* (212) takes on rich metaliterary significance: it refers to Phalaris' bull on Grosphus' shield and calls to mind its inventor's punishment, but it also serves, through allusions to Ovid, as a reminder

---

25 Bruère 1959, 237 f.; Spaltenstein 1990, ad *Pun.* 14.214; cf. Wilson 2004, 230. Also, note *Ib.* 437: *aere Perilleo veros imitere iuvencos.*

26 The phrase *conditor artis* is also found, and, again, as a clausula, in Luc. *BC* 1.636 with reference to Tages.

27 Ovid compares himself to Perillus in *Tr.* 5.1.49–54 as well.

28 Cf. *Pont.* 2.9.44 *quive repertorem torruit arte sua.*

(*monimenta* in one sense) of Ovid's own punishment. But there is still another possibility: that the 'punishment' we are witnessing is the very transmutation of the Ovidian (and Callimachean) material into the martial epic context of *Punica* 14 and the attendant perversion of their non-epic poetics by virtue of that allusive act. In this sense, the images on the shield serve as a warning (*monimenta* in another sense) of what may befall 'small' genres and their authors when appropriated by an epic poet: their own poetry may be used against them.[29] As if to put an exclamation point on all of this, Silius even identifies these victims, be it Perillus, Ovid, or the Callimachean-Ovidian tradition, with a particularly unsavory, yet appropriately Sicilian epic character: Polyphemus. After describing how victims were burned alive in Phalaris' bull, the poet turns to the fate of its inventor, which he prefaces with the phrase *haud impune quidem* (216: 'but not with impunity'). This alludes to Achaemenides' account of the death and suffering he and Ulysses' men endured at the hands of Polyphemus in *Aeneid* 3: he witnessed, he says, his companions being eaten by the Cyclops (623–627), 'but not with impunity' (*haud impune quidem*, 628), for Ulysses put a stop to it and got his revenge (628–638).[30]

What is happening on a generic level here, the epicization of non-epic models, is mimetic of what is happening on a wider scale throughout *Punica* 14. As I noted at the outset, Silius frequently associates Sicily with non-epic traditions, such as the Callimachean, neoteric, and pastoral, and, in doing so, establishes a correlation between these traditions and the relatively peaceful state of the island before her involvement in the war. But as Marcellus and the Romans invade and Sicily is mobilized for military action, we witness the ascendancy of martial epic, which perverts and subsumes Sicily's literary heritage for its own totalizing, imperialistic ends. Grosphus is one example of the epic transformation Sicily undergoes in the book, but he is at least not conquered by the Romans; he fights on their side. A Sicilian named Daphnis is less fortunate; he left the countryside to take up arms against the Romans, but meets his death in the sea battle at Syracuse later in the book (462–476). I will not go into detail about this passage, as Antony Augoustakis has recently discussed it thoroughly. It suffices to point

---

29 In *poenae monimenta vetustae* we also hear an echo of Catullus' description of Prometheus, another clever *artifex* who was punished (Cat. 64.295): *extenuata gerens veteris vestigia poenae*, 'bearing faint traces of his ancient penalty'. Also, cf. Ov. *Fast.* 2.301 (*monimenta vetusti*) and Stat. *Theb.* 12.674 (*veteres reminiscitur actus*: Theseus' shield).

30 The only other instance of this phrase in Latin literature is found in *Punica* 16, when Scipio's brother cuts off the right hand of the Cantabrian Larus (66). Later in *Punica* 14, by the way, the Roman Laronius will play the role of Ulysses, so to speak, when he kills a Sicilian named Polyphemus in the sea battle at Syracuse (522–538).

out that Daphnis' death is a relatively minor detail, briefly noted in the last line of the passage (476); more important is his namesake and ancestor Daphnis, the legendary inventor of bucolic poetry, on whom Silius lingers for eleven lines (465–475). Augoustakis well captures the significance of the passage: "if the Ur-Daphnis represents the bucolic genre by-and-large, the sailor Daphnis is configured to betoken the destruction and subsumption of the pastoral into the landscape of epic".[31] And reading the passage in connection with Syracuse's fall at the end of the book, he concludes: "Daphnis' presence marks the transition from the pastoral world of Greek Sicily to the imperial realities of an island destined to be ruled by the Romans after the Second Punic War".[32] A similar lesson may be taken from Grosphus' appearance in the catalogue, as it foregrounds the conflict between "small" genres and the "big" genre of epic and, further, testifies to the growing hegemony of the latter in Sicily.

But even if imperialism and its literary vehicle, martial epic poetry, win out in the end, Rome will herself encounter new challenges in the future, and those challenges are immediately apparent once Marcellus takes Syracuse at the end of the book. After briefly reporting the Romans' invasion of Syracuse (638–640), Silius reflects at length on the wealth of the city, which no other in the world could rival at that time (641 f.). Testifying to this fact are its many monumental buildings and structures (643–648), its spoils of war and peace-time acquisitions adorning the city (649–654), and its abundance of art and luxury items (654–665). The poet next turns his attention to the conqueror Marcellus, who, looking down upon the city and deliberating whether its walls should stand or fall (665–669), groans at the great power he possesses and shudders to think that he is permitted to do whatever he wants (670 f.). He then orders his men to spare the Syracusans and their city (671–673); thus, clemency takes the place of plunder (673 f.), and a relatively bloodless victory is won (674 f.).[33] The vanquished, no less than the victors, rejoice at this outcome (679 f.), and Marcellus is praised as a "second founder" for his merciful treatment of the city (680 f.). Immediately hereafter, we reach the end of the book, where Silius, looking to the future, puts Marcellus' achievement into historical and moral perspective (682–688):

> ergo exstat saeclis stabitque insigne tropaeum
> et dabit antiquos ductorum noscere mores.
> felices populi, si, quondam ut bella solebant,
> nunc quoque inexhaustas pax nostra relinqueret urbes!　　　　　685

---

31 Augoustakis 2012, 134.
32 Augoustakis 2012, 134.
33 A notable exception is the death of Archimedes (*Pun.* 14.676–678).

at, ni cura viri, qui nunc dedit otia mundo,
effrenum arceret populandi cuncta furorem,
nudassent avidae terrasque fretumque rapinae.

It, therefore, remains and will remain for ages a remarkable trophy and will let it be known what the moral character of our leaders was long ago. People would be happy if our peace now also left cities unplundered, just as our wars once used to do! But, if he who has now brought peace to the world were not attentively checking the unrestrained lust for despoiling everything, greedy rapine would have stripped bare land and sea.

I linger on this concluding development because it represents Silius' final engagement with non-epic content in *Punica* 14 and, specifically, with *Carm.* 2.16, which Grosphus' appearance earlier evoked, and offers a kind of resolution or easing of tensions between that content and the martial epic content of the book. As we saw above, Silius' allusions to the ode develop a contrast between his Grosphus, who has taken up arms on the Romans' behalf during Marcellus' invasion of Sicily, and Horace's, who enjoys the peace and prosperity of the Sicilian countryside. Implicit in this contrast, however, is another contrast between the poetic genres in which these Grosphi appear, lyric and epic; and, as I suggested, Silius' appropriation of this Horatian material for his own martial epic ends marks a fundamental perversion of his predecessor's lyric ethos and Callimachean program. But this reading represents only one side of the intepretive coin. Its premise is that Horace's Grosphus and the poem addressed to him, *Carm.* 2.16, stand behind, and thus inform by virtue of their anteriority, Silius' depiction of Grosphus in *Punica* 14. This is, of course, a reasonable way of proceeding, as Horace's ode predates Silius' epic by over one hundred years. But if we indulge the fiction that Silius gives us, that there was a Sicilian named Grosphus who fought in the Second Punic War, and if we, accordingly, flip the coin so that we consider Silius' Grosphus the predecessor of Horace's, then the events in Sicily, as described by Silius, appear to be predicative or causative of the future state of affairs on the island described by Horace. And, as one can see at the end of *Punica* 14, Silius is acutely aware of the long-term repercussions of Marcellus' victory at Syracuse: it marks the beginning of Roman rule in Sicily, which will make possible the prosperous and peaceful conditions for Grosphus' Horatian namesake almost two hundred years later. Viewed from this historical perspective, Silius' and Horace's poems seem to be more complementary than in conflict.

But there are other ways in which the two are complementary, although not without qualification. For one, there is some coherence between their moral messages. In *Carm.* 2.16 Horace advises Grosphus to seek *otium* or peace of mind, which, for the poet, is secured by living simply and frugally, not by pursuing military success, political power, or, as is the specific case with Grosphus, wealth. Turning to the end of *Punica* 14, we see that what the lyric poet views as threats to *otium* are the very things Marcellus struggles with when he takes Syracuse: his victory raises the prospects of widespread plunder and of his own limitless authority. And, as the book's epilogue reminds us, these will continue to pose a threat to future generations of Roman imperialists. The moral challenges of the late first century BCE that Horace foregrounds in his ode thus have their roots in Rome's military successes of the late third century BCE.[34] But while Horace and Silius may agree on what these challenges are, they differ on how to address them. Retreating from the world of *negotium* into the world of *otium*, as the lyric poet advises, is simply not possible for the epic poet, who accommodates his historical subject matter to a decidely imperialist message. We must not forget that in the *Punica* the god Jupiter himself designs the Second Punic War to revitalize Rome's flagging martial virtue and thereby sets her on a path not only toward victory in the war, but toward world domination thereafter (3.571–592; cf. 3.163–165). Beyond that await the Flavian emperors, most notably Domitian, who stands at the end – and as the "end" – of the god's prophecy in *Punica* 3 (593–629).[35] As empire-building is a central, divinely sanctioned, and non-negotiable aspect of the epic's teleology, what is needed is not Horatian withdrawal, but leaders of good moral character, like Marcellus or Domitian, who can expand and maintain Rome's empire without succumbing to the vices to which military success and the acquisition of power or wealth may lead.

But we also perceive toward the end of *Punica* 14 a lessening of generic tensions between Silian epic and Horatian lyric. Telling in this respect is line 686, where Silius begins his praise of Domitian: *at, ni cura viri, qui nunc dedit otia mundo*. The poet here uses language that is evocative of the Callimachean-neoteric tradition in Rome. The word *cura* refers, in the immediate context, to the care and attention with which the emperor keeps the rapacity of provincial ad-

---

34 Livy's influence, however, should be noted as well. Although Silius' account of Syracuse's fall deviates significantly from the historian's in several respects (see below), his portrait of Marcellus, who reacts emotionally, is influenced by Livy's depiction of the general, who weeps on that occasion (25.24.11; cf. Plut. *Marc.* 19.1). One of the ideas that Livy touches on through this depiction, as Rossi 2000, 61–63 shows, is that of "negative foreboding" not only for Marcellus himself, who will die later in the war, but for Rome, which, as Livy indicates in 25.40.1–3, will be corrupted by the influx of wealth from Syracuse. The similarity of Marcellus' reaction in *Punica* 14 and the subsequent moralizing epilogue, which, retrospectively, invites a reading of that reaction similar to that which Rossi proposes for Livy's Marcellus, would appear to confirm the historian's influence here.

35 For more, see Marks 2005b, 211f.

ministrators in check, but it might also remind us of the Callimachean virtue of laborious composition and revision, τέχνη or πόνος, also rendered in Latin by the terms *ars* and *labor*.[36] We may also wish to consider Horace's use of the word in *Carm.* 2.16, where, as was noted above, *Cura* is what hounds the military man (21). Since the word is used there in the sense of 'concern' or 'anxiety' and represents in the poem what should be avoided, it would seem to suit Domitian's administrative activities better than Horace's poetic ones. And yet, as we have seen, Horace concludes his ode in an emphatically Callimachean fashion, which suggests that the lyric poet, though rejecting *cura* in the 'negative' sense, embraces it in the poetically 'positive', Callimachean sense of τέχνη or *ars*. Consider, moreover, Silius' use of *otia* in line 686. In the immediate context, it must refer to peace throughout the empire (cf. 685 *pax*), but it has poetic connotations as well: *otium* was a term the neoterics and their successors used not only to set themselves apart as poets from those involved in politics, business, or war, but to distinguish their own literary endeavors from those that dealt with the world of *negotium*, such as historical epic or panegyric.[37] In fact, a famous use of the term appears in *Carm.* 2.16, whose first two stanzas contain the triple anaphora *otium* (1) ... *otium* (5) ... *otium* (6), and this, in turn, takes us back to another famous instance of the word, also in triple anaphora, in the last stanza of Catullus 51, a poem likewise in sapphics: *otium* (13) ... *otio* (14) ... *otium* (15).[38] Silius' use of such terms in the epilogue of *Punica* 14 suggests that there is, indeed, a place for the poetry of Callimachus, the neoterics, and Horace and that there is something to be learned from them; for while there is a time for a leader like Marcellus or Domitian to play the martial epic hero, there is also a time, when the battle is over, for him to cultivate, enjoy, and spread the benefits of a world without war or epic.

Comparable to these leaders is the poet Silius himself, who, once Syracuse is taken, tellingly eases his martial epic grip over the narrative, describing a rapid deceleration of tensions as Marcellus curbs his troops' furor (671 *propere revocata militis ira*) and prevents the despoliation of the city (672f.). I say "tellingly" because his account of the victory's aftermath is unhistorical or, at the very least, misleading: Livy speaks of 'many abominable examples of wrath and greed' (*multa irae, multa avaritiae foeda exempla*) and refers to widespread ran-

---

36 For more on *cura* in this sense and its applicability to Silius, see the works cited in n. 40, below.
37 See André 1966, 214–232, 403–429, and, with reference to Horace, 489–498.
38 For the relationship between Catullan and Horatian *otium* in this instance, see Fraenkel 1957, 211–214 and Putnam 2006, 90 f.

sacking and looting by Roman soldiers (25.31).[39] Now, as we reflect on the gentle aftermath of Syracuse's defeat, as Silius fashions it, and on his use of poetically marked language, *cura* and *otium*, in the epilogue thereafter, we might well consider how all of this speaks to his own poetic practice. And thus we might see in the easing of hostilities between the Romans and the Sicilians at the end of *Punica* 14 a rapprochement on the epic poet's part with non-epic poetic traditions. We might, further, reflect on Silius' engagement with those traditions throughout the book and acknowledge a central paradox underlying his epicizing program therein: to assert the authority of his 'big' epic over the 'small' genres of Callimachus, Horace, and Ovid he must appropriate their poetry and their erudite, allusive literary practices for his own. But in embracing such practices our poet may not be behaving so uncharacteristically as the paradox suggests, and the well-known assessment of him, offered by the younger Pliny, may support this idea (*Ep.* 3.7.5): *scribebat carmina maiore cura quam ingenio* ('he wrote poetry with greater care than talent'). Although Pliny's words have often been taken to express disparagement of Silius' poetic abilities, some have challenged that interpretation, proposing that *cura* be understood in its Callimachean-neoteric sense.[40] Whether such was Pliny's intention or not, *Punica* 14 indeed shows Silius to be a poet of *cura* in that very sense.

---

39 Silius' account owes much, rather, to the sterilized version given by Cicero, *Ver.* 2.4.116, 120–123. For more, see Burck 1984, 53–60, Ripoll 2000, 153–156, and Scaffai 2004. For more on Silius' favorable depiction of Marcellus not only here, but elsewhere in the epic, see Fucecchi 2010, 230–238 and Stocks 2014, 147–166.
40 So, Laudizi 1989, 19–24 and Pomeroy 1989, who considers (139 n. 78) "an evaluation which puts Silius on a par with Callimachus whom Ovid described as 'strong in skill, if not in talent' (*Am.* 1.15.14: *quamvis ingenio non valet, arte valet*)".

Alison Keith
Lyric resonances in Statius' *Achilleid*

Statius' intertextual appropriations of a variety of authors and genres in the *Achilleid* have received considerable attention in recent years. Primacy has naturally been given to his epic sources, especially his relations with Homer, Virgil and Ovid; but scholars have also considered his extensive debts to elegy and tragedy.[1] By contrast, his interest in the genre of lyric has garnered surprisingly little scholarly attention, despite Statius' authorship – over the course of a long professional literary career – of occasional poems, some of which he collected into four books of *Silvae*, and issued from 91 or 92 CE onwards, as his *Thebaid* neared completion and went into circulation.[2] Yet it was precisely in this period, when he was collecting and issuing the *Silvae*, that Statius seems to have conceived his new epic project on the life of Achilles and embarked upon its composition. In this paper, I wish to explore the possibility of Statius' sustained engagement with the lyric genre in his extant elaboration of Achilles' life. I shall argue that Statius draws on Horatian lyric at critical junctures in both his statement of poetic programme and his representation of Achilles; that he deploys the technical terminology of Latin lyric in his depiction of Achilles as a singer (and teacher) of lyric; and that he alludes to his own contemporary lyric collections in his development of the new epic plot.

We may begin with Statius' programmatic opening statement, which has been taken as the announcement of a grand epic project that would seem to leave little room for engagement with the genre of lyric (*Ach.* 1.1–4):[3]

My thanks to Federica Bessone and Marco Fucecchi for the invitation to participate in the original conference in Torino; to Jen Oliver for indispensible help with the bibliography; and to Lorenza Bennardo, Michael Dewar, †Elaine Fantham, and Stephen Kershner for their comments on earlier versions of this paper. I am responsible for all remaining errors and infelicities.

1 In addition to the commentators, see Fantham 1979 on Statius' debts to Ovid and Senecan tragedy; Rosati 1992, 1994a and 1994b, and Hinds 2000 on Statius' debt to Ovid; and Körte 1934, Aricò 1981, and Fantuzzi 2012 on Statius' debt to Euripides' tragedy *Skyrioi*.
2 For the difficulties of dating Statius' life and works, see van Dam 1984, 1–4; Coleman 1988, xv–xxii; Laguna 1992, 3–13; Nauta 2002, 195–204; Gibson 2006b, xxviii–xxx; and Newlands 2011, 1–3.
3 I cite Statius' *Achilleid* from Marastoni's 1974 Teubner edition of the poem, and Statius' *Silvae* from Courtney's 1990 Oxford Classical Text. Unless otherwise indicated, all translations of Latin poetry are my own.

https://doi.org/10.1515/9783110534436-016

> Magnanimum Aeaciden formidatamque Tonanti
> progeniem et patrio vetitam succedere caelo,
> diva, refer. quamquam acta viri multum inclita *cantu*
> *Maeonio,* sed plura vacant...

> Goddess, remember great-hearted Achilles, descended of Aeacus, and the offspring feared
> by the Thunderer, forbidden to succeed to his father's sky. Although the man's deeds are
> renowned in Homeric song, still more remain available...

The opening word of the poem (*magnanimum, Ach.* 1.1) is a Latin calque on the Homeric epithet μεγάθυμος, applied to Achilles in the *Iliad* (21.153, 23.168) and, in its Latin form, by Ovid in the *Metamorphoses* (13.298), as well as to the foundational Roman epic hero, Aeneas, by Virgil in the *Aeneid* (1.260, 5.17, 407, 9.204). Similarly, Statius' papponymic *Aeaciden* (*Ach.* 1.1) varies Homer's designation of Achilles by the patronymic Πηληϊάδεω in the opening line of the *Iliad* (μῆνιν ἄειδε, θέα, Πηληϊάδεω Ἀχιλῆος, *Il.* 1.1), while his invocation of the goddess (*diva, Ach.* 1.3) alludes to Homer's initial apostrophe of the Muse as 'goddess' there. And, of course, Statius' reference to 'Homeric song' (*cantu / Maeonio, Ach.* 1.3–4) clinches the poem's generic alignment with Homeric epic. Or does it?

The Latin poetic use of the adjective *Maeonius* in application to Homer derives from Horace, who in *Odes* 1.6 acknowledges the primacy of Homeric song (1.6.1–4):[4]

> Scriberis Vario fortis et hostium
> victor *Maeonii carminis* alite,
> quam rem cumque ferox navibus aut equis
>   miles te duce gesserit.

> You will be commemorated by Varius, a bird of Homeric song, as brave and a victor over the
> enemy, for whatever exploit the fierce soldier shall have accomplished either on sea or land
> under your leadership.

Nisbet and Hubbard comment *ad loc.* (1970, 84) that this is the first extant reference in Latin to Homer's Maeonian provenance (whether genealogical or geographical), and they note Horace's reuse of the adjective in *Odes* 4.9 (*Maeonius ... Homerus,* 4.9.5 f.). What they do not note is that the adjective's continuing association with Homer retains a distinctly lyrico-elegiac *color* in Latin usage, appearing next in Propertian and Ovidian elegy, as well as later in Statius' *Silvae*.[5]

---

4 Uccellini 2012, 35 ad Stat. *Ach.* 1.1. I cite Horace's *Odes* from the 1982 Teubner edition of Klingner.
5 Cf. Prop. 2.28.29, 2.34.66; Ov. *Ars* 2.4, *Rem.* 373, *Pont.* 3.3.31; Verg. *Cat.* 15.2; *Laus Pis.* 232; Mart. 7.46.2; Stat. *Silv.* 2.1.117. See further *OLD* s.v. 'Maeonius' 1b and 2.

This is not to deny that the seven-line sentence with which Statius launches his *Achilleid* is modelled on the seven-line opening sentence of the *Aeneid*, nor that the Flavian poet's avowed project, of rehearsing the whole of the hero Achilles' life up to and including his time at Troy, is the stuff of grand martial epic. But it has been well observed that Statius – like Virgil and Ovid before him – tempers epic grandeur with a stylistic delicacy normally characterized as neoteric or elegiac (*Ach.* 1.4–7):

> ... nos ire per *omnem* –
> sic amor est – *heroa* velis *Scyro*que *latentem*　　　　　　　　5
> *Dulichia* proferre *tuba* nec in *Hectore* tracto
> sistere, sed *tota iuvenem deducere Troia.*

May you wish us – such is our desire – to proceed through the hero's whole life, and to bring him forth from hiding on Scyros with Odysseus' martial trumpet, and not to end with him dragging Hector but to lead the youth through the whole Trojan war.

Despite the 'totalizing' epic ambition (as Philip Hardie has described it)[6] implied in the phrases *omnem heroa* (1.4–5) and *tota Troia* (1.7), Koster (1979, 192–196) suggested that *deducere* be interpreted metapoetically here, as signalling a desire on Statius' part 'to refine' his grand epic subject in the style of slender elegiac or lyric verse. For this sense of *deducere* we may compare programmatic passages in Catullus (64.306–322), Virgil (*Ecl.* 6.5), and Horace (*Ep.* 2.1.225 *tenui deducta poemata filo*, 'poems spun with a fine thread'). Especially relevant is Ovid's well known qualification of his grand epic subject in the proem to the *Metamorphoses*, where he requests that the gods 'refine' his continuous song (1.4 *perpetuum deducite ... carmen*).[7] Although not every recent critic has accepted the poetological interpretation of Statius' project as 'a *deductus Achilles*', i.e. 'a reduced version of the sublime hero of Homer', Ripoll and Soubiran are, in fact, remarkably isolated in disavowing any metapoetic implications in their 2008 commentary on the *Achilleid*.[8]

In further support of such a poetological interpretation, moreover, we may adduce the vatic lyric stance Statius adopts in the invocation of Apollo that follows (*Ach.* 1.8–11):

---

6 Hardie 1993, 1–10.
7 I cite the text of Ovid's *Metamorphoses* from Tarrant 2004.
8 The quotations are from Barchiesi 2005a, 70 n. 30. *Contra* Ripoll / Soubiran 2008, see further Hinds 2000; Heslin 2005; and Uccellini 2012, 39 f.

tu modo, si veterem digno deplevimus haustu,
da *fontes* mihi, *Phoebe*, novos ac fronde secunda
necte comas: neque enim Aonium *nemus* advena *pulso*   10
nec mea nunc *primis* augescunt tempora *vittis*.

> Only you, Phoebus, grant new sources [of poetic inspiration] to me, if I have exhausted the old with a worthy draught, and bind my hair with a propitious wreath: for I do not strike the ground of the Aonian grove as a stranger, nor are my temples now honoured for the first time with fillets.

Statius' aquatic imagery of poetic inspiration is familiar from Callimachus (*Ap.* 2.106–112) and Propertius (3.1.3 f. *primus ego ingredior puro de fonte sacerdos | Itala per Graios orgia ferre choros*, 'I am the first priest to enter and from your pure source to bring Italian rites through Greek dances');[9] the poet's garland, which Horace claims both for Pindar (*Carm.* 4.2.9 *laurea donandus Apollinari*, 'to be presented with Apollo's bay') and himself (*Carm.* 3.30.15 f. *mihi Delphica | lauro cinge volens, Melpomene, comam*, 'willingly crown my hair with Delphic bay, Melpomene'), from the Pythian games (Call. *Fr.* 194.33, Paus. 10.7.22–4); and the bard's entry into the grove of the Muses, from Propertius' accounts in the 'Roman Elegies' of his poetic initiation (3.1.1–8, partially quoted above; cf. 3.3.42). The opening of Statius' epicedion for his father in *Silvae* 5.3, probably contemporary in date of composition with that of the *Achilleid*, also combines many of these motifs, including the fountains and groves of poetry, there in explicit conjunction with lyric inspiration (*Silv.* 5.3.1–5):

Ipse malas vires et lamentabile carmen
Elysio de *fonte* mihi *pulsum*que sinistrae
da, genitor praedocte, *lyrae*. neque enim *antra* movere
Delia nec solitam fas est impellere Cirrham
te sine…

> You yourself, exceptionally learned father, grant me from the Elysian spring the painful strength for a song of lamentation, to strike the ill-omened lyre. For without you it is right neither to move Delius' glades nor to disturb Cirrha in the usual way.

Even Statius' reference to 'striking' the ground of the Muses' grove in the proem of the *Achilleid* (1.10) is consistent with his repeated use of the verb *pulso* of 'striking' his lyre in the *Silvae:* although at first his lyre does not 'strike' Helicon (*Silv.* 1.5.1 *Non Helicona … pulsat chelys*), he later 'knocks' to gain entry to the Muses' glades in Boeotia (*Silv.* 5.3.209–214):

---

9 I cite the text of Propertius from Fedeli 1984, and the text of Ovid's *Amores* from McKeown 1987.

me quoque vocales *lucos Boeotaque tempe*
pulsantem, cum stirpe tua descendere dixi,   210
admisere deae; nec enim mihi sidera tantum
aequoraque et terras, quae mos debere parenti,
sed *decus hoc* quodcumque *lyrae primus*que dedisti
non vulgare loqui et famam sperare sepulchro.

Me too, knocking at the sounding groves and vales of Boeotia, the goddesses admitted when I said I was descended from your stock; for you not only gave me the stars, seas and lands, which it is customary to owe to a parent, but also this glory, such as it is, of the lyre, and you first taught me no common speech but to hope for fame for my tomb.

In all three programmatic passages in the *Silvae* (5.3.1–5, 1.5.1, and 5.3.209–214), Statius employs a form of the word for 'strike' in close conjunction with the musical instrument which symbolizes the genre of lyric, just as he does here in the proem to the *Achilleid*. Finally, by calling for fillets at *Achilleid* 1.11, Statius represents himself as a priest of Apollo, like the Augustan poets of lyric and elegy. His stance is especially reminiscent of Horace, who seems to have introduced it into Latin poetry in his Roman Odes (3.1.1–4):

Odi profanum volgus et arceo.
favete linguis: carmina non *prius*
    audita Musarum *sacerdos*
        virginibus puerisque canto.

I hate the vulgar rabble and keep them away. Observe a religious silence; the priest of the Muses, I sing songs not heard before to maidens and youths.

Statius' articulation of his poetic program in the proem to the *Achilleid* is thus as indebted to lyric (and elegiac)[10] poetry as it is to Homer's epic.

When we turn from Statius' poetic program to his characterization of his hero, moreover, we find already in the proem that Achilles, in hiding on Scyros, has adopted a posture derived from Horatian lyric (*latentem*, *Ach.* 1.5). In *Odes* 1.8, Horace famously chides 'Lydia' for entrapping the handsome youth 'Sybaris' in the toils of love, thereby keeping him from the athletic and military pursuits appropriate to his age (and to Augustan ideology), like Thetis' son Achilles (1.8.13–16):

---

10 With the vatic language of initiation and ritual purity used by Horace in *Carm.* 3.1.1–4, cf. Prop. 3.1.1–8 (partially quoted in the text), and Ov. *Am.* 3.8.23 (*ille ego Musarum purus Phoebique sacerdos*, 'I am that cultivated priest of Phoebus and the Muses').

> quid *latet*, ut marinae
> > *filium* dicunt *Thetidis* sub lacrimosa Troiae
> funera, ne virilis
> > cultus in caedem et Lycias proriperet catervas?

Why does [Sybaris] lie hidden – as they say the son of marine Thetis did on the eve of mournful deaths at Troy, lest his manly dress snatch him into the slaughter and Lycian bands.

Statius' Horatian echo may be faint here (though he may recall the same passage in the phrase *hoc ... cultu* at *Ach.* 1.272), but he signals a decisive interest in Horace's lyric characterization of Achilles again later in the first book, in his description of Thetis' transformation of Achilles' appearance so as to deceive his Scyrian hosts into accepting him as a girl (Stat. *Ach.* 1.335–337):

> > ... superest nam plurimus illi
> invita virtute decor, *fallit*que tuentes
> *ambiguus* tenuique *latens discrimine* sexus.

For very much charm remains to [Achilles] though his masculinity resists, and his indeterminate sex, hidden by a slender margin, deceives onlookers.

As has long been recognized, the context and diction which Statius employs here are derived from another Horatian ode, where a similarly epicene youth is described (2.5.20–24):

> > ... Cnidiusve Gyges,   20
> quem si puellarum insereres choro,
> mire sagacis *falleret* hospites
> > *discrimen* obscurum solutis
> > > crinibus *ambiguo*que voltu.

... or Cnidian Gyges – if you set him in a ring of girls, the imperceptible difference of his flowing locks and doubtful countenance could wonderfully deceive even discerning strangers.

Dilke (1954, 103 *ad loc.*) notes Statius' appropriation of 'three important words' in this passage, and there is no dissent among the commentators about the importance of the Horatian model for Statius here.[11] Indeed, Statius has garnered praise for penetrating the allusive obscurity of Horace's lines, which, as Nisbet and Hubbard (1978, 91 *ad* 2.5.21) observe, refer "to the disguise of Achilles on Scyros", when he danced in the chorus of Lycomedes' daughters. Statius signals

---

11 Cf. Ripoll / Soubiran 2008, 202 *ad loc.*; Uccellini 2012, 229 *ad loc.*

his understanding of Horace's allusion in *Odes* 2.5.20–24, by his self-citation of an earlier Horatian allusion in the proem (*latentem*, 1.7) in conjunction with a cross-reference (*latens*) to the passage we have just considered in 1.8.13 (*latet*). Indeed, Statius' reprisal of *latens* here at 1.337 would seem to clinch the argument for allusion to *Odes* 1.8 in the proem (*latentem*, *Ach.* 1.5).

In *Allusion and Intertext*, however, although noting that Statius' allusion to *Odes* 2.5.20–24 in these lines (*Ach.* 1.335–337) offered "one of the clearest verbal and situational allusions to be found anywhere in the *Achilleid*", Stephen Hinds tendentiously denied an allusion to Horace's *Odes* here in favour of an allusion to Ovid's *Metamorphoses*.[12] While I would by no means deny Statius' pervasive use in the *Achilleid* of Ovidian models, from both the *Ars* and the *Metamorphoses*, I would suggest that we should also take Statius' allusions to Horace's *Odes* (and his own *Silvae*) in the *Achilleid* seriously. For the lyric diction of the proem, in conjunction with the strongly marked allusion to Horatian lyric at the moment of Achilles' arrival on Scyros and transformation into a cross-dressing teenager hiding on the island, invite us to interpret Statius' use of (Horatian) lyric in the *Achilleid* as both systematic and significant. Moreover, if we examine the poem for other lyric investments, we need not look far to find an associative nexus of strikingly lyric imagery in the Flavian poet's characterization of Achilles.

Statius introduces his protagonist into the poem while still under the tutelage of Chiron, as he returns from training in martial and epic pursuits. At this point in his career, Achilles has not yet achieved the status even of an ephebe, for he is still 'sweet to the sight', his childish cast of face making him look very much like his mother (*Ach.* 1.159–166):

> ille aderat multo sudore et pulvere maior,
> et tamen arma inter festinatosque labores   160
> dulcis adhuc visu: niveo natat ignis in ore
> purpureus fulvoque nitet coma gratior auro.
> necdum prima nova lanugine vertitur aetas,
> tranquillaeque faces oculis et plurima vultu
> mater inest; qualis Lycia venator Apollo   165
> cum redit et saevis *permutat plectra pharetris.*

He was there, much larger with sweat and dust, but though in the midst of arms and premature labours, still sweet to the sight: a red glow suffuses his snowy face, his hair gleams more pleasantly than yellow gold. Not yet is his first youth transformed by new down, but a quiet flame burns in his eyes and there is very much of his mother in his face; such as Apol-

---

12 Hinds 1998, 136.

lo, when he returns from hunting in Lycia and exchanges his savage quivers for the lyre's quill.

Although Statius surrounds his hero with the insignia of war and epic heroism here (1.160), Achilles is clearly no martial warrior yet. He is covered with the sweat and dust reminiscent of an athlete on the training ground (1.159), while his childish beauty (1.161–165) is that of the effeminate *puer delicatus* of elegy and lyric. Statius confirms his hero's distance in age and experience from the mature warrior of the *Iliad* in a simile comparing him to Apollo returning from the hunt and exchanging 'his savage quivers for the lyre's quill' (1.165 f.). The commentators note the Virgilian inspiration of Statius' simile (*A.* 4.143–150), but observe that the Flavian poet also employs a Horatian turn of phrase from the Roman Odes (3.1.47 f. *cur valle permutem Sabina / divitias operosiores?*, 'why would I exchange my Sabine valley for more laborious wealth')[13] in a re-working of Horace's description of Apollo in the second book of the *Odes* (2.10.18–20):[14] *quondam cithara tacentem / suscitat Musam neque semper arcum / tendit Apollo* ('Apollo sometimes rouses the silent Muse with his lyre, and does not always bend his bow'). Achilles is represented as an Apollonian ephebe throughout classical literature, of course, but Statius' emphasis here on his resemblance to the god precisely in his lyric aspect sounds a distinctively Horatian note and anticipates the occasions on which Achilles performs with the lyre later in the first book of the *Achilleid*.

Indeed, we do not have to wait long for his first performance. After Thetis' arrival and warm reception from Chiron, her son's tutor calls for the lyre, tuning it and passing it to Achilles so that he can accompany himself in song (*Ach.* 1.184–194):

> tunc libare dapes Baccheaque munera Chiron
> orat et attonitae varia oblectamina nectens   185
> elicit extremo *chelyn* et solantia curas
> *fila movet leviter*que expertas pollice *chordas*
> dat puero. canit ille libens *inmania laudum*
> *semina:* quot *tumidae* supcrarit iussa novercae
> Amphitryoniades, *crudum* quo Bebryca caestu   190
> obruerit Pollux, quanto circumdata nexu
> ruperit Aegides Minoia bracchia tauri,
> maternos in fine toros superisque *gravatum*
> Pelion...

---

13 Uccellini 2012, 144 *ad loc.*
14 Dilke 1954, 97; Ripoll / Soubiran 2008, 178; Uccellini 2012, 144–146.

Then Chiron asks her to taste the meal and the gifts of Bacchus and, contriving various delights for her astonishment, finally brings out the tortoise-shell lyre; he moves the strings that solace cares and having tested the strings gently with his thumb he gives it to the boy. He willingly sings of the mighty seeds of glory: how many orders of his haughty step-mother Hercules overcame, with what glove Pollux overwhelmed bloody Amycus, king of Bebrycia, with how great a wrestling hold Theseus burst the limbs of Minos' bull and, at the end, his mother's wedding and Pelion weighed down by the gods...

Uccellini notes Statius' predilection for the word *chelys*, Greek for 'tortoise', to designate the lyre, as here at line 186. Indeed, in contrast to his predecessors and contemporaries, who eschew the Graecism, Statius employs it frequently (27 times in total), and especially often in his *Silvae* (22 times), where it is programmatic of his lyric verse (e. g., *Silv.* 1.5.1, quoted above).[15] His description of Chiron tuning its strings in the *Achilleid*, moreover, finds choice parallels in his own contemporary *Silvae*, both in the fourth book, which he himself released into circulation (*Silv.* 4.4.53 f. *tenuis ignavo pollice chordas / pulso*, 'with my idle thumb I strike the slender strings'), and in the fifth book, which was posthumously released (*Silv.* 5.5.31 f. *nec eburno pollice* [*scil. plectro*] *chordas / pulso*, 'and not with ivory quill do I strike the strings').

In the convivial setting of after-dinner song, Achilles takes as his subject not the 'glorious deeds of heroes' (κλέα ἀνδρῶν), which he sings in the *Iliad* (9.186–189, quoted below), but their 'vast seeds' (*inmania*[16] ... / *semina, Ach.* 1.188 f.), an oxymoron that nicely encapsulates Statius' project, in the first book of the *Achilleid*, of bringing the youth from adolescent training ground to epic battlefield. Here Chiron's protégé sings of Hercules' labours, Pollux' defeat of the Bebrycian king Amycus, Theseus' victory over the Minotaur, and his parents' wedding. Though the exploits of the heroes Hercules, Pollux, Theseus, and Peleus are undoubtedly appropriate subjects of high epic, we lack classical epic authority for (at least) two (if not three) of the four.[17] Still, Uccellini (2012, 157) observes that

---

15 Used once by Ovid, the term also appears once in Valerius and three times in Silius (in both Flavian authors of Chiron): see Uccellini 2012, 155–157 *ad loc.*, citing Ov. *Ep.* 15.181, V.Fl. 1.139 *pulsat ... chelyn post pocula Chiron*; Sil. 11.408, 441, 449–451: *nam quae Peliaca formabat rupe canendo / heroum mentes et magni pectora Achillis, / Centauro dilecta chelys*. Deferrari / Eagan 1942, 137, list the following occurrences of the word in the *Silvae*: 1.2.226; 1.3.99, 102; 1.5.1, 11; 2.1.7, 11; 2.2.60, 114, 120; 3.5.64; 4.3.119; 4.4.33; 4.6.30, 98; 4.8.38; 5.1.135; 5.3.122, 156, 271, 274; 5.5.33.
16 Dilke 1954, 98 *ad* 188 f., observes that in Statius "the force of this adjective [i. e., *inmanis*, which originally meant 'savage'] is often weakened by employment in such phrases as *telum immane*, *Th.l.L.* IX, 547, 802; *certamen immane* XII, 662", where it takes on the connotation of vast size: see *OLD* s.v.
17 Pollux' boxing match appears in the Argonautic epics of both Apollonius and Valerius Flaccus, but in both poems the boxing match is a parergon to the main epic theme of the voyage of

Achilles' themes "must have formed part of the traditional musical education" of Greek ephebes, and she aptly compares Pindar's account of the Aeacides' exploits in his third *Nemean Ode*, especially Pindar's treatment of Achilles' exploits when fostered by Chiron (Pind. *N.* 3.43–53):[18]

ξανθὸς δ' Ἀχιλεὺς τὰ μὲν μένων Φιλύρας ἐν δόμοις,
παῖς ἐὼν ἄθυρε μεγάλα ἔργα· χερσὶ θαμινά
βραχυσίδαρον ἄκοντα πάλλων ἴσα τ' ἀνέμοις,   45
μάχᾳ λεόντεσσιν ἀγροτέροις ἔπρασσεν φόνον,
κάπρους τ' ἔναιρε· σώματα δὲ παρὰ Κρονίδαν
Κένταυρον ἀσθμαίνοντα κόμιζεν,
ἐξέτης τὸ πρῶτον, ὅλον δ' ἔπειτ' ἂν χρόνον·
τὸν ἐθάμβεον Ἄρτεμίς τε καὶ θρασεῖ Ἀθάνα,   50
κτείνοντ' ἐλάφους ἄνευ κυνῶν δολίων θ' ἑρκέων·
ποσσὶ γὰρ κράτεσκε. *λεγόμενον δὲ τοῦτο προτέρων*
ἔπος ἔχω·

But fair-haired Achilles, when he stayed in Philyra's house, though a child, performed great deeds; with his hands often brandishing a small-headed javelin, swift as winds, he would, in battle with them, deal bloody death to savage lions and kill boars. He used to bring their gasping bodies to Kronos' son, Chiron, the Centaur, first from the age of six, and then for the whole time after that. Artemis and daring Athena were amazed that he killed deer without dogs and cunning nets for he surpassed them in speed of feet. This tale I have was told by former poets...

Statius thus seems to have drawn on a Greek lyric model for his portrait of the young Achilles rather than on Homeric epic. Moreover, Peter Heslin has shown that the specific exploits Achilles recounts here in *Achilleid* 1 emerge in literature

---

the Argo. Similarly, Callimachus treats Theseus' contest with the bull of Marathon in the fragmentary *Hecale*, but the focus of his short epic seems to have been on the title character, the old woman Hecale, rather than on the young hero: see Hollis 1990, 5–15 and 23–26, who notes the possible existence of earlier Theseus epics. While the Hesiodic *Shield of Herakles* undoubtedly attests to Herakles' martial valour, that poem can hardly be described as a Herakles-epic.

18 Cf. Fantham 1999, 63–65, who notes Statius' debt to Pindar's ode (*Nem.* 3.43–64) in Achilles' account of his upbringing to Diomedes, in response to his inquiry concerning his childhood at the opening of the unfinished second book of the *Achilleid* (2.91–93): *quae solitus laudum tibi pandere semina Chiron / virtutisque aditus, quas membra augere per artes, / quas animum?* ('What seeds of glory did Chiron display to you, what paths to manly courage, and by what arts did he help you to develop your physical and moral development?,' trans. Fantham 1999, 63). She also makes the important observation that Chiron "is quoted four times in the *Silvae*, always in relation to Achilles and in his role as foster father and educator", drawing the parallel with Statius' own father's role as educator in *Silv.* 5.3.193–196; cf. 1.2.216, 1.4.98, 2.1.89.

(and art) of the Hellenistic period, and are not familiar from Homeric epic.[19] In addition, many scholars have noted the song's special relationship to Catullus 64, the tiny perfect 'neoteric' epic that depicts Ariadne's love for Theseus on a tapestry laid out on the bridal couch at the wedding of Peleus and Thetis.[20] Like other recent critics, therefore, I regard these themes as better suited to the *deductum carmen* Statius offers in the *Achilleid* than as the stuff of grand heroic epic. Even the accompaniment of the small tortoise-shell lyre which Achilles plays in Statius' poem links his song to the genre of lyric, in contrast to the epic songs that he plays on the larger *phorminx* in the *Iliad* (9.186–189):

τὸν δ᾽ εὗρον φρένα τερπόμενον φόρμιγγι λιγείῃ,
καλῇ δαιδαλέῃ, ἐπὶ δ᾽ ἀργύρεον ζυγὸν ἦεν,
τὴν ἄρετ᾽ ἐξ ἐνάρων πόλιν Ἠετίωνος ὀλέσσας·
τῇ ὅ γε θυμὸν ἔτερπεν, ἄειδε δ᾽ ἄρα κλέα ἀνδρῶν.

They found him delighting his heart with the shrill phorminx, beautifully worked, and on it there was a silver bridge, which he won from the spoils, when he sacked Eëtion's city. With this he was delighting his heart, and singing the glorious deeds of men.

After his departure from Chiron's care and removal to the women's quarters of Lycomedes' palace on the island of Scyros too, the young Achilles remains a singer of lyric. Indeed, he charms Deidamia precisely by teaching her a lyric song about his 'brother's' exploits (*Ach.* 1.570–579):

nunc nimius lateri non evitantis inhaeret   570
nunc levibus sertis, lapsis nunc sponte canistris,
nunc thyrso parcente ferit, modo *dulcia notae*
fila lyrae tenuesque modos et carmina monstrat
Chironis ducitque manum digitosque sonanti
infringit citharae, nunc occupat ora canentis   575
et ligat amplexus et mille per oscula laudat.
illa libens discit, quo vertice Pelion, et quis
Aeacides, puerique auditum nomen et actus
adsidue stupet et praesentem *cantat* Achillem.

Now he clings too closely to her side, though she does not avoid him, and now pelts her with light garlands or the contents of baskets, and now with restrained thyrsus. And now he shows her the melodious strings of the familiar lyre, tender music and Chiron's songs; he guides her hands and bends her fingers to the sounding cithara, and now seizes the singer's face, binds her in his embrace, and praises her with a thousand kisses. She

---

19 Heslin 2005, 89–93; *contra* Fantham 1999, 61 and 63.
20 Hinds 1998, 125–128; Heslin 2005, 88f.; cf. Ripoll / Soubiran 2008, 181f.

willingly learns on what peak Pelion rises, who Aeacus' descendant is; she constantly thrills to hear the boy's name and deeds, and she sings of Achilles in his presence.

Statius commemorates Achilles as an awkward lover, pelting Deidamia with love gifts (1.571 f.), in the tradition of the courtship of Galatea and Polyphemus in Theocritus' *Idyll* 6 or the drunken *amator* in Propertian elegy (1.3). But the youthful Achilles finds more success with his beloved than Polyphemus or the Propertian lover by teaching his beloved to play the lyre's 'melodious strings' and 'tender music', rehearsing for her pleasure the songs Chiron taught him and fitting her fingers to the instrument so that she can sing of his exploits herself. Here Statius describes the lyre and its music in the programmatic language reserved at Rome for elegy and lyric, in opposition to epic, as Horace's famous *recusatio* in *Odes* 1.6 makes clear:

> Scriberis Vario fortis et hostium
> victor *Maeonii carminis* alite,
> quam rem cumque ferox navibus aut equis
>   miles te duce gesserit.
> nos, Agrippa, neque haec dicere nec *gravem*   5
> Pelidae stomachum cedere nescii
> nec cursus duplicis per mare Ulixei
>   nec saevam Pelopis domum
> conamur, *tenues grandia*, dum pudor
> *inbellisque lyrae* Musa potens vetat   10
> *laudes* egregii Caesaris et tuas
>   culpa deterere ingeni.
> quis Martem tunica tectum adamantina
> digne scripserit aut pulvere Troico
> nigrum Merionen aut ope Palladis   15
>   Tydiden superis parem?
> nos *convivia*, nos *proelia virginum*
> sectis in iuvenes unguibus acrium
> *cantamus* vacui, sive quid urimur,
>   non praeter solitum *leves*.   20

You will be commemorated by Varius, a bird of Homeric song, as brave and a victor over the enemy, for whatever exploit the fierce soldier shall have accomplished either on sea or land under your leadership.

We humble writers, Agrippa, do not attempt to tell of these mighty deeds nor the stern wrath of Peleus' son, who did not know how to yield, nor the voyages of wily Ulysses over the sea, nor the cruel house of Pelops;

while modesty and the Musa who has power over the peaceful lyre forbid (us) to diminish the praises of Caesar and your own, by a defect of talent.

Who could worthily describe Mars clad in his steel tunic, or Meriones, black with Trojan dust, or Diomedes, by the aid of Pallas, equal to the gods above?

We sing of banquets, of the battles of maidens, their trimmed nails fiercely attacking youths; we sing whole of heart, or if we are at all fired by love, light-hearted as usual.

Horace's well known poem delimits the conventional contrast between the tender music of the peaceful lyre, whose themes are banquets and maidens' battles such as Statius describes in *Achilleid* 1, and the grand and weighty subjects of martial epic, such as Achilles' anger and Odysseus' travels – the very themes of Homeric epic that are promised for the later books of the *Achilleid*. Even the verb with which Horace characterizes lyric song in the final stanza of the ode (*cantamus*, 1.6.19) is reprised in our scene in the *Achilleid*, when Deidamia learns lyric song from the disguised Achilles (*cantat*, *Ach.* 1.579).[21] The first book of Statius' *Achilleid* thus begins within the ambit of Horatian lyric, as sketched in *Odes* 1.8, even if the poet's audience knows full well that the lyric Achilles is living on borrowed time, both on Mt. Pelion with Chiron and on the island of Scyros with Lycomedes' daughters. For the impending arrival of Odysseus and Diomedes will draw the young Achilles out of this lyric context towards the epic battlefield. When the clarion call of the martial war trumpet, promised already in the proem (*Ach.* 1.6, quoted above), finally sounds, Achilles will join Odysseus and Diomedes on the journey to Troy in the second book of the *Achilleid*, and there on the battlefield he will come into his full Homeric manhood.

But in the first book of the *Achilleid*, the hero lingers in the lyric world, ambivalent about leaving its delights behind. Statius enriches his portrait of the young Achilles by drawing on lyric models and lyric settings to characterize him as not quite ready for grand epic yet. Like his hero, moreover, Statius presents himself as having both an epic and a lyric profile in the proem of his new epic, where he is not only the accomplished author of the epic *Thebaid* (*Ach.* 1.8–10) but also a vatic bard whose wide experience in lyric shapes his choice of presentation and theme in the new poem (*Ach.* 1.10 f.). Although the proem proclaims Statius' plan to follow his hero into war and onto another epic battlefield, neither Statius nor his hero ever reach Troy and the full epic masculinity which Achilles there achieves. Cut off by Statius' death, his second martial epic was left an unfinished 'reduced' fragment of epic song, published perhaps by the same literary executor who collected the remaining lyric poems in the posthumous fifth book of his *Silvae*.[22]

---

21 Horace characteristically employs the verb *cantare* to describe his production of lyric song (e.g., Hor. *Carm.* 3.1.4, quoted above). Cf. Statius' uses of the verb at *Silv.* 1.2.197, of Stella's elegy, and 5.3.153, of Alcman.
22 Gibson 2006b, xxviii–xxx.

Antony Augoustakis

Burial scenes: Silius Italicus' *Punica* and Greco-Roman historiography

1 Introduction

In an epic poem about war, especially a long conflict such as the one with Hannibal, it comes as no surprise that the bodies of the dead are in need of the last rites, cremation and burial.[1] Silius draws on several sources for these scenes, from epic poetry (Homer through Lucan and Valerius) to historiography (from Herodotus to Livy and beyond).[2] In a long article in 1981, Erich Burck examined in detail the portrayal of epic burial scenes (*Bestattungsszenen*) from Virgil through the Flavian epicists.[3] From this systematic overview of motifs, Burck drew some general conclusions with regard to a certain typology of epic descriptions of funeral, cremation, and burial rites. But while at times detailed, his analysis of specific episodes in the *Punica* seems rather perfunctory and therefore unsatisfactory beyond the now trite assertions concerning Silius' Virgilian *aemulatio*, especially after the rehabilitation of the *Punica* in the last decade of the past and the first decade of this century:[4] to be sure, Silius makes use of Virgilian intertexts to assert the continuity of the epic tradition in the Flavian age. In this article, however, I would like to examine several episodes of cremation and burial in Silius' *Punica* with the goal of re-examining the Flavian poet's relationship with his historiographical models, especially Polybius and Livy, by

1 For Silius' Latin text, I have used Delz's 1987 Teubner edition, with Duff's Loeb 1934 translation modified. For Livy, I have used Conway's and Walters' and Conway's and Johnson's 1963 OCT edition, with de Sélincourt's (1972) Penguin translation; for Polybius, the newest Loeb edition by Paton / Walbank / Habicht 2011. Versions of this paper were also presented at Washington University, St. Louis (March 2013) and the Annual Meeting of the American Philological Association in Chicago (January 2014). This is part of a monograph project in progress, entitled 'Death, Burial, and Ritual in Flavian epic' (cf. also Augoustakis 2016). I would like to extend my warm thanks to the organisers of the Turin conference, Federica Bessone and Marco Fucecchi, for their generosity and many years of friendship.
2 There have been multiple studies on Silius' use of the previous literary tradition, especially Homer (e.g., Juhnke 1972), including the various historiographical works (surviving or lost), such as Livy and the Annalists as well as the Greek historians (e.g., Gibson 2010).
3 For Silius in particular, see the analysis in 459–464.
4 The progress towards charting a new method of approach in studying Silius' use of his historiographical sources is evidenced from studies such as Gibson 2010 and Pomeroy 2010.

https://doi.org/10.1515/9783110534436-017

addressing questions such as why Silius showcases some of these funerals by marking them as the climax in his narrative; what insights we gain concerning the protagonists at hand; and finally how Silius would like his reader to perceive the often antagonistic relationship between the *Punica* and its models in Greco-Roman historiography.

2 Real Pyres, Fake Funerals

Let us first look at instances of funerals and burial in the *Punica* that establish this type of episode as an important part of the narrative, in a literal but also figurative manner. For instance, in the second book of the *Punica*, the reader comes across two types of funeral pyres. First one finds a fake funeral, when the Saguntines decide to erect a pyre in the centre of their city where they burn all their possessions: thus Hannibal will find nothing to plunder when he takes the city (Sil. 2.599–608):[5]

certatim structus surrectae molis ad astra
in media stetit urbe rogus; portantque trahuntque   600
longae pacis opes quaesitaque praemia dextris,
Callaico vestes distinctas matribus auro
armaque Dulichia proavis portata Zacyntho
et prisca advectos Rutulorum ex urbe penates.
huc, quicquid superest captis, clipeosque simulque   605
infaustos iaciunt enses et condita bello
effodiunt penitus terrae gaudentque superbi
victoris praedam flammis donare supremis.

A pyre, zealously built, stood in the middle of the city, whose height rose to the stars; they drag and carry the wealth of a long peace and the prizes won by valour, that is the clothes embroidered by the mothers with Gallician gold, the Dulichian weapons brought by their ancestors from Zacynthus, and the household gods brought across the sea from the ancient city of the Rutulians. Here the conquered people throw whatever is left to them, and their shields too and their cursed swords. And from the bowels of the earth, they dig up what they had hidden during the war and they rejoice in giving to the last fire the booty of the arrogant victor.

That this is a funeral pyre will become evident from later episodes where the shield and armor of the deceased are burned together with the corpse, which

---

5 On the Saguntum episode in Silius, see the recent discussion and further bibliography in Augoustakis 2010a 113–136, as well as Dominik 2003 and 2006. On the mass suicide, see most recently Bernstein 2016.

of course is absent here. This pyre, the *flammae supremae*, foreshadows the mass suicide the Saguntines commit just before victorious Hannibal enters the city like a hungry lion. An obvious source for Silius' refashioning of this episode is found in Livy's account, where some of the *primores* of Saguntum pile silver and gold onto the pyre, before they also leap into it and are burnt alive (Liv. 21.14.1):

> repente primores secessione facta priusquam responsum daretur argentum aurumque omne ex publico privatoque in forum conlatum in ignem ad id raptim factum conicientes eodem plerique semet ipsi praecipitaverunt.

> Suddenly, however, the leaders of the Senate, before an answer could be given, left their places, collected all the precious metal from public buildings and private houses they could find, and flung it into a fire hastily kindled for the purpose in the Forum, and themselves leapt after it into the flames.

Silius fashions this pyre as a symbol of the breakdown of the ties between Romans and Saguntines: the Saguntines in effect burn their past. Before death, Saguntine identity is incinerated.[6] Silius emphasises the emptiness of the city when the Carthaginians storm the citadel (*irrumpunt vacuam Poeni tot cladibus arcem*, 2.694), whereas Polybius focuses on the great booty awaiting the Carthaginians: κύριος δὲ γενόμενος χρημάτων πολλῶν καὶ σωμάτων καὶ κατασκευῆς ('a great booty of money, slaves, and property fell into his hands', Plb. 3.17.10).

And this is not the only instance of a semblance of a funeral in the poem: in the sixteenth book, Scipio celebrates a fake funeral in Spain in honour of his father and uncle, just before the games commence (Sil. 16.303–311):

> iamque dies praedicta aderat, coetuque sonabat
> innumero campus simulatasque ordine iusto
> exequias rector lacrimis ducebat obortis.　　　　　　　　305
> omnis Hiber, omnis Latio sub nomine miles
> dona ferunt tumulisque super flagrantibus addunt.
> ipse tenens nunc lacte, sacro nunc plena Lyaeo
> pocula odoriferis aspergit floribus aras.
> tum manis vocat excitos laudesque virorum　　　　　　310
> cum fletu canit et veneratur facta iacentum.

> Now the appointed day came, and the plain was filled with the noise of a crowd past numbering; and Scipio, with tears in his eyes, led the semblance of a funeral procession with due rites of burial. Every Spaniard and every soldier of the Roman army brought gifts to

---

6 Augoustakis 2010a, 131: "this pyre then can be read also as a cenotaph, a tomb in which Roman identity is incinerated. In hybrid Saguntum, this becomes not a story of founding, but rather one of utter destruction". See also Augoustakis 2011 on the relationship between such cenotaphs in Silius and Lucan.

throw upon the blazing pyres. Scipio himself held goblets, filled either with milk or with sacred wine, and sprinkled fragrant flowers over the altars. Then he summoned the ghosts to rise up; he rehearsed with tears the glories of the dead and honoured their noble deeds.

Libations of milk and wine are poured, the pyre burns, flowers are sprinkled over the altars. The ritual ends with the *laudatio funebris* given by Scipio, as he recounts the noble deeds of his kinsmen, a tradition which Polybius explains in detail in the sixth book of his *Histories* (Plb. 6.53.1–3):

> ὅταν γὰρ μεταλλάξῃ τις παρ᾽ αὐτοῖς τῶν ἐπιφανῶν ἀνδρῶν, συντελουμένης τῆς ἐκφορᾶς κομίζεται μετὰ τοῦ λοιποῦ κόσμου πρὸς τοὺς καλουμένους ἐμβόλους εἰς τὴν ἀγορὰν ποτὲ μὲν ἑστὼς ἐναργής, σπανίως δὲ κατακεκλιμένος. πέριξ δὲ παντὸς τοῦ δήμου στάντος, ἀναβὰς ἐπὶ τοὺς ἐμβόλους, ἂν μὲν υἱὸς ἐν ἡλικίᾳ καταλείπηται καὶ τύχῃ παρών, οὗτος, εἰ δὲ μή, τῶν ἄλλων εἴ τις ἀπὸ γένους ὑπάρχει, λέγει περὶ τοῦ τετελευτηκότος τὰς ἀρετὰς καὶ τὰς ἐπιτετευγμένας ἐν τῷ ζῆν πράξεις. δι᾽ ὧν συμβαίνει τοὺς πολλοὺς ἀναμιμνησκομένους καὶ λαμβάνοντας ὑπὸ τὴν ὄψιν τὰ γεγονότα, μὴ μόνον τοὺς κεκοινωνηκότας τῶν ἔργων, ἀλλὰ καὶ τοὺς ἐκτός, ἐπὶ τοσοῦτον γίνεσθαι συμπαθεῖς ὥστε μὴ τῶν κηδευόντων ἴδιον, ἀλλὰ κοινὸν τοῦ δήμου φαίνεσθαι τὸ σύμπτωμα.

> Whenever any illustrious man dies, he is carried at his funeral into the forum to the so-called rostra, sometimes conspicuous in an upright posture and more rarely reclined. Here with all the people standing round, a grown-up son, if he has left one who happens to be present, or if not some other relative mounts the rostra and discourses on the virtues and successful achievements of the dead during his lifetime. As a consequence the multitude and not only those who had a part in these achievements, but those also who had none, when the facts are recalled to their minds and brought before their eyes, are moved to such sympathy that the loss seems to be not confined to the mourners, but a public one affecting the whole people.

As Polybius stresses, the adult son is responsible to deliver the eulogy, and in the case such offspring is found lacking, then τῶν ἄλλων εἴ τις ἀπὸ γένους ὑπάρχει.[7] We shall return to this passage to see that Hannibal appropriates this role in his burial of the Roman generals.

To go back to the second book, however, in the first part of the narrative and before the self-immolation of the Saguntines, the Amazon Asbyte, a literary construct in the fashion of Penthesilea and Camilla, is beheaded by her pursuer Theron.[8] As one of Hannibal's most valuable allies in the siege of Saguntum, Asbyte becomes the first important loss for the Carthaginian general in this war. Her death is marked by the first extensive reference in the poem to funeral tra-

---

7 Walbank 1957–1979, 1.737 observes that the style of the *laudatio* had to be characterised by *brevitas nuda et inornata*, as Cicero notes (*De orat.* 2.341).
8 On Asbyte, see Augoustakis 2010a, 117–129 and Keith 2010.

ditions, especially non-Roman, as the Numidians grieve and bury their leader (Sil. 2.264–269):

> at Nomadum furibunda cohors miserabile humandi
> deproperat munus tumulique adiungit honorem   265
> et rapto cineres ter circum corpore lustrat.
> hinc letale viri robur tegimenque tremendum
> in flammas iaciunt ambustoque ore genisque
> deforme alitibus liquere cadaver Hiberis.

> But the cohort of the Numidians, frantic [with grief], hasten the mournful office of burial and attach the honour of a pyre. In addition, having seized [Theron's] corpse, they go three times round her ashes. Then, they cast into the flames the deadly club of the man and his dreadful head-cover. And when his face and cheeks were burnt, they left the unsightly corpse to the Spanish birds.

François Spaltenstein points out here that the Libyans do not normally practise cremation, while some of the details of Asbyte's funeral together with the abuse on Theron's body are unique, even though the narrative acquires certain Homeric overtones with reference to Achilles and the corpse of Hector.[9] To be sure, Silius is interested in geography and ethnography: in book 13, Scipio encounters the ghost of Appius Claudius, who had recently died at Capua and now begs for immediate cremation; after he promises Appius to take care of the task promptly, Silius' Scipio indulges in a digression on the funerary rituals of various people from around the world, an episode often criticised for its lack of connection with the narrative proper (Sil. 13.468–487):[10]

> ... namque ista per omnes
> discrimen servat populos variatque iacentum
> exequias tumuli et cinerum sententia discors.   470
> tellure, ut perhibent, is mos antiquus Hibera:
> exanima obscenus consumit corpora vultur.
> regia cum lucem posuerunt membra, probatum est
> Hyrcanis adhibere canes. Aegyptia tellus
> claudit odorato post funus stantia saxo   475
> corpora et a mensis exsanguem haud separat umbram.
> exhausto instituit Pontus vacuare cerebro
> ora virum et longum medicata reponit in aevum.
> quid, qui reclusa nudos Garamantes harena

---

9 Spaltenstein 1986, 132 with Nicol 1936, 134.

10 See the discussion in Van der Keur 2013, and in particular 340: "Scipio, who shows the right mindset by making the cremation of Appius a priority, not for glory, but in recognition of his duty, forms a stark contrast with Hannibal".

infodiunt? quid, qui saevo sepelire profundo   480
exanimos mandant Libycis Nasamones in oris?
at Celtae vacui capitis circumdare gaudent
ossa, nefas, auro ac mensis ea pocula servant.
Cecropidae ob patriam Mavortis sorte peremptos
decrevere simul communibus urere flammis.   485
at gente in Scythica suffixa cadavera truncis
lenta dies sepelit putri liquentia tabo.

All over the world the practice is different in this matter, and unlikeness of opinion produces various ways of burying the dead and disposing of their ashes. In the land of Spain, we
are told (it is an ancient custom) the bodies of the dead are devoured by awful vultures.
When a king dies in Hyrcania, it is the rule to let dogs have access to the corpse. The Egyp-
tians enclose their dead, standing in an upright position, in a coffin of stone, and worship
it; and they admit a bloodless spectre to their banquets. With the peoples of the Black Sea it
is the custom to empty the skull by extracting the brain and to preserve the embalmed body
for centuries. The Garamantes, again, dig a hole in the sand and bury the corpse naked,
while the Nasamones in Libya commit their dead to the cruel sea for burial. Then the
Celts have a horrible practice: they frame the bones of the empty skull in gold and keep
it for a drinking-cup. The Athenians passed a law that the bodies of all who had fallen
in battle in defence of their country should be burnt together on a single pyre. Again,
among the Scythians the dead are fastened to tree-trunks and left to rot, and time at last
is the burier of their bodies.

Given Silius' interest in cremation and burial throughout the poem, as we shall
see with the burials of prominent generals, this is not just another digression. As
Edward Bassett has pointed, "Scipio's lecture is in keeping with the conventions
of epic poetry [...] with tendencies of the epic of the Silver Age (e. g., the digression of a scientific or quasi-scientific nature), and with a special Stoic tradition
(the question of mortuary customs) [...] illustrated by Cicero, whose account of
burial rites Silius has followed".[11] It is important to observe that Scipio's ethno-
graphic tour includes barbaric customs, from the usual suspects (the Hyrcani-
ans, the Celts, the Scythians), but also the custom of the common pyre and burial
as described by Thucydides in the second book of his *History* just before Pericles'
funeral oration (Thuc. 2.34). These are not the practices of the uncivilised, an-
thropophagous and cannibalistic groups of people, but also of the civilised Athenians who honour those who gave up life to save their *patria*. And when it comes
to burial, as we shall see next, the distinction between Roman and non-Roman,
friend and foe, civilised and uncivilised is often blurred in the *Punica*.

---

11 Bassett 1963, 89.

3 Burying the Enemy: Hannibal's Funerals

Let us now turn to three episodes in the poem where Silius recounts the burial of a prominent Roman general who has died on the battlefield: Lucius Aemilius Paulus in book 10, Tiberius Sempronius Gracchus in book 12, and Marcus Claudius Marcellus in book 15. The tenth book of the poem opens with the last stand of the consul Aemilius Paulus: at Cannae, Paulus urges his comrades to stay and fight, since nothing is left to them now but glorious death.[12] Finally in an act of extreme heroism, after surveying the battleground to find Hannibal and die by that glorious hand, Paulus is finished off by a shower of darts (Sil. 10.301–305):

> Sidoniumque ducem circumspectabat, in illa
> exoptans animam certantem ponere dextra.
> sed vicere virum coeuntibus undique telis
> et Nomas et Garamas et Celtae et Maurus et Astur.
> hic finis Paulo.   305

> Then he looked round for Hannibal, eager to yield up his life, a warrior's life, to that glorious hand. Not so: he was overcome by a shower of darts from every side, from Numidians and Garamantians, from Gauls and Moors and Asturians. Thus Paulus died.

Silius' account is drawn from Livy's similar description of the death of Paulus: *et occurrit saepe cum confertis Hannibali et aliquot locis proelium restituit* [...] *consulem ignorantes quis esset obruere telis* ('at the head of his men in close order, Paulus continued to make a number of attempts to get at Hannibal, and in several places succeeded in pulling things together [...] The consul fell under a shower of spears, his killers not knowing whom they killed', Liv. 22.49.1, 12). The only mention in Polybius is the phrase βιαίοις πληγαῖς (Plb. 3.116.9):

> ἐν ᾧ καιρῷ καὶ Λεύκιος Αἰμίλιος περιπεσὼν βιαίοις πληγαῖς ἐν χειρῶν νόμῳ μετήλλαξε τὸν βίον, ἀνὴρ πάντα τὰ δίκαια τῇ πατρίδι κατὰ τὸν λοιπὸν βίον καὶ κατὰ τὸν ἔσχατον καιρόν, εἰ καί τις ἕτερος, ποιήσας.

> It was here that Lucius Aemilius fell in the thick of the fight after receiving several dreadful wounds, and of him we may say that if there ever was a man who did his duty by his country both all through his life and in these last times, it was he.[13]

---

12 On Paulus as a character in Silius, see most recently Tipping 2010a, 75 f. with further bibliography; on the portrayal of the consul in Livy, see Levene 2010, 186–189.
13 On Polybius' death notices, see Pomeroy 1986, 413.

As becomes clear from the continuation of the narrative later in the book, Silius' purpose is to tie this episode of Paulus' efforts just before his death with Hannibal's ensuing funeral.

At the conclusion of the bloody battle at Cannae, unlike the tyrannical Creon in Statius' *Thebaid*, who forbids the burial of the Argive Seven, or Lucan's Caesar at Pharsalus, Hannibal orders the bodies of the dead to be burnt and buried on the following day after the devastating defeat. In a topos well-established from Ennius to Virgil and beyond, the Carthaginians cut down the groves and dutifully prepare the pyres (Sil. 10.535–546):[14]

funereas tum deinde pyras certamine texunt,	535
officium infelix et munus inane peremptis,	
donec anhelantes stagna in Tartessia Phoebus	
mersit equos fugiensque polo Titania caecam	
orbita nigranti traxit caligine noctem.	
post, ubi fulserunt primis Phaethontia frena	540
ignibus atque sui terris rediere colores,	
supponunt flammam et manantia corpora tabo	
hostili tellure cremant. subit horrida mentem	
formido incerti casus, tacitusque pererrat	
intima corda pavor, si fors ita Martis iniqui	545
mox ferat, hac ipsi inimica sede iacendum.	

And lastly they hastily built funeral pyres – a mournful duty and a tribute that means nothing to the dead – until Phoebus plunged his panting steeds in the waters of Tartessus, and the moon's disk departing from the sky brought on the blind darkness of black night. Then, when the chariot of the sun shone forth with dawning fire and the earth resumed its familiar colours, they kindled the pyres and burnt the corrupting bodies of their dead on a foreign soil. They felt a dreadful apprehension of the uncertain future, and an unspoken fear invaded their inmost hearts that, if the fortune of war turned against them later, they themselves must lie in this unfriendly earth.

This is an *officium infelix*, a phrase that matches the *miserabile ... munus* in the case of Asbyte's funeral, as we saw above.[15] The Carthaginian soldiers comment on the futility of the ritual: it has no meaning for the dead after all, they ponder,

---

14 Cf. Enn. *Ann. 175–179* Sk. with Skutsch 1985, 341 on the occasion of Pyrrhus' victory in Heraclea; Verg. *A.* 6.179–182 (with Horsfall 2013, 183–185); Stat. *Theb.* 6.90–117. Caesar displays similar behavior in *Gal. 1.26*.

15 Littlewood 2017, 209 notes: "Silius' conventional observation that *munus*, the offering or final duty performed to honour the dead is without value, *inane*, for the dead themselves [...] may contain a deeper implication: those so recently slaughtered in the bloodbath of Cannae will now be eternally oblivious of the struggle of the Second Punic War".

as the narrator adds a philosophical tone to the narrative. We are also invited to sympathise with the fear of the soldiers; in his notes, Ernesti (*ad loc.*) praises these masterful lines *inter lumina Siliani carminis*. What would happen if they died on Italian soil, should the outcome of the war turn against their hopes?[16] Their fear is silent (*tacitus*) and therefore most effective. It seems that the poet would like to minimise here the Carthaginian victory: the bloodbath at Cannae is also the beginning of Carthage's decline and defeat.[17]

Then Hannibal turns his attention to the burial of the consul. A note in Lucan's *De bello civili* 7, elaborating on the Livian account, functions as the immediate source for Silius: *non illum Poenus humator / consulis et Libyca succensae lampade Cannae / compellunt hominum ritus ut servet in hoste* ('The Carthaginian who buried the consul and Cannae lit by Libyan torches do not compel him to observe the customs of humanity towards an enemy', Luc. 7.799–801). Livy's statement is laconic, referring to some writers who support the veracity of this episode, perhaps Valerius Antias: *tum sepeliendi causa conferri in unum corpora suorum iussit; ad octo milia fuisse dicuntur fortissimorum virorum. consulem quoque Romanum conquisitum sepultumque quidam auctores sunt* ('Hannibal then gave orders for the bodies of his men to be collected for burial. There are said to have been about 8,000, all from his best troops. According to some writers Paulus' body, too, was searched for and given burial', Liv. 22.52.6).[18] Earlier in book 22, the Roman historian points to Hannibal's efforts to find and bury Flaminius: *Flamini quoque corpus funeris causa magna cum cura inquisitum non invenit* ('he also wished to honour Flaminius with burial, but, though his body was searched for with all diligence, it was never found', Liv. 22.7.5). It is perhaps not coincidental that in the case of Flaminius, Silius makes the Romans pile up their weapons, bodies, and hands over the corpse of Flaminius *ceu tumulo: sic densae caedis acervo / ceu tumulo texere virum* ('thus they covered him with close-packed heap of corpses for a tomb', Sil. 5.665 f.).[19]

What Silius emphasises in his narrative of Paulus' burial is absence: the lack of pomp and ceremony expected on such an occasion (Sil. 10.558–577):

> hinc citus ad tumulum donataque funera Paulo
> ibat et hostilis leti iactabat honorem.
> sublimem eduxere pyram mollisque virenti   560
> stramine composuere toros. superaddita dona,

---

16 On the function of such counterfactuals in the poem, see Cowan 2010.
17 E.g., Marks 2005a.
18 Levene 2010, 290 and n. 67.
19 On the role of the demagogues in Silius, see in particular Ariemma 2010.

funereum decus: expertis invisus et ensis
et clipeus, terrorque modo atque insigne superbum
tum laceri, fasces captaeque in Marte secures.
non coniunx native aderant, non iuncta propinquo   565
sanguine turba virum, aut celsis de more feretris
praecedens prisca exequias decorabat imago,
omnibus exuviis nudo, iamque Hannibal unus
sat decoris laudator erat. fulgentia pingui
murice suspirans inicit velamina et auro   570
intextam chlamydem ac supremo adfatur honore:
'i, decus Ausoniae, quo fas est ire superbas
virtute et factis animas. tibi gloria leto
iam parta insigni. nostros Fortuna labores
versat adhuc casusque iubet nescire futuros.'   575
haec Libys, atque repens crepitantibus undique flammis
aetherias anima exultans evasit in auras.

From here Hannibal went quickly to witness the funeral rites granted to Paulus, proud of showing honour to a dead enemy. A tall pyre was reared, and a soft bier was made of green turf, and offerings were laid upon it, to honour the dead – the shield, the sword dreaded by those who had felt it, the rods and axes taken in the battle, broken now but once a badge of power that all men feared. No wife was there, no sons, no gathering of near kinsmen; no customary masks of ancestors were borne on high litters before the corpse to grace the funeral procession. Bare was it of all trappings; but the praise of Hannibal was glory enough in itself: sighing he threw on the body a covering bright with rich purple dye and a mantle embroidered with gold and uttered this last tribute to the dead: 'Go, pride of Italy! Go where spirits may go that exult in brave deeds! To you fame is secured already by a glorious death, but I must struggle on as Fate drives me, and she hides future events from my knowledge'. So Hannibal spoke; and suddenly, amidst the crackling of the flames all around, the spirit of Paulus sprang forth and rose triumphant to the sky.

As is fitting for what he calls the *decus Ausoniae*, Hannibal provides a *funereum decus*, that is, the shield, the sword (just like in the fire of the Saguntines), the *fasces*, the *secures*. No ritual mourning by the wife or the children, no *imagines*, no proper farewell, *omnibus exuviis nudo*. Instead, Silius makes Hannibal deliver the *laudatio funebris* (*iamque Hannibal unus / sat decoris laudator erat*): as we have seen above, Polybius informs us that the role of the *laudator* is usually performed by the son of the deceased, just as in the case of the Scipios in Spain, as we saw above. Polybius continues that if there is no son available, then τῶν ἄλλων εἴ τις ἀπὸ γένους ὑπάρχει. In this case, there is no kinsman nearby, and Hannibal fulfils the role of a kinsman. I submit that this is no ironic gesture on the part of the Carthaginian: Hannibal extols Paulus' *virtus* and *facta*, and this is clearly juxtaposed to the contempt with which he treats Fabius' delaying methods or Varro elsewhere in the narrative. Hannibal's *laudatio* responds to the demands of the genre as illustrated by Polybius: λέγει περὶ τοῦ τετελευτηκότος τὰς ἀρετὰς καὶ τὰς ἐπιτετευγμένας ἐν τῷ ζῆν πράξεις, or in Latin *virtute et factis* as in 10.573.[20] For Paulus, Hannibal asserts *tibi gloria leto / iam parta insigni*. But like the soldiers, Hannibal cannot predict the future, and this is an allusion to his final speech to Scipio at Zama as reported by Livy (30.30), where he warns Scipio of the unpredictability of *fortuna*: 'what I was at Trasimene and Cannae, you are today'.[21] Hannibal could not possibly predict his *casus futuros*. The word used in 575 *casus* refers to any occurence, accidental event, or mishap; it is something which befalls, like death, and in fact like the death of Paulus. It corresponds to the Polybian σύμπτωμα, where the word has the meaning of loss, death,[22] and it is the purpose of a *laudatio funebris* to make the audience feel the loss as individual as well as communal. Ben Tipping observes with regard to this *laudatio funebris* that the poet "reasserts Hannibal's decency, diminished at 10.559 by boastfulness about honouring a fallen enemy, when he comments that Hannibal's praise alone compensates for the absence of Paulus' family and of conventional Roman trappings from his funeral".[23] By elaborating on Livy's note and breaking away from the historiographical tradition which overall remains silent concerning this episode, Silius is allowed the opportunity to portray Hannibal not in black and white, but rather in grey.[24]

The ambiguity of Hannibal's action is further heightened by the description of this funeral by Scipio himself when he encounters the ghost of the slain Paulus in the Underworld in book 13.705– 718:

> iamque aderat multa vix adgnoscendus in umbra　　　　705
> Paulus et epoto fundebat sanguine verba:
> 'lux Italum, cuius spectavi Martia facta
> multum uno maiora viro, descendere nocti
> atque habitanda semel subigit quis visere regna?'
> cui contra talis effundit Scipio voces:　　　　710
> 'armipotens ductor, quam sunt tua fata per urbem
> lamentata diu! quam paene ruentia tecum

---

20 Littlewood (2017) 217 notes: "Hannibal offers a sincerely generous propempticon to speed his illustrious enemy on his way to Elysium. His laudatory or hymnic formula of address, *decus Ausoniae* [...] has been earned by Paulus' valour, *virtute*, and feats of arms, *factis*".
21 Tipping 2010a, 59: "What we know, but the future Africanus does not, is that he will never be more successful than at Zama".
22 *LSJ* s.v. A2; and the connection between *cado* and πίπτω.
23 Tipping 2010a, 76
24 Stocks 2014, 132: "[Hannibal] fears for his future, which remains unclear to him, and he envies Paulus for the fame he has gained through death. To Hannibal, his life is nothing if he fails to realise this ambition [...] But in comparing himself to Paulus, Hannibal also emerges as a figure who actively seeks to define himself as 'Roman', the conqueror of Italy and its name".

traxisti ad Stygias Oenotria tecta tenebras!
tum tibi defuncto tumulum Sidonius hostis
constituit laudemque tuo quaesivit honore.'   715
dumque audit lacrimans hostilia funera Paulus,
ante oculos iam Flaminius, iam Gracchus et aegro
absumptus Cannis stabat Servilius ore.

Next Paulus came, hard to recognise in the dim light, and drank of the blood, and spoke thus: 'Bright star of Italy, whose martial feats, too great by far for a single man, these eyes beheld, who forces you to descend into darkness and to visit this realm where those who enter must dwell for ever?' Scipio spoke thus in answer: 'O mighty captain, how long did all Rome mourn your death! How nearly you carried down the Roman city in your fall to Stygian darkness! Also the Carthaginian, our foe, built a tomb for your dead body and sought to gain glory by honouring you!' While Paulus shed tears to hear of his burial by the enemy, Flaminius came in sight, and Gracchus, and the sad face of Servilius who fell at Cannae.

Paulus' tears are explicated indirectly in Duff's translation as the result of painful shame upon hearing of his burial by the enemy; Ruperti, however, explains (*ad loc.*) the tears as the result of Paulus' emotional outburst upon hearing of the last rites bestowed upon his corpse by Hannibal: *quae humanitas Paulum ita movet, ut lacrimas non teneat, etsi Scipio id laudis cupiditate factum dixerat.* Scipio may have intended for his statement to sound pejorative, but this is not how Paulus receives the news. Consider the ghosts surrounding Paulus at the moment: Flaminius and Gracchus, both of whom are related to Hannibal's burial acts in the war.[25] As Spaltenstein admits, we need not look far for an explanation of this difficulty: there is nothing shameful with the desire for glory, and Silius does not condemn Hannibal now for pursuing it.[26]

In 212 BCE, and while Hannibal rushes back to Capua when the city is besieged by the Romans, the Carthaginian stops to give proper burial to the body of the proconsul, Tiberius Sempronius Gracchus, who was ambushed and slain in Lucania by his local guest (Sil. 12.473–478):

exequiae tantum famam nomenque volentem
mitificae mentis tenuerunt funere laeto.
namque per insidias (infandum!) et ab hospite caesus,   475
colloquium et promissa petit dum perfida gentis

---

25 Reitz 1982, 99 correctly points to the parallel at 12.549 f., when Paulus, Gracchus, and Flaminius are grouped together again, representing the fear in the mind of the distraught women in Rome.
26 Spaltenstein 1990, 265.

Lucanae, Gracchus caeco circumdatus astu
occiderat, laudemque Libys rapiebat humandi.

One thing only made Hannibal pause: seeking a reputation for humanity, he gave burial to
Gracchus, though rejoicing at his death. For, while seeking by means of a conference to gain
the adherence of the false Lucanians, Gracchus had been treacherously and foully slain by
his host; encompassed by hidden guile he had been murdered, and Hannibal snatched at
the credit of giving him burial.

Livy lays emphasis on the ritual performed by the Spanish troops at the funeral
of Gracchus (Liv. 25.17.4–6):

funeris quoque Gracchi varia est fama. alii in castris Romanis sepultum ab suis, alii ab
Hannibale – et ea volgatior fama est – tradunt in vestibulo Punicorum castrorum rogum
exstructum esse, armatum exercitum decucurrisse cum tripudiis Hispanorum motibusque
armorum et corporum suae cuique genti adsuetis, ipso Hannibale omni rerum verborum-
que honore exsequias celebrante. haec tradunt qui in Lucanis rei gestae auctores sunt.

The accounts of his funeral also vary. Some say he was buried in camp by his own troops;
others – and this is the account more widely accepted – that Hannibal erected a funeral
pyre outside the gate of the Carthaginian camp; his troops in full armor marched past,
the Spanish contingents performing dances, each tribe going through its national movements of the body and weapon-drill, while Hannibal in person paid honour to the obse-
quies in all due acts and words. This is the version of those who maintain that Gracchus
was killed in Lucania.

Conversely, the Flavian poet showcases Hannibal's eagerness to seize the *laus
humandi*. Spaltenstein emphasises the Carthaginian general's hypocrisy here,
as opposed to the genuine bestowal of honour in Livy.[27] I believe that such a
clear-cut interpretation is not afforded by the text: Hannibal rushes back to
Capua and stops to bury Gracchus motivated by his eagerness to acquire *fama*
and a *nomen mitificae mentis*. The adjective *mitificus* is a hapax in Silius and certainly points to a potentially positive trait: the epithet *mitis* is applied elsewhere
in the poem to Jupiter and Hieron of Sicily (in addition to its employment to de-

---

27 Spaltenstein 1990, 186 f. Cf. Plb. 8.35.1 Ὅτι Τιβέριος ὁ Ῥωμαίων στρατηγὸς λόχῳ ἐνεδρευθεὶς
καὶ γενναίως ὑποστὰς σὺν τοῖς περὶ αὐτὸν τὸν βίον κατέστρεψεν. περὶ δὲ τῶν τοιούτων περιπε-
τειῶν, πότερα χρὴ τοῖς πάσχουσιν ἐπιτιμᾶν ἢ συγγνώμην ἔχειν, καθόλου μὲν οὐκ ἀσφαλὲς ἀπο-
φήνασθαι διὰ τὸ καὶ πλείους τὰ κατὰ λόγον πάντα πράξαντας, ὅμως ὑποχειρίους γεγονέναι τοῖς
ἑτοίμως τὰ παρ' ἀνθρώποις ὡρισμένα δίκαια παραβαίνουσιν ('Tiberius, the Roman proconsul, fell
into an ambush and after a gallant resistance perished with all who accompanied him. Regarding such accidents it is by no means safe to pronounce whether the sufferers are to be blamed or
pardoned, because many who have taken all reasonable precautions have notwithstanding fall-
en victims to enemies who did not scruple to violate the established laws of mankind').

scribe geographic regions, such as Campania or Parthenope). Scipio himself is often described as *non mitis*, just as Juno is *immitis*.[28] Silius once again deviates from the historiographical record, and in so doing creates an ambiguous portrait for Hannibal who rejoices in the Roman loss but does not miss the opportunity to display the Roman traits of *humanitas* and civilised mores. This is a truly Roman Hannibal.

The final scene under discussion here, the death of Marcellus in Apulia, takes place in 208 BCE;[29] Marcellus' demise is criticised by both Livy and Polybius as the result of inexplicably foolish and rushed decisions, especially Polybius:

> mors Marcelli cum alioqui miserabilis fuit, tum quod nec pro aetate – iam enim maior sexaginta annis erat – neque pro veteris prudentia ducis tam improvide se collegamque et prope totam rem publicam in praeceps dederat [...] Hannibal magnum terrorem hostibus morte consulis unius, volnere alterius iniectum esse ratus, ne cui deesset occasioni castra in tumulum in quo pugnatum erat extemplo transfert; ibi inventum Marcelli corpus sepelit. (Liv. 27.27.11 and 28.1)

> The death of Marcellus, distressing from any point of view, was made more so by the circumstances in which it occurred; for, in spite of his age (he was over sixty), and in spite of the caution he had learned as a veteran commander, he had thoughtlessly hazarded his own life and that of his colleague, and also, one might say, the safety of the country as a whole [...] Hannibal knew that the death of one consul and the wounding of the other would have had a shattering effect upon the enemy. Determined therefore to let no advantage slip through his fingers, he immediately transferred his position to the hill where the fight had taken place. He found Marcellus' body and gave it burial.

> Μάρκος μὲν οὖν ἀκακώτερον ἢ στρατηγικώτερον αὑτῷ χρησάμενος τοῖς δεδηλωμένοις περιέπεσε συμπτώμασιν· ἐγὼ δὲ παρ' ὅλην τὴν πραγματείαν πολλάκις ἀναγκάζομαι περὶ τῶν τοιούτων ὑπομιμνήσκειν τοὺς ἐντυγχάνοντας, θεωρῶν, εἰ καὶ περί τι τῶν τῆς στρατηγίας μερῶν ἄλλο, καὶ περὶ τοῦτο διαμαρτάνοντας τοὺς ἡγεμόνας, καίτοι προδήλου τῆς ἀγνοίας ὑπαρχούσης. τί γὰρ ὄφελος ἡγεμόνος ἢ στρατηγοῦ μὴ διειληφότος διότι τῶν κατὰ μέρος κινδύνων, οἷς μὴ συμπάσχει τὰ ὅλα, πλεῖστον ἀπέχειν δεῖ τὸν ἡγούμενον; τί δ' ἀγνοοῦντος ὅτι, κἂν ποτ' ἀναγκάζωσιν οἱ καιροὶ πράττειν τι τῶν κατὰ μέρος, πολλοὺς δεῖ πρότερον ἀποθανεῖν τῶν συνόντων πρὶν ἢ τὸ δεινὸν ἐγγίσαι τοῖς προεστῶσι τῶν ὅλων; (Plb. 10.32.7–10)

> Marcellus, it must be confessed, brought this misfortune on himself by behaving not so much like a general as like a simpleton. Throughout this work I am often compelled to call the attention of my readers to such occurrences, as I observe that generals are most liable to make mistakes in this matter than in any other parts of their duty as commanders,

---

28 Augoustakis 2015.

29 On Marcellus' death, see Burck 1984, 60–68, Augoustakis 2010a, 103–105, and Fucecchi 2010.

although the error is such an obvious one. For what is the use of a general or commander who does not comprehend that he must keep himself as far away as possible from all partial encounters in which the fate of the whole army is not involved? Or what use is he if he does not know that, if circumstances at times compel commanders to undertake in person such partial encounters, they must sacrifice many of their men before the danger is suffered to approach the supreme commander of the whole?

Both Livy and Polybius comment on Marcellus' lack of *providentia* and *prudentia* that leads him to this fatal ἁμαρτία. Silius repeats some of the details familiar to the reader from Paulus' own burial: the same ritual is followed with the shield and the *fasces* in the funereal procession (Sil. 15.381–396):

at postquam Tyrius saeva inter proelia ductor
infixum adverso vidit sub pectore telum,
immane exclamat: 'Latias, Carthago, timere
desine iam leges. Iacet exitiabile nomen,
Ausonii columen regni. sed dextera nostrae   385
tam similis non obscuras mittatur ad umbras.
magnanima invidia virtus caret.' alta sepulcri
protinus exstruitur caeloque educitur ara.
convectant silvis ingentia robora. credas
Sidonium cecidisse ducem. tum tura dapesque   390
et fasces clipeusque viri, pompa ultima, fertur.
ipse facem subdens 'laus' inquit 'parta perennis.
Marcellum abstulimus Latio. deponere forsan
gens Italum tandem arma velit. vos ite superbae
exsequias animae et cinerem donate supremi   395
muneris officio; numquam hoc tibi, Roma, negabo.'

But when Hannibal amid the rage of battle saw the weapon still sticking in the consul's manly heart, he gave a mighty shout: 'Carthage, you need dread no longer the dominion of Rome! That name of terror, that pillar of the Roman state, lies low. Yet one who was my peer in battle must not go down unhonoured to the shades. In heroic breasts there is no room for jealousy'. At once a sepulchral altar was raised on high. Great trees were brought from the forest; one might suppose that Hannibal himself had fallen. Then incense and meat-offerings, the consul's rods and his shield, were borne along in funeral procession. Hannibal himself lighted the pyre: 'We have gained immortal glory', he said, 'by robbing Rome of Marcellus. It may be that Italy will at last consent to lay down her arms. You, my men, march in the funeral train of that proud spirit, and give to his ashes the last tribute; never will I refuse to Rome this concession'.

The *laudatio funebris* is delivered by Hannibal, whereas Livy mentions a version of the story according to which the son of Marcellus purportedly delivered and published the oration. In this final burial of a Roman general by Hannibal, the Carthaginian boasts of the eternal praise attained and adds the empty promise that he will always honour Roman generals in this manner. Ironically, by the end of the book, Hannibal will have realised that the Carthaginians will soon lose, after the battle at Metaurus and the death of his brother Hasdrubal.[30] In his first speech that opens the passage above, Hannibal takes pride in having conquered the *columen* of Rome. In an apostrophe, however, with the second person *credas*,[31] Silius marks this funeral as a symbolic one: if you did not know, you could believe this to be Hannibal's own funeral, an event foreshadowed in the poem twice (at the end of books 2 and 13: 2.699–707 and 13.874–893).[32] In Appian's account, Hannibal praises Marcellus: καὶ αὐτοῦ τῷ σώματι ὁ Ἀννίβας ἐπιστάς, ὡς εἶδε τὰ τραύματα πάντα ἐπὶ τῶν στέρνων, ἐπήνεσε μὲν ὡς στρατιώτην, ἐπέσκωψε δὲ ὡς στρατηγόν ('when Hannibal stood over his body and saw the wounds all on his breast, he praised him as a soldier but criticised him as a general', App. *Hann.* 50);[33] in Silius, Hannibal praises himself instead. In Paulus' funeral, Hannibal had praised his opponent's *virtus* and *facta*, and he now underscores his own *magnanima virtus*.

Without doubt, Hannibal is a complex character in the *Punica*.[34] In this overview, the choice has been to focus on the burial scenes from various books to reevaluate the relationship between Silius and his Greco-Roman historiographical models. As a way of conclusion, let us return to the opening first book. To be sure, death, funeral, burial, and the Underworld play a significant role throughout the poem, expressing a deeper anxiety felt by all the protagonists concerning posthumous fame (or lack thereof).[35] In the very beginning of the first book, Hannibal is introduced to necromancy at an early age, when he is led by his father to Dido's grove, where the prophetess of Juno foresees the great successes of the future general:

> Aetolos late consterni milite campos   125
> Idaeoque lacus flagrantis sanguine cerno...
>
> iacet ore truci super arma virosque,
> tertia qui tulerit sublimis opima Tonanti...
>
>   ... venientia fata
> scire ultra vetuit Iuno, fibraeque repente
> conticuere. latent casus longique labores. (Sil. 1.125 f., 132 f., 137–139)

---

30 On Hasdrubal, see Augoustakis 2003.
31 For the nature of the second person apostrophe, see Gilmartin 1975.
32 On Hannibal's death, see Reitz 1982, 130–133.
33 Walbank 1957–1979, 3.242 f. and Burck 1984, 68.
34 Tschiedel 2011, 240: "[Silio] approfitta dell'occasione per mettere in primo piano la pietà e l'umana compassione di Annibale".
35 As becomes evident by the extensive *Nekyia* of book 13 for instance.

I see the Aetolian fields covered far and wide with soldiers' corpses, and lakes red with Trojan blood [...] Fierce is that face that lies on a heap of arms and men – the face of him who was the third to carry in triumph choice spoils to the Thunder-god [...] Then Juno forbade her to learn more of coming events, and the victims suddenly became dumb. The dangers and the endless hardships were concealed.

Two of the Roman defeats stand out in particular: Cannae and the death of Marcellus. But these are also the two events framing Hannibal's burial of his opponents (with the middle one in book 12 of Gracchus, silenced here, as are so many other events that are not disclosed by the priestess). As for the rest, *latent casus:*[36] Hannibal cannot know beyond what is allowed; Juno forbids it. Ultimately it is because of such limitations that Silius' tragic hero falls.[37] It comes as no surprise that, as the poem progresses, Hannibal becomes more and more attentive to cremation and burial as an expression of respect but also as a signal of a deep anxiety concerning his own, uncertain *casus*.

---

36 Cf. Helenus in Verg. *A.* 3.379 f.: *prohibent nam cetera Parcae / scire Helenum farique vetat Saturnia Iuno.*

37 To employ Ganiban's 2010, 97 f. language "ultimately Hannibal is a tragic hero, possessed of greatness but also of flaws. A hero who if he had been a Roman, would have certainly led his city to greatness, as Silius suggests at 17.401–405. Hannibal is admirable for his devotion to honor, family, and state, compelling for his natural ability, horrifying for his violence and treachery [...] Ultimately he is forced to play from a script whose ending has already been written but which he was never allowed to see". On the tragic hero Hannibal see also Manolaraki / Augoustakis 2012.

Christiane Reitz

Is Capaneus an Epicurean? A case study in epic and philosophy

The title of my paper alludes to a warning uttered by Fred Ahl in 1993. In one of his articles on Lucan,[1] Ahl speaks about the possible philosophical background of epic narrative and the epic narrator and warns against the "hypocrisy of ideology". I suggest to make use of one of the showpieces of Statius' *Thebaid*, the death of Capaneus, as a case study for an intertextual reading which might throw light on the understanding of the passage itself and, moreover, impart a possible metapoetic message conveyed through the epic narrative.

Statius' *Thebaid* is the only transmitted epic text that deals with the myth of the Seven against Thebes. All other versions known to us form part of the dramatic tradition.[2] So it is not astonishing that Statius' epic version has been regarded by critics as this author's competitive challenge to tragedy and its poetic means.[3] The epic as a whole has been made the object of political interpretation. The internal conflict of the hostile brothers Eteocles and Polynices has in recent years been no longer seen as a return to the conventions of mythological epic, in contrast to Lucan's de-mythologising of epic in the *Bellum Civile*.[4] Interpreters have pointed to the parallels and possible evocations of the political strain in the last years of Domitian's reign, or to the civil strife of 69, at the beginning of the Flavian era, as markers of the work's political context.[5]

However it is interpreted, the myth of the campaign of the Seven against the unlawful successor on Oedipus' throne, leading to the final catastrophe of the duel between the two brothers, is present in art and literature and well established since the 5th century BC. The names of the single warriors, their participation

---

I have to thank the organizers of the Torino conference for inviting me to this event, and to contribute to this volume. I also feel grateful to several audiences who have commented on earlier versions of this paper, esp. on the occasion of a symposium in honor of Frederick Ahl, Sept. 6–8 2013 at Cornell University.

1 Ahl 1993.
2 For Capaneus, see A. *Th.* 423–446, S. *Ant.* 127–137, E. *Ph.* 1172–1186, more positive in the evaluation of Capaneus' character, but still alluding to his death by the hand of Zeus, E. *Supp.* 860–871.
3 See e. g. the interpretation of the *teichoscopia* in *Theb.* 7: Smolenaars 1994, Reitz 2013.
4 For a brief survey of trends in Lucan scholarship, see Bartsch 2009, 494–496.
5 Dominik 1994, on Capaneus see 29–32. See McNelis 2007, 2 n. 7.

https://doi.org/10.1515/9783110534436-018

in the battle, the geographic distribution of the fighters at the seven gates and their fatal lot are all part of the tradition, not Statius' inventions.

The Argive hero Capaneus, too, forms part of this tradition. Book X of Statius' *Thebaid* ends with the *aristeia* and the death of the powerful hero. I will first give a brief survey of Capaneus' appearances during the events of the poem before looking into the final scene in more detail. I will then suggest a reading which is perhaps not obvious at first sight.[6]

Capaneus is first mentioned in the proem of the *Thebaid*. The poet, in a variation of the traditional invocation to the Muse,[7] asks Clio which hero will be the first whose fate he will have to narrate (Stat. *Theb.* 1.41–45):

> quem prius heroum, Clio, dabis? Immodicum irae
> Tydea laurigeri subitos an vatis hiatus?
> urguet et hostilem propellens caedibus amnem
> turbidus Hippomedon, plorandaque bella protervi
> Arcados atque alio Capaneus horrore canendus.   45

> Clio, which of the heroes do you offer first? Tydeus, untrammeled in his wrath? Or the laurelled seer's sudden chasm? Stormy Hippomedon too is upon me, pushing the river his enemy with corpses. And I must mourn the fight or the overbold Arcadian, and sing Capaneus in consternation never felt before.[8]

Capaneus is the last in this list of four, and we hear that he will have to be sung *alio horrore*, with a different sort of horror. This annunciation will be of special importance for my argument. Philip Hardie[9] discusses the passage and stresses the poet's claim of sublimity, his competition with Virgil, and the link to Ennius. But maybe *alius* has another meaning as well and points not just to a different stylistic level, but to a different genre altogether.

Capaneus first enters the narrative proper in Book III (*Theb.* 3.598–602):[10]

---

6 Cf. the contribution by Joy Littlewood in this volume.
7 For the topical invocation of the Muse or Muses, see the excellent overview by Schindler 2013.
8 Translations of Statius are by Shackleton Bailey 2003, those of Lucretius by Rouse 1924.
9 Cf. Hardie 2009, 135 on the subject of sublimity. Hardie compares *alio horrore* with *non solito de more* in *Theb.* 10.829 and argues that Statius' main aim is to foreground the novelty, and thereby the sublimity, of his poetic enterprise. Capaneus' *aristeia* is also discussed by Leigh 2006 in the light of the theory of the sublime.
10 Frings 1991, 10–15 offers a valuable interpretation of the exchange between Capaneus and Amphiaraus. See, too, Stover 2009.

Atque hic ingenti Capaneus Mavortis amore
excitus et longam pridem indignantia pacem
corda tumens [...]

diu tuto superum contemptor...

Capaneus was spurred by mighty love of Mars, his swelling breast had long protested
lengthy peace [...]
Long had he despised the High Ones with impunity...

He is characterized as of noble origin, but also as belligerent and wrathful, and as a *contemptor deorum*, spurner of the gods.[11] This is a role he is now playing throughout the narrative.[12] He is the one who, in a long speech, challenges the well-founded premonitions of the priest Amphiaraus and urges the old king Adrastus to war, against better wisdom and despite the prophetic warnings. This scene can be understood as the "principal internal Argive conflict".[13] In his speech Capaneus declares that he, for one, puts his faith entirely in his own fortitude (*virtus mihi numen et ensis quem teneo*); that belief and trust in the gods is the result of futile fears (3.602 *primus in orbe deos fecit timor*).[14]

His appearance in the catalogue of Argive heroes presents him as a huge man of extraordinary strength (4.165–186) equipped with spectacular armour. The breastplate is especially fearsome (4.175 *horrendum; non matris opus*), and his helmet sports the figure of a Giant.[15]

In the course of events this powerful hero has several opportunities to show off his military prowess and his lack of reverence towards any higher principle other than courage and strength. These qualities also become apparent in the interlude before the final outbreak of the war in Thebes. This sub-plot tells the story of the death of young Opheltes, who becomes the prey of a dragon-serpent, and the funeral games given in honour of this Opheltes. It is Capaneus who is

---

11 The pivotal study on the motive of the *contemptor deorum* is Nestle 1936. Klinnert 1970 still remains important for the careful analysis of the Statian characters Capaneus and Hippomedon. Delarue 2000, 140–144 points to the importance of Virgil's Mezentius as a model for Capaneus.
12 To him applies Ahl's dictum that "Statius' protagonists behave as they do because their view of themselves and their role has become fixed at some point or level. They continue to behave as if nothing has altered ..." (Ahl 1989, 1).
13 Ahl 1986, 2850.
14 Klinnert 1970, 19, who refers to Raith 1963 and Petr. *fr. 27*. See Lactantius Placidus in *Schol. Theb.* 3.602.
15 For the importance of giant-imagery see Chaudhuri 2013, 392. Chaudhuri compares Capaneus' helmet with the one worn by Flaminius, Sil. 5.130–145. On Capaneus' arms see Harrison 1992; on the imagery in general Fucecchi 2013, 113. Cf. below, n. 20.

able to kill the dragon-serpent. This monster is called *sacer horror* (5.505), and it is, at least in the belief of the rural inhabitants of the surrounding landscape, sacred to Inachius Tonans (5.511 f.). The reader might expect a direct reaction to Capaneus' slaying of the dragon, but, this time, he escapes Jupiter's wrath (*Theb.* 5.583–587):

> ipse etiam e summa iam tela poposcerat aethra
> Iuppiter et dudum nimbique hiemesque coibant
> ni minor ira deo gravioraque tela mereri   585
> servatus Capaneus; moti tamen aura cucurrit
> fulminis et summas libavit vertice cristas.

> Jupiter himself had already called for his weapons from highest heaven, and storm clouds and tempests were gathering – but that the god's wrath is not great enough[16] and Capaneus is spared to deserve a heavier missile. Yet the coursing wind of the stirred thunderbolt tasted the tip of the crest upon his head.

He is also one of the protagonists in the competitions during the funeral games for the dead Opheltes.[17] There he challenges his comrades to a boxing match (*Theb.* 6.731–825); his opponent is the young Alcidamas, who through the help of his father Pollux is about to win the match; Capaneus threatens to kill the young man. Only at the very last moment the fight is interrupted and the raving Capaneus is declared the winner against his will by Adrastus (*Theb.* 6.809–812). The characteristics in all these scenes are similar: Capaneus is *immanis*, his immense height and physical strength are stressed. The imagery here, as in other instances,[18] points to the Giants, and to the famous sinner Tityos, as has been shown by Chaudhuri and especially by Fucecchi.[19]

The impression of reckless force is also underlined in all the battle scenes in which Capaneus takes part. The first encounter costs the Theban priest Eunaeus his life; Capaneus kills the holy man despite his appeals and admonitions about the sacred origin of the city of Thebes and its special protection by Bacchus (7.649–687). And again, during the act of revenge against the Theban Hypseus, who in many respects functions like a double of Capaneus, the *contemptor deorum* (9.550) acts in character. The weapons of the slain foe are used by him as a

---

16 Shackleton Bailey adds a note on *minor* 5.585: "Or perhaps 'not so great' (as it would be when he actually did destroy Capaneus): Not 'the god restrained his wrath'."
17 On this scene, see Franchet d'Espérey 1999, 197–203 and 333 f.; Lovatt 2006, 154–162.
18 In 5.569 Capaneus declares that he would not be prevented from killing the dragon even if it 'brought a Giant against *him* above *his* body' (*non si consertum super haec mihi membra Giganta / subveheres*).
19 On comparisons with Giants and Titans see Fucecchi 2013; Ganiban 2007, 146.

means for burying his fallen comrade Hippomedon (cf. 9.563, where he explicitly mentions the opposition between traditional burial rites and his own action). In this episode Capaneus is distinguished by the epithet *magnanimus*.[20] We should keep that in mind, and also the fact that Capaneus is well aware that his act of piety can only be provisional, and that an appropriate burial (*iustos ignes*, 9.564) will have to be executed later. That this will not be possible until Theseus intervenes in the last book of the *Thebaid* has a special irony: the prophecy of the great sinner Capaneus will be fulfilled by the righteous *deus ex machina* Theseus.

Capaneus' *aristeia*, the last one before the duel of the brothers in Book XI,[21] is clearly separated from the preceding episode, the suicide of Menoeceus and the following lament of the Thebans (*Theb.* 10.827–836):[22]

> Hactenus arma, tubae, ferrumque et vulnera: sed nunc
> comminus astrigeros Capaneus tollendus in axes.
> non mihi iam solito vatum de more canendum;
> maior ab Aoniis poscenda amentia lucis: 830
> mecum omnes audete deae! sive ille profunda
> missus nocte furor, Capaneaque signa secutae
> arma Iovem contra Stygiae rapuere Sorores,
> seu virtus egressa modum, seu gloria praeceps
> et magnae data fama neci, seu laeta malorum   835
> principia et blandae superum mortalibus irae.

Thus far of arms, trumpets, of steel and wounds. But now Capaneus must be raised aloft to fight the starry vault at close quarters. No longer may I sing in the wonted fashion of poets; I must ask for a higher lunacy from Aonia's groves. Goddesses all, dare with me. Was his frenzy sent from the depth of night, did the Stygian Sisters take arms agains Jove following Capaneus' standard? Or was it valour past bounds or reckless thirst for glory and fame granted to a great death or success the harbinger of disaster and the High Ones flattering mortals in their wrath?

The break announced by the poet as he turns to his new topic – *hactenus arma, tubae, ferrumque et vulnera* – is misleading. Reading these words, one might think that something entirely different, something which has nothing to do with warfare, fighting or death might be the object of the following lines. But

---

20 An insightful discussion of this term is offered by Leigh 2006, 229 and n. 54.

21 Schetter 1960, 109 ff. has convincingly shown how the different Argives' *aristeiai* are connected by parallel and contrasting motives.

22 See Ahl 1986, 2888 on the contrast between the two heroes, but also on the ambiguity of Menoeceus' heroic act of self-sacrifice. He argues that despite or even because of the "grand gesture", in the long run Thebes becomes indefensible. See also Criado 2000, 99–109.

the contrary is true – the noise of battle and war seemed, rather, suddenly far away in the preceding passage, the lament of Menoeceus' mother Eurydice. The true meaning of the narrator's move will only become clear in the following line, where Capaneus' special exploit is foreshadowed by the words *comminus* and *astrigeros tollendus in axes*. An extraordinary exploit, indeed, but undoubtedly it is the poet who claims for himself the task of elevating his character to the stars. The following invocation *non mihi iam solito vatum de more canendum; / maior ab Aoniis poscenda amentia lucis*, stresses the identification between the poet and his subject. Whose exactly is the *furor* and the *amentia*? Not only the hero, but also the poet describing his actions has become involved, and with him all the Muses (*omnes ... deae*). The introductory line *hactenus arma...* can thus be understood as a sort of *recusatio* at a higher level. The normal means of epic poetry are not enough to fulfil the task ahead.[23] Bessone in her recent book[24] points out that here a metapoetical voice already foreshadows the competition with tragedy, which will become even more significant in the final duel between the brothers. This is certainly correct. But again, the allusions are multilayered. Tragedy, and the *furor poeticus* that inspires the tragic poet, are indeed evident here. But in the outline of the invocation yet another voice seems to join in, the voice of the didactic poet. In a famous passage at the end of the first book of *De rerum natura*,[25] the poet Lucretius also appeals to the Muses (*deae*, in the plural) to help him with his most difficult topic. Statius might be alluding not only to tragic *furor*, but to *furor* more generally. This is not as far-fetched as it may seem, when we look at *Silv.* 2.7.75 (the *Genethliacon Lucani*), where Statius praises Lucan's poetic gifts by ranking him equal to or even higher than Ennius, the *docti furor arduus Lucreti*, Varro Atacinus and Ovid.[26]

The following passage (10.831b–836) is extremely complex and precludes – deliberately, in my opinion – any unambiguous reading. Four alternative causes[27] for Capaneus' acts are enumerated: underworld powers, *virtus* grown out of proportion, an excessive desire for glory regardless of death, or, finally, *laeta malorum principia et blandae superum mortalibus irae* ('success the har-

---

[23] Leigh 2006, 234 discusses the complicity of hero and poet in their venture for the sublime.

[24] Bessone 2011, 97 and n. 2.

[25] 1.920 ff., repeated as the proem to Book IV (or the other way round), and imitated, e. g. by Verg. *G.* 3.289 ff.

[26] On the interpretation of *furor* see Barth 1664–1665 on 10.832.

[27] On the textual problem (*fama / fata*) and on the technique of giving alternatives see Feeney 1991, 349 f. On the Lucretian technique of 'multiple explanations' and its influence see Hardie 2009, 156 f.

binger of disaster and the High Ones flattering mortals in their wrath'). On the meaning of *blandae* much has been said and written. Williams, following a discussion in Barth,[28] translates 'the anger of the gods that lures mortals on'. He also points to the fact that Lactantius glosses *blandae* as *sero venientes*, comparing Juv. 13.100. In this interpretation, *blandae*, 'slow' or 'late', forms a contrast to *principia*. This would result in the meaning: 'first results success, even of evil deeds, and the bad end follows because the gods can take their time when punishing mortals'. But a reading closer to the Latin is not implausible. Capaneus in his wrath obviously has no sense of right and wrong; he dismisses the possibility of punishment by the gods. But we have to keep in mind that the list gives four different reasons both for the actions and decisions of Capaneus the epic character, and for the epic poet's wish to secure the help of the goddesses for his narrative. So one possible reason for the poet to venture upon the story of Capaneus' death is the idea of *blandae irae*, the idea of the gods' – presumed – harmlessness.

This will become clearer when we turn to the final section of Capaneus' *aristeia*. Having reached the top of the city wall, Capaneus begins to destroy this symbol of divine harmony, the walls erected through divine power. His speeches mark the escalation of events (10.874–878; 10.899–906). Between the speeches the reader witnesses a slow change of scene. During the hero's ascent towards heaven, a divine assembly is taking place (*Theb.* 10.883–886):

> Iamque Iovem circa studiis diversa fremebant
> Argolici Tyriique dei; pater, aequus utrisque,
> aspicit ingentes ardentum comminus iras   885
> seque obstare videt.

And now around Jupiter the gods of Argos and Tyre were clamouring in diverse partisanship. Fair to both, the Father surveys the mighty wrath blazing before his eyes and sees that only he can keep it in check.[29].

While Bacchus and the other deities are extremely concerned, Jupiter himself remains outwardly calm (*Theb.* 10.907–911):

> Ingemuit dictis superum dolor; ipse furentem
> risit et incussa sanctarum mole comarum,

---

28 Williams 1972 on v. 836. Barth 1664–1665 on 830: "ludibrio habere Deos res humanas dicit, ut alii infiniti auctores, quosque velint magnis malis afficere, iis successibus rerum optabilibus prius illudere (ex vet. Schol.)".

29 I give Shackleton Bailey's translation, which will have to be altered if my following considerations can be accepted.

'quaenam spes hominum tumidae post proelia Phlegrae?
tune etiam feriendus?' ait, premit undique lentum   910
turba deum frendens et tela ultricia poscit.

At his (*scil.* Capaneus') words the High Ones grieved and groaned. He (= Jupiter) himself laughed at the madman, and shaking the mass of his sacred hair 'What hope', says he, 'do men have after the battles of resumptious Phlegra? Must I strike you down too?' From all hands the crowd of deities urge their tardy chief, gnashing their teeth and demanding weapons of vengeance.

Even in response to the ultimate challenge when Capaneus addresses him directly,[30] the father of the gods reacts just by laughing (*ipse furentem risit,* 907 f.). His answer to the other gods' pressing request for vengeance is on the one hand a 'look back to history' – *quaenam spes hominum tumidae post proelia Phlegrae?* (909). Fucecchi writes: "Jupiter's laugh accentuates the difference between the struggles of the past and the one at present"[31] and interprets his laughter as "ironic disdain".

On the other hand, Jupiter asks *tune etiam feriendus?* (910). Doesn't this seem a bit odd? The most powerful of the gods is not – or not yet – taking action. The question is expressed in strictly neutral form (*tune feriendus?* – 'do you have to be struck?'), though *mihi* ('by me') could be added by the readers and hearers from their knowledge of the events which occurred during the battle of Phlegra.

While the gods insist, urging Jupiter finally to exact vengeance in the form of a lightning bolt, events rush to their finale (*Theb.* 10.913–915; 921 f.; 927 f.):

ipsa dato nondum caelestis regia signo
sponte tonat, coeunt ipsae sine flamine nubes
accurruntque imbres [...]   915

coeperat Ogygiae supra fastigia turris
arcanum mugire polus caelumque tenebris
auferri [...]

[...] talia dicentem toto Iove fulmen adactum
corripuit.

---

30 It would be interesting to further examine the exact phrasing of Capaneus' challenge to Jupiter. He claims already to have taken possession of *Semelea busta* (903). This might be seen as an intertextual link to Semele's being burned by Jupiter's lightning in Ov. *Met.* 3.308 f. Ovid refrains from giving an explicit description of Semele's actual death; *corpus mortale tumultus non tulit aetherios* is all that the reader gets to hear about it.
31 Fucecchi 2013, 113.

> The celestial region itself thunders of its own accord, no signal yet given; the clouds gather of themselves without a wind and the rains come running [...] Above the summit of the Ogygian tower the heavens began a secret rumbling and the sky to be withdrawn in darkness [...] As he spoke thus, the thunderbolt seized him, flung with all that was Jupiter [?].[32]

Nature itself revolts against the turmoil caused by Capaneus' climbing up towards heaven. While Capaneus is still threatening and roaring, the final blow reaches him: *talia dicentem toto Iove fulmen adactum / corripuit.* He burns, but even as a living torch he still stands upright and the last we hear of him at the end of Book X is that *potuit fulmen sperare secundum:* had he endured but a little longer, 'he might have hoped for a second bolt' (10.939).

What exactly happens? If we consider the words carefully, we can, I am convinced, reach an astonishing conclusion. We stand before a combination of rather well known standard situations. The myth of Capaneus climbing the walls and being struck down is well known from all the existing (tragic) versions of the story, and has been foreshadowed throughout the epic. The memory of the battle of Phlegra, a byword for human hybris and ensuing divine vengeance, has been activated several times throughout the narrative, the last time in Jupiter's statement (909). But when we look more closely, there is not a single instance of Jupiter actually taking direct action in the killing of Capaneus. He speaks to his fellow gods; he laughs, he shakes his head, but all these actions belong strictly to the divine sphere. Within the conventions of one of the standard situations of epic narrative, the council of the gods, the father of the gods behaves as befits him. But there is no interaction, no direct contact with the human sphere whatsoever. Jupiter does not assemble the clouds, he does not produce darkness and thunder, he does not take the bolt of lightning in his hand; he does not throw it actively, he does not show any reaction to Capaneus' mortal agony and death. Only at the beginning of Book XI do we hear (5 f.): *componit dextra victor concussa plagarum / Iuppiter et vultu caelumque diemque reducit ...*, 'victorious Jupiter with his right hand composes the shaken zones and with his countenance brings back sky and daylight'. Only then, looking back, are the events summed up with the words *memorandaque facta relinquens / gentibus atque ipsi non illaudata Tonanti,* 'leaving to the nations memorable deeds not unpraised of the Thunderer himself' (11.10 f.).[33]

---

32 For the translation see above, n. 30.
33 Another comparison with Tityus follows. Fucecchi 2013, 114 f. comments: "a climactic moment [...] exalting C.'s feat". He sees the *aristeia* as "a strategy orchestrated by power itself" and its outcome as a "propaganda success".

But during the entire time in which the catastrophe is happening, the phrasing remains absolutely neutral: Jupiter's reaction to what is going on (*aspicit ingentes … iras / seque obstare videt*, 886) should, in my opinion, not be translated as 'sees that only he can keep it in check', but rather: 'he sees himself resisting'. Nothing can shatter his tranquillity: *non tamen haec turbant pacem Iovis* (897). His reaction is not grief (*dolor*), as with the other deities, but laughter. The punishment of the culprit is spoken of in the passive voice: *tune etiam feriendus?* (910). Nature, clouds, thunder, rain, all act by themselves (*ipsa, sponte, ipsae*, 913, 914). The actual killing is seen as if from outside: *corripuit*,[34] 'the lightning bolt … caught him', in the perfect tense. At the moment when the hero speaks out (*dicentem*), he is already struck. And let us have a look at the juncture *fulmen adactum*.[35] Statius elsewhere uses the verb in the active for the act of throwing or striking.[36] In the passive we can adduce an interesting parallel from Lucretius, if we accept a correction already made by Marullus and followed by most editors (Lucr. 5.1222–1225):[37]

> non populi gentesque tremunt, regesque superbi
> corripiunt divum percussi membra timore,
> necquid ob admissum foede dictumve superbe
> poenarum grave sit solvendi tempus adactum?   1225

> Do not nations and peoples tremble, do not proud kings huddle up their limbs smitten with fear of the gods, lest for some base deed or proud word the solemn time of punishment be now at hand?[38]

The context of the long passage in the fifth book is a discussion of the fears and horrors experienced by men when confronted with thunder, tempests or earthquakes. The reason for these fears is the ignorance of the true causes of these

---

34 *Corripere* used for the action of fire (*flamma* etc): OLD s.v. §1d.

35 Here used as in Lucretius' passage quoted below in the text (5.1224 f.). For *adigere* see ThlL 1,677,82 ('de rebus quae pro telis usu veniunt'). For the construction with double accusative, and the accusative remaining also in the passive construction, see Kühner / Stegmann 1955³, II 34, n. 11 (the example is *animum adigere*).

36 *Theb.* 5.214 *adigit costas ferrum*.

37 Bailey 1947 on 5.1225.

38 See also Lucr. 5.1161–1168 *nunc quae causa deum per magnas numina gentis / pervulgarit et ararum compleverit urbis* […] *unde etiam nunc est mortalibus insitus horror, / qui delubra deum nova toto suscitat orbi / terrarum et festis cogit celebrare diebus, / non ita difficilest rationem reddere verbis*, 'next, what cause spread abroad the divine powers of the gods among great nations, and filled cities with altars […] whence even now there is implanted in mortals a shuddering dread, which raises new shrines of the gods over all the world, and constrains men to throng them on holy days; of all this it is not hard to give account in words'.

phenomena. And what these true causes are forms the subject matter of much of the fifth and sixth books. The natural origin of lightning, the formation of thunderstorms, the relation between winds and celestial phenomena are all treated at length at the beginning of Lucretius Book VI. There, the physical explanations for thunder and lightning are set out in great detail (6.96–378); the passage ends with the conclusion that 'this is to understand the true nature of the fiery thunderbolt, and to see by what power it plays its part' (6.380) and with a warning against searching for hidden meaning and *omina*. The whole argument serves as the background for the renewed message, central to the sixth book and to the poem as a whole, that there is no reason to fear the gods. *Denique cur numquam caelo iacit undique puro / Iuppiter in terras fulmen sonitusque profundit?*, 'Why again does Jupiter never cast a bolt on the earth and sound his thunder, when the heaven is clear on all sides?' (Lucr. 6.400 f.), the poet asks. If there is a divine will behind the manifestations of nature, then why do the bolts strike not only the guilty, but also places in the desert, or even the temples of the gods? If the gods take any part in human actions, then crime would be justly punished, as has been explained shortly before (Lucr. 6.387–392):

> quod si Iuppiter atque alii fulgentia divi
> terrifico quatiunt sonitu caelestia templa
> et iaciunt ignem quo quoiquest cumque voluptas,
> cur quibus incautum scelus aversabile cumquest   390
> non faciunt icti flammas ut fulguris halent
> pectore perfixo, documen mortalibus acre [...]?

> But if Jupiter and other gods shake the shining regions of heaven with appalling din, if they cast fire whither it may be the pleasure of each one, why do they not see to it that those who have not refrained from some abominable crime, shall be struck and breathe out sulphurous flames from breast pierced through, a sharp lesson to mankind [...]?

Lucretius argues against the idea that thunder and lightning are a means of divine justice. These natural phenomena do not provide men with a *documen*, a demonstration of punishment. In the final conclusion to the events surrounding Capaneus' death, Statius (as we saw in the passage from the beginning of Book XI: *memoranda ... gentibus*, 11.10 f.), emphatically contradicts Lucretius, explicitly stating that the results of a thunderstorm and stroke of lightning do serve as a *memorandum* for men, a reminder of the gods' retribution for those who act out of turn.

The reader of *De rerum natura* has been informed (e. g. in 2.1092) that thunder and the like are not the result of the gods' intervention, but that the visible and tangible world is subject to the movements of atoms, and that these atoms move without any impulse from the gods: *ipsa sua per se sponte omnia dis agere expers*, '(nature) herself doing all by herself of her own accord, and having no part nor lot in the gods' (2.1092). Why is that so? Because the gods in their tranquillity are not disturbed: *nam pro sancta deum tranquilla pectora pace / quae placidum degunt aevom vitamque serenam*, 'for I appeal to the holy hearts of the gods, which in tranquil peace pass untroubled days and a life serene' (1093 f.); and they do not bother themselves with directing the motion of the elements. This argument is then expanded (Lucr. 2.1097–1101):

> quis pariter [...]
> ignibus aetheriis terras suffire feracis,
> omnibus inve locis esse omni tempore praesto,
> nubibus ut tenebras faciat caelique serena   1100
> concutiat sonitu, tum fulmina mittat [...]?

> Who is [...] strong enough to warm the fruitful worlds with ethereal fires, or to be present in all places and at all times, so to make darkness with his clouds and to shake the serene sky with thunder, then to launch lightnings [...]?

Yet that is exactly what we as readers of the *Thebaid* are witnessing, and what Capaneus experiences. He is certainly guilty of crime, of impiety and of impunity. His depravity and boastfulness arouse the force of the elements whose victim he will become: *ipsa dato nondum caelestis regia signo / sponte tonat* (*Theb.* 10.913 f.). The celestial region itself thunders of its own accord, no signal being given yet – but signal of what, we may ask. The hero is not struck by Jupiter himself, by a divine avenger. Actually, Jupiter behaves exactly in the way the Epicurean poet has dismissed as impossible, and as an argument against the existence of the gods: he does wait for the clouds to gather (*nubes successere*, Lucr. 6.402) and for darkness to prevail before the final strike. The sky does go dark: *caelumque tenebris auferri* (*Theb.* 10.922 f.); Capaneus stands on the *arx* which he cannot see anymore: *quas non videt arces* (10.923). Even the difficult phrase *toto Iove fulmen adactum / corripuit* (10.927 f.), seen in this light, takes on a remarkable meaning: Capaneus is struck by the bolt of lightning while the thunderstorm gathers its force and spreads over the whole sky. To understand *toto Iove* in this way is much easier; one could compare the usage of *sub Iove* ('outside'), or similar phrases.[39] The possible double entendre – *Iupiter* as the sky, and *Iupiter* as the vengeful divine power – is, in my opinion, entirely in line with Statius' style. There is no need to take refuge in strained explanations and transla-

---

39 See *OLD* s.v. 'Iuppiter' § 2. Cf. Lucr. 6.400 f. *denique cur numquam caelo iacit undique puro / Iuppiter in terras fulmen sonitusque profundit?*

tions like 'with all Jupiter's power' (Williams 1972, *ad loc.*)[40] or 'with all that was Jupiter' (Shackleton Bailey, also adapted by Fucecchi). Williams explains *totus* by adducing a parallel from Horace (*Carm.* 1.19.9 *in me tota ruens Venus*), and takes the ablative as instrumental, for which he adduces many parallels, all but one (cf. *Silv.* 3.1.53 *ictusque Hyperione multo* [*scil. Sirius*]) with the common *ab* plus ablative. I would like to suggest that we should understand the sentence as follows: 'While he was still speaking, the bolt of lightning – hurled over the whole sky – had smashed him'.

I shall recapitulate a few points of my reading of the text, and then I will come to my conclusion. Statius, when introducing Capaneus as a character in the epic narrative, describes him as a sinister man who, though spurning the gods, nevertheless is a mighty warrior and a fearsome hero. His story as one of the Seven is well known from Greek tragedy. His words and deeds stay in character throughout the epic; his final *aristeia* and death form the culminating point of the series of *aristeiai* before the final duel between the brothers and the twelfth book, with the denouement brought about by Theseus. Capaneus' *aristeia* begins immediately after the self-sacrifice of the Theban Menoeceus. It opens with an invocation to all the Muses – as one goddess' inspiration is not enough for the task in hand. The poet astonishingly sets aside the traditional subject matter of epic poetry (*arma, tubae, ferrum, vulnera*) and calls for a *maior amentia*. The list of possible motivations for the singularity of the following events ends with *blandae superum mortalibus irae*.

I have suggested that different elements of the action, both on the part of the epic hero and on the part of the gods, are tinged with the terminology and doctrine of Epicurean philosophy as known from Lucretius' *De rerum natura*. The epic hero behaves as an *hybristes*, a *contemptor deorum*, someone acting of his own accord, regardless of religious consequences.[41] One could say he misunderstands Epicurean philosophy. The paradoxical outcome of the final act of hybris would be that the *contemptor deorum* would in the end reach heaven itself. The events that are set in motion to bring him down in the end and to prevent the worst from happening develop as if Jupiter himself had designed the mise en scène for this special case. The highest deity in heaven sets himself apart and smiles benignly – like the gods in the *intermundia* – , even in the midst of a somewhat turbulent council of the gods. He does not take action by throwing

---

40 Dante, *Inf.* 14.59 "sì com' el fece a la pugna di Flegra, / e me saetti con tutta sua forza: / non ne potrebbe aver vendetta allegra".
41 I am very grateful to Alessandro Schiesaro for making known to me, before it goes into print, his interpretation of the Phaethon episode in Ovid's *Metamorphoses* in the light of Epicurean (Lucretian) terminology and thought.

his thunderbolt himself, but waits for the elements to fulfil the task of punishing the sinner. Nature and the elements act on their own, driven by physical forces,[42] just as described in Lucretius' Epicurean doctrine. Only when the contumacious evildoer is lying on the ground, struck down by the natural cause of a lightning strike, does Jupiter become active again and resume his role as the power responsible for controlling the weather.[43] Only at this point is a possible interpretation offered: the *aristeia* and Capaneus' death are memorable (*memoranda*) and gain praise even from Jupiter himself. That the god is now metonymically called *Tonans* deserves special attention and points back to the central part of the killing, the *fulmen adactum toto Iove*.

But we may ask: is it really plausible that Statius is alluding to Lucretius, and to Epicurean philosophy? Why would he do so? Is he engaged in a philosophical discussion, e. g. refuting Epicurean doctrine in favor of some other theory? – Stoicism comes to mind, and has been suggested as a background for this passage by some scholars.[44] Do I want to argue that Statius is taking part in a philosophical discussion? And why would Statius choose the story of Capaneus for such a discourse – Stoic and Epicurean theory competing in the punishment of a well-known sinner? Isn't the sequence of events determined instead by myth, and by the literary – and, at least to us, mainly tragic – tradition? One might even adduce Dante's *Inferno* (14.43–75) for the motif of the never repenting hero. There, the inconvincible sinner claims that Jupiter will never relish his revenge ("non ne potrebbe aver vendetta allegra", 60).[45]

In recent years, I have observed a renaissance of philosophical interpretations of epic poetry. Especially for Lucan, the Stoic reading has been brought back into the scholarly discourse;[46] but, at present, no literary text seems to remain safe from philosophical exegesis. I am not joining the ranks of those who

---

42 It might be worthwhile to compare Statius here with a passage of Lucan's *Bellum civile* dealing with the Thessalian witches who assemble storms *Iove ignaro* (Luc. 6.465–469 *nunc omnia complent / imbribus et calido praeducunt nubila Phoebo, / et tonat ignaro caelum Iove: vocibus isdem / umentis late nebulas nimbosque solutis / excussere comis*, 'torrents are outpoured beneath a burning sun; and thunder roars uncaused by Jupiter. From their flowing locks vapours immense shall issue at their call').

43 An accomplishment that Gibson 2013a, 85 sees as "questionable praise". He points to the "inconsistency and paradox" of the passage and relates it to the inconsistency already present in the proem.

44 Klinnert 1970 and Schetter 1960 see fate, or "Weltgeist", at work. Criado 2013, 207 views the Statian Jupiter as subject to Fate.

45 I owe the first reference to Dante to William Kennedy. See McNelis 2007, 1 and n. 2 (Capaneus as a model for basphemers).

46 For Lucan, e. g. the study by Wiener 2006.

think poetry is a means of conveying philosophical messages. But the *Thebaid* does indeed have a message, a metapoetic message. This message is meant to persuade us that the epic genre is the most flexible and most adaptable of genres, and that epic is the supreme way of telling a story.

The supremacy and richness of the epic genre have always been duly observed by interpreters of the *Aeneid*. But Lucan and the Flavian poets are, more often than not, read with a more restricted outlook. Either a claim is made that elements of philosophical doctrine can be detected, but they are reduced to allusions to 'popular philosophy' or contemporary politics; or the literary competition between epic and tragedy is foregrounded in interpretation. Both approaches are not wrong; on the contrary, as has been rightly observed, the contest between the two most sublime genres lies already in the choice of the subject matter.

But I am convinced that it is Statius' aim, too, to argue for the supremacy of epic poetry. The poet, in our example, directs his reader to this fundamental statement in many ways: he first invokes the whole chorus of all the Muses; he then endows his epic hero with an – evidently misunderstood – Epicurean credo, and he finally unfolds a sequence of events in which the false Epicurean receives the treatment that is due to him according to the doctrines of didactic poetry. The mythological hero from Greek tragedy is taught his lesson, both a moral and a poetic one. And the epic poet once more reminds his reader that epic poetry has all the other genres at its disposal, and is the most powerful among poetic genres.[47]

---

47 Bessone 2011 *passim*. The last book of the *Thebaid* can be read as a competition with tragic poetry: the change of scene, the one thing most notably not possible in drama, is here taken to the extreme. At a conference on Flavian epic in 2011, I was able to discuss my interpretation of Capaneus' death with Pramit Chaudhuri, who was already exploring the problem in detail and has recently published a monograph on this subject (Chaudhuri 2014).

Bibliography

Abbamonte, Giancarlo (2009), "Discorsi alle truppe: documenti, origine e struttura retorica", in: G. Abbamonte / L. Miletti / L. Spina (eds.), 29–46.

Abbamonte, Giancarlo / Miletti, Lorenzo / Spina, Luigi (eds.) (2009), *Discorsi alla prova*, Napoli.

Adamietz, Joachim (1986), "Quintilians *Institutio oratoria*", in: *ANRW* II 32.4, 2226–2271.

Agnesini, Alex (2012), "*Lepos, mores, pathos, furor, risus...* Per una 'ri-sistemazione' di alcuni *carmina* catulliani", in: A.M. Morelli (ed.), *Lepos e mores. Una giornata su Catullo, Atti del convegno internazionale, Cassino, 27 maggio 2010*, Cassino, 171–202.

Ahl, Frederick M. (1986), "Statius' *Thebaid*. A reconsideration", in: *ANRW* II 32.5, 2803–2912.

Ahl, Frederick M. (1989), "Homer, Vergil, and complex narrative structures in Latin epic: an essay", in: *ICS* 14, 1–31.

Ahl, Frederick / Davis, Martha A. / Pomeroy, Arthur (1986), "Silius Italicus", in: *ANRW* II 32.4, Berlin, 2492–2461.

Albrecht, Michael von (1964), *Silius Italicus: Freiheit und Gebundenheit römischer Epik*, Amsterdam.

Albrecht, Michael von (1999), *Roman Epic: an Interpretative Introduction*, Leiden.

Anderson, William B. (ed. and transl.) (1936, 1965[2]), Sidonius Apollinaris, *Poems and Letters*, I, Cambridge, MA.

André, Jean-Marie (1966), *L'Otium dans la vie morale et intellectuelle romaine des origines à l'époque augustéenne*, Paris.

Argentieri, Lorenzo (2007), "Meleager and Philip as Epigram Collectors", in: P. Bing / J.S. Bruss (eds.), *Brill's Companion to Hellenistic Epigram*, Leiden-Boston, 147–164.

Aricò, Giuseppe (1972), *Ricerche Staziane*, Palermo.

Aricò, Giuseppe (1981), "Contributo alla ricostruzione degli *Skyrioi* euripidei", in: I. Gallo (ed.), *Studi salernitani in memoria di R. Cantarella*, Salerno, 215–230.

Aricò, Giuseppe (1986), "L'*Achilleide* di Stazio: tradizione letteraria e invenzione narrativa", in: *ANRW* II 32.5, 2925–2964.

Aricò, Giuseppe (1991), "La vicenda di Hypsipyle in Valerio Flacco e Stazio", in: M. Korn / H.J. Tschiedel (eds.), *Ratis Omnia Vincet: Untersuchungen zu den Argonautica des Valerius Flaccus*, München, 197–210.

Aricò, Giuseppe (1996), "Rileggendo l'*Achilleide*", in: F. Delarue / S. Georgacopoulou / P. Laurens / A.-M. Taisne (eds.), *Epicedion. Hommage à P. Papinius Statius 96–1996*, Poitiers, 185–199.

Aricò, Giuseppe (2008), "*Leves libelli*. Su alcuni aspetti della poetica dei generi minori da Stazio a Plinio il Giovane", in: *CentoPagine* 2, 1–11.

Ariemma, Enrico (2010), "*Fons Cuncti Varro Mali:* The Demagogue Varro in *Punica* 8–10", in: A. Augoustakis (ed.), 241–276.

Arrighetti, Graziano (1965), Epicuro, *Opere*, Torino.

Ash, Rhiannon (1999), "An Exemplary Conflict: Tacitus' Parthian Battle Narrative (*Annals* 6.34–35)", in: *Phoenix* 53, 114–135.

Ash, Rhiannon (2002), "Epic encounters? Ancient historical battle narrative and the epic tradition", in: D.S. Levene / D.P. Nelis (eds.), *Clio and the Poets: Augustan Poetry and the Traditions of Ancient Historiography*, Leiden, 253–274.

https://doi.org/10.1515/9783110534436-019

Auerbach, Erich (1965), *Literary Language and its Public in late Latin Antiquity and the Middle Ages*, transl. R. Mannheim, London.

Augoustakis, Antony (2003), *"Rapit infidum victor caput: Ekphrasis* and Gender Role Reversal in Silius Italicus' *Punica* 15", in: P. Thibodeau / H. Haskell (eds.), *Being There Together: Essays in Honor of Michael C.J. Putnam on the Occasion of his Seventieth Birthday*, Minnesota, 110–127.

Augoustakis, Antony (2010a), *Motherhood and the Other. Fashioning Female Power in Flavian Epic*, Oxford.

Augoustakis, Antony (ed.) (2010b), *Brill's Companion to Silius Italicus*, Leiden-Boston.

Augoustakis, Antony (2010c), "Silius Italicus. A Flavian Poet", in: A. Augoustakis (ed.), 3–23.

Augoustakis, Antony (2011), *"sine funeris ullo ardet honore rogus:* Burning Pyres in Lucan and Silius Italicus' *Punica"*, in: P. Asso (ed.), *Brill's Companion to Lucan*, Leiden-Boston, 185–198.

Augoustakis, Antony (2012), "Daphnis' *deductum nomen* / *carmen* in Silius' Sicilian Pastoral (*Pun.* 14.462–76)", in: *TiC* 4, 132–152.

Augoustakis, Antony (ed.) (2013), *Ritual and Religion in Flavian Epic,* Oxford.

Augoustakis, Antony (ed.) (2014), *Flavian Poetry and Its Greek Past*, Leiden-Boston.

Augoustakis, Antony (2015), "Campanian Politics and Poetics in Silius Italicus' *Punica"*, in: *ICS* 40, 155–169.

Augoustakis, Antony (2016), "Burial and Lament in Flavian Epic: Mothers, Fathers, Children", in: N. Manioti (ed.), 276–300.

Austin, Roland G. (ed.) (1965), *Quintiliani Institutionis oratoriae liber XII*, Oxford (1948[1]).

Ax, Wolfram (1986), *Laut, Stimme, Sprache – Studien zu drei Grundbegriffen der antiken Sprachtheorie*, Göttingen.

Ax, Wolfram (ed.) (2011), *Quintilians Grammatik (inst. orat. 1, 4–8)*, Berlin-Boston.

Bäblitz, Leanne (2009), "The selection of advocates for *repetundae* trials. The cases of Pliny the Younger", in: *Athenaeum* 97, 197–208.

Baehrens, Aemilius (ed.) (1893[2]), *Catulli Veronensis Liber*, II, *Commentarius*, nova ed. a K.P. Schulze curata, Lipsiae.

Bailey, Cyril (ed.) (1949), Lucretius, *De rerum natura,* ed. with trans. and comm., Oxford.

Bailey, Cyril (ed.) (1975), Epicurus, *The Extant Remains. With short critical apparatus, translation, and notes*, Hildesheim-New York.

Barchiesi, Alessandro (1995), "Figure dell'intertestualità nell'epica romana", in: *Lexis* 13, 49–67.

Barchiesi, Alessandro (1996), "La guerra di Troia non avrà luogo: il proemio dell'*Achilleide* di Stazio", in: *AION* 18, 45–62.

Barchiesi, Alessandro (2001), "Genealogie letterarie nell'epica imperiale. Fondamentalismo e ironia", in: E.A. Schmidt (ed.), *L'histoire littéraire immanente dans la poésie latine* (Entretiens sur l'Antiquité Classique 47), Vandoeuvres-Genève 21–25 août 2000, Genève, 315–354 and "Discussion", 355–362.

Barchiesi, Alessandro (2005a), "Masculinity in the 90's: the education of Achilles in Statius and Quintilian", in: M. Paschalis (ed.), *Roman and Greek Imperial Epic*, Rethymnon, 47–75.

Barchiesi, Alessandro (2005b), "The Search for the Perfect Book: a PS to the new Posidippus", in: K. Gutzwiller (ed.), *The New Posidippus. A Hellenistic Poetry Book*, Oxford, 320–342.

Barth, Caspar P. (1664–1665), *P. Statii quae extant*, Leipzig-Zwickau.

Bartsch, Shadi (2005), "Lucan", in: J.M. Foley (ed.), *A Companion to Ancient Epic*, Chichester, 492–503.

Barwick, Karl (1932), "Zur Kompositionstechnik und Erklärung Martials", in: *Philologus* 87, 63–79.

Barwick, Karl (1958), "Zyklen bei Martial und in den kleinen Gedichten des Catull", in: *Philologus* 102, 284–318.

Bassett, Edward (1963), "Scipio and the Ghost of Appius", in: *CPh* 58, 73–92.

Bauman, Richard A. (1974), *Impietas in principem*, München.

Bauman, Richard A. (1996), *Crime and Punishment in Ancient Rome*, New York.

Beck, Jan-Wilhelm (1996), *'Lesbia' und 'Juventius': Zwei libelli im Corpus Catullianum*, Göttingen.

Bellandi, Franco (2007), *Lepos e Pathos. Scritti su Catullo*, Bologna.

Benjamin, Walter (1969), "The work of art in the age of mechanical reproduction" in: H. Arendt (ed.), *Illuminations*, New York, 211–244.

Bernstein, Neil W. (2007), "Fashioning Crispinus through his Ancestors: Epic Models in Statius' *Silvae* 5.2", in: *Arethusa* 40, 183–196.

Bernstein, Neil W. (2008), *In the Image of the Ancestors: Narratives of Kinship in Flavian Epic*. Toronto.

Bernstein, Neil W. (2016), "*Mutua uulnera*: Dying Together in Silius' Saguntum", in: N. Manioti (ed.), 228–247.

Bessone, Federica (2002), "Voce femminile e tradizione elegiaca nella *Tebaide* di Stazio", in: A. Aloni / E. Berardi / G. Besso / S. Cecchin (eds.), *Atti del Seminario Internazionale I Sette a Tebe. Dal mito alla letteratura, Torino 21–22 Febbraio 2001*, Bologna, 185–217.

Bessone, Federica (2011), *La Tebaide di Stazio. Epica e potere*, Pisa-Roma.

Bessone, Federica (2013), "Critical Interactions. Constructing Heroic Models and Imperial Ideology in Flavian Epic", in: G. Manuwald / A. Voigt (eds.), 87–105.

Bessone, Federica (2014), "*Polis*, Court, Empire. Greek Culture, Roman Society, and the System of Genres in Statius' Poetry", in: A. Augoustakis (ed.), 215–233.

Bessone, Federica (2016), "The Hero's Extended Family. Familial and Narrative Tensions in Statius' *Achilleid*", in: N. Manioti (ed.), 174–208.

Bessone, Federica (forthcoming a), "Allusive (im-)pertinence in Statius' Epic", in: N. Coffee / C. Forstall / L. Galli / D. Nelis (eds.).

Bessone, Federica (forthcoming b), "*Nimis mater*. Mother Plot and Epic Deviation in the *Achilleid*", in: A. Keith / A. Sharrock (eds.), *Motherhood in Antiquity*, Toronto.

Bessone, Federica (forthcoming c), "Visions of a Hero: Optical Illusions and Multifocal Epic in Statius' *Achilleid*", in: *Helios*.

Bessone, Federica (forthcoming d), "The Hut and the Temple. Private Aetiology and Augustan Models in the *Silvae*", in: A. Lòio (ed.), *Editing and Commenting on the Silvae*.

Beye, Charles R. (1969), "Jason as Love-Hero in Apollonius' *Argonautica*", in: *GRBS* 10, 31–55.

Biles, Zachary P. (2006–2007), "Aeschylus' Afterlife. Reperformance by Decree in 5th C. Athens?", in: *ICS* 31–32, 206–242.

Biondi, Giuseppe (1984), *Il Nefas argonautico. Mythos e logos nella Medea di Seneca*, Bologna.

Bleicken, Jochen (1962), *Senatsgericht und Kaisersgericht,* Göttingen.

Bloomer, W. Martin (2010), "Roman Declamation: the Elder Seneca and Quintilian", in: W. Dominik / J. Hall (eds.), 297–306.

Bonadeo, Alessia (2010), *L'Hercules Epitrapezios Novi Vindicis: introduzione e commento a Stat. silv. 4, 6,* Napoli.

Bonadeo, Alessia (2012), "*Martem... aequare canendo* (Stat. *silv.* 5,3,11): divagazioni sulla concezione della poesia nelle *Silvae*", in: *MD* 68, 111–152.

Bonadeo, Alessia (2013), "Nella 'biblioteca' di Stazio: spigolature dalle *Silvae*", in: *BStudLat* 43, 37–86.

Bowie, Michael N.R. (1988), *Martial Book XII. A Commentary,* Diss. Oxford.

Boyle, Anthony J. (ed.) (1990), *The imperial Muse: Ramus Essays on Roman literature of the Empire, Flavian Epicist to Claudian,* Bendigo.

Boyle, Anthony J. / Dominik, William (eds.) (2003), *Flavian Rome: Culture, image, text,* Leiden.

Braun, L. (1993), "Der Aufbau der *Punica* des Silius Italicus", in: *WJA* 19, 173–183.

Bright, David F. (1980), *Elaborate Disarray: The Nature of Statius' Silvae,* Meisenheim am Glan.

Brink, Charles O. (ed.) (1971), Horace, *On Poetry: the Ars Poetica,* Cambridge.

Broich, Ulrich (1967), "*Batrachomyomachia* und *Margites* als literarische Vorbilder. Einige Bemerkungen zu einem literarkritischen Topos", in: H. Meller / H.-J. Zimmermann (eds.), *Lebende Antike. Symposion für Rudolf Sühnel,* Berlin, 250–257.

Bruère, Richard T. (1958), "*Color Ovidianus* in Silius' *Punica 1–7*", in: N.I. Herescu (ed.), *Ovidiana. Récherches sur Ovide,* Paris, 475–499.

Bruère, Richard T. (1959), "*Color Ovidianus* in Silius' *Punica VIII–XVII*", in: *CPh* 54, 228–245.

Buchheit, Vinzenz (1975a), "Chrysogonus als Tyrann in Ciceros Rede für Roscius aus Ameria", in: *Chiron* 5, 193–211.

Buchheit, Vinzenz (1975b), "Ciceros Kritik an Sulla in der Rede für Roscius aus Ameria", in: *Historia* 24, 570–591.

Buongiovanni, Claudio (2009), "Marziale, libro X. Gli epigrammi 1 e 2 tra poesia, poetica e politica", in: *Athenaeum* 97, 507–526.

Burck, Erich (1970), "Kampf und Tod des Cyzicus bei Valerius Flaccus", in: *REL* 47, 173–198.

Burck, Erich (1979), "Die *Argonautica* des Valerius Flaccus", in: E. Burck (ed.), *Das römische Epos,* Darmstadt, 208–253.

Burck, Erich (1981), "Epische Bestattungsszenen. Ein literarhistorischer Vergleich", in: E. Lefèvre (ed.), *Vom Menschenbild in der römischen Literatur. II,* Heidelberg, 429–487.

Burck, Erich (1984), *Historische und epische Tradition bei Silius Italicus,* München.

Burkert, Walter (1983), *Homo Necans. The Anthropology of Ancient Greek Sacrificial Ritual and Myth* (transl. P. Bing), Berkeley.

Busse, Adolf (1887), *Porphyrii isagoge et in Aristotelis categorias commentarium* (Commentaria in Aristotelem Graeca 4.1), Berlin.

Butler, Harold E. (ed. and transl.) (1921–1922), *The Institutio Oratoria of Quintilian with an English translation in four volumes,* I–IV, Cambridge, MA-London (repr. 1958–1961).

Cairns, Francis (1984), "The Nereids of Catullus 64,12–23b", in: *Gräzer Beitrage* 11, 95–101.

Calcante, Cesare Marco (2007), "L'antico come categoria stilistica: la teoria dell'arcaismo nell'*Institutio oratoria* di Quintiliano", in: A. Bonadeo / E. Romano (eds.), *Dialogando con il passato. Permanenze e innovazioni nella cultura latina di età flavia,* Firenze, 108–123.

Camera, Elisa (2007), "Marziale e Stazio tra inimicizia ed emulazione", in: F. Bertini (ed.), *FuturAntico* 4, Genova, 155–190.

Campbell, Gordon (2003), *Lucretius on Creation and Evolution. A Commentary on De Rerum Natura Book Five, Lines 772–1104*, Oxford.

Canali, Luca (ed.) (2000), Publio Papinio Stazio, *Selve. Silvae*, collaborazione e note di Maria Pellegrini, Locarno.

Canobbio, Alberto (2005), "Il libro VIII di Marziale e la ricerca di una identità augustea", in: F. Gasti / G. Mazzoli (eds.), *Modelli letterari e ideologia nell'età flavia. Atti della III Giornata ghisleriana di Filologia classica (Pavia, 30–31 ottobre 2003)*, Como-Pavia, 127–162.

Canobbio, Alberto (2008), "*Epigrammata longa* e *breves libelli*. Dinamiche formali dell'epigramma marzialiano", in: A.M. Morelli (ed.), 169–193.

Canobbio, Alberto (ed.) (2011a), *M. Valerii Martialis Epigrammaton liber quintus*, introduzione, edizione critica, traduzione e commento, Napoli.

Canobbio, Alberto (2011b), "Marziale e la tradizione elegiaca latina", in: *Athenaeum* 99, 437–472.

Canobbio, Alberto (2014), "Generi 'grandi' e generi 'piccoli' in Marziale e in Stazio", in: *BStudLat* 44, 442–470.

Carderi, Flavia (2008), "Le *ekphraseis* di Valerio Flacco tra novità e tradizione", in: *Hermes* 136, 214–226.

Cavarzere, Alberto (2008²), *Oratoria a Roma. Storia di un genere pragmatico*, Roma.

Chaniotis, Angelos (2005), *War in the Hellenistic World: A Social and Cultural History*, Malden, MA.

Chaudhuri, Pramit (2014), *The War with God. Theomachy in Roman Imperial Poetry*, Oxford.

Citroni, Mario (1968), "Motivi di polemica letteraria negli epigrammi di Marziale", in: *DArch* 2, 259–301.

Citroni, Mario (ed.) (1975), *M. Valerii Martialis Epigrammaton Liber I*, introduzione, testo, apparato critico e commento, Firenze.

Citroni, Mario (1988), "Pubblicazioni e dediche dei libri in Marziale. Gli epigrammi di fronte a imperatori, amici, lettori", in: *Maia* 40, 3–39.

Citroni, Mario (1989), "Marziale e la letteratura per i Saturnali (poetica dell'intrattenimento e cronologia della pubblicazione dei libri)", in: *ICS* 14, 201–226.

Citroni, Mario (1992), "Letteratura per i Saturnali e poetica dell'intrattenimento", in: *SIFC* 85, 425–447.

Citroni, Mario (1995), *Poesia e lettori in Roma antica. Forme della comunicazione letteraria*, Roma-Bari.

Citroni, Mario (2003a), "I canoni di autori antichi: alle origini del concetto di classico", in: L. Casarsa / L. Cristante / M. Fernandelli (eds.), *Culture europee e tradizione latina* (Polymnia: studi di filologia classica 1), Trieste, 1–22.

Citroni, Mario (2003b), "Marziale, Plinio il Giovane, e il problema dell'identità di genere dell'epigramma latino", in: F. Bertini (ed.), *Giornate filologiche "Francesco Della Corte" – III*, Genova, 7–29.

Citroni, Mario (2004), "Martial, Pline le jeune et l'identité du genre de l'épigramme latine", in: *Dictynna* 1, 125–153 (https://dictynna.revues.org/172).

Citroni, Mario (2005a), "Finalità e struttura della rassegna degli scrittori greci e latini in Quintiliano", in: F. Gasti / G. Mazzoli (eds.), *Modelli letterari e ideologia nell'età flavia*.

Atti della III Giornata ghisleriana di Filologia classica (Pavia, 30–31 ottobre 2003), Pavia, 15–38.

Citroni, Mario (2005b), "Orazio, Cicerone, e il tempo della letteratura", in: J.P. Schwindt (ed.), *La représentation du temps dans la poésie augustéenne. Zur Poetik der Zeit in augusteischer Dichtung*, Heidelberg, 123–139.

Citroni, Mario (2006a), "The Concept of the Classical and the Canons of Model Authors in Roman Literature", in: J.I. Porter (ed.), *Classical Pasts. The Classical Traditions of Greece and Rome*, Princeton-Oxford, 204–234.

Citroni, Mario (2006b), "Quintilian and the Perception of the System of Poetic Genres in the Flavian Age", in: R.R. Nauta / H.-J. van Dam / J.J.L. Smolenaars (eds.), 1–19.

Citroni, Mario (2009), "Marziale e l'identità dell'epigramma latino", in: R. Cardini / D. Coppini (eds.), *Il rinnovamento umanistico della poesia. L'epigramma e l'elegia*, Firenze, 15–42.

Citroni Marchetti, Sandra (1982), "*Iuvare mortalem*. L'ideale programmatico della *Naturalis Historia* di Plinio nei rapporti con il moralismo stoico-diatribico", in: *A&R* 27, 124–148.

Citroni Marchetti, Sandra (1991), *Plinio il Vecchio e la tradizione del moralismo romano*, Pisa.

Cizek, Eugen (1975), "Face à face éloquent. Encolpe et Agamemnon", in: *PP* 30, 91–101.

Claassen, Jo-Marie (1999), *Displaced Persons. The literature of exile from Cicero to Boethius*, Madison, WI.

Clement, Grace (1996), *Care, Autonomy, and Justice. Feminism and the Ethic of Care*, Boulder.

Coarelli, Filippo (1996), *Revixit ars. Arte e ideologia a Roma. Dai modelli ellenistici alla tradizione repubblicana*, Roma.

Coffee, Neil / Forstall, Chris / Galli, Lavinia / Nelis, Damien (eds.) (forthcoming), *Intertextuality in Flavian Epic*, Berlin-Boston.

Coleman, Kathleen M. (ed.) (1988), Statius, *Silvae IV*, Text, Translation and Commentary, Oxford.

Coleman, Kathleen M. (ed.) (2006), Martial, *Liber Spectaculorum*, Edited with Introduction, Translation & Commentary, Oxford.

Colson, Francis Henry (ed.) (1924), *M. Fabii Quintiliani Institutionis Oratoriae Liber I*, Cambridge (repr. Hildesheim-New York 1973).

Commager, Steele (1962), *The Odes of Horace: A Critical Study*, New Haven.

Conte, Gian Biagio (1984), *Virgilio, il genere e i suoi confini. Modelli del senso, modelli della forma in una poesia colta e 'sentimentale'*, Milano.

Conte, Gian Biagio (1985²), *Memoria dei poeti e sistema letterario. Catullo Virgilio Ovidio Lucano*, Torino.

Conte, Gian Biagio (1986), *The Rhetoric of Imitation: Genre and poetic memory in Virgil and other Latin poets* (transl. by C. Segal), Ithaca-London.

Conte, Gian Biagio (1991), *Generi e lettori. Lucrezio, l'elegia d'amore, l'enciclopedia di Plinio*, Milano (repr. Pisa 2012).

Conte, Gian Biagio (1994), *Genres and Readers* (transl. by G.W. Most), Baltimore.

Conte, Gian Biagio (2007a), *The Poetry of Pathos. Studies in Virgilian Epic* (transl. by S.J. Harrison), Oxford.

Conte, Gian Biagio (2007b), *Virgilio. L'epica del sentimento* (Nuova edizione accresciuta), Torino.

Conway, Robert S. / Johnson, Stephen K. (eds.) (1963), *T. Livi Ab Urbe Condita XXVI–XXX*, Oxford.

Conway, Robert S. / Walters, Charles F. (eds.) (1963), *T. Livi Ab Urbe Condita XXI–XXV*, Oxford.

Corsi, Stefano (ed.) (1997), M. Fabio Quintiliano, *La formazione dell'oratore*, I, Milano.

Courtney, Edward (2001), *A Companion to Petronius*, Oxford.

Courtney, Edward (ed.) (1990), *P. Papini Stati Silvae*, Oxford.

Cousin, Jean (ed.) (1976), Quintilien, *Institution oratoire*, II, Paris.

Cova, Pier Vincenzo (1990), "La critica letteraria nell'*Institutio*", in: P.V. Cova / R. Gazich / G.E. Manzoni / G. Melzani, *Aspetti della 'paideia' di Quintiliano*, Milano, 9–59.

Cowan, Robert (2006), "Absurdly Scythian Spaniards: Silius, Horace and the Concani", in: *Mnemosyne* 59, 260–267.

Cowan, Robert (2010), "Virtual Epic: Counterfactuals, Sideshadowing and the Poetics of Contingency in the *Punica*", in: A. Augoustakis (ed.), 323–351.

Craca, Clotilde (2011), *Dalla Spagna. Gli epigrammi 1–33 del XII libro di Marziale*, Bari.

Criado, Cecilia (2000), *La teología de la Tebaida Estaciana. El anti-virgilanismo de un clasicista*, Hildesheim-Zürich-New York.

Criado, Cecilia (2013), "The contradictions of Valerius' and Statius' Jupiter", in: G. Manuwald / A. Voigt 2013, 195–214.

Crook, John (1955), *Consilium principis*, Cambridge.

Dahlmann, Hellfried (1928), *De philosophorum Graecorum sententiis ad loquellae originem pertinentibus capita duo*, Diss. Leipzig.

Dahlmann, Hellfried (1932), *Varro und die hellenistische Sprachtheorie* (Problemata 5), Berlin-Zürich 1964.

Dams, Peter (1970), *Dichtungskritik bei nachaugusteischen Dichtern*, Diss. Marburg.

Daube, David (1976), "Martial, father of three", in: *AJAH* 1, 145–147.

David, Jean Michel (1983), "Le tribunal dans la basilique: évolution fonctionnelle et symbolique de la République à l'Empire", in: *Architecture et société. De l'archaïsme grec à la fin de la République. Actes du colloque de Rome (2–4 décembre 1980)*, 219–241.

Davis, Gregson (1991), *Polyhymnia: The Rhetoric of Horatian Discourse*, Berkeley.

Davis, Martha (1990), "*Ratis audax*: Valerius Flaccus' bold Ship", in: A. Boyle (ed.), 46–73.

Day, Henry J. M. (2013), *Lucan and the Sublime: Power, Representation and Aesthetic Experience*, Cambridge.

De Lacy, Phillip H. / De Lacy, Estelle A. (ed.) (1941), Philodemus, *On Methods of Inference. A Study in Ancient Empiricism*, Philadelphia.

De Sélincourt, Aubrey (transl.) (1972), *Livy: The War with Hannibal*, London.

Deferrari, Roy J. / Eagan, Clement M. (1942), *A Concordance of Statius*, Washington, DC.

Delarue, Fernand (1992), "Sur l'architecture des *Punica* de Silius Italicus", in: *REL* 70, 149–165.

Delarue, Fernand (2000), *Stace, poète épique: originalité et cohérence*, Louvain.

Delhey, Norbert (ed.) (1993), Apollinaris Sidonius, *Carm. 22*, Berlin.

Delz, Joseph (ed.) (1987), Silius Italicus, *Punica*, Stuttgart.

Deremetz, Alain (1995), *Le miroir des Muses: poétiques de la réflexivité à Rome*, Villeneuve d'Ascq.

Desbordes, Françoise (1979), *Argonautica: Trois études sur l'imitation dans la littérature antique*, Bruxelles.

Dieterich, Albrecht (1905), *Mutter Erde. Ein Versuch über Volksreligion*, Leipzig-Berlin.

Dilke, O.A.W. (ed.) (1954), Statius, *Achilleid*, Edited with introduction, apparatus criticus and notes, Cambridge.

Dix, T. Keith (1996), "Pliny's Library at Comum", in: *Libraries & Culture* 31, 85–102.

Dominik, William (1994), *The Mythic Voice of Statius. Power and Politics in the Thebaid*, Leiden-New York-Köln.

Dominik, William (2003), "Hannibal at the Gates: Programmatising Rome and *Romanitas* in Silius Italicus' *Punica* 1 and 2", in: A. Boyle / W. Dominik (eds.), *Flavian Rome: Culture, Image, Text*, Leiden, 469–497.

Dominik, William (2006), "Rome Then and Now: Linking the Saguntum and Cannae Episodes in Silius Italicus' *Punica*" in: R.R. Nauta / H-J. van Dam / J.J.L. Smolenaars (eds.), 113–127.

Dominik, William (2010), "Tacitus and Pliny on oratory", in: W. Dominik- / J. Hall (eds.), 323–338.

Dominik, William / Hall, John (eds.) (2010), *A Companion to Roman Rhetoric*, Oxford.

Dominik, William / Newlands, Carole / Gervais, Kyle (eds.) (2015), *Brill's Companion to Statius*, Leiden-Boston.

Doody, Aude (2009), "Authority and Authorship in the *Medicina Plinii*", in: L. Taub / A. Doody (eds.), *Authorial Voices in Greco-Roman Technical Writings*, Trier, 93–105.

Duff, J.D. (transl.) (1934), *Silius Italicus*, Cambridge, MA.

Dyck, Andrew R. (2008), "Rivals into partners. Hortensius and Cicero", in: *Historia* 57, 142–173.

Eckert, Alexandra (2016), *Lucius Cornelius Sulla in der antiken Erinnerung. Jener Mörder, der sich Felix nannte*, Berlin-Boston.

Eigler, Ulrich / Lefèvre, Eckard (eds.) (1998), Ratis omnia vincet 2: *Neue Untersuchungen zu den Argonautica des Valerius Flaccus*, München.

Ellis, Robinson (ed.) (1889²), *A Commentary on Catullus*, Oxonii.

Erler, Michael (1994), "Epikur"; "Die Schule Epikurs", "Lukrez", in: H. Flashar (ed.), *Grundriß der Geschichte der Philosophie, Die Philosophie der Antike. IV, Die hellenistische Philosophie*, 1. Halbbd., Basel, 29–490.

Ernesti, J.C.G. (1791–92), *Caii Silii Italici Punicorum libri septemdecim*, Leipzig.

Ernout, Alfred / Meillet, Antoine (1959⁴), *Dictionnaire étymologique de la langue latine*, Paris.

Fabbrini, Delphina (2007), *Il migliore dei mondi possibili. Gli epigrammi ecfrastici di Marziale per amici e protettori*, Firenze.

Fabre-Serris, Jacqueline (2008), *Rome, l'Arcadie et la mer des Argonautes*, Lille.

Fantazzi, Charles (ed.) (2004), Angelo Poliziano, *Silvae*, Cambridge, MA.

Fantham, Elaine (1979), "Statius' Achilles and his Trojan Model", in: *CQ* 29, 457–462.

Fantham, Elaine (1999), "*Chironis exemplum*: on teachers and surrogate fathers in *Achilleid* and *Silvae*", in: *Hermathena* 167, 59–70.

Fantham, Elaine (2011a), "Imitation and Evolution: The Discussion of Rhetorical Imitation in Cicero *De oratore* 2. 87–97 and Some Related Problems in Ciceronian Theory", in: E. Fantham, *Roman Readings. Roman Response to Greek Literature from Plautus to Statius and Quintilian*, Berlin-New York, 243–264.

Fantham, Elaine (2011b), "The Concept of Nature and Human Nature in Quintilian's Psychology and Theory of Instruction", in: E. Fantham, *Roman Readings. Roman Response to Greek Literature from Plautus to Statius and Quintilian*, Berlin-New York, 331–342.

Fantuzzi, Marco (2012), *Achilles in Love: Intertextual Studies*, Oxford.

Fedeli, Paolo (ed.) (1984), *Propertius*, Stuttgart.

Fedeli, Paolo (2004), "Marziale catulliano", in: *Humanitas* 56, 161–189.

Feeney, Denis (1982), *A Commentary on Silius Italicus Book 1*, Diss. Oxford.

Feeney, Denis (1991), *The Gods in Epic. Poets and Critics of the Classical Tradition*, Oxford.

Feeney, Denis (2002), "*Una cum scriptore meo*. Poetry, Principate and the Tradition of Literary History in the Epistle to Augustus", in: T. Woodman / D. Feeney (eds.), *Traditions & Contexts in the Poetry of Horace*, Cambridge, 172–182.

Feeney, Denis (2004), "*Tenui … latens discrimine*: Spotting the Differences in Statius' *Achilleid*", in: *MD* 52, 85–106.

Ferguson, John (1963), "Catullus and Martial", in: *PAfrClassAss* 6, 3–15.

Fordyce, Charles J. (ed.) (1961), Catullus, *A Commentary*, Oxford.

Fowler, Don (1995), "Martial and the book", in: *Ramus* 24, 31–58.

Fowler, Don (2000), *Roman Constructions: Readings in Postmodern Latin*, Oxford.

Fraenkel, Eduard (1957), *Horace*, Oxford.

Fraenkel, Eduard (1966), "*Nam satis beatus*", in: *MH* 23, 114–117.

Franchet d'Espèrey, Sylvie (1999), *Conflit, violence et non-violence dans la Thébaïde de Stace*, Paris.

Frass, Monika (2009), "Intervention und Protektion in den Briefen Plinius des Jüngeren. Empfehlungsschreiben für Voconius Romanus", in: Chr. Antenhofer / M. Müller (eds.), *Briefe in politischer Kommunikation vom Alten Orient bis ins 20. Jahrhundert*, Göttingen, 67–82.

Fredricksmeyer, Hardy C. (2001), "A diachronic reading of Sappho fr. 16 LP", in: *TAPhA* 131, 75–86.

Frère, Henri / Izaac, H.J. (eds.) (1944), Stace, *Silves*, I–II, Paris.

Friedlaender, Ludwig (ed.) (1886), *M. Valerii Martialis epigrammaton libri*, I–II, Leipzig.

Frings, Irene (1991), *Gespräch und Handlung in der Thebais des Statius*, Stuttgart.

Frisby, Danielle M. (2013), *Epic Precedence: Statius' Thebaid and its Intertextual Links to the Iliad of Homer*, Diss. Nottingham.

Froesch, Hermann H. (1968), *Ovids Epistulae ex Ponto I–III als Gedichtsammlung*, Diss. Bonn.

Fröhlich, Uwe (2000), *Regulus, Archetyp der römischer Fides: Das sechste Buch als Schlüssel zu den Punica des Silius Italicus*, Tübingen.

Fucecchi, Marco (1996), "Il restauro dei modelli antichi: tradizione epica e tecnica manieristica in Valerio Flacco", in: *MD* 36, 101–165 [repr. in: A. Augoustakis (ed.) (2016), *Flavian Epic* (Oxford Readings in Classical Studies), Oxford, 80–110].

Fucecchi, Marco (2009), "Ovidio e la nuova bucolica di Calpurnio: osservazioni e proposte", in: L. Landolfi / R. Oddo (eds.), *'Fer propius tua lumina': Giochi intertestuali nella poesia di Calpurnio Siculo* (Incontri sulla poesia latina di età imperiale 2), Bologna, 41–65.

Fucecchi, Marco (2010), "The Shield and the Sword: Q. Fabius Maximus and M. Claudius Marcellus as Models of Heroism in Silius' *Punica*", in: A. Augoustakis (ed.), 219–239.

Fucecchi, Marco (2013a), "Looking for the Giants. Mythological Imagery and Discourse on Power in Flavian Epic", in: G. Manuwald / A. Voigt (eds.), 107–122.

Fucecchi, Marco (2013b), "With (a) God on Our Side; Ancient Ritual Practices and Imagery in Flavian Epic", in: A. Augoustakis (ed.), 17–32.

Fucecchi, Marco (2014a), "The Philosophy of Power. Greek Literary tradition and Silius' *On Kingship*", in: A. Augoustakis (ed.), 305–324.

Fucecchi, Marco (2014b), "War and Love in Valerius Flaccus' *Argonautica*", in: M. Heerink / G. Manuwald (eds.), 115–135.

Fucecchi, Marco (2015), "Passato da rimuovere e passato da rivivere: l'incubo della guerra civile (e la sua 'metabolizzazione') nell'epica flavia", in: P. Esposito / Chr. Walde (eds.), *Letture e lettori di Lucano*, Pisa, 231–253.

Fucecchi, Marco (forthcoming a), "Constructing (super-)characters: the case study of Silius' Hannibal", in: N. Coffee / C. Forstall / L. Galli / D. Nelis (eds.).

Fucecchi, Marco (forthcoming b), "Flavian Epic: Roman Ways of 'Metabolizing' a Cultural Nightmare?", in: L. Ginsberg / D. Krasne (eds.), *After 69 CE: Writing Civil War in Flavian Rome*, Berlin-Boston.

Fuhrmann, Manfred (1997), "Zur Prozesstaktik Ciceros. Die Mordanklage gegen Sextus Roscius von Ameria und Cluentius Habitus", in: U. Manthe / J. von Ungern-Sternberg (eds.), *Grosse Prozesse der römischen Antike*, München, 48–61.

Fusi, Alessandro (ed.) (2006), *M. Valerii Martialis Epigrammaton liber tertius*, introduzione, edizione critica, traduzione e commento, Hildesheim-Zürich-New York.

Fusi, Alessandro (2013), "La recensio gennadiana e il testo di Marziale", in: *S&T* 11, 79–122.

Fusillo, Massimo (ed.) (1988), [Omero], *La battaglia delle rane e dei topi. Batrachomyomachia*, prefazione di Franco Montanari, appendice di Caterina Carpinato, Milano.

Gagliardi, Lorenzo (2002), *"Decemviri" e "centumviri"*, Milano.

Galli, Daniela (ed.) (2007), *Valerii Flacci Argonautica I: Commento*, Berlin-New York.

Gamberini, Federico (1983), *Stylistic Theory and Practice in the Younger Pliny*, Hildesheim-Zürich-New York.

Ganiban, Randall T. (2007), *Statius and Virgil. The Thebaid and the Reinterpretation of the Aeneid*, Cambridge.

Ganiban, Randall T. (2010), "Virgil's Dido and the Heroism of Hannibal in Silius' *Punica*", in: A. Augoustakis (ed.), 73–98.

Garson, R.W. (1964), "Some Critical Observations on Valerius Flaccus. I", in: *CQ* 14, 267–279.

Gärtner, Thomas (2010), "Überlegungen zur Makostruktur der *Punica*", in: F. Schaffenrath (ed.), *Silius Italicus. Akten der Innsbrucker Tagung vom 19.–21. Juni 2008*, Frankfurt am Main, 77–96.

Gärtner, Ursula (1998), *"Quae Magis Aspera Curis Nox:* Zur Bedeutung der Tageszeiten bei Valerius Flaccus", in: *Hermes* 126: 202–220.

Gavi, Emanuele (2007), "Riprese di Catullo in Marziale", in: *FuturAntico* 4, 119–154.

Genette, Gérard (1987), *Seuils*, Paris.

Gentili, Bruno (1985), "Cultura dell'improvviso. Poesia orale colta nel Settecento italiano e poesia greca dell'età arcaica e classica", in: B. Gentili / G. Paioni (eds.), *Oralità. Cultura, letteratura, discorso. Atti del convegno internazionale (Urbino 21–25 luglio 1980)*, Roma, 365–408.

Gibson, Bruce (2006a), "The *Silvae* and Epic", in: R. Nauta / H.-J. van Dam / J.J.L. Smolenaars (eds.), 163–183.

Gibson, Bruce (ed.) (2006b), Statius, *Silvae 5*, Edited with Introduction, Translation and Commentary, Oxford.

Gibson, Bruce (2010), "Silius Italicus: A Consular Historian?" in: A. Augoustakis (ed.), 47–72.

Gibson, Bruce (2013a), "Praise in Flavian epic", in: G. Manuwald / A. Voigt (eds.), 67–86.

Gibson, Bruce (2013b), "Pliny and the Letters of Sidonius: from Constantius and Clarus to Firminus and Fuscus", in: *Arethusa* 46, 333–355.

Gibson, Roy K. (2003), "Pliny and the art of (in)offensive self-praise", in: *Arethusa* 36, 235–254.

Gibson, Roy K. / Morello, Ruth (2012), *Reading the Letters of Pliny the Younger*, Cambridge.

Gilligan, Carol (1982), *In a Different Voice. Psychological Theory and Women's Development*, Cambridge, MA.

Gilmartin, K. (1975), "Rhetorical Figure in Latin Historical Style: The Imaginary Second Person Singular", in: *TAPhA* 105, 99–121.

Ginsberg, Lauren / Krasne, Darcy (eds.), (forthcoming), *After 69 CE: Writing Civil War in Flavian Rome*, Berlin-Boston.

Goldhill, Simon (1991), *The Poet's Voice: Essays on Poetics and Greek Literature*, Cambridge.

Gombrich, Ernst Hans (1966), "The Debate on Primitivism in Ancient Rhetoric", in: *Journal of the Warburg and Courtauld Institutes* 29, 24–38.

Grasmuück, E. L. (1978), *Exilium. Untersuchungen zur Verbannung in der Antike,* Paderhorn.

Grebe, Sabine (2000), "Kriterien für die *Latinitas* bei Varro und Quintilian", in: A. Haltenhoff / F.-H. Mutschler (eds.), *Hortus litterarum antiquarum. Festschrift für Hans Armin Gärtner zum 70. Geburtstag*, Heidelberg, 191–210.

Grewe, Stephanie (1998), "Der Einfluss von Senecas *Medea* auf die *Argonautica* des Valerius Flaccus", in: U. Eigler / E. Lefèvre (eds.), 173–190.

Grewing, Farouk (1996), "Möglichkeiten und Grenzen des Vergleichs: Martials 'Diadumenos' und Catulls 'Lesbia'", in: *Hermes* 124, 333–354.

Grewing, Farouk (ed.) (1997), Martial, *Buch VI. Ein Kommentar*, Göttingen.

Grewing, Farouk (ed.) (1998), *Toto notus in orbe. Perspektiven der Martial-Interpretation*, Stuttgart.

Groag, Edmund (1931), "Cornelius Orfitus" n. 359, in: *RE* IV A 1 1931, 1506–1507.

Gutzwiller, Kathryn (1998), *Poetics Garlands. Hellenistic Epigrams in Context*, London.

Håkanson, Lennart (2013), *Unveröffentlichte Schriften.* I, *Studien zu den pseudoquintilianischen Declamationes maiores,* hrsg. von Biagio Santorelli, Berlin-Boston.

Hardie, Alex (1983), *Statius and the Silvae. Poets, Patrons and Epideixis in the Graeco-Roman World*, Liverpool.

Hardie, Philip (1993), *The Epic Successors of Virgil. A Study in the Dynamics of a Tradition*, Cambridge.

Hardie, Philip (1997), "Virgil and Tragedy", in: Ch. Martindale (ed.), *The Cambridge Companion to Virgil*, 312–326.

Hardie, Philip (2009), *Lucretian Receptions*, Cambridge.

Hardie, Philip / Moore, Helen (eds.) (2010), *Classical Literary Careers and Their Reception*, Cambridge-New York.

Harries, Jill (1994) *Sidonius Apollinaris and the Fall of Rome*, Oxford.

Harrison, Stephen J. (1992), "The arms of Capaneus. Statius, *Thebaid* 4,165–77", in: *CQ* 42, 247–252.

Hartz, Cornelius (2007), *Catulls Epigramme im Kontext hellenistischer Dichtung*, Berlin-New York.

Hauser, Manfred (1954), *Der römische Begriff 'cura'*, Diss. Basel.

Häussler, Reinhard (1978), *Das historische Epos von Lucan bis Silius und seine Theorie. Studien zum historischen Epos der Antike.* II, *Geschichtliche Epik nach Virgil,* Heidelberg.

Heerink, Mark / Manuwald, Gesine (eds.) (2014), *Brill's Companion to Valerius Flaccus,* Leiden-Boston.

Held, Virginia (2005), *The Ethics of Care: Personal, Political, and Global,* Oxford.

Heldmann, Konrad (1980), "Dekadenz und literarischer Fortschritt bei Quintilian und bei Tacitus. Ein Beitrag zum römischen Klassizismus", in: *Poetica* 12, 1–23.

Heldmann, Konrad (1982), *Antike Theorien über Entwicklung und Verfall der Redekunst,* München.

Helzle, Martin (ed.) (2003), *Ovids Epistulae ex Ponto. Buch I–II. Kommentar,* Heidelberg.

Henriksén, Christer (1998), "Martial und Statius", in: F. Grewing (ed.), *Toto notus in orbe. Perspektiven der Martial-Interpretation,* Stuttgart, 77–118.

Henriksén, Christer (ed.) (1999), Martial, *Book IX. A Commentary,* Uppsala.

Heraeus, Wilhelm (ed.) (1976²), *M. Valerii Martialis epigrammaton libri,* Editionem correctiorem cur. I. Borowskij, Lipsiae.

Hershkowitz, Debra (1998), *Valerius Flaccus' Argonautica: Abbreviated Voyages in Silver Latin Epic,* Oxford.

Heslin, Peter J. (2005), *The Transvestite Achilles. Gender and Genre in Statius' Achilleid,* Cambridge.

Heurgon, Jacques (1969), "Les sortilèges d'un avocat sous Trajan", in: J. Bibauw (ed.), *Hommages à Marcel Renard,* I, Bruxelles, 443–448.

Hill, Donald E. (ed.) (1996), *P. Papini Stati Thebaidos Libri XII,* Leiden.

Hinds, Stephen (1985), "Booking the Return Trip: Ovid and *Tristia* 1", in: *PCPS* 31, 13–32.

Hinds, Stephen (1998), *Allusion and Intertext. Dynamics of Appropriation in Roman Poetry,* Cambridge.

Hinds, Stephen (2000), *Essential Epic: Genre and Gender from Macer to Statius,* in: M. Depew / D. Obbink (eds.), *Matrices of Genre: Authors, Canons, and Society,* Cambridge, MA-London, 221–244.

Hinds, Stephen (2007), "Martial's Ovid/Ovid' Martial", in: *JRS* 97, 113–154.

Hinz, Vinko (2001), *Nunc Phalaris doctum protulit ecce caput. Antike Phalarislegende und Nachleben der Phalarisbriefe,* München-Leipzig.

Hollis, Adrian S. (ed.) (1990), Callimachus, *Hecale,* Oxford.

Holzberg, Niklas (2002), *Martial und das antike Epigramm,* Darmstadt.

Holzberg, Niklas (2004), "*Illud quod medium est:* middles in Martial", in: S. Kyriakidis / F. De Martino (eds.), *Middles in Latin Poetry,* Bari, 245–260.

Horsfall, Nicholas (ed.) (2013), Virgil, *Aeneid 6: A Commentary,* Berlin.

Howell, Peter (1980), *A Commentary on Book One of the Epigrams of Martial,* London.

Hunter, Richard (1987), "Medea's Flight: The Fourth Book of the *Argonautica*", in: *CQ* 37, 129–139.

Hunter, Richard (ed.) (1989), Apollonius of Rhodes, *Argonautica Book III,* Cambridge.

Hunter, Richard (1993), *The Argonautica of Apollonius Rhodius: Literary Studies,* Cambridge.

Hutchinson, Gregory O. (1988), *Hellenistic Poetry,* Oxford.

Hutchinson, Gregory O. (2014), *Greek to Latin: Frameworks and Contexts for Intertextuality,* Oxford.

Jansen, Laura (ed.) (2014), *Roman Paratext. Frame, Texts, Readers,* Cambridge.

Jauß, Hans Robert (1974⁴), "Literaturgeschichte als Provokation der Literaturwissenschaft", in: H.R. Jauß, *Literaturgeschichte als Provokation*, Frankfurt am Main, 144–207.

Johannsen, Nina (2006), *Dichter über ihre Gedichte. Die Prosavorreden in den Epigrammaton libri Martials und in den Siluae des Statius*, Göttingen.

Jonca, Maciej (2009), "The scope of *exilium voluntarium* in the Roman republic", in: B. Santalucia (ed.), *La repressione criminale nella Roma repubblicana fra norma e persuasione*, Pavia, 77–91.

Juhnke, Herbert (1972), *Homerisches in römischer Epik flavischer Zeit. Untersuchungen zu Szenennachbildungen und Strukturentsprechungen in Statius' Thebais und Achilleis und in Silius' Punica*, München.

Kaufmann, Helen (2015), "Papinius Noster: Statius in Roman Late Antiquity", in: W. Dominik / C. Newlands / K. Gervais (eds.), *Brill Companion to Statius*, Leiden, 481–496.

Kay, Nigel M. (ed.) (1985), Martial, *Book XI. A Commentary*, London.

Keith, Alison M. (2000), *Engendering Rome. Women in Latin Epic*, Cambridge.

Keith, Alison M. (2010), "Engendering Orientalism in Silius' *Punica*", in: A. Augoustakis (ed.), 355–376.

Keith, Alison M. (2014a), "*Poetae Ovidiani*. Ovid's *Metamorphoses* in Imperial Roman Epic", in: J. Miller / C. Newlands (eds.), 70–85.

Keith, Alison M. (2014b), "Valerius and Ovid", in: M. Heerink / G. Manuwald (eds.), 269–289.

Kelly, Gordon P. (2006), *A history of Exile in the Roman Republic*, Cambridge.

Kennedy, George (1969), *Quintilian*, New York.

Kennedy, George (1972), *The Art of Rhetoric in the Roman World*, Princeton.

Kennedy, George (1978), "Encolpius and Agamemnon in Petronius", in: *AJPh* 99, 171–178.

Kenney, Edward J. (1984), "The Mosella of Ausonius", in: *G&R* 31, 190–202.

Ker, Walter C.A. (ed. and transl.) (1919–1920), Martial, *Epigrams*, I–II, London-New York.

Kershner, Stephen M. (2008), *Self-fashioning and Horatian Allusion in Statius's Silvae*, Diss. SUNY-Buffalo.

Kirk, Geoffrey S. (1985), *The Iliad: A Commentary. Volume 1: Books 1–4*, Cambridge.

Kleywegt, Anton (ed.) (2005), Valerius Flaccus, *Argonautica Book 1: A Commentary*, Leiden.

Klingner, Friedrich (ed.) 1982, Horatius, *Opera*, Stuttgart.

Klinnert, Thomas C. (1970), *Capaneus – Hippomedon. Interpretationen zur Heldendarstellung in der Thebais des P. Papinius Statius*, Diss. Berlin.

Knight, Virginia H. (1995), *The Renewal of Epic: Response to Homer in the Argonautica of Apollonius Rhodius*, Leiden.

Korfmacher, W. Ch. (1946), "Pliny and the gentleman of Cicero's Offices", in: *CW* 40, 50–53.

Korn, Mathias / Tschiedel, Hans Jürgen (eds.) (1991), *Ratis omnia vincet: Untersuchungen zu den Argonautica des Valerius Flaccus*, Hildesheim.

Körte, Alfred (1934), "Euripides' *Skyrier*", in: *Hermes* 69, 1–12.

Koster, Severin (1979), "Liebe und Krieg in der *Achilleis* des Statius", in: *WJA* 5, 189–208.

Krevans, Nita (2002–2003), "Dido, Hypsipyle, and the bedclothes", in: *Hermathena* 173/4, 175–183.

Kroll, Wilhelm (ed.) (1989⁷), *Catull*, Stuttgart.

Kühner, Raphael / Stegmann, Carl (1955³), *Ausführliche Grammatik der lateinischen Sprache*, Teil 2: Satzlehre, I–II, Hannover.

Kullmann, Wolfgang (1980), "Zu den historischen Voraussetzungen der Beweismethoden des Lukrez", in: *RhM* n.F. 123, 97–125.

Küppers, Joachim (1986), *Tantarum causas irarum: Untersuchungen zur einleitenden Bücherdyade der Punica des Silius Italicus,* Berlin.

Labate, Mario (1987), "Elegia triste ed elegia lieta. Un caso di riconversione letteraria", in: *MD* 19, 91–129.

Labate, Mario (1990), "Forme della letteratura, immagini del mondo. Da Catullo a Ovidio", in: A. Schiavone (ed.), *Storia di Roma*, 2 (*L'impero mediterraneo*). I (*La repubblica imperiale*), Torino, 923–965.

Laguna, Gabriel (ed.) (1992), Estacio, *Silvas III. Introducción, Edición crítica, traducción y comentario*, Madrid.

Laguna Mariscal, Gabriel (2006), "Satirical elements in Statius' *Silvae:* A literary and sociological approach", in: R.R. Nauta / H.-J. van Dam / J.J.L. Smolenaars (eds.), 245–255.

Laudizi, Giovanni (1989), *Silio Italico: il passato tra mito e restaurazione etica,* Galatina.

Laurens, Pierre (1965), "Martial et l'epigramme du Ier siècle ap. J.-C.", in: *REL* 43, 315–341.

Laurens, Pierre (2012²), *L'abeille dans l'ambre. Célébration de l'épigramme de l'époque alexandrine à la fin de la Renaissance*, Paris.

Lausberg, Marion (1982), *Das Einzeldistichon. Studien zum antiken Epigramm*, München.

Lawall, G. (1966), "Apollonius' *Argonautica:* Jason as Anti-Hero", in: *YCS* 19, 119–169.

Lazenby, John F. (1978), *Hannibal's War: A Military History of the Second Punic War,* Warminster.

Lazenby, John F. (1996), "Was Maharbal right?", in: T. Cornell / B. Rankov / P. Sabin (eds.), *The Second Punic War: A Reappraisal* (BICS Supplement 67), London.

Leach, Eleanor W. (1994), "Horace *Carmen* 1.8: Achilles, the Campus Martius, and the Articulation of Gender Roles in Augustan Rome", in: *CP* 89, 334–343.

Leary, Timothy J. (ed.) (1996), Martial, *Book XIV. The Apophoreta,* text with introduction and commentary, London.

Leary, Timothy J. (ed.) (2001), Martial, *Book 13: The Xenia*, text with introduction and commentary, London.

Leberl, Jens (2004), *Domitian und die Dichter. Poesie als Medium der Herrschaftsdarstellung*, Göttingen.

Lechi, Francesca (1978), "La palinodia del poeta elegiaco: i carmi ovidiani dell'esilio", in: *A&R* 23, 1–22.

Leeman, Anton D. (1974), *Orationis ratio. Teoria e pratica stilistica degli oratori, storici e filosofi latini*, tr. it., Bologna.

Lefèvre, Eckard (2009), *Vom Römertum zum Ästhetizismus. Studien zu den Briefen des jüngeren Plinius*, Berlin-New York.

Lehmann, Erwin (1931), *Antike Martialsausgaben*, Diss. Jena.

Leigh, Matthew (2006), "Statius and the sublimity of Capaneus", in: M.J. Clarke / B.F.G. Currie / and R.O.A.M. Lyne (eds.), *Epic Interactions. Perspectives on Homer, Virgil, and the Epic Tradition. Presented to Jasper Griffin*, Oxford, 217–241.

Levene, David S. (2010), *Livy on the Hannibalic War*, Oxford.

Levick, Barbara (1985), "L. Verginius Rufus and the four emperors", in: *RhM* 127, 318–346.

Liberman, Gauthier (ed. and transl.) (1997), Valerius Flaccus, *Argonautiques, Chants I–IV,* Paris.

Liberman, Gauthier (ed.) (2010), Stace, *Silves. Édition et commentaire critiques*, Paris.

Liebs, Detlef (1967), "Die Herkunft der Regel *bis de eadem re ne sit actio*", in: *ZRG* 84,104–132.

Lindsay, Wallace M. (ed.) (1929²), *M. Valeri Martialis Epigrammata*, Oxonii.

Littlewood, R. Joy (2013), "Upstaging Juno: Minerva's (Flavian) role in Proteus' Judgement of Paris (Silius Italicus, *Punica* 7. 409–93)", in: H. Wiegand / R. Düchting (eds.), *Aridus Frugifer, Michael von Albrecht zum achtzigsten Geburtstag*, Heidelberg.

Littlewood, R. Joy (2017), *A Commentary on Silius Italicus' Punica 10*, Oxford.

Lobato, Jésus H. (2010), "*Sterilis Camena*. El Carmen 9 de Sidonio Apolinar o la muerte de la poesia", in: *Acme* 63.1, 97–133.

Lobur, John A. (2007), "*Festinatio* (Haste), *Brevitas* (Concision), and the Generation of Imperial Ideology in Velleius Paterculus", in: *TAPhA* 137, 211–230.

Lomanto, Valeria (1994), "Il sistema del *sermo latinus* in Quintiliano", in: *Voce di molte acque. Miscellanea di Studi offerti a Eugenio Corsini*, Torino, 237–256.

Lorenz, Sven (2002), *Erotik und Panegyrik. Martials epigrammatische Kaiser*, Tübingen.

Lorenz, Sven (2004), "Waterscape with Black and White: Epigrams, Cycles, and Webs in Martial's *Epigrammaton Liber Quartus*", in: *AJPh* 125, 255–278.

Lorenz, Sven (2007), "Catullus and Martial", in: M. B. Skinner (ed.), *A Companion to Catullus*, Malden, MA, 418–438.

Lovatt, Helen V. (1999), "Competing endings: re-reading the end of Statius' *Thebaid* through Lucan", in: *Ramus* 28, 126–151.

Lovatt, Helen V. (2005), *Statius and Epic Games: Sport, Politics and Poetics in the Thebaid*, Cambridge.

Lovatt, Helen V. (2007), *Statius' Thebaid and the Poetics of Civil War*, Cambridge.

Lovatt, Helen V. (2013), *The Epic Gaze: Vision, Gender and Narrative in Ancient Epic*, Cambridge.

Malamud, Martha A. (2007), "A Spectacular Feast: *Silvae* 4.2", in: *Arethusa* 40, 223–244.

Malaspina, Ermanno (2013), "La formation et l'usage du titre *Silvae* en latin classique", in: P. Galand / S. Laigneau (eds.), *La silve. Historie d'une écriture libérée en Europe de l'antiquité au XVIIIᵉ siècle* (Latinitates 5), Turnhout, 17–43.

Manioti, Nikoletta (ed.), 2016, *Family in Flavian Epic*, Leiden-Boston.

Manolaraki, Eleni (2005), "A picture worth a thousand words: Revisiting Bedriacum (Tacitus *Histories* 2.70)", in: *CPh* 100, 243–267.

Manolaraki, Eleni (2010), "Silius' Natural History: Tides in the *Punica*", in: A. Augoustakis (ed.), 293–321.

Manolaraki, Eleni / Augoustakis, Antony (2012), "Silius Italicus and Tacitus on the Tragic Hero", in: V. Pagán (ed.), *Blackwell Companion to Tacitus*, Malden, MA, 386–402.

Manuwald, Gesine (1999), *Die Cyzicus-Episode und ihre Funktion in den Argonautica des Valerius Flaccus*, Göttingen.

Manuwald, Gesine / Voigt, Astrid (eds.) (2013), *Flavian Epic Interactions* (Trends in Classics Supplementary Volumes 21), Berlin-Boston.

Marastoni, Aldo (ed.) (1974), *P. Papini Stati Achilleis*, Stuttgart.

Marchesi, Ilaria (2008), *The Art of Pliny's Letters*, Cambridge.

Marks, Raymond (2005a), "*Per vulnera regnum*: Self-Destruction, Self-Sacrifice and *Devotio* in Punica 4–10", in: *Ramus* 34, 127–151.

Marks, Raymond (2005b), *From Republic to Empire: Scipio Africanus in the Punica of Silius Italicus*, Frankfurt am Main.

Marks, Raymond (2008), "Getting Ahead: Decapitation as Political Metaphor in Silius Italicus' *Punica*", in: *Mnemosyne* 61, 66–88.

Marks, Raymond (2010), "Silius and Lucan", in: A. Augoustakis (ed.), 127–153.

Marks, Raymond (2013), "Reconcilable Differences: Anna Perenna and the Battle of Cannae in the *Punica*", in: A. Augoustakis (ed.), 287–301.

Marks, Raymond (forthcoming), "A Medial Proem and the Macrostructures of the *Punica*", in: Chr. Schmitz (ed.), *Anfänge und Enden. Narrative Potentiale des antiken und nachantiken Epos*, Heidelberg.

Marpicati, Paolo (1999), "Silio 'delatore' di Pompeo (*Pun.* 5. 328ss; 10. 305ss)", in: *MD* 43, 191–202.

Marsilio, Maria S. (2008), "Mendicancy and Competition in Catullus 23 and Martial 12,32", in: *Latomus* 67, 918–930.

Martin, Michel (1980), "Le Carmen Bucolique dans l'Univers Épique: Daphnis et le 'Pseudo-Daphnis' ou le Reflet Trompeur (Silius Italicus, *Punica* XIV)", in: *Orphea Voce: Cahiers du Groupe de recherches sur la poésie latine*, Bordeaux, 149–175.

Martin, Michel (1990), "Silius Italicus lecteur d'Horace", in: *Orphea Voce: Cahiers du Groupe de recherches sur la poésie latine*, Bordeaux, 135–158.

Mastrorosa, Ida (2010a), "*Principes in Caesaris amicitia:* oratori e consenso 'negoziato' in età flavia", in: G. Petrone / A. Casamento (eds.), *Studia ... in umbra educata. Percorsi della retorica latina in età imperiale*, Palermo, 173–187.

Mastrorosa, Ida (2010b), "La pratica dell'oratoria giudiziaria nell'alto impero: Quintiliano e Plinio il Giovane", in: P. Galand-Hallyn / F. Hallynt / C. Lévy / W. Verbaal (eds.), *Quintilien: ancien et moderne. Études réunies*, Turnhout, 125–152.

Mattiacci, Silvia (2007a), "Marziale e la fortuna del neoterismo nella prima età imperiale", in: S. Mattiacci / A. Perruccio, *Anti-mitologia ed eredità neoterica in Marziale. Genesi e forme di una poetica*, Ospedaletto (Pisa), 137–218, partially reprinted in: Mattiacci 2007b, 178–195.

Mattiacci, Silvia (2007b), "Marziale e il neoterismo", in: A. Bonadeo / E. Romano (eds.), *Dialogando con il passato. Permanenze e innovazioni nella cultura latina di età flavia*, Firenze, 177–206.

Mattiacci, Silvia (2016), „"I *lascivi versus* di Augusto citati da Marziale e la tecnica dell'epigramma nell'epigramma", in: B. Pieri / D. Pellacani (eds.), *Si verba tenerem. Studi sulla poesia latina in frammenti*, Berlin-Boston, 111–132.

Mayer, Roland G. (2003), "Pliny and *gloria dicendi*", in: *Arethusa* 36, 227–234.

Mazzoli, Giancarlo (1970), *Seneca e la poesia*, Milano 1970.

McGuire, Donald T. (1995), "History Compressed: Roman Names of Silius' Cannae Episode", in: *Latomus* 54, 110–118.

McGuire, Donald T. (1997), *Acts of Silence: Civil War, Tyranny and Suicide in the Flavian Epics,* Hildesheim.

McKeown, James C. (ed.) (1987), Ovid, *Amores. Text, Prolegomena and Commentary in four volumes. I, Text and Prolegomena*, Liverpool.

McNelis, Charles (2004), "Middle-March: Statius' *Thebaid* 7 and the Beginning of Battle Narrative", in: F. De Martino / S. Kyriakidis (eds.), *Middles in Latin Poetry*, Bari, 261–310.

McNelis, Charles (2007), *Statius' Thebaid and the Poetics of Civil War,* Cambridge.

Merli, Elena (1993), "Ordinamento degli epigrammi e strategie cortigiane negli esordi dei libri I–XII di Marziale", in: *Maia* 45, 229–256.

Merli, Elena (1998), "Epigrammzyklen und 'serielle Lektüre' in den Büchern Martials. Überlegungen und Beispiele", in: F. Grewing (ed.), 139–156.

Merli, Elena (2000), *Arma canant alii: materia epica e narrazione elegiaca nei Fasti di Ovidio*, Firenze.

Merli, Elena (2006a), "Identity and irony. Martial's tenth book, Horace, and the tradition of Roman satire", in: R.R. Nauta / H.-J. van Dam / J.J.L. Smolenaars (eds.), 257–270.

Merli, Elena (2006b), "Martial between Rome and Bilbilis", in: R.M. Rosen and I. Sluiter (eds.), *City, Contryside and the Spatial Organisation of Value in Classical Antiquity*, Leiden-Boston, 327–347.

Merli, Elena (2008), "*Cenabis belle*. Rappresentazione e struttura negli epigrammi di invito a cena di Marziale", in: A.M. Morelli (ed.), 299–326.

Merli, Elena (2009), "L'illusione callimachea. Acqua ispiratrice e strategia di comunicazione in Marziale 8, 70", in: *Quaderni del Dip. di Filologia linguistica e tradizione classica "Augusto Rostagni"* n.s. 8, 43–63.

Merli, Elena (2013), *Dall'Elicona a Roma. Sorso ispiratore e lima poetica nell'Ovidio dell'esilio e nella poesia flavia di omaggio*, Berlin-Boston.

Méthy, Nicole (2007), *Le lettres de Pline le Jeune. Une représentation de l'homme*, Paris.

Mette, Hans Joachim (1961), "*Genus tenue* and *mensa tenuis* bei Horaz", in: *Museum Helveticum* 18, 136–139.

Meyer, Heinrich (1842), *Oratorum Romanorum fragmenta ab Appio inde Caeco et M. Porcio Catone usque ad Q. Aurelium Symmachum*, Turici (= ORF²).

Mezzanotte, Alessandro (1995), "Echi del mondo contemporaneo in Silio Italico", in: *RIL* 129, 357–388.

Micozzi, Laura (2007), *Il catalogo degli eroi: Saggio di commento a Stazio Tebaide 4,1–344*, Pisa.

Miller, John F. / Newlands, Carole E. (eds.) (2014), *A Handbook to the Reception of Ovid*, Malden, MA-Oxford-Chichester.

Miltner, Franz (1931), "*Sulpicius*" n. 30, in: *RE* IV A 1, 745–746.

Mindt, Nina (2013), *Martials 'epigrammatischer Kanon'*, München.

Morelli, Alfredo M. (2003), "Cicerón, epigrama 1 Soubiran: cuestiones de atribución e interpretación histórica y lingüística", in: *Myrtia* 18, 169–187.

Morelli, Alfredo M. (2007), "Hellenistic Epigram in the Roman World. From the Beginnings to the End of the Republican Age", in: P. Bing / J. Bruss (eds.), *Brill's Companion to Hellenistic Epigram*, Leiden-Boston, 521–541.

Morelli, Alfredo M. (ed.) (2008), *Epigramma longum. Da Marziale alla tarda antichità. From Martial to Late Antiquity. Atti del Convegno internazionale, Cassino, 29–31 maggio 2006*, I-II, Cassino.

Morelli, Alfredo M. (2008a), "Epigramma longum: in cerca di una *basanos* per il genere epigrammatico", in: A.M. Morelli (ed.), 17–51.

Morelli, Alfredo M. (2008b), "Gli epigrammi erotici 'lunghi' in distici di Catullo e Marziale. Morfologia e statuto di genere", in: A.M. Morelli (ed.), 81–130.

Morelli, Alfredo M. (2009), "Sighs of lost love: The Rufus cycle in Martial (Mart. 1.68 and 1.106)", in: *CPh* 104, 34–49.

Morelli, Alfredo M. (2012), "Il *lepos* di Catullo", in: *Eikasmos* 23, 467–488.

Morelli, Alfredo M. (forthcoming a), "*Ceveant versiculi*. Per l'esegesi di Catull. 16,9–11", forthcoming in: *MD*.

Morelli, Alfredo M. (forthcoming b), "Entre le petit et le ridicule. Pour une histoire comparée dé l'épigramme satirique grecque et latine", forthcoming in: D. Meyer / C. Urlacher-Becht (eds.), *La rhétorique du petit dans l'épigramme grecque et latine*.

Moreno Soldevila, Rosario (2004), "Algunas apreciaciones sobre la estructura del libro IV de Marcial", in: *Faventia* 26, 99–109 (http://ddd.uab.es/pub/faventia/02107570v26n2p99.pdf).

Mori, Anatole (2008), *The Politics of Apollonius Rhodius' Argonautica*, Cambridge.

Moskalew, Walter (1982), *Formular Language and Poetic Design in the Aeneid*, Leiden.

Mratschek, Sigrid (2003), "*Illa nostra Italia*. Plinius und die 'Wiedergeburt' der Literatur in der Transpadana", in: L. Castagna / E. Lefèvre (eds.), *Plinius der jüngere und seine Zeit*, München, 219–244.

Mudry, Philippe (ed.) (1982), *La préface du De medicina de Celse. Texte, traduction et commentaire*, Roma.

Mueller, Melissa (2010), "Helen's Hands: Weaving for Kleos in the *Odyssey*", in: *Helios* 37, 1–21.

Münkel, Gabriele (1959), *Redner und Redekunst in den historischen Schriften des Tacitus*, Diss. Würzburg.

Murgatroyd, Paul (2009), *A Commentary on Book 4 of Valerius Flaccus' Argonautica*, Leiden-Boston.

Murphy, Trevor (2004), *Pliny the Elder's Natural History. The Empire in the Encyclopaedia*, Oxford.

Myers, S. (2005), "*Docta Otia:* Garden Ownership and Configurations of Leisure in Statius and Pliny the Younger", in: *Arethusa* 38, 103–129.

Nagle, Rebecca (2009), "Statius' Horatian Lyrics, *Silvae* 4.5 and 4.7", in: *CW* 102, 143–157.

Nauta, Ruurd R. (2002), *Poetry for Patrons. Literary Communication in the Age of Domitian*, Leiden-Boston-Köln.

Nauta, Ruurd R. (2006), "The *recusatio* in Flavian Poetry", in: R.R. Nauta / H.-J. van Dam / J.J.L. Smolenaars (eds.), 21–40.

Nauta, Ruurd R. (2008), "Statius in the *Silvae*", in: J.J.L. Smolenaars / H.-J. van Dam / R.R. Nauta (eds.), 143–174.

Nauta, Ruurd R. / van Dam, Harm-Jan / Smolenaars, Johannes J.L. (eds.) (2006), *Flavian Poetry*, Leiden-Boston.

Neger, Margot (2012), *Martials Dichtergedichte: das Epigramm als Medium der poetischen Selbstreflexion*, Tübingen.

Németh, Béla (1971), "Notes on Catullus, c. 23", in: *ACD* 7, 33–41.

Nestle, Wilhelm (1936), "Legenden vom Tod der Gottesverächter", in: *Archiv für Religionswiss.* 33, 246–269.

Newlands, Carole (1988a), "*Naturae opus mirabor:* Ausonius' challenge to Statius", in: *TAPhA* 108, 403–419.

Newlands, Carole (1988b), "Horace and Statius at Tibur", in: *ICS* 13, 95–111.

Newlands, Carole (2002), *Statius' Siluae and the Poetics of Empire*, Cambridge.

Newlands, Carole (2008), "Statius' Prose Prefaces", in: *MD* 61, 229–242.

Newlands, Carole (2009), "Statius' Self-Conscious Poetics: Hexameter on Hexameter", in: W. Dominik / J. Garthwaite / P.A. Roche (eds.), *Writing Politics in Imperial Rome*, Leiden, 387–404.

Newlands, Carole (ed.) (2011), Statius, *Silvae Book II*, Cambridge-New York.

Newlands, Carole (2012), *Statius, Poet between Rome and Naples*, London.

Newman, John K. (1990), *Roman Catullus and the Modification of the Alexandrian Sensibility*, Hildesheim.

Newmyer, S.T. (1979), *The Silvae of Statius: structure and theme*, Leiden.

Nicol, John (1936), *The Historical and Geographical Sources Used by Silius Italicus*, Oxford.

Niemann, Karl-Heinz, (1975), *Die Darstellung der römischen Niederlagen in den Punica des Silius Italicus,* Bonn.

Nisbet, Robin G.M. / Hubbard, Margaret (1970), *A Commentary on Horace Odes, Book I*, Oxford.

Nisbet, Robin G.M. / Hubbard, Margaret (1978), *A Commentary on Horace Odes, Book II*, Oxford.

Nisbet, Robin G.M. / Rudd, Neil (2004), *A Commentary on Horace Odes, Book III*, Oxford.

Noddings, Nel (1984), *Caring: A Feminine Approach to Ethics and Moral Education*, Berkeley.

O' Bryhim, Shawn (2007), "Catullus 23 as Roman Comedy", in: *TAPhA* 137, 133–145.

O' Connor, Eugene (1990), "Mamurianus and Martial's Revenge (Epigrams 1,92)", in: *CB* 66, 93–95.

Obermayer, Hans P. (1998), *Martial und der Diskurs über männliche 'Homosexualität' in der Literatur der frühen Kaiserzeit*, Tübingen.

Offermann, Helmut (1980), "*Uno tibi sim minor Catullo*", in: *QUCC* 5, 107–139.

Orentzel, Anne (1974), *Pliny and the Orators*, Diss. Univ. Pennsylvania.

Orentzel, Anne (1978a), "Declamation in the Age of Pliny", in: *CB* 54, 65–68.

Orentzel, Anne (1978b), "Quintilian and the Orators", in: *CB* 55, 1–5.

Orentzel, Anne (1980), "Pliny and Domitian", in: *CB* 56, 49–52.

Osgood, Josiah (2006), *Caesar's legacy: civil war and the emergence of the Roman Empire*, Cambridge.

Pagán, Victoria E. (2000), "The mourning after: Statius *Thebaid* 12", in: *AJPh* 121, 423–452.

Pagán, Victoria E. (2010), "The power of epistolary preface from Statius to Pliny", in: *CQ* 60, 194–201.

Parkes, Ruth (ed.) (2012), Statius, *Thebaid 4*, Oxford.

Paton, W.R. / Walbank, F.W. / Habicht, C. (transl.) (2011), *Polybius*, Cambridge, MA.

Patterson, Lee (1991), *Chaucer and the Subject of History*, Madison, WI.

Paukstadt, Rudolph (1876), *De Martiale Catulli imitatore*, Diss. Halle.

Peek, Philip S. (2002), "Feeding Aurelius' hunger: Catullus 21", in: *AClass* 45, 89–99.

Pelliccia, Hayden (1992), "Sappho 16, Gorgias' *Helen* and the Preface to Herodotus' Histories", in: *YCS* 29, 63–84.

Peterson, W. (ed.) (1891), M. Fabii Quintiliani *Institutionis Oratoriae Liber Decimus*, Oxford (repr. Hildesheim 1967).

Pflips, Heribert (1973), *Ciceronachahmung und Ciceroferne des jüngeren Plinius. Ein Kommentar zu den Briefen des Plinius über Repetundenprozesse (epist. 2,11; 2,12; 3,9; 4,9; 5,20; 6,13; 7,6)*, Münster.

Picone, Giusto (1977), *L'eloquenza di Plinio*, Palermo.

Pini, Licia (2006), "Omero, Menandro e i 'classici' latini negli *Apophoreta* di Marziale: criteri di selezione e ordinamento", in: *RFIC* 134, 443–478.

Pomeroy, Arthur (1986) "Polybius' Death Notices", in: *Phoenix* 40.4, 407–423.

Pomeroy, Arthur (1989), "Silius as *Doctus Poeta*", in: *Ramus* 18, 119–140.

Pomeroy, Arthur (2010), "To Silius through Livy and his Predecessors", in: A. Augoustakis (ed.), 27–46.

Poortvliet, Harm M. (ed.) (1991), C. Valerius Flaccus, *Argonautica Book 2*, Amsterdam.

Pöschl, Viktor (1991²), *Horazische Lyrik: Interpretationen*, Heidelberg.

Preisshofen, Felix (1979), "Kunsttheorie und Kunstbetrachtung", in: *Le classicisme à Rome aux 1ers siècles avant et après J.-C.* (Entretiens sur l'Antiquité Classique 25), Vandœuvres-Genève, 263–282.

Prioux, Évelyne (2008), *Petits musées en vers. Épigramme et discours sur les collections antiques*, Paris.

Procchi, Federico (2012), *Plinio il Giovane e la difesa di C. Iulius Bassus. Tra norma e persuasione*, Pisa.

Puelma, Mario (1997), "Epigramma: osservazioni sulla storia di un termine greco-latino", in: *Maia* 49, 189–213.

Putnam, Michael C.J. (2006), *Poetic Interplay: Catullus and Horace*, Princeton.

Raina, Giampiera (2008), "*Contendere potius quam sequi* (*Inst. or.* 10, 2, 9). Dinamiche del rapporto con i grandi del passato in Quintiliano", in: L. Castagna / C. Riboldi (eds.), *Amicitiae templa serena. Studi in onore di Giuseppe Aricò*, II, Milano, 1387–1409.

Raith, Oskar (1963), *Petronius, ein Epikureer*, Nürnberg.

Reed, Joseph D. (2009), *Virgil's Gaze: Nation and Poetry in the Aeneid*, Princeton.

Reinhardt, Tobias (2008), "Epicurus and Lucretius on the Origins of Language", in: *CQ* n.s. 58, 127–140.

Reinhardt, Tobias / Winterbottom, Michael (eds.) (2006), Quintilian, *Institutio Oratoria*, Book 2, Oxford.

Reitz, Christiane (1982), *Die Nekyia in den Punica des Silius Italicus*, Frankfurt am Main.

Reitz, Christiane (2013), "Does mass matter? The epic catalogue of troops as narrative and metapoetic device", in: G. Manuwald / A. Voigt (eds.), 229–243.

Riggsby, Andrew M. (1995), "Pliny on Cicero and oratory: self-fashioning in the public eye", in: *AJPh* 116, 123–135.

Rimell, Victoria (2008), *Martial's Rome: Empire and the Ideology of Epigram*, Cambridge-New York.

Ripoll, François (2000), "Silius Italicus et Cicéron", in: *LEC* 68, 147–173.

Ripoll, François (2002), "Martial et Stace, un bilan de la question", in: *BAGB* 3, 303–323.

Ripoll, François / Soubiran, Jean (eds.) (2008), Stace, *Achilléide*, Leuven.

Rivière, Yann (2002), *Les délateurs sous l'Empire romain*, Roma.

Roberts, Michael (1989), *The Jeweled Style. Poetry and Poetics in Late Antiquity*, Ithaca, NY.

Robinson, Fiona (2011), *The Ethics of Care. A Feminist Approach to Human Security*, Philadelphia.

Rogers, Robert S. (1960), "A group of Domitianic treason-trials", in: *CPh* 55, 19–23.

Rosati, Gianpiero (1992), "L'*Achilleide* di Stazio, un'epica dell'ambiguità", in: *Maia* n.s. 44, 233–266.

Rosati, Gianpiero (1994a), "Momenti e forme della fortuna antica di Ovidio: l'*Achilleide* di Stazio", in: M. Picone / B. Zimmermann (eds.), *Ovidius redivivus, von Ovid zu Dante*, Stuttgart, 43–62.

Rosati, Gianpiero (ed.) (1994b), Stazio, *Achilleide*, Milano.

Rosati, Gianpiero (1994c), "L'*Achilleide* di Stazio, un'epica *en travesti*", in: G. Rosati (ed.), 5–61.

Rosati, Gianpiero (2002), "Muse and Power in the Poetry of Statius", in: E. Spentzou / D. Fowler (eds.), *Cultivating the Muse: Struggles for Power and Inspiration in Classical Literature*, Oxford, 229–251.

Rosati, Gianpiero (2003), "*Dominus/domina:* moduli dell'encomio cortigiano e del corteggiamento amoroso", in R. Gazich (ed.), *Fecunda licentia. Tradizione e innovazione in Ovidio elegiaco*, Milano, 49–69.

Rosati, Gianpiero (2005), "Elegy after the Elegists: from Opposition to Assent", in: F. Cairns (ed.), *Papers of the Langford Latin Seminar* 12 (Greek and Roman Poetry. Greek and Roman Historiography), Cambridge, 133–150.

Rosati, Gianpiero (2006), "Luxury and Love: The Encomium as Aestheticisation of Power in Flavian Poetry", in: R.R. Nauta / H.-J. van Dam / J.J.L. Smolenaars (eds.), 41–58.

Rosati, Gianpiero (2008), "Statius, Domitian and Acknowledging Paternity. Rituals of Succession in the *Thebaid*", in: J.J.L. Smolenaars / H.-J. van Dam / R.R. Nauta (eds.), 176–250.

Rosati, Gianpiero (2013), "Un aedo in posa. Stazio e la coscienza di un poeta professionista", in: H. Casanova-Robin / A. Billault (eds.), *Le poète au miroir de ses verses. Études sur la représentation du poète dans ses oeuvres*, Grenoble, 81–100.

Rosati, Gianpiero (2014a), "Ovid in Flavian Occasional Poetry (Martial and Statius)", in: J. Miller / C. Newlands (eds.), 55–69.

Rosati, Gianpiero (2014b), "Memory, Myth, and Power in Statius's *Silvae*", in: G. Karl Galinsky (ed.), *Memoria Romana: Memory in Rome and Rome in Memory*, Ann Arbor, 71–81.

Rosati, Gianpiero (2015), "The *Silvae*: Poetics of Impromptu and Cultural Consumption", in: W. Dominik / C. Newlands / K. Gervais (eds.), 54–72.

Rose, A. (1985), "Clothing Imagery in Apollonius's *Argonautika*", in: QUCC 3, 29–44.

Rossi, Andreola (2000), "The Tears of Marcellus: History of a Literary Motif in Livy", in: *G&R* 47, 56–66.

Rostagni, Augusto (1961[2]), *Virgilio minore. Saggio sullo svolgimento della poesia virgiliana*, Roma.

Rouse, William Henry Denham (ed. and transl.) (1924), Lucretius, *De rerum natura*, Cambridge, MA-London.

Rühl, Meike (2006), *Literatur gewordener Augenblick. Die Silven des Statius im Kontext literarischer und sozialer Bedingungen von Dichtung*, Berlin-New York.

Ruperti, G.A. (ed.) (1795–98), *Caii Silii Italici Punicorvm libri septemdecim*, Göttingen.

Russell, Donald A. (ed. and transl.) (2001), Quintilian, *The Orator's Education*, Cambridge, MA-London.

Rutledge, Steven H. (2010), "Oratory and Politics in the Empire", in: W. Dominik / J. Hall (eds.), 109–121.

Sacerdoti, Arianna (2012), *Novus unde Furor: una lettura del dodicesimo libro della Tebaide di Stazio*, Pisa.

Santalucia, Bernardo (1998), *Diritto e processo penale nell'antica Roma*, Milano.

Sapsford, Francesca (2009), "Linking the Epigrams with a Theme: The Example of Martial, Books Two and Three", in: *Rosetta* 6, 44–62 (http://www.rosetta.bham.ac.uk/issue6/linking-the-epigrams.pdf).

Scaffai, Marco (2004), "Il console Marcello e Archimede nei *Punica* di Silio Italico", in: *Paideia* 59, 483–509.

Scarcia, Riccardo (1984), *"Ad tantas opes processit.* Note a Plinio il Giovane", in: *Labeo* 30, 291–316.

Scherf, Johannes (1998), "Zur Komposition von Martials Gedichtbüchern 1–12", in: F. Grewing (ed.), 119–138.

Scherf, Johannes (2001), *Untersuchungen zur Buchgestaltung Martials*, München.

Scherf, Johannes (2008), "*Epigramma longum* and the arrangement of Martial's book", in: A.M. Morelli (ed.), 195–216.

Schetter, Willy (1959), *Die Buchzahl der Argonautica des Valerius Flaccus: Beobachtungen zur Ausgestaltung des Kriegsthemas in den Argonautica*, München.

Schetter, Willy (1960), *Untersuchungen zur epischen Kunst des Statius*, Wiesbaden.

Schindler, Claudia (2013), "Musen", in: *RAC* 25, 184–220.

Schubert, Cristoph (1998), *Studien zum Nerobild in der lateinischen Dichtung der Antike*, Stuttgart.

Schubert, Werner (1984), *Jupiter in den Epen der Flavierzeit*, Frankfurt am Main.

Schuster, Michael (1961), "Voconius" n.6 in: *RE* IX A 1 Hb., 698–704.

Schwindt, Jürgen P. (2000), *Prolegomena zu einer "Phänomenologie" der römischen Literaturgeschichtsschreibung. Von den Anfängen bis Quintilian* (Hypomnemata 130), Göttingen.

Scodel, Ruth S. / Thomas, Richard F. (1984), "Virgil and the Euphrates", in: *AJPh* 105, 339.

Scott, William C. (2005), "The Patterning of the Similes in Book 2 of the *Iliad*", in: E.J. Rabel (ed.), *Approaches to Homer*, Swansea, 21–53.

Sedley, David N. (ed.) (1973), "Epicurus, *On nature, Book xxviii*", in: *CErc* 3, 5–83.

Seel, Otto (1977), *Quintilian oder Die Kunst des Redens und Schweigens*, Stuttgart.

Seelentag, Sabine (ed.) (2012), *Der pseudovergilische Culex*, Text, Übersetzung, Kommentar, Stuttgart.

Sevehuijsen, Selma (1998), *Citizenship and the Ethics of Care. Feminist Considerations on Justice, Morality and Politics*, London-New York.

Shackleton Bailey, David R. (1978), "Corrections and explanations of Martial", in: *CPh* 73, 273–296.

Shackleton Bailey, David R. (1983), "Notes on Quintilian", in: *HSCP* 87, 217–240.

Shackleton Bailey, David R. (ed.) (1990), M. Valerius Martialis, *Epigrammata*, Stuttgart.

Shackleton Bailey, David R. (1992²), *Onomasticon to Cicero's Speeches*, Stuttgart.

Shackleton Bailey, David R. (ed. and transl.) (1993), Martial, *Epigrams*, I–III, Cambridge MA-London.

Shackleton Bailey, David R. (ed. and transl.) (2003), Statius, *Thebaid, Books 1–7*; *Thebaid, Books 8–12, Achilleid*, I–II, Cambridge, MA-London.

Shapiro, H.A. (1980), "Jason's Cloak", in: *TAPhA* 110, 263–286.

Shelton, Jo-Ann (2013), *The Women of Pliny's letters*, London-New York.

Sherwin-White, Adrian Nicholas (ed.) (1966), *The Letters of Pliny: A Historical and Social Commentary*, Oxford.

Siebenborn, Elmar (1976), *Die Lehre von der Sprachrichtigkeit und ihren Kriterien: Studien zur antiken normativen Grammatik*, Amsterdam.

Skutsch, O. (ed.) (1985), *The Annals of Q. Ennius*, Oxford.

Slusanschi, Dan (1974), "Le vocabulaire latin du gradus aetatum", in: *Revue roumaine de linguistique* 19, 103–121; 267–296; 345–369; 437–451; 563–578.

Smolenaars, Johannes J.L. (1991), "Quellen und Rezeption. Die Verarbeitung Homerischer Motive bei Valerius Flaccus und Statius", in: M. Korn / H.J. Tschiedel (eds.), *Ratis omnia vincet*, Hildesheim, 57–71.

Smolenaars, Johannes J.L. (1994), *Statius Thebaid VII: A Commentary*, Leiden.

Smolenaars, Johannes J.L. / van Dam, Harm-Jan / Nauta, Ruurd R. (eds.), *The Poetry of Statius*. Mnemosyne, Supplementa 306, Leiden-Boston 2008.

Spaltenstein, François (1986), *Commentaire des Punica de Silius Italicus (livres 1 à 8)*, Genève.

Spaltenstein, François (1990), *Commentaire des Punica de Silius Italicus (livres 9 à 17)*, Genève.

Spaltenstein, François (2002), *Commentaire des Argonautica de Valerius Flaccus. (livres 1 et 2)*, Brussels.

Spaltenstein, François (2004), *Commentaire des Argonautica de Valerius Flaccus. (livres 3, 4 et 5)*, Brussels.

Sparagna, Sara (2010), "L'occhio di Mamuriano (Mart. I, 92)", in: *GIF* 1, 173–185.

Spoerri, Walter (1959), *Späthellenistische Berichte über Welt, Kultur und Götter: Untersuchungen zu Diodor von Sizilien* (Schweizerische Beiträge zur Altertumswissenschaft 9), Basel.

Stein, Arthur (1950), "Mettius Modestus", in: *RE* xv 2, 1499–1502.

Steinmetz, Peter (1964), "Gattungen und Epochen der griechischen Literatur in der Sicht Quintilians", in: *Hermes* 92, 454–466.

Steinmetz, Peter (1982), *Untersuchungen zur römischen Literatur des zweiten Jahrhunderts nach Christi Geburt*, Wiesbaden.

Stocks, Claire (2014), *The Roman Hannibal: Remembering the Enemy in Silius Italicus' Punica*, Liverpool.

Stover, Tim (2008), "The Date of Valerius Flaccus' *Argonautica*", in: *PLLS* 13, 211–229.

Stover, Tim (2009), "Apollonius, Valerius Flaccus, and Statius: Argonautic elements in *Thebaid* 3.499–647", in: *AJPh* 130, 439–455.

Stover, Tim (2012), *Epic & Empire in Vespasianic Rome. A new reading of Valerius Flaccus's Argonautica*, Oxford.

Stramaglia, Antonio (ed.) (2013), [Quintiliano], *L'astrologo. Declamazioni maggiori 4,* Cassino.

Sullivan, John P. (1991), *Martial: The Unexpected Classic*, Cambridge.

Swann, Bruce W. (1994), *Martial's Catullus. The Reception of an Epigrammatic Rival*, Hildesheim.

Swann, Bruce W. (1998) "*Sic scribit Catullus:* The Importance of Catullus for Martial's *Epigrams*", in: F. Grewing (ed.), 48–58.

Sweeney, Robert D. (1997), *Lactantii Placidi in Statii Thebaida commentarii libri XII*, Stuttgart.

Syme, Ronald (1958), *Tacitus*, Oxford.

Syme, Ronald (1968), "People in Pliny", in: *JRS* 58, 135–151.

Syndikus, Hans P. (1972), *Die Lyrik des Horaz. Eine Interpretation der Oden. I, Erstes und zweites Buch*, Darmstadt.

Syndikus, Hans P. (2017⁴), *Catull. Eine Interpretation*, Darmstadt.

Taisne, Anne-Marie (1996), "Echos épiques dans les *Silves* de Stace", in: F. Delarue / S. Georgacopoulou / P. Laurens / A.-M. Taisne (eds.), *Epicedion. Hommage à P. Papinius Statius, 96–1996*, Poitiers, 215–234.

Tarrant, Richard J. (ed.) (2004), *P. Ovidi Nasonis Metamorphoses*, Oxford.

Thomas, Richard (1982), "Catullus and the Polemics of Poetic Reference (Poem 64, 1–18)", in: *AJPh*, 103, 144–164.

Thomas, Richard (2007), "Horace and Hellenistic Poetry", in: S. Harrison (ed.), *The Cambridge Companion to Horace*, Cambridge, 50–62.

Thomson, Douglas F.S. (ed.) (1997), *Catullus*, Ed. with a Textual and Interpretative Commentary, Toronto.

Tipping, Ben (2004), "Middling epic? Silius Italicus' *Punica*", in: S. Kyriakidis / F. De Martino (eds.), *Middles in Latin Poetry*, Bari, 345–370.

Tipping, Ben (2007), "*Haec tum Roma fuit*: Past, Present, and Closure in Silius Italicus' *Punica*", in: S.J. Heyworth / P.G. Fowler / S.J. Harrison (eds.), *Classical Constructions: Papers in Memory of Don Fowler*, Oxford, 221–241.

Tipping, Ben (2010a), *Exemplary Epic: Silius Italicus' Punica*, Oxford.

Tipping, Ben (2010b), "Virtue and Narrative in Silius Italicus' *Punica*", in: A. Augoustakis (ed.),193–218.

Traglia, Antonio / Aricò, Giuseppe (eds. and transl.) (1980), Publio Papinio Stazio, *Opere*, Torino.

Trisoglio, Francesco (ed. and transl.) (1973), *Opere di Plinio Cecilio Secondo*, Torino.

Tronto, Joan C. (1993), *Moral Boundaries. A Political Argument for an Ethic of Care*, London-New York.

Tschiedel, Hans J. (2011), "Annibale come padre e marito", in: L. Castagna / G. Galimberti Biffino / Ch. Riboldi (eds.), *Studi su Silio Italico*, Milano, 231–244.

Uccellini, Renée (2012), *L'arrivo di Achille a Sciro. Saggio di commento a Stazio Achilleide 1, 1–396*, Pisa.

Vallat, Daniel (2008), *Onomastique, culture et société dans les Épigrammes de Martial*, Bruxelles.

van Dam, Harm-Jan (ed.) (1984), *P. Papinius Statius, Silvae Book II. A Commentary*, Leiden.

van Dam, Harm-Jan (2006), "Multiple imitation of epic models in the *Silvae*", in: R.R. Nauta / H.-J. van Dam / J.J.L. Smolenaars (eds.), 185–205.

Van der Keur, Michiel (2013), "Funeral Rites in Silius and Statius", in: G. Manuwald / A. Voigt (eds.), *Flavian Epic Interactions*, Berlin, 327–342.

Van Waarden, Johannes A. (ed.) (2010), *Writing to Survive. A Commentary on Sidonius Apollinaris Letters Book 7*, Leuven.

Vannini, Giulio (2009), "Il capitolo 5 del *Satyricon*: una proposta di lettura", in: F. Gasti (ed.), *Il Romanzo latino: modelli e tradizione letteraria. Atti della VII Giornata Ghisleriana di Filologia classica (Pavia, 11–12 ottobre 2007)*, Pavia, 31–46.

Varwig, Freyr Roland (1976), *Der rhetorische Naturbegriff bei Quintilian. Studien zu einem Argumentationstopos in der rhetorischen Bildung der Antike*, Heidelberg.

Venini, Paola (1972), "Su alcuni motivi delle *Argonautiche* di Valerio Flacco", in: *BStudLat* 2, 10–19.

Venini, Paola (1994), "Valerio Flacco e il *nefas* argonautico", in: F. Curti / C. Crimi (eds.), *Scritti classici e cristiani offerti a Francesco Corsaro*, Catania, II, 733–738.

Verlinsky, Alexander (2005), "Epicurus and his predecessors on the origin of language", in: D. Frede / B. Inwood (eds.), *Language and Learning. Philosophy of Language in the Hellenistic Age. Proceedings of the Ninth Symposium Hellenisticum*, Cambridge, 56–100.

Vinchesi, M.A. (1999), "Alcune considerazioni sul caso di Dafni nel XIV libro delle *Guerre Puniche* di Silio Italico", in: F. Conca (ed.), *Ricordando Raffaele Cantarella. Miscellanea di Studi*, Bologna, 247–255.

von der Mühll, Friedrich (1914), "*Roscius*" n. 6, in: *RE* I A 1, 1116–1117.

von Fritz, Kurt (1949), "Ancient Instruction in 'Grammar' According to Quintilian", in: *AJPh*, 70, 337–366.

von Rohden, Paul (1895), "Aquilius" n. 34, in: *RE* I A 2, 331f.

Wacht, Manfred (1991), *Juppiters Weltenplan im Epos des Valerius Flaccus*, Stuttgart.

Walbank, F.W. (1957–1979), *A Historical Commentary on Polybius*, Oxford.

Washburn, Daniel A. (2013), *Banishment in the later roman empire, 284–476 CE*, New York-London.

Watson, Lindsay (2003), "Bassa's Borborysms: on Martial and Catullus', in: *Antichthon* 37, 1–12.

Watson, Lindsay (2004), "Martial 12.32: An Indigent Immigrant?", in: *Mnemosyne* 57, 311–324.

Watson, Lindsay (2006), "The Unity of Martial's *Epigrams*", in: R.R. Nauta / H.-J. van Dam / J.J.L. Smolenaars (eds.), 271–284.

Watson, Lindsay / Watson, Patricia (eds.) (2003), Martial, *Select Epigrams*, Cambridge.

Watson, Patricia (1982), "Martial's Fascination with Lusci", in: *G&R* 29, 71–76.

Wehrli, Fritz (1944), 'Horaz und Kallimachos', in: *Museum Helveticum* 1, 69–76.

Weinreich, Otto (1928), *Studien zu Martial. Literarhistorische und religionsgeschichtliche Untersuchungen*, Stuttgart.

Weische, Alfons (1989), "Plinius d.J. und Cicero. Untersuchungen zur römischen Epistolographie in Republik und Kaiserzeit", in: *ANRW* II 33.1, 375–386.

West, David (1998), *Horace, Odes II: Vatis Amici*, Oxford.

Wiener, Claudia (2006), *Stoische Doktrin in römischer Belletristik: das Problem von Entscheidungsfreiheit und Determinismus in Senecas Tragödien und Lucans Pharsalia*, München.

Williams, Craig A. (2002), "*Sit nequior omnibus libellis:* Text, Poet and Reader in the *Epigrams* of Martial", in: *Philologus* 146, 150–171.

Williams, Craig A. (ed.) (2004), Martial, *Epigrams Book Two*, Edited with Introduction, Translation and Commentary, Oxford.

Williams, Robert D. (ed.) (1972), *P. Papini Stati Thebaidos liber decimus*, Edition and Commentary, Leiden.

Wilson, Marcus (1993), "Flavian variant: History. Silius' *Punica*", in: A.J. Boyle (ed.), *Roman Epic*, London, 218–236.

Wilson, Marcus (2004), 'Ovidian Silius', in: *Arethusa* 37, 225–249.

Winniczuk, Lidia (1982), "De C. Plinio Secundo Minore M. Tulli Ciceronis aemulatore", in: *Meander* 37, 85–97.

Winterbottom, Michael (1975), "Quintilian and Rhetoric", in: T.A. Dorey (ed.), *Empire and Aftermath. Silver Latin II*, London-Boston, 79–97.

Wistrand, Erik (1979), "The Stoic opposition to the principate", in: *StudClas* 28, 93–101.

Woodman, Anthony J. (1975), "Questions of Date, Genre and Style in Velleius: Some Literary Answers", in: *CQ* 25, 272–306.

Wray, David (2001), *Catullus and the Poetics of Roman Manhood*, Cambridge.

Wray, David (2007), "Wood: Statius' *Silvae* and the Poetics of Genius", in: A. Augoustakis / C. Newlands (eds.), *Statius' Silvae and the Poetics of Intimacy*, in: *Arethusa* 40, 127–143.

Zeiner, Noelle K. (2005), *Nothing Ordinary Here: Statius as Creator of Distinction in the Silvae*, New York-London.

Zellner, Harold (2007), "Sappho's alleged proof of aesthetic relativity", in: *GEBS* 47, 257–270.

Zetzel, James E.G. (1983), "Catullus, Ennius and the Poetics of Allusion", in: *ICS* 8, 251–266.

Zissos, Andrew (1999), "Allusion and Narrative Possibility in the *Argonautica* of Valerius Flaccus", in: *CP* 94, 289–301.

Zissos, Andrew (2002), "Reading Models and the Homeric Program in Valerius Flaccus' *Argonautica*", in: *Helios* 29, 69–96.

Zissos, Andrew (2003–2004), "Navigating Genres: Martial 7, 19 and the *Argonautica* of Valerius Flaccus", in: *CJ* 99, 405–422.

Zissos, Andrew (2004a), "Terminal Middle: the *Argonautica* of Valerius Flaccus", in: S. Kyriakidis / F. De Martino (eds.), *Middles in Latin poetry*, Bari, 311–344.

Zissos, Andrew (2004b), "L'ironia allusiva: Lucan's *Bellum Civile* and the *Argonautica of Valerius Flaccus*", in: P. Esposito / E.M. Ariemma (eds.), *Lucano e la tradizione dell'epica latina,* Napoli, 21–38.

Zissos, Andrew (ed.) (2008), Valerius Flaccus, *Argonautica: Book I*, Edited with Introduction, Translation and Commentary, Oxford.

Zissos, Andrew (2009), "Navigating Power: Valerius Flaccus' *Argonautica*", in: W. Dominik / J. Garthwaite / P.A. Roche (eds.), *Writing Politics in imperial Rome,* Leiden-Boston, 351–366.

Zissos, Andrew (2012), "The King's Daughter: Medea in Valerius Flaccus' *Argonautica*", in: *Ramus* 41, 94–118.

Zissos, Andrew (2014), "Stoic Thought and Homeric Reminiscence in Valerius Flaccus' *Argonautica*", in: M. Garani / D. Konstan (eds.), *The philosophizing Muse: The Influence of Greek Philosophy on Roman Poetry*, Newcastle upon Tyne, 269–297.

Zissos, Andrew (ed.) (2016), *A Companion to the Flavian Age of Imperial Rome*, Malden, MA-Oxford-Chichester.

List of Contributors

Antony Augoustakis is Professor of Classics and Langan Professorial Scholar at the University of Illinois – Urbana-Champaign. He is editor of *The Classical Journal* and author of *Statius, Thebaid 8* (Oxford 2016), *Motherhood and the Other: Fashioning Female Power in Flavian Epic* (Oxford 2010), and *Plautus' Mercator* (Bryn Mawr 2009). Most recently he has edited the *Oxford Readings in Flavian Epic* (Oxford 2016), *Flavian Poetry and its Greek Past* (Leiden 2014) and is co-editor of *Spartacus: Reimagining an Icon on Screen* (Edinburgh 2016).

Thomas Baier is Professor of Classical Philology at the University of Würzburg. He is author of *Valerius Flaccus. Argonautica, Buch VI. Einleitung und Kommentar* (Zetemata), *Werk und Wirkung Varros im Spiegel seiner Zeitgenossen* (Hermes-Einzelschriften) and *Geschichte der römischen Literatur* (Beck). He has also edited several volumes on Flavian Epic, Roman Comedy and Neo-Latin Literature.

Andrea Balbo is Researcher of Latin Language and Literature at the University of Turin and teaches Latin literature at USI in Lugano (CH). He is vice-president of the SIAC. He has published extensively on Roman oratory, rhetoric and declamation, late antique literature, the presence of classical authors in modern literatures, and the history of classical philology. He is author of *I frammenti degli oratori romani dell'età augustea e tiberiana. Parte prima. Età augustea*; *Parte seconda. Età tiberiana* (Alessandria 2007²; 2007).

Alessia Bonadeo is Researcher in Latin Language and Literature at the University of Pavia. She is interested in the relations between myth and science in the ancient world, Flavian poetry, love poetry (Catullus and elegy), and ancient metapoetic reflection. She is author of *Mito e natura allo specchio. L'eco nel pensiero greco e latino* (Pisa 2003), *Iride: un arco tra mito e natura* (Firenze 2004), and *L'Hercules Epitrapezios Novi Vindicis. Introduzione e commento a Stat. silv. 4,6* (Napoli 2010).

Sandra Citroni Marchetti, former Professor of Latin Literature at the Universities of Siena and Florence, is author of *Plinio il Vecchio e la tradizione del moralismo romano* (Pisa 1991), *La scienza della natura per un intellettuale romano. Studi su Plinio il Vecchio* (Pisa 2011), and a book on political, sociological and psychological aspects of Roman friendship (*Amicizia e potere nelle lettere di Cicerone e nelle elegie ovidiane dall'esilio*, Firenze 2000). She has also studied several aspects of moral philosophy in Latin poets and prose writers, especially Cicero and Seneca.

Mario Citroni is Emeritus Professor of Latin Literature at the Scuola Normale Superiore, Pisa and Florence. He is the author of an edition and commentary on Martial Book I (Firenze 1975), studies on the author-public relationship in Latin poetry, including *Poesia e lettori in Roma antica: forme della comunicazione letteraria*, Roma-Bari 1995), and on various aspects of the relations between literature and society in the Roman world, especially in the Augustan and Flavian ages. Some of his recent papers treat literary canons in ancient literature and the origin of the concept of 'classic'.

Alberto Canobbio is Associate Professor of Latin Language and Literature at the University of Pavia. He is the author of a literary-juridical study about the *lex Roscia theatralis* and Martial's book five (Como 2002) and of a critical edition, translation and commentary of the whole *Epigrammaton liber quintus* (Napoli 2011). He has published many articles on Martial, as well as on archaic poetry (particularly Ennius), satire, imperial epic, and epistolography (especially on intertextuality in Pliny the Younger).

Jacqueline Fabre-Serris is Professor of Latin at the University of Lille. She is the autor of *Mythe et Poésie dans les Métamorphoses d'Ovide* (1995), *Mythologie et littérature à Rome* (1998), and *Rome, l'Arcadie et la mer des Argonautes. Essai sur la naissance d'une mythologie des origines en Occident* (2008). She has published many articles on Augustan poetry, mythology and mythography, and gender studies. She is co-director of the electronic reviews *Dictynna, Eugesta*, and *Polymnia*, and of the series "Mythographes" (Presses du Septentrion).

Alison Keith is Director of the Jackman Humanities Institute and Professor of Classics and Women's Studies at the University of Toronto. She is the author of *The Play of Fictions: Studies in Ovid's Metamorphoses II* (Ann Arbor 1992), *Engendering Rome* (Cambridge 2000), and *Propertius, Poet of Love and Leisure* (London 2008). Her research focuses on gender and genre in Latin literature and Roman culture. She is currently completing a book on Virgil for IB Tauris in their series "Understanding Classics".

Joy Littlewood is predominantly interested in historical epic and religion. She has published commentaries on Ovid's *Fasti*, Book 6 (Oxford 2006), Silius Italicus' *Punica* 7 (2011), and *Punica* 10 (2017). She is currently writing a commentary on *Punica* 3, with Antony Augoustakis, with whom she is also editing a conference volume: *Campania in the Flavian Poetic Imagination*. She has recently undertaken to complete the fourth and final volume of Jim McKeown's monumental commentary on Ovid's *Amores*.

Helen Lovatt is Professor of Classics at the University of Nottingham and has published widely on Flavian epic. Her first book was *Statius and Epic Games* (Cambridge 2005); recently she has been working on epic visuality (*The Epic Gaze*, Cambridge 2013; *Epic Visions*, ed. with Caroline Vout, Cambridge 2013), and is now writing a cultural history of the Argonaut myth.

Raymond Marks is an Associate Professor at the University of Missouri. He has published extensively on Silius Italicus, including his book *From Republic to Empire: Scipio Africanus in the Punica of Silius Italicus* (2005). His current work focuses on the influence of Ovid on post-Augustan epic poets.

Elena Merli studied Classics at the Scuola Normale Superiore in Pisa and is Associate Professor of Latin Literature at the University of L'Aquila since 2004. Her main field of research is Latin poetry, especially Ovid and Martial, with a focus on formal aspects of that literature (genre, intertextuality, poetry books) and its ideology (poets and emperors, patronage, Roman values). She is the author of a book on Ovid's *Fasti* (*Arma canant alii*, Firenze 2000), and of *Dall'Elicona a Roma* (Berlin 2013), on poetologic images in Flavian poetry.

Alfredo Mario Morelli is Associate Professor in Latin language and Literature at the University of Cassino. He has published extensively on Greek and Roman poetry, and is the author of *L'epigramma latino prima di Catullo* (Cassino 2000). He has organized two international conferences and edited the proceedings (*Epigramma longum. From Martial to late Antiquity*, Cassino 2008; *Lepos e mores. Una giornata su Catullo*, Cassino 2012).

Carole Newlands teaches Classics at the University of Colorado – Boulder. She is author of *Playing with Time: Ovid and the Fasti* (Ithaca 1995); *Statius Siluae and the Poetics of Empire* (Cambridge 2002); *Siluae Book 2* (Cambridge 2011); *Status: a Poet between Rome and Naples* (London 2012); *Ovid: an introduction* (London 2015). She is also co-editor of the *Wiley-Blackwell Companion to Ovid* (Oxford 2014), *The Brill Companion to Statius* (Leiden 2015), and *Ancient Campania: Poetics, Location, and Identity* (Illinois 2015).

Christiane Reitz is Professor of Latin at the University of Rostock. She has published extensively on epic poetry, is co-editor of *Lucan's Bellum civile* (Berlin 2010), *Tradition und Erneuerung: mediale Strategien in der Zeit der Flavier* (Berlin 2010), *Von Ursachen sprechen: eine aitiologische Spurensuche* (Hildesheim 2014), and is working at a companion on the structures of epic. Other fields of her research are classical reception studies and the transfer of knowledge in late antiquity (she co-edited *Condensing texts – condensed texts*, Stuttgart 2010).

Andrew Zissos is Professor and Chair of Classics at the University of California – Irvine. He is the author of numerous articles on imperial Roman literature and its reception, along with a commentary on Book 1 of Valerius Flaccus' *Argonautica* (OUP 2008). He is also editor of *A Companion to the Flavian Age of Imperial Rome* (Wiley-Blackwell 2016), and co-editor, with Ingo Gildenhard, of the volume *Transformative Change in Western Thought: a History of Metamorphosis from Homer to Hollywood* (Legenda 2013).